Trade and Money

Analecta Isisiana: Ottoman and Turkish Studies

93

A co-publication with The Isis Press, Istanbul, the series consists of collections of thematic essays focused on specific themes of Ottoman and Turkish studies are brought together in Analecta Isisiana. These scholarly volumes address important issues throughout Turkish history, offering in a single volume the accumulated insights of a single author over a career of research on the subject.

Trade and Money

The Ottoman Economy in the Eighteenth and Early Nineteenth Centuries

Elena Frangakis-Syrett

The Isis Press, Istanbul

gorgias press

2010

Gorgias Press LLC, 954 River Road, Piscataway, NJ, 08854, USA

www.gorgiaspress.com

Originally published in 2007

2010 ○

ISBN 978-1-61719-102-2

Printed in the United States of America

Elena Frangakis-Syrett is Professor of History at Queens College of the City University of New York. Born in Alexandria, of Greek origin, she grew up in Athens and London and currently resides in New York. She holds a B.A. (Honours) in Modern History from University College, London University and a Ph.D. in Ottoman Economic History from King's College, London University. Frangakis-Syrett has also pursued post-graduate studies at the School of Oriental and African Studies, London University and at the École des Hautes Études in Paris as a French Government Scholar.

A Fellow of the Royal Historical Society, in England, Frangakis-Syrett has also been Visiting Research Fellow at the London School of Economics, London University and at the Skilliter Centre for Ottoman Studies, Newnham College, Cambridge University. Her research specializations are Ottoman commercial and monetary history, late 17th to early 20th centuries, and in particular, the economic history of western Anatolia and the Aegean islands, with special emphasis on İzmir. Her research interests also relate to the commercial history of the wider eastern Mediterranean region, 18th to early 20th centuries. Her publications include *The Commerce of Smyrna in the Eighteenth Century, 1700-1820* (1992), *Οι Χιώτες έμποροι στις διεθνείς συναλλαγές, 1750-1850* (1995) and numerous articles in international journals.

For David

CONTENTS

SECTION III: İZMİR, THE EMPIRE'S PREMIER PORT

SECTION IV: TRADE AND MONETARY PRACTICES

ACKNOWLEDGMENTS

This is a selection of my articles on the economic history of the Ottoman empire in the eighteenth and early nineteenth centuries, with special reference to İzmir. With the exception of two studies, which appear here for the first time, all the other articles in the volume have been published in the years between 1985 and 2003.

It is a pleasant duty to thank all the individuals and editors for the hospitality they offered me in publishing my work which is contained in this volume: Dr. Kate Fleet; Professor Daniel Panzac; Professor John Armstrong; Professor Jacques Thobie; Dr. Salgur Kançal; Dr. Michele Bernardini; Professor Reşat Kasaba; Professor Çağlar Keyder; Professor Şevket Pamuk; Dr. Alexander H. de Groot ; Professor Vasilis Panayotopoulos ; Professor Alastair Hamilton; Professor Marcel Bazin; Dr. Maurits H. van den Boogert; Professor Constantine Svolopoulos; Professor Faruk Tabak; Dr. Andreas Kunz; Professor Samir Saul; Dr. Jean-David Mizrahi; Professor Yavuz Tekelioğlu; Dr. Walid Arbid. I take here the opportunity to express my thanks to Professor Malcolm Wagstaff with whom I co-authored one of the articles in this volume. I would also like to thank the following journals: ***Revue du Monde Musulman et de la Méditerranée; Oriente Moderno; New Perspectives on Turkey; Eurasian Studies***; ***Balkan Studies***. In addition, I would like to extend my thanks to the following publishers and institutions: İzmir Büyükşehir Belediyesi Yayıncılık; Association for the Study of Modern Hellenism; Institute of Neohellenic Research/National Hellenic Research Foundation; International Association for South-Eastern European Studies; the Cartographic Unit of the University of Southampton.

Research for many of the articles in this book has been supported, in part, by the City University of New York PSC-CUNY Research Award Program and the preparation of this volume has been assisted by a Scholar Incentive Award from Queens College, City University of New York. I would like to thank them as well as the staff of the Rosenthal Library of Queens College of the City University of New York for all their support.

Finally, I would like to extend my thanks to the Isis Press and in particular to Sinan Kuneralp for giving me the privilege of publishing this volume in their Analecta series.

Elena Frangakis-Syrett
Professor of History Queens College,
City University of New York
August 2006

LIST OF ILLUSTRATIONS

LIST OF APPENDICES

ABBREVIATIONS

ANF AE Bi	Archives Nationales de France, Série Affaires Étrangères: sous-série Bi
ANF AE Biii	Archives Nationales de France, Série Affaires Étrangères: sous-série Biii
ANF Marine B/7	Archives Nationales de France, Marine, Série B/7
ANF F/12	Archives Nationales de France, Série F/12
AMAE CCC	Archives du Ministère des Affaires Étrangères, Série Correspondance Consulaire et Commerciale
AMAE NS	Archives du Ministère des Affaires Étrangères, Nouvelle Série
ACCM I	Archives de la Chambre de Commerce de Marseille, Série I
ACCM LIX	Archives de la Chambre de Commerce de Marseille, Série LIX, Fonds Roux
ACCM MQ, 5.1	Archives de la Chambre de Commerce de Marseille, Série MQ, 5.1
MAE, CADN, FC	Ministère des Affaires Étrangères, Centre des Archives Diplomatiques de Nantes, Fonds Ambassade de Constantinople.
ARA	Algemeen Rijksarschief
NA, RG 84	National Archives, Washington D.C., Record Group 84
PRO, SP/105	Public Record Office, State Papers, Series 105
PRO, SP/110	Public Record Office, State Papers, Series 110
PRO, FO/78	Public Record Office, Foreign Office, Series 78
PRO, FO/195	Public Record Office, Foreign Office, Series 195
TNA: (PRO)	The National Archives of the United Kingdom (see PRO)

INTRODUCTION

Studies in this volume have been published over a period of eighteen years. They examine different aspects of the Ottoman economy in the eighteenth and early nineteenth centuries, namely, monetary conditions, trade and the local market as well as the forces that shaped them, including imperial government policy. In particular, studies in this volume deal with the nature of and long-term dynamics in the commercial relationship of the Ottoman Empire with Europe, within the context of long-distance international trade and through the perspective of a pre-industrial eighteenth-century world economy. Special emphasis is given to the western Anatolian city-port of İzmir (Smyrna), which emerged as the single most important port in the Empire's trade with Europe, a process which started in the early eighteenth century and reached its apex in the early nineteenth century.

Articles in the first section examine the characteristics of the Ottoman monetary system ; the way it functioned and impacted upon commercial activities, especially in relation to the fiscal and specie substitution policies of the state, and the way the local market responded to such policies as well as adjusted to such phenomena as specie scarcity, volatility of the local currency and recurring fiscal crises, whilst registering on-going economic growth. Special attention is paid to the extensive mechanisms of credit and to the speculative monetary practices that developed as a result of such economic conditions and their impact upon Ottoman trade.

Studies in the second section seek to illustrate the *raison d'être* of the Ottoman maritime world, namely the creation of an equilibrium between production and consumption, surpluses and needs, within its vast imperial domains in order to ensure the effective provisioning of its markets. Further, studying the Ottoman maritime world from the perspective of the three major ports, Istanbul, İzmir and Alexandria, two trends become apparent : namely, the degree to which external and internal trade overlapped and how İzmir commanded the largest number of coastal and blue water routes which, given its primary position in Ottoman-European trade, further reenforced its central role in the Empire's internal maritime trade, too.

The third and fifth sections examine the causes and process by which, in the course of the eighteenth and early nineteenth centuries, İzmir came to acquire such a pivotal position in Ottoman-European as well as Ottoman coastal trade and the local and international economic conditions that made it possible. As a result of such developments, by the early nineteenth century, İzmir had become the *plaque tournante*, or central wheel, from whose axes the most extensive commercial networks and routes, with Europe as well as within the Empire, at sea as well as in land, emanated.

Studies in the fourth section analyze the nature, structure and *modus operandi* of the trading networks and the strategies and practices of the merchants, both Ottoman and European, who manned them as well as the role that these networks played in ensuring the flow of goods, money and information over short and long distances, both in the long-term and in the daily conduct of Ottoman-European trade. Further, the articles explore the interlocking relationships of the European merchants that were key to the company organizations that underpinned their trading networks and the role that ties of blood and trust or, in the parlance of the time, ties of kinship and 'friendship', played in these relationships. Special attention is paid to their business strategies, put in place to overcome problems inherent in long-distance international trade and what made their enterprises profitable. Parallel to the Europeans the volume studies the Ottoman merchants who, along with the westerners, were key players in Ottoman-European trade. Articles examine how the locals dominated the internal commercial networks that linked markets in the Ottoman interior and how they expanded their activities to Europe at the turn of the century. Studies in this volume look at specializations in the commercial activities between Europeans and Ottomans, at the dynamics in their relationship and at the way such dynamics evolved in the course of the eighteenth and early nineteenth centuries as a result of changes in the international political, military and economic arenas.

Overall, the volume illustrates the way Ottoman-European trade was affected by developments in the world economy as well as by the close interrelation between war and trade, namely, how the various conflicts, in land or at sea, between the Ottoman Empire and Iran in the East and the Empire and Europe in the West as well as inter-European conflicts affected the development of European-Ottoman and Ottoman maritime trade and had a lasting effect on the fortunes of the participants. Since 1985, when articles from this volume first appeared, the history of İzmir and Ottoman-European trade have been endowed with a growing bibliography, including the author's books on the subject. It is nevertheless hoped that the present studies, which go beyond the author's monographs, will further contribute to Ottoman commercial and monetary history.

THE OTTOMAN ECONOMY AND İZMİR IN PERSPECTIVE*

This book is a collection of articles on the economic history of the Ottoman Empire in the eighteenth and early nineteenth centuries. It focuses on monetary issues and commerce in the empire and in particular on Ottoman maritime trade with Europe. Its special emphasis is İzmir which became, in the eighteenth and early nineteenth centuries, the most important port in the trade of the Ottoman Empire both internally and with Europe.

The articles in this volume are based on multiple archival western sources from countries which were principal participants in the trade of the Empire with Europe and whose nationals were established at that time in a number of Ottoman ports, including İzmir, for the purpose of trade. The studies make particular use of the rich British sources on Ottoman trade with Europe and of the even richer French archival collections in Paris and Marseilles (and more recently Nantes) as well as Dutch and Greek archives. The articles both pre-date and follow on from the author's book on the commerce of İzmir in the eighteenth century, published in 1992.[1] In relation to the author's book, the articles in the volume both introduce and develop further questions related to Ottoman commercial and monetary history in the eighteenth and early nineteenth centuries that have not been included in the above publication.

When the first of the articles in this volume appeared, in 1985, there were relatively few studies treating exclusively Ottoman trade with Europe in the eighteenth century. Perhaps the earliest published work on this subject is that of Nicos Svoronos on the commerce of Salonica, 1700-1789, which appeared in 1956.[2] It was followed in 1967 by the book of Ralph Davis on the trade of Aleppo with Britain in the eighteenth century,[3] although Ottoman-British trade in Aleppo during the first half of the eighteenth century

---

*First publication.

[1] Elena Frangakis-Syrett, *The Commerce of Smyrna in the Eighteenth Century, 1700-1820* (Athens, 1992).

[2] Nicos Svoronos, *Le Commerce de Salonique au XVIIIe siècle* (Paris, 1956).

[3] Ralph Davis, *Aleppo and Devonshire Square. English Traders in the Levant in the Eighteenth Century* (London, 1967).

had already been the subject of two unpublished Ph.D. theses written in the 1930s by Gwylim Ambrose[1] and Clarence Matterson[2] respectively. In 1987 Katsumi Fukasawa published his work on the trade of Aleppo with France in the eighteenth century.[3] The book of Bruce Masters on Aleppo's regional and international trade, placed within the context of Ottoman-European economic relations and from the viewpoint of western economic dominance of the Ottoman empire, during the seventeenth and first half of the eighteenth centuries appeared in 1988,[4] while Abraham Marcus studied the international trade of Aleppo in the eighteenth century within the context of a socio-economic analysis of the city[5] and Maurits van den Boogert has recently completed a Ph.D. dissertation on Ottoman dragomans and European Consuls in Aleppo in the eighteenth century.[6]

With the exception of the first book of Kremmydas on the trade of the Peloponnese (Morea), published in 1972,[7] a number of other studies appeared in the 1980s dealing with the trade of Ottoman port-cities or islands in the Aegean Sea with Europe in the eighteenth century; namely, George Siorokas on the commerce of Arta;[8] Maria Efthymiou-Hadzilacou on the trade of the island of Rhodes;[9] Yolande Triantafyllidou-Baladié[10] and Molly Greene[11] on the trade of the island of Crete; Patrick Boulanger on the trade of the island of

---

[1]Gwylim Ambrose, "The Levant Company mainly from 1640-1753" (unpublished Oxford University B. Litt. thesis, 1933).

[2]Clarence Matterson, "English Trade in the Levant, 1693-1753" (unpublished Harvard University Ph.D. dissertation, 1936).

[3]Katsumi Fukasawa, *Toilerie et commerce du Levant d'Alep à Marseille* (Paris, 1987).

[4]Bruce Masters, *The Origins of Western Economic Dominance in the Middle East. Mercantilism and the Islamic Economy in Aleppo, 1600-1750* (New York, 1987).

[5]Abraham Marcus, *The Middle East on the Eve of Modernity. Aleppo in the Eighteenth Century* (New York, 1989).

[6]Maurits H. van den Boogert, "Ottoman Dragomans and European Consuls: The Protection System in Eighteenth-Century Aleppo" (unpublished Ph.D. dissertation, Leiden University, 2001).

[7]Vasilis Kremmydas, *Το εμπόριο της Πελοποννήσου στο 18° αίωνα,* 1715-1792 (*Με βάση τα γαλλικά αρχεία*) (*The Commerce of the Peloponnese in the 18th century, 1715-1792)* (Based on the French Archives) (Athens, 1972); *Idem, Ευγκυρία και εμπόριο στην ηροεπαναστατική πελοπόννησο, 1793-1821 (Conjuncture and Commerce in Pre-Revolutionary Peloponnese, 1793-1821)* (Athens, 1980).

[8]George A. Siorokas, *Το γαλλικό προξενίο της Αρτας (1702-1789) (The French Consulate of Arta, 1702-1789)* (Ionnina, 1981).

[9]Maria Efthymiou-Hadzilacou, *Rhodes et sa région élargie au 18ème siècle: les activités portuaires* (Athens, 1988).

[10]Yolande Triantafyllidou-Baladié, *Το εμπόριο και η οικονομία της Κρήτης,* (1669-1795) (*The Commerce and Economy of Crete, 1669-1795*) (Iraklion, Crete, 1988).

[11]Molly Greene, *A Shared World* (Princeton, NJ, 2000).

Mitylene.[1] Daniel Panzac has written on different issues related to Ottoman and Ottoman-European trade, namely on Ottoman coastal trade,[2] piracy,[3] and on plague in the Ottoman empire in the eighteenth century.[4] Plague was a constant and major health risk factor in the eighteenth and early nineteenth centuries, which greatly impacted the demography and economy of the empire's ports. Robert Mantran has examined Ottoman-European trade in the seventeenth and eighteenth centuries[5] and primarily the economy and trade of Istanbul in the seventeenth century.[6] Others have contributed to the historiography of Ottoman-European trade in the eighteenth century by studying related aspects as, for instance, André Raymond, who studied Ottoman-European trade through the port of Alexandria, within the context of Ottoman urban history, in his work on Cairo in the eighteenth century;[7] Ali İhsan Bağış has studied the question of *beratlı* merchants,[8] and Rudi Matthee studied the Persian silk export trade to Europe, which has similarities with Ottoman-European trade.[9]

A study of Ottoman-European trade naturally includes the merchant communities, Ottoman and European, that have participated in this trade. Some have studied European merchants trading with Europe from the Ottoman empire whilst others have looked at Ottoman merchant communities trading with the Ottoman empire from Europe in the eighteenth and early nineteenth centuries. Olga Katsiardi-Hering has studied the Greek merchant community of Trieste in the eighteenth and early nineteenth centuries;[10] Despina Vlami has

---

[1]E.g., Patrick Boulanger, "L'ile de Mitylène et le négoce français au XVIIIe siècle", D. Panzac ed., *Les villes dans l'Empire ottoman: activités et sociétés* (Paris, 1991), vol. I, pp. 273-298, see also, E. Siphneou, *Λέσβος* (*Lesbos*) (Athens, 1996).

[2]Daniel Panzac, *Commerce et navigation dans l'Empire ottoman au XVIIIe siècle* (Istanbul, 1996); see also, *idem*, ed., *Les villes dans l'Empire ottoman: activités et sociétés* (Paris, 1991).

[3]Daniel Panzac, *Les corsaires barbaresques: la fin d'une épopée, 1800-1820* (Paris, 1999).

[4]Daniel Panzac, *La Peste dans l'Empire ottoman, 1700-1850* (Louvain, Belgium, 1985), *idem, Quarantaines et lazarets, l'Europe et la peste d'Orient* (Aix-en-Provence, 1986).

[5]E.g., Robert Mantran, "Commerce maritime et économie dans l'empire ottoman au XVIIIe siècle", Jean-Paul Bacqué-Grammont & Paul Dumont, eds., *Économies et sociétés dans l'Empire ottoman (fin du XVIIIe - début du XXe siècles)* (Paris, 1983), pp. 289-96.

[6]Robert Mantran, *Istanbul dans la seconde moitié du XVIIe siècle* (Paris, 1962); see also, *idem, Histoire d'Istanbul* (Paris, 1996).

[7]André Raymond, *Les artisans et commerçants du Caire au XVIIIe siècle* (Damascus, 1973 74), 2 vols; see also, *idem*, "L'impacte de la pénétration européenne sur l'économie de l'Égypte au XVIIIe siècle", *Annales Islamologiques* (1982), Vol. XVIII, pp. 217-235.

[8]Ali Ihsan Bağış, *Osmanlı ticaretinde gayri müslimler* (Ankara, 1983); on a related question, see also, Bruce Masters, "The Sultan's Entrepreneurs: The Avrupa Tüccaris and the Hayriye Tüccaris in Syria" *International Journal of Middle East Studies* (1992), Vol. 24/4, pp. 579-597.

[9]Rudi Matthee, *Silk for Silver: Iran's Silk Trade and the Safavid Political Economy, 1600-1730* (Cambridge, 1999).

[10]Olga Katsiardi-Hering, *Η παροικία της Τεργέστης, (1751-1830), (The Greek Community of Trieste, 1751-1830)* (Athens, 1986), 2 vols. *Idem, Λησμονημένοι ορίζοντες ελλήνων εμπόρων. Το πανηγυρι της* Seniqallia *(Forgotten Horizons of Greek merchants: the Fair at Seniqallia)* (Athens, 1989).

recently published her work on the Greek merchant community of Livorno in the eighteenth and nineteenth centuries.[1] We also have the published letters of Stamatis Petrou on the Ottoman Greek merchants of Amsterdam in the eighteenth century,[2] and the work of Pierre Échinard on the commercial activities of Ottoman Greeks in Marseilles in the late eighteenth and early nineteenth centuries.[3] All four city-ports had a most flourishing trade with the Ottoman empire in the eighteenth and early nineteenth centuries, which is the period that concerns us here. Besides Greek, there were flourishing Ottoman Jewish and Armenian merchant communities in the above ports, and elsewhere in Europe, trading with the Ottoman empire.[4] Following the publication of the author's study on the commercial activities of the Ottoman Greek community from the island of Chios (Sakız) in the Aegean Sea with Europe,[5] there has been another study that deals with the trade of the Ottoman empire with Europe, for the eighteenth century, namely the book of Edhem Eldem on the commerce of Istanbul.[6]

Besides Ottoman-European trade, the present volume naturally also pertains to the history of İzmir. There has been a flourishing of publications, many of which have appeared in recent years, that deal with various aspects of the history of Ottoman İzmir, and especially of its economy, at different periods of time. References that follow here are by no means exhaustive of this bibliography. The social and economic development of İzmir in the fifteenth and sixteenth centuries has been studied by Mübahat Kütükoğlu.[7] The commercial history of İzmir from mid-sixteenth to mid-seventeenth centuries has been studied by Daniel Goffman.[8] The trade of İzmir with Europe in the late seventeenth century has been studied by Sonia Anderson.[9]

---

[1]Despina Vlami, *Το φιορίνι, το σιτάρι και η οδός του κήπου. Ελληνες έμποροι στο Λιβορνο, 1750-1868. (Florin, Wheat and Garden Street. Greek Merchants in Livorno, 1750-1868)* (Athens, 2000).

[2]Stamatis Petrou, *Γράμματα απο το Αμστερντάμ* (Letters from Amsterdam) (Athens, 1976).

[3]Pierre Échinard, *Grecs et Philhellènes à Marseille de la révolution française à l'indépendance grecque* (Marseilles, 1973).

[4]E.g., J.G. Nanninga, ed., *Bronnen tot de Geschiedenis van den Levantschen Handel. Derde deel: 1727-1765* ('S-Gravenhage, 1952) and *idem, Bronnen tot de Geschiedenis van den Levantschen Handel. Vierde deel: 1765-1826* ('S-Gravenhage, 1966).

[5]Elena Frangakis-Syrett, *Οι Χιώτες έμποροι στις διεθνείς συναλλαγές,* 1750-1850 (*Chiot Merchants in International Trade 1750-1850)* (Athens, 1995).

[6]Edhem Eldem, *The Commerce of Istanbul in the Eighteenth Century* (Leiden, 1999).

[7]Mübahat S. Kütükoğlu, *XV ve XVI. Asırlarda İzmir Kazasının Sosyal ve İktisadi Yapısı* (İzmir, 2000); see also, *idem, İzmir Tarihinden Kesitler* (İzmir, 2000).

[8]Daniel Goffman, *İzmir and the Levantine World, 1550-1650* (Seattle, 1990); see also, Edhem Eldem, Daniel Goffman, and Bruce Masters, *The Ottoman City between East and West. Aleppo, İzmir, and Istanbul* (Cambridge, 1999).

[9]Sonia Anderson, *An English Consul in Turkey* (Oxford, 1989).

Necmi Ülker in his unpublished Ph.D. dissertation has studied the trade of İzmir with Europe in the late seventeenth and early eighteenth centuries.[1] Yugo Nagata has studied the Karaosmanoğulları family, who were landowners and administrators in western Anatolia (including the regions of İzmir and Manisa) in the eighteenth and early nineteenth centuries.[2] Bozkurt Ersoy has studied the hans of İzmir.[3] For the nineteenth century, Orhan Kurmuş has studied the trade of İzmir within the context of European-Ottoman economic relations,[4] whilst the economy and trade of İzmir with Europe, from the viewpoint of the incorporation of the Ottoman empire into the world economy, has been studied by Reşat Kasaba.[5] Marie-Carmen Smyrnelis has recently completed a Ph.D. thesis on the social history of İzmir and its communities in the eighteenth and nineteenth centuries.[6] İnci Kuyulu Ersoy has studied the cultural history of İzmir in the nineteenth century.[7] Tuncer Baykara has written on the history of İzmir overall.[8] Rauf Beyru has studied the social history of nineteenth-century İzmir[9] and Engin Berber, in particular, early twentieth-century İzmir.[10] E. Serce has written on İzmir in the second half of the nineteenth and in the early twentieth centuries.[11] O. Ergenç,[12]

---

[1] Necmi Ülker, "The rise of İzmir, 1688-1740" (University of Michigan Ph.D. dissertation, 1974). Some of his findings have been published in *idem, XVII. ve XVIII. Yüzyıllarda İzmir Şehri Tarihi* (İzmir, 1994).

[2] Yuzo Nagata, *Tarihte Ayanlar Karaosmanoğulları üzerinde bir inceleme* (Ankara, 1997); see also, Çağatay M. Ulücay, "Karaosmanoğullarına ait vesikalar" *Tarih Vesikaları Dergisi* (1942), pp. 117-126; 193-207; 430-440.

[3] Bozkurt Ersoy, *İzmir hanları* (Ankara, 1991).

[4] Orhan Kurmuş, "The Role of British Capital in the Economic Development of western Anatolia, 1850-1913" (unpublished University of London Ph.D. thesis, 1974); see also, *idem, Emperyalizmin Türkiye'ye Girişi* (Ankara, 1982).

[5] Reşat Kasaba, *The Ottoman Empire and the World Economy* (Albany, NY, 1988); see also, *idem*, "Was there a Comprador Bourgeoisie in Mid-Nineteenth Century Western Anatolia?", *Review*, Vol. 10 (1988), pp. 215-228 and R. Kasaba, Ç. Keyder & F. Tabak, "Eastern Mediterranean Port Cities and their Bourgeoisies: Merchants, Political Projects, and Nation States", *Review*, Vol. 10/1 (1986), pp. 121-135.

[6] Marie-Carmen Smyrnelis, "Une société hors de soi. Identités et relations sociales à Smyrne aux XVIIIe et XIXe siécles", (unpublished thèse de doctorat, École des Hautes études et Sciences Sociales, Paris, 2000).

[7] Inci Kuyulu Ersoy, "Cultural Contributions of the Levantines in İzmir", *Kolokyum 19. yy.'da Mersin ve Akdeniz Dünyası* (Mersin, 2002), pp. 73-39.

[8] Tuncer Baykara, *Izmir Şehri ve Tarihi* (İzmir, 1974).

[9] Rauf Beyru, *19. Yüzyılda İzmir'de Yaşam* (Istanbul, 2000).

[10] Engin Berber, *Sancılı yıllar: İzmir 1918-1922. Mütareke ve Yunan işgali döneminde İzmir sancağı* (Ankara, 1997).

[11] Erken Serce, *Tanzimat'tan Cumhuriyet'e İzmir'de belediye, İzmir* (İzmir, 1998); see also, *idem, İzmir, 1905* (İzmir, 2000).

[12] O. Ergenç, *Salnamelerde İzmir* (İzmir, 1990). See also, Nahide Şimşir, *Osmanlı Araştırmaları* (Istanbul, 2004); *idem*, İzmir'in Sosyal ve Ekonomik Tarihi (1730-1792) (Ege Üniversitesi doktora tezi, İzmir, 1999) and Sibel Zandi-Sayek, Public Space and Urban Citizens: Ottoman Izmir in the Remarking, 1840-1890 (University of California Ph.D dissertation, Berkeley, CA, 2001).

Zeki Arıkan[1], A. Martal,[2] H. Rifat,[3] and Melih Gürsoy[4] have all written on different aspects of the social, administrative or economic history of İzmir in the nineteenth and early twentieth centuries, while Serap Yılmaz has studied the French community of the city-port,[5] and Jan Schmidt has studied the opium trade and the Dutch community of İzmir in the nineteenth century.[6]

With the exception of Necmi Ülker, who deals in detail with the trade of İzmir in the early decades of the eighteenth century, as does also the author of this volume, none of the above works on İzmir study the commercial and monetary history of the city throughout the eighteenth and early nineteenth centuries, what can be termed "the long eighteenth century" — namely, c. 1700-1820. It is this gap in Ottoman historiography that the articles in the present volume, in part, seek to fill. Especially since this was a time when İzmir dominated Ottoman-European trade and was central to the empire's internal trade, too. During this time İzmir also played an important role in alleviating some of the monetary problems that the empire faced in the process becoming one of the major financial markets of the empire. Some of the recurrent themes in the present articles thus deal with monetary issues and the mechanisms and practices that İzmir's market developed to overcome problems such as currency volatility and monetary shortage. There has been a long tradition of studies on such issues in Ottoman historiography as for instance the studies of Halil Sahillioğlu.[7] Amongst other authors that have more recently looked at Ottoman monetary issues and state policy, for the eighteenth century, have been Şevket Pamuk in his recent book on Ottoman monetary history,[8] Yavuz Cezar in his studies on Ottoman finance and state fiscal policies[9] and Mehmet Genç in his studies on Ottoman taxation and

---

[1]E.g. Zeki Arıkan, "XVIII.-XIX. Yüzyıllarda İzmir", *21. Yüzyıl Eşiğinde İzmir. Uluslararası Sempozyum* (İzmir, 2001).

[2]A. Martal, *Değişim sürecine İzmirde Sanayileşme* (İzmir, 1999).

[3]H. Rıfat, *İzmir, 1914* (İzmir, 1999).

[4]M. Gürsoy, *Tarihi, Ekonomisi ve İnsanlarıyla bizim İzmirmiz* (İzmir, 1993).

[5]Serap Yılmaz, "XVII-XIX. Yüzyıllarda İzmir'de Fransızlar", *Çağdaş Türkiye Tarihi Araştırmaları Dergisi* (1993), Vol. 1/3 pp. 117-132.

[6]Jan Schmidt, *From Anatolia to Indonesia. Opium Trade and the Dutch Community of İzmir, 1820-1940* (Istanbul, 1998).

[7]E.g., Halil Sahillioğlu, "Fatih'in Son Yıllarında Bakir Para Basılması ve Dağıtılması ile İlgili Belgeler", *Belgelerle Türk Tarih Dergisi* (1968), No. 6, pp. 72-75; see also, *idem*, "Sivis Year Crises in the Ottoman Empire", M.A. Cook, ed., *Studies in the Economic History of the Middle East* (Oxford, 1970), pp. 230-249.

[8]Şevket Pamuk, *A Monetary History of the Ottoman Empire* (Cambridge, 2000); see also, *idem*, "Money in the Ottoman Empire, 1326-1914", Halil İnalcık & Donald Quataert, eds., *The Ottoman Empire: Its Economy and Society, 1300-1914* (Cambridge, 1995), pp. 497-980.

[9]Yavuz Cezar, *Osmanlı Maliyesinde Bunalım ve Değişim Dönemi (XVIII. yy'dan Tanzimat'a Mali Tarih)* (Istanbul, 1986).

fiscal policies.[1] In his above-cited book on Istanbul and in his book on the Ottoman Bank, Eldem has studied monetary issues relating to the eighteenth and nineteenth centuries.[2] The present volume hopes to contribute further, primarily through the prism of İzmir, to Ottoman monetary history in the eighteenth and early nineteenth centuries.

Apart from the obvious importance of Ottoman archives for Ottoman economic history, amongst the European archives used by scholars of Ottoman-European trade, in the eighteenth century, the British archives figure prominently. However, there is an even more extensive use of French archival sources. Many of the books on eighteenth-century Ottoman-European trade cited above are based exclusively on French sources and some study exclusively Ottoman-French trade in that century. There are a number of reasons for this. Firstly, France was the principal trading partner in the trade of the empire with Europe in the eighteenth century. Secondly, the extensive nature of French sources on the trade of France as well as of other European countries with the Ottoman empire, in part due to the requirements of the *ancien régime*, where the state sought to document and regulate extensive areas of the economy, have left us extremely good records to work from. Certainly, one must keep in mind that these were documents mostly written by French officials or merchants usually for other French officials, merchants or civil servants; that is, they were written from a certain point of view. Nevertheless the writers did address and were familiar with the Ottoman reality, often being either first-hand witnesses or active participants in Ottoman-European trade and, within certain constraints, in the Ottoman social milieu, too. The extensive use of French sources is also due to the fact that these archives contain systematic statistical data — a trait of the Enlightenment — which is pivotal for undertaking any effective study of trade. Moreover, since the eighteenth century was the Age of Reason and promoted verifiable scientific inquiry, there was also a conscious effort on the part of the French officials, or merchants acting as commission agents for their employers in France, for accuracy in the statistical tables they compiled or in the information they included and judgments they made in their reports. There is also a strong tradition amongst French historians, many of them from the Marseilles/Aix-en-Provence region, in the south of France, of

[1]Mehmet Genç, *Osmanlı İmparatorluğunda Devlet ve Ekonomi* (Istanbul, 2000); see also, *idem*, "A Study of the Feasibility of Using Eighteenth Century Ottoman Financial Records as an Indicator of Economic Activity", in Huri Islamoğlu-İnan, ed., *The Ottoman Empire and the World Economy* (Cambridge, 1987), pp. 345-373.

[2]Edhem Eldem, *A History of the Ottoman Bank* (Istanbul, 1999); on Ottoman finance, see also C. Clay, *Gold for the Sultan* (London, 2000).

studying this subject. This is perhaps also the result of the historically strong economic links between Marseilles and the Levant. Starting with the works of Paul Masson, published in the late nineteenth and early twentieth centuries,[1] we have more recently the publications by L. Bergasse and G. Rambert,[2] Robert Paris,[3] Charles Carrière,[4] Ferreol Rebuffat & Marcel Courdurié,[5] Carrière, Courdurié & Rebuffat,[6] C. Carrière & M. Morineau,[7] Carrière & Courdurié.[8] Panzac, Raymond, Mantran, Boulanger, cited above, and in many respects Eldem, too, can also be considered part of this tradition. The author, having availed herself of the above bibliography in her research, hopes to contribute to it further through the present volume.

II

The volume is divided into separate but interrelated parts which concern different aspects of the Ottoman economy in the eighteenth and early nineteenth centuries: the monetary conditions in the empire and their impact upon trade; the long-term dynamics in the commercial relationship of the Ottoman empire and Europe; Ottoman coastal trade routes and markets; the role and position of İzmir in the empire's external and internal trade; commercial and monetary practices and networks of European and Ottoman merchants in the conduct of Ottoman-European trade. More specifically, the second article in the volume, following this introductory study, compares the way the Ottoman empire, Britain and France tried to raise revenues and deal with state debt and the fiscal policies that were followed to attain such objectives. The third article examines the way the Ottoman monetary system functioned in relation to the specie substitution policies of the state and the way the local market responded as well as adjusted to such policies, including

[1]Paul Masson, *Histoire du commerce français dans le Levant au XVIIIe siècle* (Paris, 1911); see also, *idem, Histoire du commerce français dans le Levant au XVIIe siècle* (Paris, 1896).

[2]L. Bergasse & G. Rambert, *Histoire du commerce de Marseille. Vol. IV. De 1559 à 1660* (Paris, 1954).

[3]Robert Paris, *Histoire du commerce de Marseille. Vol. V. Le Levant de 1660 à 1789* (Paris, 1957).

[4]Charles Carrière, *Négociants marseillais au XVIIIe siècle* (Marseilles, 1973), 2 vols.

[5]F. Rebuffat & M. Courdurié, *Marseille et le négoce monétaire international, 1785-1790* (Marseilles, 1966).

[6]C. Carrière, M. Courdurié & F. Rebuffat, *Marseille, ville morte. La peste de 1720* (Marseilles, 1968).

[7]E.g., C. Carrière & M. Morineau, "Draps du Languedoc et commerce du Levant au XVIIIe siècle", *Revue d'histoire économique et sociale* (1968), Vol. 46, pp. 108-121.

[8]E.g., C. Carrière & M. Courdurié, "Un sophisme économique. Marseille s'enrichit en achetant plus qu'elle ne vend. Réflexions sur les mécanismes commerciaux levantins au XVIIIe siècle", *Histoire, Économie et Société* (1984), pp. 7-51.

the speculative monetary practices that developed as a response to such conditions. Trade in money was one of those practices, and one which the fourth article examines using statistical data concerning monetary flows between İzmir and Marseilles in the decades between 1750s-1780s. Such an analysis shows that it was not only the market of İzmir that needed and received inflows of specie and bills, either in order to boost its circulating medium or to send funds onto the imperial capital, but at times, also Marseilles. Movements of funds between Marseilles and İzmir also formed part of the international flows of bullion through the Europe-centered international payments system of the eighteenth century in which a major Ottoman market, such as that of İzmir, formed an integral part.

Early on in my studies of Ottoman-European trade in the context of long-distance international commerce within an eighteenth-century world economy, I became aware of the importance of monetary issues not only for the Ottoman but for the European economies, too. This was due to the, perhaps obvious, fact that, besides the use of barter, the commercial interaction between the two economies was taking place through the medium of money in the form of specie and of various instruments of payments. As a result monetary issues impacted the commercial relationship in fundamental ways. There was another reason, too: in the eighteenth century, and one can certainly extend the argument to the late seventeenth century, which is a period the present volume touches upon, monetary conditions were still evolving in the world economy. European and Ottoman governments were still exploring new and more efficient ways of raising taxes at peacetime. Fiscal solvency, especially at times of war, as well as in the immediate aftermath following a protracted period of conflict, was a challenge for most states. In the private sector, too, monetary resources could still be limited. The efficiency of bills of exchange as credit mechanisms and as international instruments of payment was still evolving. Banking, as a specialized and regulated sector of the European economies, representing considerable capital resources and being able to finance trade and industry, was still developing. Chronic monetary shortages and periodic imbalances between availability and demand for the circulating medium could still occur in active money markets or commercial centers. However such phenomena affected the various countries, or regions within Europe and the Empire, differently. For instance, Britain and the Netherlands had distinctly more developed capital markets and banking sectors than the Italian city-states. In the Ottoman empire, İzmir had a more developed money market compared to smaller urban centers in Anatolia.

A number of factors, including level of economic development and the needs of the Treasury, especially at wartime, affected the adequacy, or otherwise, of the circulating medium in an area. The many wars that the Ottoman empire had to fight, from the late seventeenth to the early nineteenth centuries, placed an extraordinary burden on its budget. It accentuated monetary shortages at home and further weakened abroad an already weak and volatile piastre.[1] Yet the Ottoman empire was not alone in battling with problems of inadequacy of the circulating medium and a weak, debased currency. As the articles in the first section of the volume endeavor to illustrate, in different ways, these were some of the basic problems that also confronted European governments. They, too, sought out new policies in order to meet state expenditure and their markets innovated on ways to add to the volume of their circulating medium, which ranged from coin clipping in late seventeenth-century England to the use of bills "payable en compensation" in late eighteenth-century Marseilles.

Pressed for revenue, the Ottoman state, too, instituted new policies, or extended the scale and scope of existing ones, in order to increase the volume of liquid funds in the economy and in its coffers. These policies included borrowing from the domestic market, farming state taxes and selling state offices in order to raise funds or, if all else failed, debasing the currency. The Ottoman government was not alone in doing so. For instance, the protracted wars of the late seventeenth and early eighteenth centuries, that the European states had to fight both against each other as well as against the Ottoman empire, strained their finances, too, and led to borrowing as one of the principal policies they pursued to raise revenue. As shown in the second article in this volume France, in particular, followed policies that were in many respects quite similar to those of the Ottoman empire with, at times, quite similar results. In the course of the eighteenth century, both France and the Ottoman empire had growing debts, mostly short-term, maintained through revolving lines of credit from their financiers. In the 1720s, in order to raise revenue to meet its debts and alleviate monetary scarcity, France undertook a series of debasements of the louis d'or. Following each debasement, the French government attempted to float the currency above its intrinsic value. However, the markets rejected the "official" value of the coin and instead let it circulate at a level that was more representative of both its metal content and demand for the coin in the market. The currency markets in the major commercial centers of the Ottoman empire reacted in exactly the

[1]I have tended to use the term piastre, rather than *guruş*, as this was the term used in the western archives at the time to denote the Ottoman currency.

same manner whenever the Porte sought to set, by decree, the value of recently debased coinage.[1]

In the course of the eighteenth and in the early nineteenth centuries, the British government, too, continued to borrow in order to face the mounting expenditure of further large-scale conflicts — from the War of the Spanish Succession through the Napoleonic Wars — thereby considerably increasing the size of its National Debt. Repayment of this debt placed a strain on its finances: in 1817 the annual interest alone of the debt was about three-quarters more than what the entire pre-war government budget had been in the late eighteenth century. However, the British government was able to organize the repayment of its debt and to do so without stifling investment in the economy. Capital remained available for the needs of trade, industry and infrastructure development such as canal building or, by the early nineteenth century, railroad construction. The existence of the relevant institutional infrastructure, particularly in the latter part of our period, in the form of London and provincial stock exchanges and personnel that could channel available capital to new enterprises certainly facilitated such investment.[2] Inflows of capital from the Netherlands may have also helped the private sector besides alleviating budget deficits.[3] Nevertheless, there was a concerted state policy, too: following the War for the Spanish Succession, Britain, more than any other state in Europe, made fiscal solvency and borrowing at low interest rates, a priority. It was able to do so for a number of reasons. The establishment of the Bank of England, in the late seventeenth century, allowed the state to streamline its borrowing and to adopt, at the end of the war in 1714, 5% as its legal maximum rate of interest. This was considerably lower than the former level of 10-14% that had been current in the 1690s.[4] The adoption of such a low rate of interest was also the result of a highly developed credit and capital market in London. Further, by reorganizing its finances and revenues, including the restructuring of its system of taxation and

[1]The National Archives of the United Kingdom (TNA): PRO, London, Series SP 105/128, Consul Werry, İzmir, 17 Sept. 1801 to Levant Company, London. Hereafter these archives will be cited as PRO. Please also note that until recently these archives have been known as Public Record Office, London (PRO) and they have been cited in this manner in all the articles in this volume.

[2]L.E. Davis & R.E. Gallman, *Evolving Financial Markets and International Capital Flows* (Cambridge, 2001), pp. 51-54.

[3]This point is still being contested in the relevant literature. E.g., E.S. Brezis, "Foreign Capital Flows in the Century of Britain's Industrial Revolution: New Estimates, Controlled Conjectures", *Economic History Review* (1995), Vol. XLVIII/1, pp. 46-67; R.C. Nash, "The Balance of Payments and Foreign Capital Flows in Eighteenth-Century England: A Comment", *Economic History Review* (1997), Vol. L/1, pp. 110-128.

[4]M.M. Postan, "Some Recent Problems in the Accumulation of Capital", *Economic History Review* (1935), Vol. VI, pp. 1-12.

collection, the British state was able to raise revenues in a viable and sustainable manner to repay its debt. This, in turn, allowed it to enjoy a high credit rating whenever it had to borrow from London, or other money markets in Europe, while lower interest rates lowered its debt burden overall. Finally, Britain was able to render its public debt into an asset, by transforming it into a sound system of public credit. Other developments, including structural changes and growth of the banking sector in England and Scotland, in the course of the eighteenth century, further enabled the British government to manage its debt effectively in the long term.[1]

As for the Ottoman empire, it used tax farming as a crucial instrument to meet its domestic borrowing goals.[2] It was not alone in doing so: France used tax farming to raise revenue in the seventeenth and eighteenth centuries. Moreover it was in 1695, a time of financial crisis for both Europe and the empire, that the latter instituted important changes in tax farming. It expanded the system to make it more effective in rendering the required revenue as well as to enable it to borrow on a longer term basis. Later modifications, carried out in mid-eighteenth century, and again in the early nineteenth century, led to further modifications in the tax farming system; however, they all fell short of the desired results. Even if tax farming had been rendered more effective, it was essentially flawed as an effective and efficient system of revenue collection, as the French experience also indicates. Indeed, when Britain reorganized its finances, early on in the eighteenth century, one of its primary policies was putting an end to tax farming altogether.

Although the Ottoman Treasury was, at times, replenished by imports of specie from Europe and its bankers may themselves have borrowed funds from the West, the Ottoman state did not contract any loans abroad throughout the period under study. Tax farming, however inadequate it might have been, acted as the primary source through which the state raised or borrowed revenue. In other words, the Ottoman state met its fiscal needs essentially through the monetary resources of the empire. In doing so, however, it drew too much capital from other sectors of the economy, such as trade, and contributed to the lack of specie in the empire's markets as well as to the slow rate of growth in investment capital. State securities were the most favorite

[1] John Brewer, *The sinews of Power. War, money and the English State, 1688-1783* (London, 1988), *passim.*

[2] Ariel Salzman, "An Ancien Régime Revisited : 'Privatization' and Political Economy in the Eighteenth-Century Ottoman Empire", *Politics & Society* (1993), Vol. 21/4, pp. 393-423 ; see also, Murat Cizakça, *A Camparative Evolution of Business Partnerships in the Islamic World and Europe with specific references to the Ottoman Archives* (Leiden, 1996), pp. 140-45, 158-64, 170-73.

investment both in Britain and in the Ottoman empire, in the eighteenth century. In the latter, moneylending was another favorable investment. In Britain, investment in state securities did not preclude investment in other sectors of the economy. In the empire, however, preference for non-productive investments by the Ottoman élite, due to the lucrative nature of such investments, which outperformed investments in trade or manufacture, together with a general lack of confidence in the long-term prospects of the economy on the part of the investors, further contributed to the inadequate levels of capital growth particularly for long-term investment.[1] Despite an advanced and sophisticated system of credit through the widespread use of promissory notes and networks of bills of exchange that functioned efficiently within the extensive Ottoman domains, the rates of interest remained at very high levels, even in its urban markets, reflecting an on-going tightness of capital. In other words, there was an inadequate level of development in the capital and credit markets to meet demands resulting from economic growth as well as demands arising from the Ottoman Treasury.

Before the nineteenth century and the widespread development of banking in western Europe, it was not only pressures placed on governments to meet expenditure, accentuated at wartime, but also the rate of growth of the economy which rendered the available amount of the circulating medium all the more inadequate and made monetary scarcity in certain European markets all the more acute. In the Ottoman empire, where large urban markets were already monetized by the seventeenth century, monetary shortage was a problem that increased further not only owing to Ottoman fiscal policies and needs but also as a result of the growing volume of trade and of the overall economic growth that was registered, in particular in the second half of the eighteenth and in the early nineteenth centuries. A number of factors, specific to the Ottoman empire, placed additional stress on the circulating medium. The vast size of the empire led to the appearance of semi-autonomous regional markets, and economies, and contributed to the lack of unification of the Ottoman domestic market. As a result the Ottoman currency was able to circulate at different rates of exchange, simultaneously, in different Ottoman markets,[2] making attempts by the state to standardize and regulate the currency, with a view to strengthening it, all the more difficult. Although it is impossible to quantify it, commerce must have received smaller flows of

[1]Mehmet Genç, "Osmanlı İktisadi Dünya Görüşünün İlkeleri", *İ.Ü. Edebiyat Fakültesi Sosyoloji Dergisi*, 3 (Istanbul, 1989), *passim*.

[2]Halil Sahillioğlu, "The role of international monetary and metal movements in Ottoman monetary history, 1300-1750", J.F. Richards, ed., *Precious Metals in the Later Medieval and Early Modern Worlds* (Durham, N.C., 1983), pp. 269-304.

capital as a result of Ottoman investors' preferences, fiscal policies and the persistent problems of a chronically inadequate circulating medium. Yet trade as a sector grew in the eighteenth century. There was growth in the external maritime trade of the empire with the West, judging from statistical figures available, and in the coastal trade, judging from the proliferation of trade routes and active markets in Ottoman coastal waters.[1]

That such commercial growth was possible, despite the problems referred to above, was due to a number of reasons amongst them being the way the Ottoman monetary and credit systems functioned on the level of the market. There was in fact a degree of flexibility, inherent in the Ottoman monetary system which could be activated through a discount mechanism, called *agio*, to enable a local market to adjust to monetary conditions and even, at times, to increase, at least temporarily, the amount of circulating capital. Through the application of an *agio*, or discount, on the rates of exchange between the Ottoman piastre and the European currencies,[2] circulating in a certain Ottoman market at a given point in time, the Ottoman currency could be favored and acquire a premium over and above its intrinsic metal or even market value. The exact amount of premium applied varied according to overall conditions in the market. This was done so as to draw specie and business to the market. For instance, if a rate of discount favoring the local currency were applied in İzmir, the city attracted specie in the local currency away from other provincial markets, for instance Bursa, where no such premium existed at the time. Local merchants found it more profitable to do business in İzmir than in Bursa and went to the city-port with their funds and, for a whole host of other reasons specific to a given market, those dealing in or holding western currencies were willing to accept an inflated local currency. Leaving aside other factors which could impact business dynamics in a local market, the lifting of *agio* too early could have the opposite result leading to a flight of specie and business to other markets. By enabling upward adjustments to take place in the amount of specie circulating in a market, the *agio* alleviated, at least temporarily, monetary scarcity but also volatility in the currency. For a local market could also modify the exchange rates by deciding the amount of *agio*, or discount, to be applied and to do so

[1]For archival sources, see Archives de la Chambre de Commerce de Marseille, Marseilles ; Série I, 19-20, 26-28 ; Archives Nationales de France, Paris; Série Affaires Étrangères, AE Bi 1011, 1014 and AE Biii 271-274. Thereafter the above archival collections will be cited as ACCM and ANF respectively. For statistics on the import and export trade of the empire with France, see Frangakis-Syrett, *The Commerce of Smyrna ..., passim.*

[2]Richard Hayes, *The Negotiator's Magazine* (London, 1719), p. 210; see also, Macé de Richebourg, *Essai sur la qualité des monnaies étrangères et sur leurs différents rapports avec les monnaies de France* (Paris, 1764), p. 55.

for a period of time that it could control, since it could decide when, and if, to modify, or end the application of *agio*, given that other conditions favoring such a discount policy were also present.

Within the Ottoman empire, the market of İzmir is quite representative of the way a major provincial urban center adapted to the monetary conditions of the eighteenth century and the role and uses of the *agio* in facilitating the achievement of such aims, as shown in different articles in this volume. As part of the self-regulatory mechanism of the Ottoman monetary system the *agio*, which was present in almost every commercial transaction, could be activated by the market forces to bring order to the monetary disorder in the city's market and often held the key to its effective functioning. Besides attracting specie to a market, as argued in greater detail in the third article in the volume, commodity prices could also be affected through application of the *agio*. In addition, the *agio* played a crucial role in Ottoman-French trade by calculating the exchange rate value of the livre tournois *vis-à-vis* the Ottoman piastre. A fixed exchange rate of three livres tournois to one Ottoman piastre was used throughout the eighteenth century. This rate was further adjusted, and modified, through application of the *agio*, so as to arrive at a precise exchange rate which took into account not only the precious metal value of the two coins but also their market value as set by the forces of supply and demand prevalent at that moment in time. This was because both coins no longer represented an intrinsic value based on their metal content. Already from the start of the eighteenth century, the livre tournois served as money of account. By the latter part of the century the Ottoman coin had departed so much from its initial intrinsic metal value that it, too, had become in many respects money of account, whose symbolic value facilitated primarily the keeping of accounts. However, the Ottoman piastre was also very real in monetary terms, since the Ottoman coin functioned as an important medium of exchange in the empire as well as in international commerce. Its fluctuating value, and hence exchange rate *vis-à-vis* the livre tournois, in the marketplace, was effected through the application of the *agio*. Besides the livre tournois, a large number of different currencies circulated in an active money market such as İzmir's and exchange rates could change daily. By the early nineteenth century, exchange rates could change even in the course of a single day. The *agio* had the flexibility and refinement that were necessary to render precisely such fluctuating exchange rates.

Besides the application of *agio,* major trading centers in the Ottoman empire were also able to develop an extensive, though sustainable, system of credit that added to the circulating medium without creating unsustainable levels of speculative credit. In other words the markets continued functioning, and even registering growth, because they were able overall to maintain confidence in the volume of promissory notes and other instruments of credit circulating within them. They did so despite the relatively high interest rates of at least 12%, and often even more, which were being charged. Nevertheless high interest rates probably diminished the potential for even further growth from taking place. Whatever the case might have been, the example of İzmir shows that monetary scarcity could be overcome to the degree necessary to register very considerable commercial growth as was the case especially in the last quarter of the eighteenth and in the first quarter of the nineteenth centuries. Of course it can also be argued that İzmir, with its active trading links with the West, had advantages that smaller markets in the interior did not have. Yet İzmir was also not unique, either within the empire or within the world economy, in the resourceful manner its market dealt with prevailing monetary conditions. There are parallels between İzmir and Bursa, Aleppo or Salonica; there are also parallels with Marseilles, as the articles in the first section in this volume indicate. The market of the French port, too, functioned through an extensive system of credit where paper increasingly substituted for specie. There was even innovation in this area whereby commercial paper was bought and sold through the means of further commercial paper rather than specie. It was a system that allowed its merchants as well as *courtiers*, or brokers, who devised it, to multiply the volume of the circulating medium to meet the needs for capital which was the result, at least in part, of the considerable commercial growth that Marseilles, like İzmir, experienced in the latter part of the eighteenth century. Excessive amount and use of credit may well have worsened the impact on Marseilles of the European financial crisis of 1774. Following the crisis, adjustments had to be made to the credit system in Marseilles to render it more accountable and less speculative. Nevertheless, judging from the way the French port recovered from the crisis and its continued commercial vibrancy, subsequently, the credit system had overall worked well in promoting economic growth.

The use of *agio* also promoted further growth in the city's informal commercial banking sector by turning some of the more problematic features of the Ottoman monetary system into opportunities for profit through arbitrage and monetary speculative operations. Profits from such activities may well have contributed to the further growth of the local economy since many of those practicing them were merchants, Ottoman or European, and would have put back, at least part of, their profits into their on-going commercial ventures. Nevertheless, with such activities one also ran the risk of creating not merely a very active and lucrative currency market, as was the case in İzmir at various points in the period under study, but an over-speculative one that could further add to the volatility of the Ottoman currency. One need not, however, consider speculative monetary activities as necessarily harmful to a local economy, if the market could sustain its confidence and continue functioning which, with some temporary exceptions to the contrary, seems to have been the case in İzmir.

As any student of Ottoman commerce would discover, dealing in money and dealing in goods was almost interrelated. Throughout the eighteenth century, but especially in the latter part and in the early nineteenth century, a whole array of speculative monetary practices went hand in hand with commercial activities and feature in many of the articles in this volume. All groups, whether Ottoman or European, Muslim or non-Muslim, practiced such activities, at times neglecting commodity trading. They had to be savvy about them or else they did not succeed in business. The westerners were at home with such practices since some of these activities were also practiced by merchants-cum-bankers in Europe. Given the relative lack of institutionalized banking in the West, merchanting and banking operations often overlapped. For instance, the Marseilles-based house of Roux Frères, which traded in the Ottoman empire through its agents, combined commerce, merchant-banking, maritime transportation and insurance in its global activities.[1] London merchants often dealt in bills of exchange or discounted bills as part of their overall business. It was all the more so in the Ottoman empire where capital, whether in specie or in bills of exchange, carried a very high premium. Ottoman merchants, their capital resources permitting, often combined moneylending and/or money changing in their trading activities. In İzmir, Istanbul or in other major Ottoman centers the Europeans, and at times the locals too, practiced arbitrage and dealt in bills of exchange. They did so in different ways: they discounted bills of exchange as well as bought and sold them making their profits by speculating on the differences in the rates of exchange and premium, and hence ultimate costs, of bills in relation to specie. There were many factors that could affect the exchange rates of specie or the premium of a bill based upon supply and demand for bills or specie or upon

[1]E.g., ACCM, Série LIX/735, R. Franchetti, İzmir, 13 Aug. 1788 and 8 Jan. 1790 to Roux Frères, Marseilles; LIX/750, Denis Rolland & Cie, İzmir, 13 Dec. 1788, 5 Jan. 1789 and 19 March 1790 to Roux Frères, Marseilles.

other special needs in a market at a given point in time. For instance, at the height of the export season in İzmir, the demand for the local currency to pay for the purchase of goods was very strong and the rates of exchange were accordingly affected. The situation, however, could change as far as bills of exchange were concerned if the need to remit funds abroad emerged at a given point in time. This was more difficult to predict given that the import trade took place all year round. Furthermore, speculators at times sought to manipulate the price of bills by influencing the amount of the circulating medium in either bills or specie to benefit from selling their bills. Similarly they could attempt to impact transactions in a given currency, which resulted in the market favoring one currency over another, in order to profit from the added premium in the rates of exchange which that currency might then carry. Trade in money, which entailed importing, and to a lesser extent exporting, specie or bills to and from the Ottoman markets and the West, was probably the most widespread speculative activity practiced mostly by the Europeans throughout the period under study.[1]

It was not only the markets that attempted to increase the circulating medium in a variety of ways; the Ottoman state, too, sought to achieve the same aim through a series of debasements of the coinage. Debasement is a classic policy that has been followed by states long before the eighteenth century. It can be temporarily effective, since by minting more coins out of the same amount of precious metal the volume of coinage is actually increased. In the late seventeenth century, pressed for extra monetary resources to meet the remittance program of King William III without visibly decreasing the amount of bullion in the British economy, the government resorted to a policy that one could call 'indirect debasement'. It allowed the circulation of clipped silver coins in the realm at full value although they represented, in essence, a lower amount of precious metal. Since there was no adequate amount of good coins to go around, the markets, too, accepted them at full value. This was a time of a Europe-wide monetary scarcity, accentuated even if not triggered by the wars. Perhaps not surprisingly, it coincided, too, with the worst and most extensive phenomenon ever of counterfeited European coins entering the Ottoman markets where, for a certain period, they circulated at values that were way above their metal content. The recoinage in Britain, in 1696, put an end to the circulation of clipped coins. The minting of the Ottoman piastre, the guruş, for the first time in 1690, also aimed at putting an end to the monetary problems of the empire. Subsequent debasements in the empire are evidence of only partial success in the Ottoman case.

---

[1]PRO, SP 105/118, Levant Company, 27 Aug. 1750 to Consul Crawley, İzmir; see also, SP 105/337, Memorandum, Consul Hayes, İzmir, 15 May 1789.

Even when temporarily effective, extensive and persistent debasements ultimately became counter-effective; they triggered inflation and/or the hoarding of good coins, both of which decreased the circulating medium either in relative and/or in absolute terms. Since they were of a lesser value, one needed more coins, in order to transact business while the disappearance of good coins placed further stress on the circulating medium. Persistent debasement of the guruş which was followed by the Ottoman government in the latter part of the eighteenth and in the early nineteenth centuries, resulted in its continuous decline in the international rates of exchange. This trend is illustrated well in the changes in the exchange rates of the guruş to the Venetian sequin, details of which are given in the third article in the volume. Debasement also resulted in inflation. For instance, by the 1790s, it was estimated that there had been a seven-fold increase, since the previous two decades, in the cost of daily living in İzmir.[1] On the short term however, debasement also gave a necessary replenishment to the Ottoman Treasury as well as a boost to Ottoman-European trade. For inflation made Ottoman goods cheaper in the western markets, which contributed to further stimulating trade between the empire and Europe in the latter part of the eighteenth and in the early nineteenth centuries. However, growth in the world economy was a bigger stimulus and accounts far more than inflation for the robust growth registered in the trade between the empire with Europe.

Increase in trade also helped increase the circulating medium. For whilst growth of trade stood to place further demands on the circulating medium, it also added to it both in specie and in bills. It did so in a number of ways. Besides the accumulation of capital from profits realized, the empire received actual inflows of specie through a trade in money. Further, through international trade the empire was linked to the Europe-centered international payments system, whose aim was twofold: to facilitate multilateral payments amongst merchants in great distances and to overcome the need for specie, since bills of exchange were used extensively. As a participant, the empire benefited from this system. For instance, it received funds through the circulation in Ottoman markets that acted as regional banking centers, such as Istanbul or İzmir, of foreign bills of exchange drawn on European centers for the payment of purchases of Ottoman goods. By the latter part of the eighteenth century the exchange rates for an array of European currencies were routinely quoted in European merchants' correspondence, trading to and from Istanbul or İzmir, evidence of an open and constant interaction, by then, of

[1] PRO, SP 105/126, British Factory, 15 Jan. 1798 to Levant Company, İzmir; SP 105/127, British Factory and Consul Werry, İzmir, 17 Sept. 1799 to Levant Company, London.

these cities with Europe. Although bills drawn on Istanbul or İzmir must have had a very limited circulation in Europe, nevertheless these centers also received funds through a speculative trade in bills of exchange besides the circulation of paper for commercial use. As a result, European bills circulated alongside Ottoman bills in major Ottoman markets such as Alexandria or Salonica, besides Istanbul or İzmir; the two networks of bills of exchange often overlapped adding to the overall volume of the circulating medium in the empire. Increasing interaction through bills of exchange between major Ottoman markets and economic centers in Europe, either for commercial payments or for arbitrage operations, further integrated the former into the European financial circuits.

Such an integration had beneficial effects on the further development of the merchant-cum-banking sector, including credit and capital markets, in Ottoman centers. An examination of data concerning the transfers of specie and bills of exchange in and out of İzmir, and their relation to the balance of trade between the Ottoman port and Marseilles, included in the fourth article in this volume, shows that such flows were guided not only by needs to cover trade deficits but also by the need to replenish monetary resources in either market. Nevertheless, funds also traveled. A good part of specie or bills from Marseilles ultimately reached the Treasury in Istanbul, whilst another part of the funds left the western Anatolian port for Alexandria or other Ottoman centers, in the process entering the internal flow of bullion in the empire. A certain part of the funds may also have gone, through trade, further East to Iran or India, or indeed even back to Europe. Inflows of funds into Marseilles from İzmir may have stayed in the local economy or may have gone to other markets in France or elsewhere in Europe. Flows of funds to the French port tended to coincide with times of strain to local monetary resources, such as during the commercial crises that affected the region in 1734 and in 1774, or during wars, such as the Seven Years' War. However, there were also outflows of specie and bills from İzmir to the French port when there were neither wars nor economic crises. This was because flows in and out of İzmir and Marseilles were also part of speculative monetary operations. In the late 1780s transfers of money to İzmir, representing a large part of the total trading activity of the port and answering a strong need for coinage in the Ottoman economy, attained their highest levels. By then, İzmir had become the port of entry *par excellence* for specie in the empire, while speculating in monetary operations seems to have overtaken commodity trading amongst French merchants.

Movements of specie and paper between European and Ottoman centers also formed part of the global monetary flows. The empire's positive balance of trade with Europe, for most of the eighteenth century, provided it with at least some of the funds for its trade with the East and the Far East with which areas it had a negative balance of trade. In the process, it contributed to the movement of silver from West to East. There were also monetary flows going from East to West, that is, from the empire to Europe in the form of repatriated profits of westerners trading in Ottoman centers or of payments for freight or insurance premium to European captains, who were active participants in Ottoman coastal trade as shown in the second section of this volume. There were also profits sent to Europe from speculative monetary operations in centers like İzmir or Istanbul where specie was traded against bills of exchange and profits were sent back either in bills of exchange or specie according to whichever means were more profitable. With specific figures lacking, it is difficult to prove in a quantifiable manner, whether there was an overall deficit, and the amount of this deficit, in the balance of payments for the empire in its trade with Europe, even if one can plausibly argue that the potential for such a deficit did exist.[1] What we can say with greater certainty is that the overall picture is much more complex than the positive balance of trade, that was registered between the Ottoman empire and Europe for most of the eighteenth century, would imply.

III

The empire had its own 'internal' system of monetary flows which besides connecting it with markets in Europe also served the needs of its own regional markets. They were in part the result of state policy that aimed to create an equilibrium in its imperial domains between needs and resources as well as to keep large urban cities, in particular, supplied with goods.[2] A by-product of this system was channeling funds to markets internally, to the extent that it was possible given overall availability of the circulating medium, so as to create a better balance in monetary liquidity as well as to fulfill the needs of the Treasury. An important monetary flow within the empire was one that went from the provinces to the capital for the payment of taxation and purchase of state offices by the investing élite. Another monetary flow channeled part of the surplus accumulated in ports trading with Europe

[1]Carrière & Courdurié, "Un sophisme économique. Marseille s'enrichit en achetant plus...", pp. 7-51.

[2]Mehmet Genç, "Osmanlı Maliyesinde Malikane Sistemi", O. Okyar & H.U. Nalbantoğlu, eds., *Türkiye İktisat Tarihi Semineri* (Ankara, 1975), pp. 231-296.

further East to cover the empire's trade with India and the Far East, while another part of the surplus was sent to Istanbul. Some of the funds sent to the capital may have been sent on to Europe since Istanbul imported more goods than it exported. Most of the funds realized from the sale of European goods in Istanbul were not sent West however. Instead they made their way to other centers in the empire, where there were Europeans, for the purchase of Ottoman goods. In the process they constituted a reverse flow of funds, from the capital to the provinces, which was mostly realized through local and European networks of bills of exchange. Although trade with Europe represented only a certain amount of the overall trading activity of the empire, the flow of funds put into motion by the Europeans for their own trading activities, whether it was sending funds from Istanbul, or Marseilles, to İzmir to pay for purchases of olive oil in Mitylene, or whether it was sending funds from Istanbul, or London, to Aleppo to cover silk purchases, such remittances stood to compliment the internal flow of funds and networks of bills of exchange.

Creating an equilibrium between resources and needs was fundamental to the *raison d'être* of the commercial maritime world of eighteenth-century Ottoman empire, as shown in greater detail in articles in the second section of this volume. It also affected the dynamics of Ottoman internal trade where major ports complimented each other and were crucial in the transportation of goods from places of production to markets within the empire's vast domains. The sea, which allowed the empire's considerable coastline to be put into good use, was crucial in the implementation of such dynamics. For instance, Alexandria received specialized goods of near-by regions and sent them on to other parts of the empire together with its own, locally produced, goods. It also ran a deficit with certain areas — the Balkans, Anatolia and especially Istanbul — and a surplus with other regions. İzmir sent some of its surplus, from its trade with Europe, to Alexandria thus restoring some of the deficit of the Egyptian port, which the latter had acquired from buying goods from India and the Far East. İzmir sent another part of its surplus to the capital, as we noted above. Istanbul used some of these funds to buy wheat and other foodstuffs from Ottoman merchants in Salonica and Alexandria, the latter often freighting European ships to carry the goods to the capital.[1] Within the Ottoman maritime world, internal and external trade overlapped in many ways. Although the latter was primarily the result of market forces in the world

[1]Panzac, *Commerce et Navigation ... passim*; see also, Rhoads Murphey, "Provisioning Istanbul: the state and subsistence in the early modern Middle East", *Food and Foodways* (1998), Vol. 2, pp. 217-263.

economy, to which the empire was increasingly being drawn in the course of the eighteenth and early nineteenth centuries, it also became part of internal market forces and of the government's policies of maintaining its urban centers supplied. The proliferation of maritime routes and the different clusters of traffic patterns that were formed around major, medium and small-size markets, for the provisioning of their hinterland, was a characteristic feature of the eighteenth-century Ottoman maritime world as well as evidence of the vibrancy of Ottoman trade.[1] It was not only the major ports that had cluster(s) of maritime routes which revolved around them — with İzmir being the central hub of what was probably the biggest such cluster — but minor ports, too, as shown in the relevant articles. The result was a constant interaction between minor, medium and major markets, primarily through the medium of the sea, that related both to the internal and external trade of the empire.

Like the Ottoman monetary system that allowed the circulation of foreign coins in the empire alongside its own coinage so, too, was the Ottoman coastal trade open to all nationalities. Although most European countries tended to have a protectionist policy in relation to their coastal trade, European ships were able to ply Ottoman sea lanes carrying goods of local merchants, both Muslim and non-Muslim, from one port to another. The exception were certain maritime routes, such as the one between İzmir and Istanbul or short feeder routes that channeled goods from near-by coastal harbors to major ports. There, Ottoman carriers predominated almost exclusively. Besides goods, European captains carried money for their clients; in fact, bullion routinely formed part of their cargo. At times they even financed the trading activities of their charterers by advancing them funds for the latter to purchase their goods; the money was repaid, with interest, once the goods had reached the market where they were destined for sale. At other times the captains not only transported but also bought the goods on behalf of their clients following detailed instructions by the latter. The maritime contracts concluded between European captains on the one hand, and their Muslim as well as non-Muslim Ottoman clients on the other, which stipulated what was to be done, details of which are given in articles in the second section of the volume, show an interaction between the two groups that was both open and fluid as well as respected and seen as legally-binding by all parties. In this manner, the European captains not only took part in the carrying trade of the empire but also participated in local trade and in some respects in the local economy, too.

[1]ANF, AE Bi 1068, Consul Amoureux, İzmir, 3 June 1778 to Minister, Paris and AE Biii 242, Consul Fourcade, Mémoire sur le commerce de Smyrne, c. 1812.

For the European captains who were involved in Ottoman coastal trade, it was a profitable operation. For the French, who were the most active participants amongst the Europeans in Ottoman coastal trade, this was an integral part of their operations. Once they had left Marseilles, they expected to stay in the Levant for two years approximately. Their return cargo was acquired from freight earned from coastal trade and the French state, in particular, took care to foster and promote their activities. Such participation did not only make economic sense for the Europeans but also for the Ottomans. As the circulation of European coins was an effective policy of coin substitution, which added to the circulating medium, so was the presence of European carriers in Ottoman waters, alongside local ships, an effective policy that offered more opportunities for the transportation of local goods and created greater competition in freight rates and services to the benefit of local trade. It could, of course, also be argued that it took potential business away from local carriers. In addition, profits realized by European captains and shipowners, through Ottoman coastal trade, did not stay in the region but were, at least partly, repatriated to Europe. Yet the growth of local merchant marines that took place in the last quarter of the eighteenth and in the early nineteenth centuries, as was the case with the Ottoman Greek merchant marine, would indicate that the potential for growth of the sector was, overall, realized.

IV

The emergence of İzmir to dominance in the trade of the empire, in the course of the eighteenth century, was a gradual and complex process as argued, in particular, in the seventh, eleventh and concluding studies in the volume. Once in place, İzmir emerged as the premier Ottoman port. Moreover, given the propitious background created by a growing world economy, at the time, the foundations were there for a considerable and sustainable commercial take off to occur in the latter part of the eighteenth century. In the first half of the century, whilst İzmir had not yet attained its later commercial dominance, the port of Alexandria rivaled it in both the internal and external trade of the Empire. By the second half of the century, İzmir had overtaken the Egyptian port in the European trade. For a whole host of reasons, and strengthened by its position in the empire's trade with Europe, İzmir came to dominate internal Ottoman trade, too, so that by the beginning of the nineteenth century, it was commanding the most extensive trading networks in the empire. As argued in the second section of the volume, within the Istanbul-İzmir-Alexandria route, which was the most frequented maritime trading axis in the empire, İzmir became the most important link. As the biggest single urban market in the empire, Istanbul was another rival to İzmir in the import trade from Europe as well as in the internal maritime trade. Supplying Istanbul with foodstuffs was the driving force for one of the most important internal axis of trade. However, its political and administrative functions ultimately left the empire's landed and maritime networks for İzmir to provision. Unlike İzmir, Istanbul did not, to any great extent, attract goods from the Ottoman interior for export to Europe, nor did it import goods for distribution widely in the Ottoman interior.[1] Such functions were left, increasingly in the course of the eighteenth century, to İzmir: neither Salonica, İskenderun nor the Aegean islands, all of which had registered considerable trading activity with Europe in the first half of the eighteenth century, could rival the steady commercial growth of İzmir from the second half of the century onwards. In addition, during this period, there was considerable increase in Ottoman-European trade, in large part as a result of growth in the Ottoman and European economies, greater commercialization of Ottoman agriculture and growing demand for Ottoman exports in the expanding European markets. İzmir was part of these economic trends. As a result, it saw its share of the empire's European trade as well as its own commercial sector grow, both in relative and in absolute terms in this period. After 1746, in particular, the rate of growth of İzmir's export trade to France, the empire's biggest trading partner, surpassed that of the empire, even growing in years when the empire's exports fell. İzmir held an equally dominant position in the empire's import trade with Europe, and particularly with France, in the second half of the eighteenth century, far surpassing Istanbul and registering an increase in both absolute and relative terms in the value of goods imported, as shown in articles in the third section of the volume. Following the onset of the Industrial and French Revolutions, by the early nineteenth century, Britain had replaced France as the empire's and the city-port's principal trading partner. During this period, there was a further and quite spectacular increase in İzmir's exports to Europe, and especially Britain, whilst its imports quadrupled in value, reflecting on-going growth in the Ottoman domestic market.

For İzmir to surpass major and established ports in Ottoman-European trade such as Alexandria, Istanbul or Salonica, it had to have a number of special assets such as the ability to offer, at sustainable quantities and at competitive prices, all the major Ottoman exports that the European markets sought. Equally, it had to offer access to Ottoman markets for European and colonial goods at a larger scale and at more competitive prices than its rivals.

[1] Eldem, *French Trade in Istanbul ...*, pp. 34-42.

Acquiring a hinterland that covered large parts of Anatolia and stretched as far as the Persian market are important factors that enabled İzmir to fulfill the above conditions. For instance, İzmir specialized in medium-quality French cloth, one of the most important commodities in Ottoman-European trade at the time and imported it in increasing quantities exactly because it suited both the Anatolian and Persian markets. In addition, İzmir exported in equally growing amounts cotton and cotton yarn which, unlike silk and mohair yarn, were not luxury items. Moreover, given that barter was a popular medium of exchange in Ottoman-European trade, the exchange of Anatolian cotton or cotton yarn for French cloth made the most economic sense.

With an array of exports for which there was strong demand in the European markets and with a secure and large hinterland, İzmir was able to establish extensive as well as competitive commercial networks that covered short-and long-distance caravan routes in the interior of Anatolia. In the process İzmir was able to undercut other Anatolian commercial centers, such as Bursa or Ankara, in the export of their goods to Europe, doing it cheaper through its own networks, which extended both East and West. For instance, some of its imports from Europe, such as Habsburg Austrian thalers (dollars), reached markets as far as Africa where the coins were particularly sought after and partly explains why İzmir imported them in even greater quantities than Spanish piastres. In the volatile and still unpredictable markets of the eighteenth century, İzmir thus came to possess a very important advantage that distinguished it from other major Ottoman ports: it could almost always guarantee cargo of Ottoman goods for west-bound ships and European and colonial goods, besides local goods, for east-bound caravans and ships. İzmir was also a major regional banking center. This enabled it to combine commercial activities with an active currency market and merchant banking activities, which further solidified its position in European-Ottoman trade.

What ultimately 'made' İzmir was a tremendous combination of all the necessary factors for commercial prominence in long-distance eighteenth-century international trade: namely, an excellent geographic position; command of a large hinterland and of an extensive network of commercial routes both in land and at sea, with both West and East; an open and interactive economic milieu encompassing an enterprising local and western mercantile community; a vibrant money market and an array of commercial and financial products and services that allowed the city-port to carry on trading, at an increasing rate, in the course of the period under study.

The study on the port of Patras in the Morea (Peloponnese) presently southern Greece, co-authored with the historical geographer Malcolm Wagstaff, included in the third section, serves as an example of the way Ottoman-European trade impacted western maritime regions of the empire, besides İzmir or Aleppo (through Iskenderun). As argued in the article, changes in population, height zonation and in the pattern of rural settlements in the hinterland of Patras, in the course of the eighteenth century, indicative of a more intensive use of land, were the results of demographic and economic growth in the region. These were in turn re-enforced by the external forces of the market. This study further shows how the world economic and political events in the late eighteenth and early nineteenth centuries offered new opportunities for trade and shipping to the local communities in the eastern Mediterranean. Patras developed as a result both of its trade activities with the West, within the framework of Ottoman-European trade, and of the economic growth that the empire, and the Mediterranean region, experienced in this period. By the early nineteenth century Patras, like İzmir, was growing faster than any other port in the Morea and was sending a growing share of the region's produce to the European markets.[1]

V

The articles in the fourth section of this volume deal with the actors of Ottoman-European trade. They examine the various ways in which European and Ottoman merchant communities interacted with each other in İzmir, and in the empire, at large, and the evolving dynamics that shaped their relationships. The studies look at merchants' trading practices and the networks they set up as they sought to adapt to the opportunities and challenges of long-distance trade within an eighteenth-century world economy. The articles serve to illustrate, among other things, that despite the separation in the living quarters that existed in the empire's urban areas, in the marketplace, locals, both Muslims and non-Muslims, interacted with each other as well as with the Europeans in a totally open and fluid manner. In analyzing the way different merchant communities set out long-term goals and organized daily trading activities, these articles further seek to show what made trading from and with the Ottoman empire a viable and profitable enterprise, despite periodic fluctuations, for all participants concerned. These studies also show that both groups were often well matched and could prove formidable competitors

[1]Between 1793-1815 Patras shipped 30% of all Morea's exports; this doubled in the years 1815-1820. Kremmydas, *Συγκυρία και εμπόριο...*, p. 59.

to each other. Whereas there were certainly differences between the European and Ottoman merchants' activities, there were also many similarities, particularly in the latter part of the eighteenth and in the early nineteenth centuries, and the divisions that separated them were more fluid than they might at first appear or may have been portrayed in the historiography including the author's earlier articles.

An analysis of the role of 'friendship' and kinship and their importance in European-Ottoman trade is undertaken in the first article in this section of the volume. These relationships provided the underpinning for the commercial networks upon which the entire organizational edifice of this trade was built and held the key to their success. They were to be found not only amongst the Europeans but also amongst the Ottomans. In the parlance of the eighteenth century, ties of kinship and friendship, could denote a whole array of relationships that ranged from a long- or short-term partnership to a transaction-specific co-operation. For instance, a group of 'friends' could be invited by a merchant to participate in the sale of European or colonial goods or in the purchase of Ottoman goods. In the former case, the commodities would have been bought by the merchant in Europe who was organizing the commercial transaction and had brought the group together and in the latter case by his agent in the empire. Where Ottoman goods had been purchased, they would usually be destined to the most profitable European market, at the time of the purchase, which could mean anywhere in the non-Ottoman Mediterranean or the Atlantic economies that this group had access. Access was usually acquired through further 'friend(s)', or associate(s) of a member of the group. In Ottoman-European trade where markets were miles away and where the means of communication and transportation could still be hazardous, there was clearly the need to pool resources together by inviting fellow merchants one trusted to participate in a commercial venture as in the above example. Thus one shared not only profits but also risks. Since it could take up to two years for a transaction to be successfully completed, before any returns could be realized on one's initial capital outlay, and given the limitations of one's capital resources, sharing out a commercial deal also spread out investment costs and ensured that one did not have more funds than necessary tied up for any length of time. The very meticulous and precise methods used to account for the smallest amounts of money that a partner, or a participant in a transaction, might use of his own funds for the good of the group, so that he could be credited with interest and the others debited with the same amount, show the paramount importance of sharing out costs at all times and how group participation made this possible.

Whether it was a formal, legally contracted partnership or a more informal, transaction-specific co-operation, in order to be effective, it had to be based on trust, since the merchants involved were often located in different port-cities in the Ottoman empire and Europe. In such circumstances, and putting aside kinship where trustworthiness was more obvious, the use of the term 'friend' was by no means perfunctory but quite real. It enabled the merchant in London to invite his agent in Livorno, who was most likely an independent merchant trading in his own right, too, to participate in the purchase of silk that the London merchant's factor in Aleppo would be buying. Once purchased, the goods might be sent to the agent in Livorno for sale there or to any other non-Ottoman Mediterranean or European Atlantic market that offered the best terms. The factor would purchase the silk either from Aleppo or if better prices were offered elsewhere in the empire, then another factor of the London merchant, who might be stationed in Cyprus or İzmir, would be instructed, from Aleppo, to buy the goods. Funds for the purchase may already be in the hands of any of these factors, perhaps from the sale of goods the London merchant had sent them earlier. It was more likely to be the case, however, that funds were sent to the relevant factor by means of a bill of exchange from a merchant-cum-banking house in the Ottoman capital who acted as the banker and 'friend' of the London merchant. The Istanbul house might also act as his factor taking on different roles according to the specific transaction being carried out, as the articles in this section of the volume show. Amongst the merchants invited by the London house to participate in the commercial transaction, besides the agent in Livorno, may have been the factor in Aleppo, the merchant-cum-banker in Istanbul and quite possibly another merchant in London, or elsewhere, who was often, but not always, his London partner. Whilst formal partners might not always be included in a particular transaction, those who were included always considered each other 'friends'.

Ties of kinship become particularly important in the selection process of factors. The latter were often younger brothers, sons, or nephews of the London merchant, or of his partner(s). They might also come from a family whose members were considered 'friends' of the London merchant, or of his partner(s). Ties of friendship, which were further re-enforced by ties of kin and blood, were the best guarantors for the success of the principal/factor relationship. Equally in existence amongst the French and Dutch, this was the most basic relationship and the foundation on which the entire structure of the *Levant trade* was based, the central piece in the edifice built by networks of kinship and friendship. Moreover, this was so largely amongst Ottoman merchants, too. Whilst the existence and importance of this relationship is known in the historiography, studies in the present volume show how it worked in ways that the author hopes will contribute to the debate concerning commercial networks and their role in the organization of long-distance trade in the eighteenth century.

By the third quarter of the century, networks of kinship and 'friendship' similar in nature, scope and extent as the Europeans' networks, were to be found also amongst Ottoman, mostly non-Muslim, merchants. Their ability to create such overlapping and extensive networks, which allowed them access to multiple markets in Europe and the Ottoman empire, at the same time, was the result of their success in establishing, simultaneously in a number of markets, agencies of their trading houses, which they manned with members of their extended families and 'friends'. That they were able to do so in the latter part of the eighteenth century, and not much earlier, as the available archival data would suggest, was in part due to the rate of capital accumulation which these communities were, by then, experiencing that allowed them to expand their commercial activities. Their greater capital resources were themselves the consequence partly of a prospering Ottoman-European trade and partly of the internal dynamics of a growing Ottoman economy. On both counts, such developments made economic sense and answered the forces of the market. This is shown, for example, in the way trade developed between the Ottoman empire and the Netherlands in the second half of the eighteenth and in the early nineteenth centuries. Whilst Dutch-Ottoman trade remained robust in this period it was increasingly conducted not only by Dutch and British houses but also by Ottoman Armenian, Jewish and Greek firms, as the latter became integral parts of the Dutch trading activities and networks. The Ottoman merchants' prospering networks and growing access to multiple European and Ottoman markets also reflect the changes that the world economy underwent in the late eighteenth and early nineteenth centuries, which resulted in even formerly fiercely protectionist markets, such as the French, favoring Free Trade.[1] Not surprisingly, this period registered the biggest expansion not only in commercial but also in speculative monetary activities as well as in the carrying trade of non-Muslim Ottoman merchants — and of the Greeks more than the Armenians or the Jews — as illustrated in the final two articles in this section.

[1]ANF, AE Biii 242, Sur l'article 30 de l'ordonnance du 20 Sept. 1810, Commerce du Levant, 28 Sept. 1814.

Another issue that the articles in this section deal with is the role of the local merchants in the empire's trade with Europe. What becomes clear, for instance, in the opening study in this section, is that once the Ottoman merchants — mostly Armenians, Jews or Greeks — had access to capital and markets that were in any way similar, though not necessarily equal, to those of the Europeans they, too, behaved in ways that were similar, and equally as effective, in carrying out Ottoman-European trade. Yet there is a tendency in the historiography — of which there is evidence in the earlier publications in this volume of the present author, too — to undermine their role or to see their activities, especially in the earlier part of the eighteenth century, as secondary to, or dependent upon, those of the Europeans. However, further research undertaken by the author, over the years, has led her to reappraise her position on this issue. A closer examination of the dynamics in the daily conduct of trade in Ottoman ports as well as of the way the internal and external trade sectors complimented each other in Ottoman markets reveals a different story. For instance, as some of the later studies in this section of the volume show, even when Ottoman, mostly non-Muslim, merchants were employed as brokers by the Europeans, they occupied a key position in the organization of external Ottoman trade. Moreover, those non-Muslim merchants who could enjoy the status of *beratlı*, — although their number was limited —, traded with Europe directly throughout the eighteenth century. In addition, together with Muslim merchants they held in their hands the internal Ottoman trade as well as dominated sectors of the market which were essential for the functioning of the external trade. Even before they went to Europe, in any considerable number, in order to trade with the Ottoman empire, they understood well the effectiveness of kinship and 'friendship' when setting up channels of communication and business contacts in the Ottoman interior. The examples of the Ankara mohair yarn or the Bursa silk trades show how Muslim and non-Muslim merchants alike were able to set up commercial networks that could compete successfully with the Europeans. As independent merchants, they further competed with the Europeans in the purchase of Ottoman goods thus contributing to making the Ottoman market a seller's market.

Certainly there were economic areas where the Europeans did find themselves in a stronger position than the locals. After all, it was growth of the western textile industries and need for raw materials that propelled the growth in Ottoman-European trade. European economies had greater capital liquidity and more developed economic systems overall. In addition, the Capitulations gave the westerners legal advantages and certain privileges. The

Europeans, as a result, dominated the external trade sector in the first three quarters of the eighteenth century. Other areas where the Europeans were dominant were insurance and the carrying trade not only between Europe and the Ottoman empire but also in Ottoman waters. Even taking into account the fact that the westerners' sources of capital could still be volatile, and at times even artificially restricted due to European state policies concerning capital flows, Ottoman merchants disposed overall of lower levels of capital resources than the Europeans. Nevertheless, both groups, to varying degrees, often had to overcome monetary scarcity in order to conduct trade or had to decide how best to face currency volatility or how best to invest any spare liquid funds. Such conditions led to the overlapping of local and western networks of credit and paper in the major Ottoman markets and created dynamics that tended to level the playing field between them. Issues of monetary liquidity were of primary concern to all participants in trade and played a key role in their business strategies as shown in the correspondence of the British merchant, Colvill Bridger. His trading activities in mid-eighteenth century Aleppo and his concerns as well as his relationships with the local merchants, described in this section, can be considered as representative of a European trading in the Ottoman empire at the time.

VI

Until the mid-nineteenth century, integration took place primarily through trade and impacted principally the empire's western maritime regions. Its major ports, which were almost all situated in those regions, became instrumental in this process. İzmir's commercial growth as well as dominance of the empire's external and internal trade were concurrent with this integration process, which started to be markedly more perceptible in the second half of the eighteenth century. Nevertheless, even then, trade with Europe represented only a small percentage of the empire's overall trade. In other words, during the period under study, the forces that drove Ottoman economic development were still to be found within the empire. The empire's integration into the world economy progressed considerably further in the course of the nineteenth century to reach its peak in the closing decades of Ottoman rule. In the process, it impacted a number of sectors of the Ottoman economy, besides trade, where it had formerly been most evident.[1] By the early twentieth

[1]E.g. Salgur Kançal, "La conquête du marché ottoman par le capitalisme industriel concurrentiel (1838-1881)", J.-L. Bacqué-Grammont & Paul Dumont, eds., *Économies et sociétés dans l'empire ottoman (fin du XVIIIe siècle-début du XXe siècle)* (Paris, 1983), pp. 355-409; *idem*, "Fin de l'empire ottoman: insertion dans la division internationale du travail (1880-1931)", *V. Milletlararası Türkiye Sosyal ve İktisat Tarihi Kongresi Tebliğler* (Ankara, 1990), pp. 395-407.

century, western capital affected most notably such sectors as the development of banking throughout the empire, the level of interest rates and of capital liquidity in the local economy,[1] as well as in the investment and construction of large-scale infrastructure projects, including transportation and utilities in Ottoman urban areas.[2] The two articles in the final section of this volume examine issues concerning the process of integration of the empire into the world economy, through the case study of İzmir, and the impact this process had on the city's economic development from the eighteenth into the early twentieth centuries.

*

Articles in this volume have been published over a period of eighteen years. Studies that have been published earlier are concerned primarily with the organization of commerce and monetary practices, whilst later publications also reflect the increasing interest of the author with the Ottoman monetary system and, in particular, specie shortage. Other recent articles also include a greater elaboration of the role of İzmir within the empire's internal maritime trade and the dynamics in this sector as well as the way it related to the empire's trade with the West. As it can be expected, over the years, the author's understanding of the Ottoman economy, İzmir, trade, merchants, and money has evolved although it has not radically changed. The exception to the above has been her own underestimation of the role and dynamism of the local merchants in the empire's trade with Europe, for most of the eighteenth century, although the author did record correctly their growing prosperity and commercial expansion in the decades spanning from the late eighteenth to the early nineteenth centuries. One theme that has been constant throughout the author's research and writings has been the emergence, by mid-eighteenth century, to commercial prominence of İzmir in Ottoman-European and Ottoman internal trade and the vibrancy of its currency market. This has enabled the study of issues related to Ottoman trade and money to be undertaken in ways that the author hopes contribute to Ottoman historiography.

---

1 Elena Frangakis-Syrett, "The Role of the European Banks in the Ottoman Empire in the Second Half of the Nineteenth and in the Early Twentieth Centuries", A. Teichova, G. Kurgan-van-Hentenryk & D. Ziegler, eds., *Banking, Trade and Industry in Europe* (Cambridge, 1997), pp. 263-276.

2 E.g., Şevket Pamuk, *The Ottoman Empire and European Capitalism, 1820-1914* (Cambridge, 1987), *passim;* Jacques Thobie, *Intérêts et impérialisme français dans l'empire ottoman (1895-1914)* (Paris, 1977), *passim.*

MONETARY SHORTAGE AND THE OTTOMAN ECONOMY: LATE SEVENTEENTH TO THE LATE EIGHTEENTH CENTURIES*

From the latter part of the seventeenth century to the end of the eighteenth, important changes took place in the areas of state finance and credit as much in the Ottoman empire as in Europe propelled, to a large extent, by the needs of war and economic growth. A protracted period of war, that spanned the closing decades of the seventeenth and the beginning of the eighteenth centuries, forced both the Ottoman and European states to seek new sources of revenue, whilst the rate of growth of the world economy that took place in the course of the eighteenth century placed increasing pressures on the circulating medium which sought new forms of credit.

Inadequacy of the circulating medium had been a chronic problem for the Ottoman economy; it continued to be so until the dissolution of the empire. The intensity of specie scarcity, however, did vary within any particular period of time and this was so for the late seventeenth and eighteenth centuries, too. Moreover, it was a problem that the Ottoman economy did not experience in isolation. Most European economies, perhaps with the exception of Great Britain and the Netherlands, experienced periodic inadequacies in their circulating medium in the course of the period under study. For instance, in the late eighteenth century, at certain times of the year, the markets of the Italian ports, flourishing centers of international trade, could face acute scarcity of specie.[1] Given the lack of an institutionalized and regulated banking sector, as it emerged in the nineteenth century, which would have created the confidence and milieu for paper money to circulate within the economy, varying degrees of inadequacy in the circulating medium were to be expected. Moreover, economic growth made such inadequacy all the greater. In the absence of an institutionalized banking sector, private bankers-cum-merchants in the Ottoman empire, *courtiers* in Marseilles or country bankers in the English provinces signed promissory notes and circulated local or

---

*W. Arbid, S. Kançal, J.-D. Mizrahi & S. Saul, eds., *Méditerranée, Moyen-Orient: deux siècles de relations internationales. Recherches en hommage à Jacques Thobie* (L'Harmattan & IFEA: Paris, 2003).

[1]Archives Nationales de France, Paris, AE Bi 600, Consul Raulin, Genoa, 14 Jan. 1793 to Minister, Paris. Hereafter this archive will be cited as ANF.

'inland' bills of exchange and other commercial paper to finance economic activities. Lack of money was legion, in the American colonies in the seventeenth and eighteenth centuries, too. As a result, paper money, in various forms of money bills, were periodically legislated into existence by the colonial assemblies[1] and acceded to, reluctantly, by London. The reasons for such reluctance on the part of the British government were not very different than those that European merchants felt when faced with an increasing circulation of promissory notes in the Ottoman provincial market of İzmir — namely, that no economy or local market could sustain, for long, an over-extension of credit without dire consequences.[2] In the absence of a modern banking sector, in a commercially active market such as İzmir, where credit backed almost every economic activity, a complex and delicate balance had to be attained between over-extension of credit and dampening of business through its restriction. As a result, however, a high degree of market volatility and monetary speculation were also prevalent in İzmir. Volatility and speculation were also evident in Marseilles culminating in the early 1770s when credit, based on paper, had become, by then, particularly widespread.

In the course of the first half of the nineteenth century a number of western European economies were able to establish a banking sector with a regulatory code of practice. In many respects the foundations for such a sector were laid in the latter part of the eighteenth century and bankers from London and the provinces played an important role. By contrast, although there was growth amongst the private bankers in the Ottoman provinces and greater sophistication in their banking practices, their level of capital accumulation remained modest. Given the absence of an active and diversified securities market in the empire, the range of their assets was also limited. For instance, although shares of tax farms were publicly traded, the Ottoman securities market could not compare in size or diversity with the securities markets that developed, in the course of the eighteenth century, in Amsterdam, London or Paris. Moreover, Ottoman private bankers were mostly small-scale entrepreneurs who could not make the change-over into full-scale banks as their English counterparts were able to do in the end of the eighteenth century. The exception were perhaps the Galata bankers who had larger monetary resources and who, through their trading and other activities, had direct access to and contacts with the western European money markets. They mostly dealt in internal loans to the state and in tax farming.

---

[1]Public Record Office, London, ADM 106/ 2560, 16 Feb. 1743. Hereafter this archive will be cited as PRO.

[2]PRO, FO 195/178, J. F. Hanson *et al.*, İzmir, 23 July 1843 to the Porte. Although the reference is for the nineteenth century, similar conditions could be found earlier, too.

There were a number of reasons why the Ottoman empire did not follow the European example in establishing a banking sector by the first half of the nineteenth century. Amongst the various reasons were lack of confidence in the long-term prospects of the economy, inadequate levels of capital growth, increasingly higher levels of military expenditure by the state, coupled with an inability to collect revenues effectively, as well as non-productive patterns of investment by the élite. Moneylending was a sought after investment by the wealthy, indeed by anybody with some cash available, given the high premium that specie always carried in the Ottoman empire. With interest rates officially limited at 15-20 %, but in fact much higher especially in the large rural sector, there was even less inducement for investment in trade or manufacture, which would have improved the level of capital growth in the Ottoman economy.[1] This was all the more so since, through the strict fixing and control of prices, profits officially allowed in trade or in handicraft were 5-10 % — clearly below moneylending. In controlling prices, the Ottoman state sought to protect its consumers; by allowing as well as by encouraging foreign imports in its domains, it sought to ensure the supply of its markets with necessary goods. Such policies were not designed to stimulate the accumulation of money which would have also added to the circulating medium. The French state, faced with specie scarcity in the economy and an inability to raise adequate revenues for its needs, sought to develop luxury exports, through ventures such as the Manufactures Royales,[2] in order to decrease imports in those goods and draw specie into the country. For a number of reasons such a policy was not viable to the Ottoman state.

The low level of investment in other sectors of the economy, such as agriculture, by the Ottoman administrative élite in favor of investment in tax farming or office holding, besides money-lending, became more evident as the state's ability to meet its growing fiscal needs through taxation revenue decreased. Pressure upon its finances, especially at wartime, was a phenomenon that the Ottoman state did not experience in isolation in the later seventeenth and eighteenth centuries. European states experienced it, too. Given the growth of far-flung empires in that period, as for instance in the case of Britain, public finance for successful military exploits and maintenance of the Empire was of paramount importance.[3] In the late seventeenth and early

[1]Mehmet Genc, "Osmanlı İktisadi Dünya Görüşünün İlkileri" *I. Ü. Edebiyat Fakültesi Sosyoloji Dergisi*, 3 (Istanbul, 1989), *passim*.
[2]ANF, AE Bi 1054, Consul Charles de Peyssonnel, İzmir, 23 Sept. 1753 to Minister, Paris.
[3]J. Brewer, *The sinews of power: war, money and the English state, 1688-1783* (London, 1989), *passim*.

eighteenth centuries, Britain was able to finance its wars and meet monetary commitments in many areas of the world simultaneously without depleting its specie by exporting it and thus negatively impacting the value of its currency. Britain was able to achieve this because it had a number of assets concerning tax collection, government borrowing or the transfer of funds abroad, which the Ottoman state either did not dispose of or not to the same degree. For instance, during the War of Spanish Succession (1701-1715), in order to meet military expenditure, Britain was able to make substantial overseas remittances, to many areas including the Ottoman empire, through bills of exchange and using the system of international payments that already existed for the purposes of international trade thus by-passing the need to send specie. For example, in 1702-1710, the British government remitted to İzmir and İskenderun £ 8,666, "for foreign service on contract", through bills of exchange at 40 days sight.[1] Like Britain, the Ottoman empire, too, was part of such a system of international payments. For instance, bills of exchange at 30 or 45 days sight drawn on Amsterdam regularly linked İzmir with the Dutch financial market.[2] However, what the British state had also at its disposal was a credit network in every major money market, encompassing the world of European finance, set up by agents from established houses in the City of London.[3] Moreover, London was emerging at the time as a strong capital market in Europe, with increasing links with Amsterdam, the premier financial market. As such, both markets attracted capital and commanded credit from all over Europe.

The money market of Istanbul received capital, to a great extent, as a direct result of state policies, which included regular and extraordinary flows of tax revenue from the provinces, as well as surplus from its trade with Europe.[4] It did, in theory, have access, although relative, to funds in the European money markets through the contacts of its bankers. Indeed in the 1840s the Ottoman government was able to remit funds to cover military expenditure to London, using as agents, Ottoman Greek houses established in the British capital.[5] However, the Porte would not have been able to do likewise a century or so earlier. The Capitulations, for one thing, would have not allowed the establishment of such houses in London. Ottoman Armenian,

---

[1]PRO, ADM 110/5, 10 March 1711.

[2]Jean-Pierre Ricard, *Le Négoce d'Amsterdam* (Rouen, 1723), p. 558.

[3]B. J. Sperling, "The International Payments Mechanism in the Seventeenth and Eighteenth Centuries", *Economic History Review*, Vol. 14 (1961-62), pp. 463-465.

[4]Edhem Eldem, *French Trade in Istanbul in the Eighteenth Century* (Leiden, 1999), pp. 120-25.

[5]PRO, FO 195/178, Niven, Kerr, Black & Co., Istanbul, 17 Dec. 1841 to Ch. Bankhead, H.M. Minister Plenipotentiary, Istanbul; see also, C.S. Hanson, Istanbul, 27 Oct. 1842 to Sir Stratford Canning, H.M. Ambassador, Istanbul.

Jewish or Greek commercial houses were nevertheless established in other European centers, such as Amsterdam or Livorno, in the course of the later seventeenth and eighteenth centuries. Whilst the empire benefited from their presence, the combined capital resources and credit network of such enterprises, even if they could all be cost-effectively mobilized at once, could not compare with what London could dispose of at home and in the Continent. Since the Ottoman state could only rely on an international network of credit of limited resources, it had to rely even more on internal networks of credit through tax farming and short-term loans. Indeed, the fact that the most developed money market in the empire, that of Istanbul, existed primarily in order to supply the fiscal needs of the Ottoman state meant that it was probably drawing too many monetary resources to the capital to the detriment of the empire's other markets and was impacting negatively the rate of capital accumulation. İzmir was perhaps the only provincial market that was the least affected by such state of affairs. Certainly, the constant needs for specie by the capital could, periodically, cause a drain on its monetary resources. However, the premier position of İzmir in the external and internal trade of the empire meant that it had developed its own currency market and credit networks both within the empire and abroad. As a result, İzmir was both a net importer of specie and of bills of exchange as well as figured independently in the financial networks of major European markets.

The Ottoman state was certainly not the only state in Europe to have recourse to its élite, through tax farming, or to its own bankers for short-term loans. France, which had fiscal problems that were more akin to those in the Ottoman empire than in Britain, did likewise. For instance, the great bankers of France, who were also its tax farmers, or ***Fermiers Généraux,*** frequently provided the King with credit in the form of bills of exchange at 6 or 8 months sight with a 12% annual interest rate. These bankers, like the agents of the British state, had access to a Europe-wide supply of bills of exchange to finance such operations. Should the King in France be unable to meet his obligations when the bills came due, the credit was rolled over with further bills of exchange of similar duration offered so that, in essence, he disposed of a continuous turn-over of credit, but also entered into an on-going cycle of debt.[1] The Galata bankers, too, may have thus financed, at least in part, their loans to their sovereign. However, until the latter part of the eighteenth century, the circulation of their bills of exchange would have been mostly, though not exclusively, internal. Nevertheless they may have been able to contract loans with Jews or Armenians in Amsterdam or in other European centers.

---

[1]British Library, Portland Loan, 29/54, John Drummond, Amsterdam, 6 Feb. 1705 to Robert Harley, London. Hereafter this library will be cited as BL.

Efficient raising and collection of taxation, would have reinforced public credit and enabled a state to finance on a long-term and fairly stable basis any internal borrowing that it had to undertake. Financing the National Debt successfully allowed the British government to find a way out of the fiscal problems it had faced in the late seventeenth and early eighteenth centuries. Moreover, it was able to turn its debt into an asset by transforming it into a sound system of public credit. In the late eighteenth century, the United States would do the same. An important measure for such success, in the British case, was moving away from short-term loans in the form of bills, or of interest-bearing bonds, that had customarily been issued by various departments of the government and its replacement by long-term loans based upon the flotation of government stock or fixed-term redeemable annuities. Capital growth in the London money market, in the late seventeenth and eighteenth centuries, as shown by the growth of the insurance sector, and the emergence of a market of transferable securities, were further factors that led to the success of such measures by the British government.[1] For the confidence that the government was able to create by making regular payments of such loans meant that investors were willing to buy shares knowing that they could both trade in their stock and liquidate it should they so wish. Of crucial importance to the success of such a measure was the restructuring of the system of taxation and collection, that Britain undertook in the eighteenth century, and which made its ability to raise revenue the envy of Europe, for this was what enabled it to make regular payments. The taxation system was based on three principles: the end of tax farming; no tax exemptions, as far as possible, for individuals or social classes and prudence as well as efficiency in the raising of indirect taxes.[2] Unlike France, Britain was willing to tax its landed aristocracy. And unlike both France and the Ottoman empire, Britain was aware of the need, as much as possible, not to overtax its poor, so as not to destroy their purchasing power or court their protest. High confidence in public credit could also have another important result for the economy — it allowed public securities, whose market value also increased, to be used in lieu of specie, adding to the circulating medium. Transferable securities, acting as money, could also be used as collateral by an entrepreneur in order to increase his assets which would allow him to expand his business. This was another way in which public credit could alleviate specie scarcity as well as induce greater capital growth as the Americans — who were also experiencing

[1]H.V. Bowen, *War and British Society, 1688-1815* (Cambridge, 1998), pp. 21-24.

[2]E.g., Brewer, *The sinews of power* ..., pp. 91-114; Bowen, *War*..., pp. 25-27. For a detailed study of British taxation in the eighteenth century, see also J.E.D. Binney, *British public finance and administration, 1774-1792* (Oxford, 1958), *passim*.

acute specie scarcity as well as had a large public debt — found out when they organized their debt and established their first bank.[1]

Tax farming had always been a primary instrument of domestic borrowing used by European and Islamic states. In the Ottoman case political considerations — the need to create alliances with various élite groups both in the capital and in the provinces — may have played a role in the government's decision, in the late seventeenth and early eighteenth centuries, to develop further its tax farming system.[2] The need to forge political alliances through venality and tax farming could be found in France, too. However, it was pressing financial considerations — made more acute at times of war when state expenditure increased whilst the economy was less able to produce the usual tax revenue, coupled with decreasing state revenue due to the economic problems the empire faced in the seventeenth century — that ultimately led to the further development and expansion of tax farming. The protracted wars of the late seventeenth and early eighteenth centuries did not only strain the European states' finances but also those of the Ottoman state. The growing budget deficits that the Ottoman state faced, in the period 1660-1699, forced it, in view of an inadequate system of public credit, to turn to tax farming in order to raise the extra revenue.[3] With short-term tax farms, which had become an important means of internal short-term state borrowing, also in crisis, the state instituted in 1695 — a year of financial crises all over Europe — important changes to make the tax farming system more effective in yielding the required revenue.[4] It created life-term tax farms, called *malikâne muqataa*, which gave the holder the right to collect taxes for life in return for a fixed annual payment to the state. In doing so the state tried, unsuccessfully,

---

[1]Harold C. Syrett, ed., *Papers of Alexander Hamilton* (New York, 1961-1987), Vol. VI, pp. 65-111.

[2]Ariel Salzman, "An Ancien Régime Revisited: 'Privatization' and Political Economy in the Eighteenth-Century Ottoman Empire", *Politics & Society*, Vol. 21/4 (1993), pp. 402-05.

[3]Mehmet Genç, "Osmanlı Maliyesinde Malikane Sistemi", O. Okyar & H. Ü. Nalbantoğlu, eds., *Türkiye İktisat Tarihi Semineri* (Ankara, 1975), p. 236.

[4]With its fixed income being continuously diminished by inflation and the inability of peasants to pay their dues, in the early seventeenth century, the state had already been forced to institute a new system of tax farming, called *iltizam:* feudal lands (*timars*) that reverted back to the state at the death of the holder, were rented for a year to whichever tax farmer (*mültezim*) could offer the highest bid to the treasury. The tax farmer could then sublet his tax farm for a higher amount to another bidder who in his turn would auction his rights to the land for an even higher sum. In order to recoup his profits, the second or third sub-letter of the tax farm ultimately exhorted dues from the peasants that were considerably higher than what was originally paid to the state for these lands. Elena Frangakis-Syrett, *The Commerce of Smyrna in the Eighteenth Century (1700-1820)* (Athens, 1992), p. 3; see also, Murat Cizakça, "Tax-farming and Financial Decentralization in the Ottoman Economy, 1520-1697", *Journal of European Economic History*, Vol. 22/2 (1993), pp. 219-250 and Yuzo Nagata and 'Abdul Rahim 'Abdul Rahman, "The iltizam system in Egypt and Turkey — a comparative study", *Journal of Asian and African Studies*, Vol. 14 (1977), pp. 181-82.

to curb the ever-increasing cycle of subletting a piece of land, farmed for a short period of time, that had evolved especially since agricultural production had deteriorated in many areas making many of these short-term tax farms unprofitable and thus unattractive. In order also to attract agrarian tax farmers, the state also conferred greater control over their tax farms. As it was the established practice in Ottoman tax farming, life-term tax farms were auctioned to the highest bidder. The latter acquired the right to collect taxation on agricultural production, for life, undisturbed by the state. In return the person had to offer, upon accepting the contract, a considerable advance to the state which was estimated at several times the annual profit. As with short-term tax farms, life-term tax farms could also be sublet as well as divided into shares, which could be traded, as transferable public securities, as long as the holder paid the appropriate registration fees to the state. The investor could also own part shares in a number of tax farms from different sectors of the economy making up a portfolio of diverse investments to spread his risks and increase his profits.[1] Upon the death of the owner(s), the shares could be sold to his male heirs on the payment to the government of a new advance. The state had thus rescinded its control over long-term sources of revenue in favor of short-term monetary relief in the form of payment of the advance by the new owner of a tax farm. At the same time, using the life-term tax farm as collateral, the state was also attempting to borrow on a longer term basis.

The intention of the state to increase the revenue of its tax sources for the long term, through life-term tax farms, whilst also increasing the amount it received on the short term, from each new owner, did not materialize. Any increase in surplus agricultural production or in the prices of agricultural goods which were increasingly commercialized in the eighteenth century, as the considerable growth in Ottoman-European trade testifies,[2] went to individual tax farmers and their financiers whilst the income to the state remained fixed.[3] In mid-eighteenth century, in an effort to raise cash, besides carrying out considerable currency devaluation, the state retracted some of the *malikane* tax farms and introduced the *esham* system of tax farming. In doing

---

[1]Murat Cizakça, *A Comparative Evolution of Business Partnerships in the Islamic World and Europe with specific references to the Ottoman Archives* (Leiden, 1996), pp. 140-45, 158-64, 170-73.

[2]For trade figures on Ottoman exports to Europe, including exports of cotton and cotton yarn, which constituted two of the most important exports of the empire, see Frangakis-Syrett, *The Commerce of Smyrna...*, pp. 138, 155-77, 231-47, 257-60, 270-77; see also, *idem*, "The Ottoman City-Port of İzmir in the Eighteenth Century", *Revue de l'Occident Musulman et de la Méditerranée*, Vol. 39/1 (1985), pp. 160-62 and Eldem, *French Trade in Istanbul...*, p. 14.

[3]Mehmet Genç, "A Study in the Feasibility of Using 18th-Century Ottoman Financial Records as an Indicator of Economic Activity," Huri Islamoglu-Inan, ed., *The Ottoman Empire and the World Economy* (Cambridge, 1987), pp. 347-48.

so, the state had a twofold aim: to broaden the base of its tax farmers to include smaller lenders and to gain greater control of its revenue sources.[1] As the state experienced further fiscal crises, despite the even greater commercial growth that occurred in the third quarter of the eighteenth century, the *esham* system was modified in the course of the Russo-Ottoman War (1768-1774). Tax farmers were able, once more, to hold on to their *esham* (shares) for their lifetime sometimes even passing them on to their heirs. Whilst it was overall more profitable than the *malikâne* system,[2] the inability of the state to control the new system more effectively diminished the financial benefits it could derive from it.[3] In the Russo-Austro-Ottoman War (1787-1792) fiscal needs nearly led to the unthinkable: the government turned to western European governments and private financiers for a loan.[4] Failing that, the enveloping fiscal crisis of the French Revolutionary and Napoleonic Wars that followed (1792-1801 and 1803-1815), led to further attempts to reorganize the tax farming system.

The alternative of confiscating the wealth of some of its most powerful financiers was also at times sought for by the Ottoman empire and France. However, the lesser the confidence in a state's ability, or willingness, to honor its debts the higher the interest rates it had to give to attract lenders. Yet a way of lessening the burden of state borrowing on the economy and increasing the ability of the state to repay its debts, was by lowering the interest rates at which it borrowed. The British government was able to lower interest rates, from 10-14% in the 1690, to 5-6% in the 1700s, by establishing the Bank of England in 1694 as well as by a viable and innovative system of short- and long-term borrowing. Some of the innovations included loans from the financially-strong chartered companies in London, at times, in exchange for the granting of their charters.[5]

---

[1]The esham tax farming system worked as follows: after the annual income of a revenue was reassessed, it was divided into shares (esham) which yielded to the buyer, for 8-10 years, a fixed interest rate of 5% per year. For more information on this system of tax farming see Çizakça, *A Comparative Evolution...*, pp. 179-87.

[2]In the *malikane* tax farming system the state's fixed income could be changed only when the tax farm was renegotiated at the death of an owner.

[3]Şevket Pamuk, *A Monetary History of the Ottoman Empire* (Cambridge, 2000), pp. 190-92.

[4]Pamuk, *A Monetary History...*, p. 192. The scale of the fiscal crisis, that led them to make such a decision, can be gauged from the extreme reluctance that the Porte felt when it did negotiate its first external loan, more than half a century later, with western financiers and which is evident in the archives of the later period.

[5]P.G.M. Dickson & John Sperling, "War and Finance, 1689-1714" in *The New Cambridge Modern History*, Vol. VI, *The Rise of Great Britain and Russia, 1688-1725* (Cambridge, 1970), pp. 288, 314.

Life-term tax farms became an important source of wealth for the Muslim élite. The financing of such ventures, which in case of large-scale tax farms could be considerable, led to the pooling of resources by several partners with investors in Istanbul having the pride of place even for some of the tax farms located in the provinces. Such partnerships came about not only in order to pool resources together but also in order to spread the risks of the investment.[1] The privileged position of Istanbul in the Imperial network that financed tax farming could in some respects be paralleled with the position that Paris had in the financing of tax farming. Most of the large number of indirect tax farms that existed in eighteenth-century France, collectively known as "the receipts of the General Farms" were nearly all administered by the *Fermiers Généraux*, who were based in Paris and disposed of a network of agencies in the provinces.[2] The Muslim élite were themselves often financed by non-Muslim bankers whose ranks grew as a result of the expansion of tax farming.[3] Although non-Muslims, they could also be tax farmers themselves. These non-Muslim financiers, together with their agents or associates, both in the capital and in the provinces, disposed of contacts and had access to a network of bills of exchange in order to transfer funds or make payments to Istanbul on behalf of their clients in the provinces. Access to such networks of credit also allowed them to bypass specie scarcity whilst profits from such ventures allowed them to increase their capital assets. From financiers to such clients, they evolved to bankers and financial agents for the state. In France the sale of offices was undertaken by a syndicate of office-jobbers (*traitans*) who sold state offices to prospective investors paying the state a fixed price and then reselling at a profit.[4] The sheer capital necessary to carry out such operations meant that a state strapped for cash came to rely upon such financiers, whose fortunes it also increased. An inability by the state to repay its debts could also bring about the ruin of such bankers whose fortunes were tied so closely to the state.

*

[1]Cizakça, *A Comparative Evolution ...*, pp. 153-57, 173.

[2]Dickson & Sperling, "War and Finance"..., p. 300.

[3]Onik Jamgocyan, "Les finances de l'empire ottoman et les financiers de Constantinople, 1732-1853" (Unpublished thèse de doctorat, University of Paris I [Panthéon-Sorbonne], 1988), 2 vols., *passim;* see also, *idem*, "Une famille des financiers arméniens au XVIIe siècle: les Serpos", D. Panzac, ed., *Les villes dans l'empire ottoman: activités et sociétés* (Paris, 1991), vol. I, p. 365.

[4]Dickson & Sperling, "War and Finance ...", p. 301.

Diminishing output of silver mines in the Ottoman empire in the latter part of the seventeenth century, together with an absence of copper coins, further contributed to the scarcity of specie. The inability of the Ottoman government to mint new silver and the urgent financial needs of a protracted military campaign (the war for the capture of Crete from Venice, 1645-1664) led to the biggest ever importation of counterfeit coins to the empire from Europe.[1] Evidence of acute specie scarcity and of a mostly illicit trade in debased coins in İzmir, a major port of entry of foreign specie for the empire, abounds in the contemporary sources of the period.[2] It was in 1665, a year after the end of the war, that French, Italian and Dutch merchants first started importing to the empire, mostly through İzmir and Istanbul, counterfeit coins, called temins.[3] Suitable for small payments, these coins started circulating with great success in the Ottoman markets.[4] For a while, they even rivaled the hitherto popular Spanish piastres, also called pieces of eight, imported regularly into İzmir by the French from Marseilles. When such exports were prohibited or when the circulation of piastres in the Provence was altogether forbidden, the French imported them to İzmir through the Italian ports.[5] Circulation of debased coinage remained volatile with the market being, at any point in time, likely to lose confidence in it and reject it. There were also limits as to how far a coin could be debased as shown in the case of the temins whose debasement finally reached unacceptable levels in 1669 and was rejected in the Ottoman markets. This was despite the further scarcity in specie that was thus caused. Another debased coin sought to take the place of the discredited temin. In 1669, the year of the rejection of the temin, French and Genoese counterfeit versions of the Dutch silver lion dollar, or asselani, probably less debased than the temin had by then become, appeared in the

[1]Sonia Anderson, *An English Consul in Turkey, Paul Rycaut at Smyrna, 1667-1678* (Oxford, 1989), pp. 178-185; see also, Şevket Pamuk, "In the Absence of Domestic Currency: Debased European Coinage in the Seventeenth-Century Ottoman Empire", *The Journal of Economic History*, Vol. 57/2 (1997), pp. 348-50.

[2]E.g., J.B. Tavernier, *Nouvelle Rélation de l'intérieur du Serrail* (Paris, 1675), pp. 45-54 and Sir Paul Rycaut, *The History of the Turkish Empire from the year 1623 to the year 1677* (London, 1680), pp. 258-60.

[3]Also called Luigini or Ottavi in Europe due to their resemblance to these coins, the temins were worth approximately five pence in England. Tavernier, *Nouvelle Rélation...*, p. 45 and Rycaut, *History of the Turkish Empire ...*, p. 258.

[4]PRO, SP 105/152, Levant Company General Court Meeting, London, 3 Oct. 1667; see also, SP 105/113, Levant Company, London, 14 Dec. 1668 to British Consul, İzmir and *ibid.*, Levant Company, 14 Dec. 1668 to British Consul, Aleppo and Rycaut, *History of the Turkish Empire...*, p. 258.

[5]PRO, SP 105/152, Levant Company General Court Meeting, London, 28 April 1668 and 28 May 1669; see also, ANF, AE Biii 235, Commerce du Levant, Louvigny Dorgemonts, Mémoire au sujet des piastres et asselanis, Genoa, 15 July 1687; and *ibid.*, Mémoire sur les monnoyes de faire entrer dans le commerce et convertir en espèces étrangères par la voie de Marseille, 1695.

market of İzmir.[1] Dutch asselani[2], imported from the Italian ports in a counterfeit form, were still popular in İzmir in the 1680s for French merchants sought permission from the French authorities to mint asselani in France specifically for export to the Levant.[3] The circulation of counterfeit coins did not only bring confusion and uncertainty to the Ottoman markets but also to Ottoman-European trade. For instance, it created, for a time, a glut of Ottoman goods in the European markets, some of which had been purchased with debased currency and hence were very cheap. Throughout this whole incident, despite being prohibited by their authorities, most European merchants in the Levant dealt in these currencies to some extent or other.[4]

Counterfeiting was not a new phenomenon nor was the import of European coins in the empire. The Ottoman monetary system had always been an open system and the host of an extensive number of European coins.[5] Since the latter part of the sixteenth century these coins circulated side by side with and, as periodic specie scarcity started to emerge, at times in lieu of the Ottoman currency. However, the scale of counterfeiting of the late seventeenth century, 200 million coins were sent to the Levant in a relatively short span of time,[6] and the success of the circulation of the counterfeit coins in the Ottoman empire makes this incident rather exceptional, although some of its root causes were not so exceptional: namely, acute specie scarcity and pressing needs for funds for military expenditure by the state. Had the Ottoman empire not been experiencing such an acute monetary shortage, it would not have allowed, and certainly not to the extent that it did, the circulation of counterfeit coins. Yet another reason for such counterfeiting may have been the acute lack of specie that the European economies were also experiencing at the time. Had the European economies not been experiencing a number of fiscal and monetary problems besides silver shortages — output from American silver mines had declined by then —, which were already creating problems in their trade with the Levant and Asia — both of which were bullion consuming regions —, there may not have been any large scale counterfeiting.

---

[1]Anderson, *An English Consul...*, pp. 182-83.

[2]Dutch coins, also called lion dollars, in non-counterfeit form, were particularly sought after in the market of İzmir. PRO, SP 105/113, Levant Company, London, 1 Sept. 1670 to Treasurer Richard Hardy, İzmir.

[3]ANF, AE Biii 235, Mémoire touchant la fabrique des asselanis en Provence, Jan. 1699.

[4]PRO, 105/152, Levant Company, General Court Meeting, London, 16 June 1668; see also, *ibid.*, Levant Company, London, 14 Dec. 1668 to British Consul, Aleppo.

[5]Halil Sahillioğlu, "The Role of International Monetary and Metal Movements in Ottoman Monetary History", J.F. Richards, ed., *Precious Metals in the Later Medieval and Early Modern Worlds* (Durham, NC, 1983), pp. 269-304.

[6]Pamuk, "In the Absence of Domestic Currency...", p. 345.

The latter part of the seventeenth century was also the period when chipped coins made their last appearance in the British economy, one of the stronger economies in terms of capital liquidity in Europe. Such a phenomenon had its origin in the acute need to increase the amount of silver coins in the realm. Whilst the British government was able, during the War for the Spanish Succession (1701-1714), to use the credit system of bills of exchange to make remittances abroad and keep fluctuations in the exchange rates within acceptable limits, it had not been able to do so earlier during the War of the League of Augsburg (1688-1697). Coming on the heel of the political upheaval of the Glorious Revolution of 1688, in England, and at a time of Europe-wide monetary problems and specie scarcity, clipped coins appeared in circulation. They answered the necessity to export silver to pay for bills of exchange drawn on London, from Amsterdam, to meet the needs of King William III's remittance program centered in the Dutch financial city. Since exporting English coins or melting them into bullion for export were both illegal, but exporting foreign silver coins was not, the answer laid in taking silver from English coins and reshaping it into foreign coins which could then be legally exported. Moreover, the acceptance and circulation of such clipped coins at full unit of account within the English economy for a period of years is poignant evidence of the monetary problems faced in England at the time.[1] Clipping, at a modest scale, first started in the 1670s. It was intensified in 1685 and went on for a decade or until the recoinage of 1696. Whilst clipping went on, contemporary observers were astonished at the full acceptance and circulation of these coins. The wondrous tone of their accounts was not very different from what one could read, at the time, on the circulation of heavily debased coins in the Ottoman empire.

> Within half a dozen years after the Revolution [of 1688], there was scarce a single hammered shilling or half Crown to be met with in any sum of money, but what was extremely clipped and diminished. Yet all such pieces were received and passed as current, as when they were of full weight and value; this encouraged, and vended the money they had clipped in all places without any check or fear from the laws.[2]

The result of reducing the silver content of a coin, whilst keeping the face value of the coin constant, was to effectively increase the price of silver remaining in the coin.[3] It thus allowed for silver bullion to be exported without registering a corresponding diminution in the amount of silver coins

[1] BL, Landsdowne MS 801, Haynes, Brief Memoirs.

[2] BL, Landsdowne MS 801, Haynes, Brief memoirs.

[3] Stephen Quinn, "Gold, silver, and the Glorious Revolution: arbitrage between bills of exchange and bullion", *Economic History Review*, Vol. XLIX/3 (1996), p. 481.

circulating in the domestic economy. In late seventeenth-century Britain, coin clipping became in essence a coin substitution measure that the market called for and the government had to tolerate. By 1695 the average silver content of circulating coins was less than half their original mint weight. At that point the British government put a stop to it by re-minting silver coins back to their full weight and never again allowing any loss in precious metal content. The Ottoman government, too, aware of the economic and political problems of large volumes of counterfeit coins circulating in its realm, used the revenue from copper coin minting in the 1680s, to undertake the minting of a new Ottoman silver coin, the kuruş, for the first time, in 1690. However, in the course of the eighteenth century, unlike the British coinage, the silver content of the kuruş did not remain unchanged.[1]

In the War of Spanish Succession (1701-14), the greater strength of British finances, by then, the ability of the City of London to raise credit through bills of exchange and the improved state of the system of international payments were all part of the process that allowed the British state to finance its overseas military expenses without neither the government tolerating nor the market having recourse to such measures as coin clipping. And this is where the difference between the Ottoman empire and Britain lies. The latter was not able to do away with such coin substitution measures. Ottoman debased coinage continued to circulate well into the nineteenth century.[2] For the Ottoman provincial markets, such coins were better than no coins at all. Besides they served another purpose: not good enough to be hoarded, they remained in circulation, at times valued above their silver content, and facilitated exchange. With specie remaining scarce, coins were often regarded as merchandise and traded as such. In the eighteenth century, trade in money of which the merchants were the experts, remained a very lucrative area of Ottoman-European trade. In the second half of the century it also became an important source of additional specie for the empire. One of the most popular currencies exported to the empire remained the Spanish piastre. The Austrian thaler, the attractive appearance of which made it more popular than its silver content would warrant, was also a sought-after currency in the Ottoman markets.[3] As in earlier periods, these coins usually made their way to the Levant via the Italian ports.[4] İzmir imported mostly, but not

[1]Pamuk, *A Monetary History...*, pp. 159-163.

[2]On Ottoman debased coinage in the nineteenth century see, e.g., PRO, FO 78/1111, Consul D. Sandison, Bursa, 15 Jan. 1855 to Foreign Office, London and *ibid.*, FO 78/1771, Sandison, Bursa, 11 March 1863 to Foreign Office, London.

[3]Charles Carrière, *Négociants marseillais au XVIIIe siècle* (Marseilles, 1979), vol. I, p. 18.

[4]Le Moine de l'Espine, *Le Négoce d'Amsterdam* (Amsterdam, 1694), pp. 187, 202-03.

exclusively, thalers which were particularly useful in its trading with the East, for the thaler was equally sought-after in the Ottoman as in the African markets.[1] Istanbul imported mostly piastres.

In 1715, following the end of the wars in the Ottoman empire and Europe, there was a period of peace. It coincided with an increasing output from the silver mines, not only in the empire but in Europe, too. This was also the time when the new Ottoman silver currency took its final form and was fixed at 40 paras or 120 akçes. Although in the first half of the century, the currency retained, to a relative degree, its silver content, even then its rate of debasement — at 40 % in the years 1720s to 1760s — was not insignificant.[2] Debasement was biggest in the 1750s which was also the time when the Ottoman state tried, without much success, to reorganize its tax farming system in order to tap more revenue through it. As the fiscal crises worsened, coupled with greater pressure on the circulating medium due to the rate of growth of the economy and possibly also due to a diminishing output from silver mines,[3] the Ottoman state undertook, in the closing decades of the eighteenth and in the early nineteenth centuries, extensive debasement of the currency.[4] Through such a policy, the Ottoman state aimed to meet its fiscal needs and possibly also to alleviate monetary shortage in the economy. The latter aim was certainly not realized. As other states in Europe found out when pursuing extensive devaluation, — France in the late seventeenth and early eighteenth centuries and England in the late seventeenth century, — such measures had rather the opposite effect. Instead of alleviating specie shortage, they destroyed public confidence in the currency. They could also lead to hoarding of good coins and thus to a further reduction in the circulating medium.[5]

---

[1]In the closing decades of the eighteenth century, from which specific data is available, most of the specie coming into the empire from the West was in the form of thalers and came through İzmir. E.g., Archives de la Chambre de Commerce de Marseille, LIX/735, R. Franchetti, İzmir, 13 Aug. 1788, 8 January, 20 October & 10 March 1790 to Roux Frères, Marseilles; *ibid.* LIX/750, Dennis Rolland & Cie, İzmir, 18 December 1788, 24 March & 13 July 1789 to Roux Frères, Marseilles.

[2]Pamuk, *A Monetary History*..., pp. 162-63.

[3]Mehmet Genç, "Precious Metal Production in the Ottoman Empire during the Eighteenth Century", paper presented to the Conference on 'Money and Mints in the Ottoman Empire, 1690-1850', Institut français d'études annatoliennes, Istanbul, November 1997.

[4]Felix de Beaujour, *Tableau du commerce de la Grèce formé d'après une année moyenne depuis 1787 jusqu'en 1797* (Paris, 1800), vol. I, p. 181 and ANF, AE Biii 242, Consul Fourcade, İzmir, c. 1812.

[5]Dickson & Sperling, "War and Finance...", p. 303.

In the Ottoman empire, too, a policy of debasement had the opposite, than desired, effect. Rising prices, in addition to possible hoarding, in the closing decades of the eighteenth century, the result to a great extent of a considerably debased coinage, further accentuated monetary shortage. It also impacted negatively upon the rates of exchange of the Ottoman currency which fluctuated greatly in the European markets and which fell, overall, considerably. For instance, in 1708 there were 3 kuruş to 1 Venetian ducat; in 1766 the ratio was increased to 4 kuruş and in 1800, it had doubled to 8 kuruş.[1] Such a situation brought considerable stress and uncertainty to the local markets of the empire. Repeated debasement made the Ottoman coin unpopular in these markets which increasingly turned to European specie considering it 'good' money and thus ensuring a brisk import trade in money. The distinction between 'good' and 'bad' coinage, and the preference for the settling of accounts or payments of debts in a specified 'good' coinage, the acceptance of which carried different terms and conditions, was periodically in evidence in the Ottoman empire in the period under study.[2] Trying to legislate the value of the currency, rather than accept its market price, the state at times brought further havoc to the provincial markets. In İzmir, where there was an active currency market, there were daily fluctuations in the rates of exchange in the early nineteenth century.[3] With constant fluctuations in the rates of exchange and in the amount of the circulating medium, entrepreneurs turned to monetary speculative activities. In the late eighteenth century, operations involving specie and bills of exchange became as important as commodity trading in the market of İzmir. These operations consisted in the importation of foreign currencies into İzmir, profiting from the fluctuations in the rates of exchange, and purchasing with such profits bills of exchange on Europe; such purchases were made in particular when the margins in the premium of specie to bills of exchange allowed for further profits to be made. Such activities led to an overlapping of roles and expertise amongst merchants, both Ottoman and European, who acted as merchants-cum-bankers, as well as to another source of profits which further helped the growth of İzmir's market.

*

---

[1]N. Svoronos, *Le Commerce de Salonique au XVIIIe siècle* (Paris, 1956), p. 82.

[2]Archives du Ministère des Affaires Étrangères, CCC, Vol. 36, Consul E. David, İzmir, 3 Jan. 1821 to Minister, Paris. See also, Charles Carrière, "Réflexions sur le problème des monnaies et des métaux précieux en Méditerranée orientale au XVIIIe siècle", *Commerce de gros, commerce de détail dans les pays méditerranéens, XVIe-XIXe siècles* (Nice, 1976), pp. 1-20.

[3]ANF, AE Biii 242, Consul Fourcade, İzmir, c. 1812.

Since the sixteenth century, as the economy of Europe became further monetized, rarity of specie continued to be felt, at varying degrees, particularly amongst merchants engaged in long-distance international trade. As a result, various means were sought to overcome it, including barter and short-term credit through bills of exchange or other instruments of payment, such as promissory notes. Barter was used extensively in inter-European trade in the sixteenth and seventeenth centuries and in Ottoman-European trade until the end of the eighteenth century. Nevertheless some money was still necessary. For example, in the Ottoman Empire, paying for insurance and transportation of goods usually necessitated cash expenditures, whilst a certain amount of ready cash, which varied according to the state of the market at the time of purchase or sale of the goods, was also needed in order to get the best terms possible. Thus most commercial transactions in Ottoman-European trade were effected partly in barter, partly in cash and partly in credit. Besides barter, credit, which could last from three months to two years, was almost routinely extended by the Europeans to Ottoman merchants who purchased their goods. Ways were even devised to overcome prohibitions in order to ensure that credit could go on being extended. Regulations against extending credit emanated, at times, from European state authorities when such practices were considered as becoming too risky. However, it was not only the Ottomans who bought on credit. The Europeans, too, at times bought on credit. Moreover moneylending was a widespread activity and both Europeans and Ottomans participated in it.[1]

Another way of adding to one's capital resources and at the same time reducing the risks to one's investment was by sharing with fellow merchants one trusted commercial transactions that revolved around the purchase of Ottoman goods for sale in a European market or the reverse.[2] Ledgers and journal books of European merchants, trading in the Levant at the time, abound with the details of such transactions including the share(s) of each of

[1]Elena Frangakis-Syrett, "Trade Practices in Aleppo in the Middle of the Eighteenth Century. The case of a British Merchant", *Revue du Monde Musulman et de la Méditerranée*, Vol. 62/4 (1991), pp. 123-132. This article is based on the Private Papers of Colvill Bridger, who traded in Aleppo in the middle of the eighteenth century. For more information on British trade in Aleppo in the seventeenth and eighteenth centuries see, Bruce Masters, *Origins of Western Economic Dominance in the Middle East* (New York, 1989), *passim* and *idem*, "Aleppo: the Ottoman Empire's caravan city", Edhem Eldem, Daniel Goffman & Bruce Masters, eds., *The Ottoman City Between East and West* (Cambridge, 1999), pp. 29-48.

[2]Elena Frangakis-Syrett, "Les réseaux commerciaux et l'intégration au marché mondial de la Méditerranée orientale, un aperçu historique", M. Bazin, S. Kançal, J. Thobie & Y. Tekelioğlu, eds., *Méditerranée et Mer Noire entre Mondialisation et Régionalisation* (Paris, 2000), pp. 190-91; see also, *idem*, "Networks of Friendship, Networks of Kinship: Eighteenth-Century Levant Merchants", *Eurasian Studies*, Vol. I/2 (2002), pp. 189-212.

the participating merchants.[1] The monetary values that these shares represented were meticulously recorded and rolled over, if necessary, from one commercial transaction to the next. Profits and losses were apportioned to each participant from those commercial transactions that had been concluded. Sometimes participations in commercial ventures were made more formal through partnerships of varying duration. Such partnerships proliferated amongst merchants trading in and with the Levant.[2]

A further means of creating credit as well as of making long-distance payments, without the use of specie, was through bills of exchange. Besides the governments, it was the merchants who mostly sought out and refined this instrument of payment.[3] Both in Europe and the Ottoman empire bills of exchange were used extensively to make payments abroad as well as between major internal markets.[4] Partly due to the concerns of mercantilists in relation to outflows of bullion from the national economies of Europe, partly due to the tendency of European governments to implement specie restriction policies, of which the European merchants trading in the Ottoman empire were very much a case in point, as well as due to actual specie scarcity, amongst other factors, it was through the development of a complex and sophisticated system of bills of exchange, rather than bullion, that world trade evolved and international payments were ultimately effected. It was a system that encompassed all of Europe and the areas that Europe traded with in the world. It also included the Ottoman empire and was vital in integrating it in the financial networks and monetary resources of the major economic centers of Europe. Bills of exchange could be negotiated anywhere within this system. Amsterdam was one of the most important hubs, if not the most important center in this system. All the important commercial centers of the empire,

---

[1]Such practices are recorded in the ledgers of Ottoman Greek companies, such as the Ralli Brothers, in the closing decades of the eighteenth century. The firm was partly based in İzmir and partly in various ports of Europe where its associates, often family members, were established. For more details see Elena Frangakis-Syrett, *Οι Χιώτες εμποροι στις διεθνείς συναλλαγές, 1750-1850 (Chiot Merchants in International Trade, 1750-1850)* (Athens, 1995), *passim;* see also, *idem,* "İzmir and the Ottoman Maritime World of the Eighteenth Century", Kate Fleet, ed., *The Ottomans and the Sea* in *Oriente Moderno*, Vol. XX/1 (2002), p. 121-128.

[2]For examples of partnerships amongst British merchants, see Elena Frangakis-Syrett, "Commerce in the Eastern Mediterranean from the Eighteenth to the Early Twentieth Centuries: The City-Port of İzmir and its Hinterland", *International Journal of Maritime History,* Vol. X/2 (1998), pp. 127-28; for examples of partnerships amongst Dutch and Ottoman Greek merchants, see, *idem,* "Networks of Friendship...", pp. 195-199, 207-211.

[3]J.A., *A General Treatise of Monies and Exchanges* (London, 1707), pp. 8-23.

[4]E.g. PRO, SP 105/113, Levant Company, London, 15 Feb. 1665 to Treasurer Richard Langley, İzmir; *ibid.*, Levant Company, London, 1 Sept. 1670 to Hardy, İzmir; SP 110/36, Thomas Lansdown, Aleppo, 3 & 19 Sept. 1759 to Messrs. Ashby & Humphrys, Istanbul.

from Istanbul to Aleppo, had financial links with Amsterdam.[1] As early as 1694 Le Moine de L'Espine, whilst in Amsterdam, poignantly noted:

> On y pourrait même trouver dans le besoin des lettres de change pour Copenhague en Danemark, pour Stockholm en Suède, pour Riga, Lubeck, Archange en Moscou et pour Smyrne et Alep dans le Levant, quoi qu'il n'y ait point de change ordinaire pour ces Places.[2]

By the latter part of the eighteenth century the exchange rates for an array of European currencies were routinely quoted in the merchants' correspondence, trading to and from İzmir or Istanbul, evidence of an open and constant interaction, by then, of the Ottoman cities with major European currency markets.[3]

In a Europe-centered international trading and payments system, it was multilateral payments through bills of exchange that mostly maintained such a system in motion and overcame specie scarcity. Moreover, multilateral payments ensured that the entire system tended towards equilibrium. Hard currency flows were kept to a minimum. Certain amounts of bullion were necessary to effect some transfers of specie to maintain the equilibrium of the system, either because specie was hoarded or because some trading areas within the system, amongst them the Ottoman empire, were bullion consuming regions as far as Europe was concerned. However, there were also inflows of bullion into the system: for instance, trade with Spanish America brought bullion into Europe. Furthermore, whilst the Ottoman empire had a net surplus in its balance of trade with Europe, the empire experienced a deficit in its balance of trade with the East and Far East, thus returning to the international payments system some of its monetary surplus, at least to the degree that some bullion, particularly gold, did return to the West from the East and the Far East. Part of the trade deficit between the empire and Europe may not, of course, have been realized in bullion but in bills of exchange. Indeed, specie did flow into İzmir from Europe — a major port of entry for both specie and goods — not only in order to cover trade deficit but also for the more lucrative and speculative trade in money. Furthermore, the flourishing trade in bills of exchange, both for commercial and speculative purposes, in the market of İzmir in the eighteenth century, demonstrates that commercial paper could be as good as specie. Ultimately, within the Europe-

[1]Ricard, *Le Négoce...*, pp. 556-68.
[2]Le Moine de l'Espine, *Le négoce ...*, pp. 12-13.
[3]For example, such data exists in the correspondance between the Marseilles-based company Roux Frères and its agents in İzmir or Istanbul.

centered system, as a whole, bullion primarily flowed to and from Amsterdam and London, rather than between actual points of trade, because it was between these two financial markets that payments were finally cleared.[1]

The Ottoman empire had its own 'internal' system of monetary flows that was both connected to the European financial markets and answered the needs of its own local markets, in the process aiming to create an equilibrium within the empire between needs and resources. It was also another way to deal with specie scarcity. An important monetary flow was from the provinces to Istanbul in the form of taxation and for the purchase of high offices by investors who went to the capital at certain times of the year, namely March and April, to do so. Major ports in the empire's internal and external trade, such as İzmir and Alexandria, sent part of their surplus in silver from their trade with the West to Istanbul; another part of the surplus was used in the East Indian trades. In the case of İzmir, funds went East both directly and after passing first through Alexandria. Some of the surplus sent to the capital made its way back to Europe, either in bills of exchange or in specie, since Istanbul was a port that primarily imported goods from the West. However most of the trade surplus, that European merchants trading in the capital realized from the sales of their goods, made its way to other markets in the empire where there were Europeans trading, to cover their purchases of Ottoman goods for the western markets or to meet other needs for commercial paper. Thus the flow of funds from the capital to the provinces, that was initiated by the Europeans, stood to compliment the pre-existing internal flow of funds from the provinces to the capital. For instance, Europeans in Cyprus or Aleppo drew on their counterparts in Istanbul whilst Ottoman administrators in the capital sold bills on Aleppo.[2] Although such transactions were carried out mostly by bills of exchange, specie could also, at times, be used.[3] Then there were the external flows, mostly in bills of exchange, between Istanbul and European centers, mostly Marseilles, to repatriate the profits of European merchants. There were also external monetary flows between Ottoman centers, mostly İzmir, and major European centers, mostly in bills of exchange, for the

---

[1]Sperling, "The International Payments Mechanism...", pp. 450-452, 460-62.

[2]E.g., PRO, FO 105/36, Thomas Lansdown, Aleppo, 27 and 30 July, 3 and 10 September 1759 to Messrs. Ashby & Humphrys, Istanbul.

[3]If a cash purchase had to be made specie could also be carried by ship. We have examples of European captains, plying the Ottoman coastal waters and covering all major routes from North Africa to the capital, carrying such specie. Yolande Triantafyllidou-Baladié, "Transports maritimes et concurrence en Méditerranée orientale au XVIIIe siècle: l'exemple de Crète", *Actes du IIe colloque international d'histoire* (Athens, 1985), vol. I, p. 24; see also, Daniel Panzac, "Affréteurs ottomanes et capitaines français à Alexandrie: la caravane maritime en Méditerranée au milieu du XVIIIe siècle", *Revue de l'Occident Musulman et de la Méditerranée,* Vol. XXXIV (1982), pp. 23-38.

purposes of monetary speculation as the correspondence of the commercial and banking house of Roux Frères clearly illustrates. As in Europe, so in the empire, networks of bills of exchange greatly facilitated not only payments but also the flow of funds as well as contributed not only to the circulating medium but also to alleviating specie scarcity.

*

Given the rate of economic growth, and particularly of trade, that occurred in the empire in the eighteenth century, specie scarcity had to have been, at least in part, overcome. An active provincial market in the Ottoman empire, İzmir experienced very considerable commercial growth, particularly in the second half of the eighteenth century. In order to achieve such rate of growth, its market had to devise successful specie substitution mechanisms, such as the use of credit through, amongst other means, an extensive circulation of promissory notes, or a widespread use of bills of exchange and/or the manipulation of the exchange rates through the application of *agio* in such a way as to give a premium to the Ottoman currency in the local market and thus to attract specie to İzmir away from other Ottoman markets.[1] Without altogether destabilizing the local money market, such practices lent it periodically a high degree of volatility and made speculative monetary practices widespread. Although one could speculate that there might have been an even greater rate of commercial growth, had there been more specie available and lower interest rates, nevertheless such practices also allowed the city, to a great extent, to carry out trade and increase very considerably its volume of business.

There are some similarities between İzmir and Marseilles in the eighteenth century. Both cities had close trading links with each other. Indeed, Marseilles was İzmir's premier trading partner although the reverse was not the case. The commercial sectors of both cities grew manifold, in the eighteenth century, although both suffered from monetary shortages and from underdevelopment of institutionalized credit. Despite or perhaps because of the banks in Lyons there was no bank in Marseilles. Instead there was an increasing use of commercial paper — whose volume and circulation grew manifold — in order to increase the circulating medium to enable, in part,

[1]For an analysis of specie substitution mechanisms in İzmir in the eighteenth century, see Elena Frangakis-Syrett, "The Ottoman Monetary System in the Second Half of the Eighteenth and in the Early Nineteenth Centuries: A View from the Provinces", paper presented to the Conference on 'Money and Mints in the Ottoman Empire', Institut français d'études anatoliennes, Istanbul, November 1997.

commercial growth which did occur at a rate commensurate to that of İzmir's growth. Unlike the case of İzmir, greater availability of credit in Marseilles lowered the interest rates and brought greater stability to the exchange rates.[1] Crucial to the dispensing of this credit and the circulation of paper were the *courtiers* in Marseilles whose position became very strong in the city's business circles. Besides trade, they financed a whole host of other activities. They were able to concentrate in their hands a more extensive array of business than did brokers in İzmir — besides merchant banking operations they also undertook chartering and insurance.

Over-extension of credit and its abuse, at times, made the market of Marseilles, like that of İzmir, volatile, speculative and unstable. It also contributed to the bankruptcies in 1774. Abuses included the circulation of fictitious commercial paper, which did not represent any commercial transactions at its origin as well as the ability to settle paper with further paper, in essence without having to have resort to any specie. The latter practice owed its origin to the way that brokers and others in Marseilles started in the 1760s and early 1770s to interpret the clause on its bills, "*payable en compensation*", to mean in essence with further paper.[2] With public confidence on the quality of Marseilles paper starting to diminish, since such paper was increasingly the only medium of exchange that circulated in the local market, and with little specie or non-locally issued paper around, bills of exchange drawn on the city started to lose in value. As a result, not only specie but also bills of exchange drawn on other centers started to carry a similar premium and hence discount rate — in other words, both instruments of payment had become equally expensive. In the early 1770s, as the financial crisis was gathering storm, Marseilles sought remittances in specie and bills of exchange from İzmir, as one of the ways to replenish its reserves.[3] In the European financial crisis of 1774, during which İzmir was not affected, Marseilles paper was totally discredited. However, following the crisis, the economy of Marseilles recovered swiftly testifying to the growth of wealth and capital that had, by then, occurred. Of course, it should also be noted that following the crisis, the Chamber of Commerce of Marseilles had to re-

---

[1] Paul Masson, *Histoire du commerce français dans le Levant au XVIIIe siècle* (Paris, 1911), pp. 231-245.

[2] L. Bergasse & G. Rambert, *Histoire du Commerce de Marseille, IV, de 1559 à 1660* (Paris, 1954), p. 632.

[3] For more information on such remittances, see Elena Frangakis, "The Balance of Trade and the Balance of Payments Between İzmir and France, 1700-1789", *Communications grecques présentées au Ve Congrès international des études du Sud-Est européen* (Athens, 1985), pp. 127-138.

regulate the *courtiers* — whose office and rights as they existed came to an end — and partially bail them out.[1]

Unlike the *courtiers* in the French city, in İzmir, throughout the period under study, all commercial and complimentary activities, including merchant banking, remained competitive and open to all; besides the petty bankers, merchants often acted also as bankers. Moreover, despite the extensive use of credit, interest rates remained high testifying to an on-going tightness of credit. Exchange rates continued to be primarily affected by the debasement of the currency. As a result, they continued to fluctuate especially in the closing decades of the century and in the early nineteenth. Despite the volatility and the tightness of credit, the market of İzmir had learnt to function under such conditions and grow. Indeed by the late eighteenth century İzmir was entering a period of spectacular commercial growth which lasted into the early nineteenth century.

*

In conclusion, it can be argued that in the absence of institutionalized banking and of extensive note-issue, and given the overall diminishing output of silver mines and growth of the world economy in the eighteenth century, it was to be expected that shortages of the circulating medium would occur. What made monetary shortages especially acute, however, were the mounting expenditure that protracted periods of war brought about in the late seventeenth and early eighteenth centuries, when the world economy was not as yet experiencing a robust rate of growth. This made Ottoman and European governments actively seek new institutions and forms of credit in order to improve, not only on the short but also on the long term, their fiscal revenues. The latter was crucial if public debt were to become an asset rather than a liability. The Ottoman government, like its European counterparts, sought ways to remint its silver currency and place it on a more secure footing. It also repeatedly attempted the re-organization of its tax-farming system, although not with much success, which constituted its major source of revenue as well as of internal borrowing. Likewise, state policies in Europe, such as the recoinage of the currency or the re-organization of the taxation system undertaken by the British government, aimed at regulating public revenue as well as at placing state debt on a basis which would ensure its repayment.

[1] Bergasse & Rambert, *Histoire du Commerce de Marseille*..., pp. 656-57.

The Ottoman state did ultimately find, within the empire, the monetary resources to fight the wars for it did not contract any loans abroad. However, in the process it drew too much capital from other sectors of the economy, such as trade, contributing to the lack of specie in the empire's markets as well as slowing down the rate of capital growth. The latter was already not encouraged by other state policies that aimed to protect the consumer. Yet the alleviation of specie scarcity was also aided by other policies of the state which set in motion a flow of goods and funds within the empire and which tended to balance resources with needs within the Ottoman world. The active and sophisticated network of bills of exchange that circulated within the empire, besides allowing the movement of funds around efficiently, also added to the circulating medium thus further aiding in the alleviation of specie scarcity. Of importance in improving monetary shortage, as far as the economy was concerned, was also the integration of the major economic centers of the empire within the European financial networks, as well as within the Euro-centered international payments mechanism, that had developed by the eighteenth century. Such a system, based primarily on the circulation of bills of exchange, served the purposes of trade as well as state finances. It also became an efficient and effective system of short-term credit besides adding to the monetary resources of the Ottoman economy.

Unable to get the revenue it needed from tax farming, the Ottoman state turned to debasement as an alternative revenue-producing policy. The increasing implementation of such a policy, in the late eighteenth century, had detrimental effects on specie scarcity in the economy. However, it did not deter the considerable economic, and in particular commercial, growth that occurred, for a number of reasons, in the empire, at the time. For if the state could not get the revenue that was due to it from the tax farmers, because the latter kept it, this meant that individuals prospered economically, further contributing to growth in the private sector. Local markets, in the maritime regions of the empire in particular, also grew. In order to achieve and maintain this growth, specie substitution mechanisms were developed to overcome specie inadequacy and monetary practices evolved to overcome the uncertainty of greatly fluctuating rates of exchange. Local markets, led by İzmir, also sought to import specie from abroad. Although such imports had the possibility of being potentially detrimental, not only for the Ottoman economy but also for Ottoman-European trade, as was the case with the counterfeiting incident of the seventeenth century, such dangers were kept to a minimum. The uniqueness of this incident testifies to this. Trade in money, of course, did lend volatility to the markets but it also became an important source of profit for entrepreneurs.

Unlike the western European economies, where low interest rates became the norm, the high interest rates that persisted in the Ottoman empire, well beyond the period under study, testify to the fact that specie scarcity remained a problem. The Ottoman state continued to seek ways to overcome it, as shown in the issue of the kaimes and in the negotiations with European capitalists for a state loan as well as the establishment of a national bank that the Ottoman state pursued in the first half of the nineteenth century.

THE OTTOMAN MONETARY SYSTEM IN THE SECOND HALF OF THE EIGHTEENTH AND IN THE EARLY NINETEENTH CENTURIES: A VIEW FROM THE PROVINCES*

Introduction

The present study[1] sets out to examine the Ottoman monetary system, how it functioned and, in particular, the way it adapted to and served the needs of the Ottoman markets in the second half of the eighteenth and in the early nineteenth centuries.[2] This will be done primarily, although not exclusively, through an analysis of the economic activities in İzmir — a major commercial and financial market in the Empire at the time.

There are a number of reasons which render İzmir an excellent case-study for an analysis of the Ottoman monetary system. The most important is its emergence as the leading commercial center both in the Empire's external and internal trade, in the process linking together large areas of the Empire.[3] In addition to its dominance of the commercial sector, İzmir also emerged as a major financial center in the Empire serving the banking needs primarily of Anatolia and the Aegean islands and, to a lesser extent, of the Balkan peninsula and the Arab lands. What is equally important for our purposes here is the fact that both the commercial and the financial sectors of İzmir grew considerably in the period under study. This growth, particularly in the commercial sector, was at times spectacular. Equally spectacular, however, were the monetary problems and challenges that, at times, formed the background to this hectic commercial and financial activity. As a result of this, a set of practices and business strategies evolved in order to meet the monetary challenges.

---

*First publication

[1] Different parts of this study were given at two international meetings, namely: 'Conference on Money and Mints in the Ottoman Empire' organized by the Institut Français d'Études Anatoliennes and held in Istanbul, November 1997 and at the Fifteenth Symposium of the International Committee on Pre-Ottoman and Ottoman Studies, held at the London School of Economics, July 2002. I wish here to thank the organizers of both these events and the participants for their useful comments.

[2] Research for this study was supported, in part, by the City University of New York PSC-CUNY Research Award Program.

[3] For a commercial history of İzmir in the long eighteenth century, see Elena Frangakis-Syrett, *The Commerce of Smyrna in the Eighteenth Century, 1700-1820* (Athens, 1992).

In the largely agricultural economy of eighteenth-century Ottoman Empire, trade was the most advanced sector of the economy in terms of its organization and level of monetization, functioning in a mutual interdependency with the financial sector. Moreover, the way each sector functioned affected the other and both sectors were affected, to a lesser or greater extent, by the imperial government's monetary policies. A case in point were government policies of currency debasement and the periodic efforts to fix the value of the currency even if that overrode market valuations. Such government policies in turn led to a whole system of practices, such as the use of *agio*, put in place by the market in order to counteract and/or mediate, as the case might be, the effect of such policies. Ottoman and western private financiers and merchants, who worked within the Ottoman monetary system — one could also call them merchants-cum-bankers for they often combined both activities — adapted their business strategies accordingly. In the process, they were able to turn potentially unfavorable situations into profitable ones; at the same time the monetary system was rendered more flexible and effective for the functioning of growing local markets. In other words, and in the absence of a *de jure* financial system, a *de facto* system emerged in İzmir, as it did in other major economic centers of the Empire based on the needs of the local market forces.

The Ottoman Monetary System

Even before the second half of the eighteenth century, the Ottoman monetary system was characterized by certain overriding features amongst which were chronic monetary scarcity and a general absence of investment capital. Another important feature was the policy of periodic currency devaluation pursued, for a number of reasons, by the Ottoman government and which contributed to inflation. In the latter part of the eighteenth century and in the early nineteenth, devaluation and inflation reached particularly high levels.[1] Both these phenomena accentuated further the problem of monetary scarcity in the Ottoman economy.[2] However, monetary scarcity had to be relatively overcome in order to ensure the functioning, growth as well as increasing monetization of certain sectors of the Ottoman economy, such as

---

[1]Archives de la Chambre de Commerce de Marseille, Marseilles, LIX/739, Garavaque & Cusson, İzmir, 21 Feb. 1764 to Roux Frères, Marseilles; LIX/735, Ruben Franchetti, İzmir, 25 Sept. 1789 to Roux Frères, Marseilles. Hereafter, these archives will be cited as ACCM. See also, Félix de Beaujour, *Tableau du commerce de la Grèce formé d'après une année moyenne depuis 1787 jusqu'en 1797* (Athens, 1974, reprint), vol. II, pp. 203-204.

[2]E.g., Archives Nationales de Fance, Paris, AE Biii 242, Consul Fourcade, Mémoire, İzmir, c. 1812. Hereafter, these archives will be cited as ANF.

trade. At the same time, the commercial growth that was registered, not only in centers like İzmir, but in sectors such as the external trade of the Empire as a whole, points to the fact that monetary scarcity was, in part, overcome. Of course, monetary scarcity may have also inhibited, at least in part, an even greater potential for commercial growth. Whatever is the case, one thing can be certain: the absolute commercial growth that was registered in the Empire at the time, must have placed additional demands on the circulating medium, thus accentuating specie scarcity.

Another important characteristic was the non-unified nature of the Ottoman monetary system[1] which had both positive and negative effects. It contributed to the liberal nature of the financial system and to free flow of bullion in and out of the Ottoman economy.[2] It also allowed for the extensive circulation of western currencies to take place, at all levels of the Ottoman economy, at times even substituting for local coins. However, it also resulted in the circulation, within the territories of the Empire of many different local currencies, both gold and silver, for the Ottoman Government did not attempt to impose a unified monetary system even in the core areas of its Empire, nor did the Government try to impose a fixed legal rate of exchange between the gold and silver coins circulating in the Empire.[3] The result of such developments was a confusing situation as far as the currency market was concerned. For there were not only different currencies circulating at different rates of exchange in the Empire but the same currencies were also simultaneously circulating at different rates of exchange within the different regions of the Empire. Such a system brought forth endless possibilities for arbitrage operations and other related activities in currency speculation. Of course, spatially variable rates of exchange for the same currencies were not only due to the non-unified nature of the Ottoman monetary system but to a whole host of other reasons too, such as, the non-unified state of the Ottoman domestic market and the existence within the Empire of fairly separate regional economies.

[1]Halil Sahillioğlu, "The role of international monetary and metal movements in Ottoman monetary history, 1300-1750", in J. F. Richards, ed., *Precious Metals in the Later Medieval and Early Modern Worlds* (Durham, N.C., 1983), pp. 278-279.

[2]Elena Frangakis, "The Balance of Trade and Balance of Payments Between İzmir and France, 1700-1789", *Communications grecques presentées au Ve Congrès International des Études de sud-est Européen* (Athens, 1985), pp. 127-138.

[3]Haim Gerber, "The Monetary System of the Ottoman Empire", *Journal of the Economic and Social History of the Orient*, Vol. XXV/III (1982), pp. 308-324.

Government Policies and Trade in Money

The combination of a non-unified monetary system with chronic specie scarcity, which became at times acute and which was not alleviated but rather worsened by the policy of currency debasement followed periodically by the Ottoman government, was one of the factors that led to an influx, since the sixteenth century, of foreign coins in the Ottoman Empire.[1] For instance, in late-seventeenth-century İzmir, European merchants were sending to the city-port gold coins such as the Venetian sequins and silver currencies such as the Austrian thalers, Dutch asselani, Spanish piastres and French écus, either for outright circulation in the Ottoman Empire or for minting purposes.[2] Such coins were either brought into the Empire through economic means or were imported outright, sometimes even in a counterfeited form.[3] The importation of foreign coins was, at times, the result of the needs by the state for precious metals in the minting of Ottoman coins.[4] At wartime such needs became more acute since the state had to provide for additional fiscal expenditure. Since wars were frequent for the Ottoman state, in the period under study, its fiscal expenditure had to be often increased accordingly.

Importing foreign coins resulted in a trade in money, or *commerce de banque*, as it was called. By the second half of the eighteenth century, as it will be argued below, İzmir was a major port of entry, even more than Istanbul, for such activities.[5] In such a trade, specie became a commodity to be used in a number of ways once it entered the Empire: it could enter circulation and facilitate trade, both internal and external, or it could be absorbed by the Ottoman Mint; in some cases, it could also be hoarded. Foreign specie could also become part of purely speculative arbitrage operations. In such a case, a large part of the specie could, at times, leave the Ottoman economy as soon as it had entered it. Flows of bullion in and out of the Empire, for monetary speculation, did not alleviate to any lasting degree the scarcity of specie in the Ottoman economy. Yet this was one of the main reasons for which the Ottoman state had initially tolerated the circulation of foreign coins in its territories; at the same time, however, it could also not

---

[1]Frangakis-Syrett, *The Commerce...*, pp. 139-140.

[2]ANF, AE Biii 235, Commerce du Levant, Mémoire sur les sequins, 1686.

[3]Şevket Pamuk, "The Disintegration of the Ottoman Monetary System During the Seventeenth Century", *Princeton Papers*, No. 2 (1993), pp. 75-76; see also, Sonia Anderson, *An English Consul in Turkey. Paul Rycaut at Smyrna, 1667-1678* (Oxford, 1989), pp. 178-185.

[4]ANF, AE Bi 1057, Consul Charles-Claude de Peyssonnel, Précis du Mémoire ... en faveur de l'agio sur les éspèces, İzmir, 29 April 1769.

[5]At times, and for reasons which will be discussed below, the reverse flow could also take place whereby specie was sent from İzmir to the West.

prevent the flow of such currencies out of its territories. There were certainly other, non-speculative, reasons for the flow of specie out of the Empire: a deficit in the Ottoman-Persian trade, or a potentially passive balance of payments in the Ottoman-European trade overall.[1] For such reasons, the Ottoman government did try at times to legislate against outflows of specie but, of course, with little tangible effect.[2] The result was a *de facto* open Ottoman monetary system with a free circulation of bullion.

Apart from the importation of foreign coins, the Ottoman government resorted periodically to debasement too, as referred to above, in order to increase the circulating medium in the economy and in the process improve its tax revenue and thus its solvency. By the latter part of the eighteenth and in the early nineteenth centuries, since the needs of the state were so pressing that long-term policies could not always be entertained, the government resorted to debasement for short-term relief[3] which, in the long term, had the opposite result: a weaker currency, which in the face of inflation, was even more inadequate in meeting certainly the nation's needs for specie, even if the state's needs were thus being met on the short term. The state then turned to legislation as an alternative policy to bolster the currency, and thus increase the circulating medium in another manner. It aimed to set, by decree, the rate of exchange of the Ottoman currency at a higher level vis-à-vis foreign currencies than it was circulating in the local markets. With the international rates of exchange of the Ottoman currency increasingly falling in the late eighteenth and early nineteenth centuries, such government decrees brought only havoc to the marketplace which refused to accept artificial values for the circulating medium.[4] Besides, as the process of integration of certain areas of the Ottoman Empire into the world economy increased, in the latter part of the eighteenth and in the early nineteenth centuries, and as some of the principal monetary networks of the Empire, such as those of Istanbul and İzmir, became more integrated into the western financial circuits, the forces of the market had more success in setting the rates of exchange than did Ottoman government decrees.[5]

---

[1]Charles Carrière & Marcel Courdurié, "Un sophisme économique: Marseille s'enrichit en achetant plus qu'elle ne vend", *Histoire, Économie et Société* (1981), pp. 37-38; see also, Frangakis-Syrett, *The Commerce*..., pp. 153-154.

[2]E.g., Gerber, "The Monetary System ...", pp. 316-317.

[3]In the last quarter of the eighteenth and in the early nineteenth centuries, the Ottoman government followed a policy of debasement which is reflected, among other things, in the exchange rates of the Ottoman piastre vis-à-vis western currencies during this period. Such data has been collected by the author as part of a bigger work on the subject.

[4]Public Record Office, London, SP 105/128, Consul Francis Werry, İzmir, 17 Sept. 1801 to Levant Company, London. Hereafter, these archives will be cited as PRO.

[5]ANF, AE Biii 242, Consul Fourcade, Mémoire, İzmir, c. 1812.

Finally an important factor in the capital liquidity of a commercial market, such as İzmir, was the degree of monetary liquidity at the disposal of the western merchants, established in the city-port. For the latter constituted an important element in the external trade of İzmir with the West, which was in itself an important sector in the local economy. These merchants — French, British, Dutch or Italians — came from some of the most advanced economies of the West where they enjoyed greater capital resources and more regulated monetary and banking systems than in the Ottoman Empire. Nevertheless one should also not overestimate the capital resources of those merchants either, since they came from European economies of essentially a pre-Industrial Revolution period. For instance, the Italian city-states could still experience periodic specie scarcity,[1] whilst the European-wide financial crisis of 1774 was felt specially strongly in France, which was the Ottoman Empire's leading trading partner at the time.[2] And, of course, the mercantilist policies of the major European economies, such as those of France or Britain, meant that efforts were made, on the part of those states' authorities, to control, as far as possible, bullion exports to the Levant. So that even when western merchants could dispose of higher capital resources in their trading activities in the Ottoman markets, they might have had to go through circuitous routes to get the actual funds. The result was that westerners in İzmir, Aleppo or elsewhere in the Levant, like their Ottoman counterparts, also disposed of overall limited capital resources.

Credit and Barter as Specie Substitutes

Given such conditions, therefore, an elaborate system of specie substitution emerged to facilitate commercial transactions: credit and barter were part of such a system. Whenever, and for whatever reasons, the local money supply became particularly low, trade relied heavily on barter and credit. The extent to which merchants relied on credit and barter was also determined by the availability of European money. Transactions carried out through barter or credit were complex as well as elaborate and required a precise knowledge of both the local and western markets, for they impacted directly on the price of the goods and hence on the profitability of the entire enterprise.

---

[1]ANF, AE Bi 600, French Consul Raulin, Genoa, 14 Jan. 1793 to Minister, Paris.
[2]ANF, AE Bii 241, Mémoire sur l'argent, c. 1774-1775; see also, François-Xavier Emmanuelli, *La crise marseillaise de 1774 et la chute des courtiers* (Paris, 1979), *passim.*

Given the dynamics of the market, certain goods were in high demand and could only be bought for cash. Such was the case with Ottoman exports of wheat, olive oil or wax. By contrast, 'colonial' goods re-exported to the Levant, such as cochineal or indigo, could easily be bartered for the produce of the country. The situation was mixed as far as other goods were concerned. For instance, in the early nineteenth century demand in the İzmir market for western cloth was such that it was generally difficult to buy it, solely through a barter exchange, without using some cash to complete the purchase. So that if one wanted to buy 1,000 Ottoman piastres worth of cloth, one would have had to barter local goods worth 2,000 to 2,500 piastres and still have a balance to pay in cash.[1] However, many factors could intervene, in what was still a very volatile market, to weaken the position of the cloth seller. For instance, temporary over-abundance of cloth in the local market could make the western merchant more willing to offer credit terms for the remaining balance. There were other reasons also why "money goods", such as western cloth, could be "sacrificed" for a barter sale against, for instance, silk. This could be either because the western merchant did not have the cash to buy silk with or because he was pressed to conclude a sale, by a set date, and was thus willing to offer more attractive terms.[2] Whenever a barter exchange was not at all feasible, or as a way of complementing a transaction, credit could also be used. Although Ottoman merchants were the ones who experienced specie scarcity the most and hence resorted to credit the most frequently, westerners, both when buying and selling, also used credit extensively and often in contravention to the regulations of their home countries. Indeed, they had devised various ways to get round such regulations. For instance, a westerner could sell his stock of cloth for a bag of money which he never opened, but handed back to the Ottoman merchant, being given a note for it. The money was to be paid when the next caravan arrived.[3] More frequently however, a westerner in the Levant was instructed by his principal (s) "to sell for time",[4] that is, to extend a credit period that usually lasted from ninety-three days to fifty-four months. Nevertheless, should the economic fortune of the debtor suddenly improve with the arrival of a caravan or a particularly good harvest,

[1] A.B. Cunningham, ed., "The Journal of Christophe Aubin: A Report of the Levant Trade in 1812", *Archivum Ottomanicum*, Vol. 8 (1983), p. 38.

[2] Private Papers, Colvill Bridger Collection, C. Bridger, Aleppo, 30 May 1755 to E. & A. Radcliffe, London; and C. Bridger, Aleppo, 30 May 1755 to R. Stratton, London. I would like here to thank Mr. James Bridger for making his family papers available to me. Hereafter this collection will be cited as PP/CBC.

[3] PRO, SP 105/116, Levant Company, London, 22 June 1715 to Consul Pilkington, Aleppo.

[4] PP/CBC, C. Bridger, Aleppo, 11 Sept. 1759 to W. Hammond, London; see also, C. Bridger, Aleppo, 10 March 1755 to J. Harding, London and C. Bridger, Aleppo, 24 April 1755 to Ch. Frye, London.

the local merchant could pay off his debt early, although it was with goods instead of with money that he was paying it off.

A similar system that involved receiving, rather than extending, credit in kind was also favored by western merchants. Unlike Istanbul, where the westerners had a trading surplus, in other Ottoman markets, such as İzmir or Aleppo, it was usual for local merchants to lend to the westerners when the former were in need of cash. However, it was goods, rather than money, that they were lending to them. For instance, a westerner in İzmir could sell some of his cloth for cash and use all or part of the proceeds to buy olive oil, wheat or wax, which could only be bought for cash, and with the balance pay off any outstanding bills of exchange drawn on him. He then worked out a bartering plan according to which the local merchant supplied him with, for instance, cotton wool, mohair yarn or cotton yarn against cloth or 'colonial' goods. However, since the westerner may not have had any of his goods in hand yet, the Ottoman merchant advanced him goods on credit. The debt was to be paid off, in kind, by the westerner when his next shipment of goods arrived. It was credit in kind — only instead of advancing money, it was goods.[1] Besides İzmir, similar credit practices also operated in Aleppo where western merchants bought silk on credit from Ottoman merchants with the understanding that they would pay for it with cloth when their next ship arrived.[2]

When monetary shortage in the local markets was particularly acute, credit could also be extended "indefinitely". Although the debt was finally and most likely paid off, the "flexibility" in the payment date that was implicit in such a situation, at times, frustrated westerners. For these were practices that had evolved over time in order to cope with a periodically acute specie shortage without affecting mortally the functioning of the local market. Whether it was in İzmir, Aleppo or elsewhere in the Ottoman Empire, the local markets had become accustomed to sustaining a certain level of credit, overall, successfully. Of course, it was a volatile and risky situation. Certainly over-ambitious or merely imprudent businessmen, as well as dishonest ones, could easily default in such a market causing in their wake a series of bankruptcies among both local and western merchants.[3] However, when the market became over-heated, or too risky, the business community itself devised regulatory mechanisms. For instance, in early nineteenth-century

[1]ANF, AE Bi 1052, Consul Charles de Peyssonnel, İzmir, 29 Jan. 1749 to Minister, Paris.
[2]R. Davis, *Aleppo and Devonshire Square* (London, 1967), pp. 185-186.
[3]ANF, AE Bi 1052, Charles de Peyssonnel, İzmir, 5 March 1749 to Minister, Paris.

İzmir, western and Ottoman importers of cloth formed an association to collect their debts from merchants in the bazaars, who were themselves represented by the Union of Greek and Armenian shopkeepers, to exact more rigorous terms of credit, and to decide upon retaliatory action in case of fraudulent bankruptcies.[1] For the westerner, who could not easily discern a debtor who procrastinated, by force of circumstances, from a willful one, who never intended paying, or for the westerner who could not accommodate himself with the "rhythm" of business in the Levant, such practices were simply either wrong or lacking in integrity. Yet there were also those westerners who understood the system well and were ready to play within it.

Agio and the Market

Whenever specie scarcity became particularly acute, and specie substitution methods as described above were not being effective, other adjusting mechanisms could also come into place to ease monetary liquidity in a local market. Such a mechanism was the *agio*, also called discount or *bénéfice*. It was used in a number of ways. As a discount mechanism, it could be applied to reflect the actual market value of the Ottoman currency and thus to calculate and adjust the exchange rates between the Ottoman and the French currency — the livre tournois. It could also be applied so as to favor the Ottoman currency in the exchange rates and thus attract specie to a local market. Through its application on the exchange rates, the *agio* could also be used to affect directly the pricing of western imports. That is, on the basis of the expected future devaluation of the Ottoman currency, the *agio* discounted such prices, thus making them more attractive to the local consumer. As a discount system, it could also be applied on the types of currencies used to make payments, by everybody concerned, in the local market. This was more likely to happen when circulation of base coinage became particularly extensive. Given the frequent debasement of the currency that took place in the late eighteenth and early nineteenth centuries, an *agio* varying in amount from 2-3 per cent began to be applied at the time in the market of İzmir on all transactions made with 'good money'. This was in order to induce payments to be made in non-abusive coinage.[2]

[1]ACCM, MQ, 5.1, Agreement proposed by the deputies of the European and Ottoman Greek cloth importers, İzmir, 5 Sept. 1820.

[2]Archives du Ministère des Affaires Étrangères, Paris, CCC, Vol. 36, Consul E. David, İzmir, 3 Jan. 1821 to Foreign Minister, Paris. Hereafter these archives will be cited as AMAE.

As a quite complex discount system, the *agio* thus reflected the forces of the market at any given moment in the various economic centers of the Ottoman Empire and the ability of the market forces to compete with and influence each other within the Ottoman economy. Applied locally, the *agio* could modify government policies concerning debasement of the currency, or the arbitrary setting of exchange rates; it could also impact capital liquidity in a given market. The *agio* varied from one market to another in the Empire. Reflecting the ebb and flow of the market forces at work in any given market, the *agio* fluctuated in amount whilst its application varied in duration. Indeed the fact that the *agio* could fluctuate so much was what rendered it so effective.

Agio and the Exchange Rates

Product of the lack of institutionalized banking and of the need to regulate a highly volatile local currency market, an important use of the *agio* was in calculating the exchange rate between the Ottoman and western currencies, and in particular the French livre tournois. To do this, the *agio* was calculated on the basis of the real, not the nominal, rate of exchange between the Ottoman piastre and the Venetian gold sequin.[1] This exchange rate was then applied to the rate of exchange between the Ottoman piastre and the livre tournois. This is how it worked: the French kept, throughout the eighteenth century, the same rate of exchange between the livre tournois and the Ottoman piastre despite the fact that the latter had fallen considerably in value and despite the fact that this depreciation fluctuated greatly. They were able to do this because the *agio* adjusted the difference in the exchange rate between the two currencies by adding or subtracting an amount equivalent to the fluctuations in the real value of the Ottoman piastre. For instance, at an *agio* rate of 25 per cent, 100 piastres at 3 livres tournois per piastre, which was the official exchange rate, yielded 225 livres not 300.[2] Given the importance of France in the commercial and financial dealings of the Ottoman Empire with the West, in the period under study, by impacting the exchange rates between the piastre and the livre tournois, the *agio* played an important role in the Ottoman markets.

---

[1]Between 1717 and 1799, the rate of the Ottoman piastre to the Venetian sequin increased from 3 piastres to 7 piastres 90 aspres per sequin. There were 120 aspres to a piastre. N. Svoronos, *Le Commerce de Salonique au XVIIIe siècle* (Paris, 1956), pp. 82, 116.

[2]ANF, Marine, B/7, 444, Procédé de dépenses et de recettes pour la comptabilité de la Chambre de Commerce de Marseille avec les échelles du Levant, 1780 in Ferréol Rebuffat & Marcel Courdurié, *Marseille et le négoce monétaire international, 1785-1790* (Marseilles, 1966), pp. 129-130.

The application of *agio* in calculating the exchange rates allowed not only the downward but also the upward fluctuations of the Ottoman currency, vis-à-vis a western currency, to be taken into account. It was thus an intervention by the local market forces to set exchange rates that reflected both the precious metal content and the market value of the Ottoman currency. The *agio* could also be used to check a politically-induced over-evaluation of the Ottoman currency. In this way, the *agio* eliminated the problems that could ensue when arbitrary rates of exchange were being forced on a market whilst providing the needed flexibility, locally, to set the exchange rates that imperial government policies could not do.[1] Moreover, given the volatility of the Ottoman currency, especially in the early nineteenth century, as a system of fluctuating discounts the *agio* ultimately helped cushion the impact of such volatility by allowing the monetary system to be more flexible and more regulated as well as more responsive to the market.[2]

Agio and Specie Scarcity

The *agio* was also applied in order to attract specie to a particular market, out of the overall pool of specie in the Empire, and thus alleviate acute monetary scarcity in that market. There were a number of reasons that could cause specie to be drained away from any given market in the Empire thus causing specie scarcity. In İzmir, as already referred to above, some of the factors that could cause specie scarcity had to do with the balance of trade, the needs of Istanbul for specie and the pattern of banking activities and other monetary activities that were carried out. Other factors that could cause specie scarcity were plague and poor harvests, due to climatic conditions in the Ottoman interior, both of which could have an adverse effect on all trading and monetary activities and hence on the market's specie reserves. Indeed, natural disasters, such as an earthquake or a particularly heavy plague epidemic, could temporarily seriously drain specie from İzmir, by disrupting the city's commercial networks and causing merchants to flee or to stay away from it, thus greatly decreasing business activity in the city.[3]

1 Such a case was in 1801 when the Porte raised the rates of exchange artificially in favor of the Ottoman piastre which brought havoc to the market in İzmir as payments of debts and other monetary transactions were temporarily suspended. PRO, SP 105/128, Werry, İzmir, 17 Sept. 1801 to Levant Company, London.

2 For the use of *agio* in western European banking, see e.g., J. C. Dillen, ed., *History of the Principal Public Banks* (New York, 1965), p. 85.

3 ACCM, LIX/728, Cailhol, İzmir, 22 May 1781 to Roux Frères, Marseilles.

In the course of the eighteenth and early nineteenth centuries, İzmir had an overall positive balance of trade with its western partners. Although we lack the data to know for certain, there was, quite likely, the potential for a passive balance of payments for İzmir, and the Ottoman Empire overall, with its European partners: for capital did go to the West in the form of repatriated profits of westerners, who had been active in Ottoman ports for a period of time, or in the form of freight payments to European captains for goods carried in Ottoman coastal waters, insurance premiums or through other means.[1] Money was also absorbed in the trade of İzmir with the East and the Far East, which was carried out often through Alexandria, Mecca and Baghdad, and with which it had a deficit.[2] Another important source of specie drain for İzmir was Istanbul, as already referred to above, either as a recipient of taxes and other government revenue or as a recipient of bullion for its Mint. This was particularly so at times of war, when government expenditure increased. In such cases considerable amounts of specie and bills of exchange could be taken out of the market of İzmir and sent to Istanbul.[3]

Another factor that impacted the flow of specie, and of other instruments of payment in the market of İzmir, was the volume of banking activities that it could undertake at a given time. For İzmir acted as a clearing house for purchases made by merchants, western and local, in Bursa, Konya, the Aegean islands, Antalya, Crete, even in Morea in Greece, or Tripoli in Syria and beyond.[4] Thus, at various points in time, İzmir could be called upon to make considerable payments and cover bills of exchange drawn upon it, which could affect the volume of its circulating medium. A further factor that could lead to a drain of capital in the market of İzmir was a need for capital in the western markets and particularly in Marseilles,[5] which was İzmir's greatest

---

[1]See, for instance, Charles Carrière & Marcel Courdurié, "Balance du commerce, balance des paiements", unpublished paper, University of Aix-en-Province, 16 May 1982.

[2]ANF, AE Biii 243, Félix de Beaujour, Inspection générale du Levant, İzmir, 5 June 1817.

[3]For instance, in 1787, at the start of the Russo-Ottoman War, the Porte set out to attract foreign specie to its Mint to convert them into a debased Ottoman piastre. In order to attract Austrian thalers, which were always in demand for the purpose of trade in the Ottoman markets, the government decreed an Empire-wide exchange rate for it which was less than the rate that was current in Istanbul. Given the proximity of İzmir to the capital and the fact that the operation was successful, as far as the Porte was concerned, the market of the western Anatolian city-port must have experienced at least a temporary drain in its circulation of thalers. ACCM, LIX/748, Porry Tornézy & Cie, İzmir, 18 Sept. 1787 to Roux Frères, Marseilles; see also, ACCM, *LIX*/734, Escalon & Cie, İzmir, 12 Aug. 1790 to Roux Frères, Marseilles.

[4]ANF, AE Bi 1053, Charles de Peyssonnel, Mémoire, İzmir, 22 Nov. 1751.

[5]The European crisis of 1774 is a case in point; see, ANF, AE Biii 241, Mémoire sur l'argent, c. 1774-1775. However, relatively greater flows of capital from İzmir to Marseilles occurred also in 1721 and 1734 which were both years of crisis for Marseilles. For more information, see Frangakis-Syrett, *The Commerce...*, pp. 139-143 and on the state of the market of Marseilles in 1721, see Ch. Carrière, M. Courdurié & F. Rebuffat, *Marseille, ville morte. La peste de 1720* (Marseilles, 1968), pp. 310-338.

European trading partner in the second half of the eighteenth century. It may be worthwhile to note here that the ability of İzmir to attract and to send considerable bullion, when needed, to the West, in both specie and bills of exchange, was also indicative of the extent and effectiveness of its financial networks. Such activities, however, necessitated even further the circulation of specie, in adequate levels, in the market of İzmir. Speculative monetary activities, as a result of which specie could leave İzmir for Marseilles at greater amounts than it came from the French port, could also cause an outflow of capital from the Ottoman city-port.[1] As it will be shown below, such activities became especially prominent, for a number of reasons, in the latter part of the eighteenth and in the early nineteenth centuries.

The extensive commercial and banking activities of İzmir were not only a source of specie drain for its market, but also attracted specie to it in a number of ways: namely, through positive trade balances or the settling of accounts through İzmir's merchants-cum-bankers. At the same time, monetary speculative operations also attracted specie in the local economy in the form of profits. Given the considerable vibrancy and growth of İzmir's commercial and financial sectors, such economic development also placed continuous and increasing demands for money that its market had to meet. Ultimately the market of İzmir, like any other major Ottoman provincial market, experienced constant fluctuations in the amount of specie that circulated within it at any given time.

So that whenever, and for whatever reasons, specie scarcity reached a particularly high level, a market-induced system of *agio* could be used to alleviate the problem. By influencing locally the exchange rates in favor of the Ottoman currency, the *agio* attracted specie to that particular market, even at the detriment of another market within the Empire. A variable *agio* of around 10 per cent — it could fluctuate up or down depending on the overall conditions of the market — was usually applied to the Ottoman currency in the market of İzmir in order to draw specie to it from other markets in the Empire. Whenever the Europeans decided to let their currencies circulate in the local market in their full strength and the *agio* was totally suspended, specie was drained from İzmir for Ottoman merchants took their business to another provincial market, where an *agio* was in force. A further specie drain followed with the local currency being absorbed by Alexandria and the foreign currencies going to other Ottoman markets, for instance, to Bursa. In addition, the European markets that were sending specie or bills to İzmir temporarily

[1]Frangakis, "The Balance of Trade and Balance of Payments...", pp. 135-138.

ceased, or decreased the extent of their operations, for there was probably little purchasing power or demand for them. And in anticipation of better business, Ottoman coins were hoarded locally which only made matters worse.[1] Certainly, İzmir did continue to receive specie from the West through trade. For instance, the Italian ports, serving as entrepots for other European markets, often exported specie to İzmir in return for Ottoman goods.[2] Nevertheless, unlike other markets, such as Istanbul, which was usually in receipt of considerable amounts of money in view of the state's collection of taxes, or for other reasons, İzmir often had to apply an *agio* in order to attract specie to its market from other areas within the Ottoman Empire, and thus alleviate a specie scarcity, which could become periodically acute, whilst the total absence of *agio* could in itself bring about an important specie drain.[3]

Agio and the Pricing of Goods

At times, the *agio* also mitigated the effects of a rapidly devalued currency by being linked to the price of imports, as opposed to only the rates of exchange. For an Ottoman merchant who bought goods from a westerner in İzmir might not sell them until several months later when he reached other markets in the Anatolian hinterland or in Persia. In the meantime, the rate of exchange of the piastre *vis-à-vis* the European currencies may well have fallen further leaving the Ottoman merchant either with uncompetitive goods or with having to sell at a loss. However, the application of the *agio* on the exchange rates, in anticipation of fluctuations in the currency market, and which was included in the price, allowed the merchant to sell profitably.

In such a case, the *agio* functioned on a sliding scale taking also into account the other market forces that played a role in the overall transaction. That is, if there was strong demand for the goods in question, a lesser discount might be given; conversely, if the market were flat, a higher *agio* might be necessary in order to attract a buyer. Initially, the price of a commodity was arrived at on the basis of a cash sale, with neither credit nor any *agio* being applied. The price was then modified according to the amount of discount, or *agio*, being applied (on the exchange rates) and according to whether shorter or longer periods of credit were being offered. Generally speaking the *agio* could

[1]ANF, AE Bi 1057, Charles-Claude de Peyssonnel, Précis du Mémoire ..., 1769.
[2]ANF, AE Bi 168, French Consul Benincasa, Ancôna, 24 Feb. 17885 to Minister, Paris.
[3]ANF, AE Bi 1057, Charles-Claude de Peyssonnel, Précis du Mémoire ..., 1769. See also, Svoronos, *Le Commerce de Salonique* ..., pp. 334; 337-39.

be counterbalanced by shorter or longer periods of credit, but the biggest price reductions were given on *comptant* sales, that is, cash purchases made without any *agio* or credit terms. For instance, in 1761 prices of the French cloth, Londrins Seconds, which was one of the most popular items in the market of İzmir, fluctuated from 220 to 235 aspres with the *agio* rate ranging from 3.5 per cent to 10 per cent and depending also on the length of the credit period being given.[1]

The *agio*, as a fluctuating and adjustable system of discount in favor of the Ottoman currency, was thus being applied on western imports with the aim of reducing their prices. Such price reductions benefited, theoretically, the local consumers. However, the goods changed many hands, which resulted in several price increases before they reached the local consumers. Without such a discount, nevertheless, these goods would have been even more expensive. The price discount was mostly absorbed by the western importers who included it in their overall business costs. In any case, the latter could do quite well when buying Ottoman goods for export to the West. Strong demand in the western markets for Ottoman goods and the devalued Ottoman currency usually left fairly good margins for profit to the westerners.[2]

*

The *agio* was thus part of the monetary system and practices that had evolved in the Ottoman markets. It was certainly not unique to İzmir, for it was used in all large urban markets of the Empire in the eighteenth and early nineteenth centuries.[3] It acted as a successful adjustment mechanism in the rates of exchange that took into account not only the precious metal content of the Ottoman currency but also the relative value of the currency given to it by the market forces at work. As such, the *agio* became part of a self-

[1]ANF, AE Bi 1058, Charles-Claude de Peyssonnel, Éclaircissements sur la suputation qui a été faite du prix des Londrins Seconds de Carcassonne à Smyrne, İzmir, 20 Nov. 1767; see also, ANF, AE Bi 1053, Charles de Peyssonnel, Mémoire, İzmir, 22 Nov. 1751.

[2]There is disagreement in the historiography on the profit margins of western merchants trading in the Levant in the eighteenth and early nineteenth centuries. Whilst further research is necessary to resolve this issue, the present author considers it imperative, when calculating the profits of these merchants, to take into account all possible venues of activity, including both speculative monetary activities and commodity trading, for they were all important components in the business strategies of the entrepreneurs in the Ottoman Empire.

[3]E.g. for Salonica, see Svoronos, *Le Commerce de Salonique* ..., pp. 115-116. For the Peloponnese, see V. Kremmydas, *Το εμπόριο της πελοποννήσου στο* 18° *αίωνα* (1715-1792) *The Commerce of the Peloponnese in the Eighteenth Century, 1715-1792* (Athens, 1972), p. 117. For Arta, see G. Siorokas, *Το γαλλικό προξενεtίο της Αρτας,* 1702-1789) (The French Consulate of Arta, 1702-1789) (Ioannina, 1981), p. 229. For Istanbul, see Edhem Eldem, *French Trade in Istanbul in the Eighteenth Century* (Leiden, 1999), pp. 161-164.

regulatory mechanism of the Ottoman monetary system, activated by the market forces. By allowing adjustments in the amount of specie circulating in the various Ottoman markets, the *agio* also facilitated the further monetization and effective functioning of those markets. In the final analysis, the *agio* was an important mitigator in the Ottoman markets for the two most serious problems in the Ottoman monetary system at the time, namely, specie scarcity and an overall weak and volatile currency. The *agio* can also be seen as part of the inherent flexibility of the Ottoman monetary system and of its responsiveness to the market forces. As such it had a beneficial effect on the Ottoman economy and was one of the factors that contributed to the overall growth, in the period under study, of urban economic centers, such as İzmir, in the Empire.

Speculative Arbitrage and the Ottoman Monetary System

Given the high premium that cash carried in the Ottoman economy there had always been a certain amount of monetary activities that an entrepreneur, Ottoman or western, carried out alongside his other business in the Levant. This allowed him to put to good use, even if only temporarily, any surplus capital that he may have had. One of the most important of such activities was moneylending. Indeed everybody lent in the Ottoman Empire: from an Ottoman administrator to a wealthy local heiress to a western or local merchant. Moreover, everybody was equally liable to borrow as well as to lend.[1]

Furthermore, the specificity of the Ottoman monetary system — specie scarcity coupled with an open monetary system — led to a number of other monetary activities, some of which were quite speculative. They consisted principally of arbitrage operations in specie or in bills of exchange, or in exchanging specie for bills of exchange, or trade in money. Such activities became integral parts of their overall business strategies and reflected as well as reinforced the dual identity of Ottoman and western entrepreneurs in the Empire, as merchants-cum-bankers.[2]

---

[1]Elena Frangakis-Syrett, "Trade Practices in Aleppo in the Middle of the Eighteenth Century", *Revue du Monde Musulman et de la Méditerranée,* No. 62/4 (1991), pp. 123-132; see also, Bruce Masters, *The Origins of Western Dominance in the Middle East* (New York, 1988), pp. 153-164.

[2]For more information, see Frangakis-Syrett, *The Commerce ...*, pp. 138-148.

As we saw above, there had been a lucrative trade in money,[1] at various points in Ottoman history.[2] In the period under study, whilst specie was being actively imported in many Ottoman markets, not only in Istanbul or İzmir,[3] preferences for specific currencies could also exist in these markets. Thus Austrian thalers were principally imported into İzmir and Spanish piastres and Austrian thalers into Istanbul.[4] The prominence of Maria-Theresa's Austrian thalers in the market of İzmir reflected their popularity in the commercial world of the Levant at the time. Given the extensive commercial networks that İzmir had within the Ottoman Empire as well as to the East, where thalers were also a particularly sought after currency, its market could be expected to be always in need of such a currency.[5]

Given the scarcity of specie in the Ottoman economy overall, bills of exchange were an instrument of payment that was used widely. Besides, the territorial expanse of the Empire and the need of the state to move funds, such as taxes from the provinces to Istanbul, had resulted, since the seventeenth century, in an extensive use of bills of exchange as a secure and effective way of moving funds around.[6] Growth of trade in the major markets of the Empire, in the period under study, had contributed further to the use of bills of exchange with the result that the Empire had a very well-developed internal network of bills of exchange. Moreover, the openness of the Ottoman financial system and the growth of international trade also meant that bills of exchange in different currencies circulated widely within the various Ottoman economic centers and could be drawn on different European markets. Indeed, the following example illustrates well the vibrancy and complexity of Ottoman networks of bills of exchange as well as the close interaction of locals and westerners in such networks: a bill of exchange for 1,300 piastres was drawn by a certain Poulhariés in Marseilles on a Gazan in Istanbul to the order of A. Rey in Marseilles. The bill was then successively endorsed to the

[1] In the late eighteenth century, profits from such trade could be as high as 12 per cent. PRO, SP 105/337, Consul A. Hayes, Memorandum, İzmir, 15 May 1789.

[2] For instance, on the importation and circulation of western coins in the Ottoman economy in the seventeenth century, see, ANF, AE Biii 235, Commerce du Levant, Mémoire, 1686 and ANF, AE Biii 235, Mémoire, 1687; see also, Şevket Pamuk, "Money in the Ottoman Empire, 1326-1914" in Halil Inalcık & Donald Quataert, eds., *An Economic and Social History of the Ottoman Empire, 1300-1914* (Cambridge, 1994), pp. 964-965.

[3] E.g., ACCM, J, 463, Consul d'Amirat, Koron in the Peloponnese, 20 Aug. 1748 to Minister, Paris.

[4] Rebuffat & Courdurié, *Marseille...*, p. 142; see also, ACCM, LIX/750, Denis Rolland & Cie, İzmir, 24 March 1788 to Roux Frères, Marseilles.

[5] Marcel-Maurice Fischel, *Le Thaler de Marie-Thérèse* (Paris, 1912): for the use of thalers amongst the Arabs see, pp. 107-131; for the use of thalers in the Levantine trade, see pp. 79-106.

[6] For more information on this issue, see Jacques Savary, *Le parfait négociant* (Paris, 1749 ed.), 2 vols., *passim*.

order of the merchants Gilly in Aleppo and Blanc in Tripoli; it was then bought by another merchant, Routier, in Aleppo and endorsed to a Guérin in Latakia, where it was finally bought by Hacı Ahmed Ağa Sali Effendi, who was the tobacco customs official of Latakia. The official had it then endorsed to the order of Hacı İbrahim Ağa in Istanbul where the latter finally received payment from Gazan.[1]

Given the wide circulation of bills of exchange and the considerable volatility in the exchange rates in the Ottoman markets in the period under study, opportunities also existed for speculative monetary operations. Indeed, in the late eighteenth and early nineteenth centuries in particular, activities such as speculative arbitrage in specie or in bills of exchange, or exchanging specie for bills of exchange became part of an overall strategy of the entrepreneurs. This was done, partly, in order to offset possible losses from commodity trading, *agio* operations or from other sources, or indeed in order to turn specie scarcity and volatility in the exchange rates into opportunities for profit.[2] Both European and Ottoman merchants with contacts, or associates, in the western financial markets participated in such operations. For these were closely connected to, and indeed were part of, the European financial-cum-commercial circuits. Moreover, given the state of the bullion markets in Europe in the late eighteenth and early nineteenth centuries, such activities played a particularly prominent part in the overall business activities of an entrepreneur in the Levant and came to be considered as more lucrative than some of their commercial activities.

Thus, apart from trade, entrepreneurs in İzmir, as elsewhere in the Empire, and westerners in particular, used bills of exchange for speculation: that is, moving bills of exchange from one place to another in order to profit from the difference in the rates of exchange which they tried to influence in their favor. For the number of bills of exchange that circulated at a given moment in a local market, if successfully regulated by the arbitrageurs, could affect the rate of exchange and thus the success of their operations, that is, the price of their bills. For a merchant did not buy a bill of exchange unless it was discounted, so that by selling it either at face value or above the discount level he realized a profit. Conversely, the seller did not give a discount unless

[1]AMAE, Chancery of the French Embassy, Vol. 38, bill dated 30 November 1764 in Edhem Eldem, "The Trade of Precious Metals and Bills of Exchange in Istanbul in the Second Half of the Eighteenth Century", *V. Milletlerarası Türkiye Sosyal ve İktisat Tarih Kongresi, Tebliğler* (Ankara, 1990), p. 583.

[2]Profits from speculative monetary operations could be as high as 25 per cent, although there could also be losses. Charles Carrière, *Négociants marseillais au XVIIIe siècle* (Marseilles, 1973), Vol. I, pp. 409-410.

it was less than the cost of transferring specie to that market. For instance, it was profitable to send Spanish piastres to İzmir when there was an abundance of circulating bills of exchange that had to be honored; then the piastres were in high demand and so enjoyed a favorable rate of exchange *vis-à-vis* the Ottoman currency.[1] Conversely, if there was a dearth in bills of exchange and an abundance of specie in the local market, or a strong demand for bills of exchange to send funds to Europe with, then the bills fetched a higher price.

Furthermore, an attempt to profit from the fluctuating rates of exchange of the various currencies and from the variable prices of bills of exchange led to a more complex speculative activity between the Ottoman and western financial markets, that involved both precious metals, in the form of specie, and bills of exchange. In such an operation profits were basically made from the difference in the exchange rates. It was a two-part operation and involved dealing first in foreign currencies and then in bills of exchange.[2] Such operations are best illustrated by the activities of the İzmir correspondents, or agents, of the commercial-cum-banking house of Roux Frères, based in Marseilles and operating world-wide.

These agents imported specie into İzmir sent to them by other correspondents of the house of Roux, who were themselves based in various European economic centers. The İzmir agents proceeded to sell their imports of western currencies making their profits from the rates of exchange. These profits they sent back to Roux Frères in the form of bills of exchange, which they purchased in İzmir in the most advantageous currency and which were drawn upon any economic center in Europe that would give them the highest return, the funds making their way finally back to the house of Roux in Marseilles.[3] Moreover, İzmir was not the only market where these practices were taking place. Istanbul had also a lively circuit of similar speculative activities.[4] Nevertheless, İzmir figured prominently in such activities, within the Ottoman Empire, and may have had a primacy over Istanbul in this sector.[5] For instance, in the late eighteenth century, from over 1,000,000

---

[1] C. Carrière, M. Courdurié, M. Gusatz & R. Squarzoni, *Banque et capitalisme commercial* (Marseilles, 1976), pp. 107-109; 137-39.

[2] Elena Frangakis-Syrett, "The Economic Activities of Ottoman and Western Communities in Eighteenth-Century İzmir", Kate Fleet, ed., *The Ottoman Empire in the Eighteenth Century* in *Oriente Moderno*, Vol. XVIII/1 (LXXIX), n.s. (1999), pp. 22-24.

[3] ACCM, LIX/735, R. Franchetti, İzmir, 13 Aug. 1788 to Roux Frères, Marseilles; LIX/750, Denis Rolland & Cie, İzmir, 13 Dec. 1788 & 5 Jan. 1789 to Roux Frères, Marseilles; LIX/735, R. Franchetti, 8 Jan. 1790 to Roux Frères, Marseilles; LIX/750, Denis Rolland & Cie, İzmir, 19 March 1790 to Roux Frères, Marseilles.

[4] ACCM, LIX/997, David Cuny, Istanbul, 18 June 1778 to Roux Frères, Marseilles.

[5] ANF, F 12/549-550, Mémoire sur le commerce avec le Levant en général, 1777.

Austrian thalers and 150,000 Sevillian piastres that were sent to the Ottoman Empire by Roux Frères, which was one of the most important houses for such operations at the time, there was an overwhelming preference for İzmir which received three-quarters of these funds.[1]

Handsome profits could thus be made. Yet these were also highly speculative activities for, at any point, there could be a flood of western specie in the market of İzmir lowering their exchange rates *vis-à-vis* the Ottoman currency. There could also be dearth of suitable bills of exchange to remit the profits to Europe with, causing the bills to become expensive and thus cutting away at the profits from the first part of the operation.[2] It was as difficult to predict the best time for one's shipment of specie to arrive in İzmir as it was to wait for a long time for the bills to become abundant, for thus capital remained idle when it could have been put to profitable use.[3] It was not only the westerners who practiced such speculative arbitrage.[4] A very large number of bills of exchange which the Europeans purchased in İzmir or Istanbul were underwritten by Ottoman, mostly non-Muslim merchants, whose credit worthiness the Europeans constantly monitored. Indeed, half of all bills of exchange bought or sold in İzmir in the course of such speculative operations were Ottoman bills, signed for by Greek and Jewish brokers, who were responsible for the payment of such bills. Equally 20 per cent of all bills of exchange circulating in Istanbul were signed for by Ottoman merchants.[5] Moreover, these bills of exchange were often drawn upon the associates of the İzmir merchants who were themselves established in various financial centers in Europe, such as Amsterdam, Trieste, Ancôna, Livorno or Vienna.[6] The considerable flux in the European money markets in the late eighteenth and in the early nineteenth centuries, due to the European-wide wars and need to raise funds to cover military expenditure, made such speculative operations both widespread and worthwhile for all concerned with benefits for the local economy, too.

---

[1] "Une prédominance écrasante pour l'échelle de Smyrne", is how Rebuffat & Courdurié have described İzmir's dominance in this sector, in Rebuffat & Courdurié, *Marseille...*, p. 156.

[2] E.g., ACCM, LIX/735, Ruben Franchetti, İzmir, 20 Oct. 1790 to Roux Frères, Marseilles.

[3] E.g. ACCM, LIX/735, Ruben Franchetti, İzmir, 10 March 1790 to Roux Frères, Marseilles.

[4] The term is taken from R. Squarzoni in Carrière *et al, Banque et capitalisme commercial ...*, p. 108.

[5] Edhem Eldem, "La circulation de la lettre de change entre la France et Constantinople au XVIIIe siècle" in Hamit Batu & Jean-Louis Bacqué-Grammont, eds., *L'Empire ottoman, la République de Turquie et la France* (Istanbul-Paris, 1986), pp. 87-97; see also, *idem, French Trade...*, pp. 178-183.

[6] ACCM, LIX/750, Denis Rolland & Cie, İzmir, 18 Dec. 1788, 24 March & 13 July 1789 and 10 Aug. & 27 Nov. 1790 to Roux Frères, Marseilles.

Considerable flows of capital in and out of İzmir's market, which were not used in the purchase of goods, were one of the results of such monetary speculative operations.[1] Another result were temporary changes in the exchange rates caused by a draining or flooding of the market in İzmir with foreign specie or bills of exchange in a certain currency or currencies. That is, such speculative activities could contribute further into making the local currency market even more volatile than it already was. This in turn increased the level of uncertainty concerning even medium-term investment and could lead to rises in the interest rates as well as in the prices of goods — as the local currency was either losing its value or was becoming more scarce — which ultimately hurt most the Ottoman borrower and consumer.

Such activities impacted positively on the local economy, too. They increased the level of monetization of the local market due to the influx of specie or bills of exchange that came into the market even temporarily. At the same time, profits from such operations, which remained in the hands of local entrepreneurs, contributed to the accumulation of capital in the local economy. Equally importantly, the market of İzmir — or other major markets in the Empire, such as Istanbul — became, partly as a result of such activities, better connected to the European financial markets. This, in turn, helped the further integration of such markets in the international economy. However, the economic growth experienced in a number of major urban markets in the Empire could not, by itself, result in enough capital accumulation to resolve either the scarcity of specie or of investment capital in the economy of the Ottoman Empire overall. Moreover, economic growth in such markets, including increases in their level of monetization, did not carry enough momentum, nor was it adequate by itself, to radically change the entire Ottoman monetary system. Indeed, it was not till the second half of the nineteenth century, when the combined forces of the Anglo-French financial markets, in the form of the Imperial Ottoman Bank, backed by the Ottoman Government, attempted with some success, to restructure certain aspects of the Ottoman monetary system, such as the stabilization in the international rates of exchange of the Ottoman gold currency.

Conclusion

In the latter part of the eighteenth and in the early nineteenth centuries, the Ottoman monetary system included both weak and strong features, if one

[1]ACCM, LIX/748, Porry Tornézy & Cie, İzmir, 17 Nov. 1787 to Roux Frères, Marseilles.

can use such terms. Some of its weak, or problematic, features were part of the Ottoman economy overall. Such was the case with scarcity of specie, which reflected the low level of capitalization in the economy overall. Another such feature was the overall weakness and volatility of the currency in the international rates of exchange which worsened as a result of the government policies of debasement, in particular, in the late eighteenth and early nineteenth centuries. It may well be that such government policies were necessary at the time to alleviate other problems of the Ottoman monetary system or of the overall economy; nevertheless, they did impact negatively on the monetary system. The Ottoman monetary system had also strong features — it was an open system and, by the second half of the eighteenth century, infinitely more complex and flexible as well as more market-responsive than usually thought of. Among the strong features of the Ottoman monetary system were the various practices that evolved on the level of the local market that substituted for specie, such as credit or barter, or compensated for potential losses in the exchange rates, or turned potential weaknesses of the monetary system into opportunities for profit. If the territorial expanse of the Ottoman Empire made it difficult for Empire-wide government policies to regulate the monetary system effectively, and contributed to the non-unification of the Ottoman economy, on the level of the local markets the monetary system also included adjusting mechanisms such as the *agio* — which were part self-regulatory and part market-induced — which rendered it more flexible and more effective as far as the continued functioning of the local market was concerned. Moreover, the activation of *agio* also reflected the forces of the market and the prominence of market forces over politics in the Ottoman economy. As such its application showed the degree of a market-induced economy that already existed, at least in some areas of the Ottoman Empire, by the second half of the eighteenth and in the early nineteenth centuries and the degree of integration of such areas into the world economy, including the European financial circuits.

THE BALANCE OF TRADE AND THE BALANCE OF PAYMENTS BETWEEN İZMIR AND MARSEILLES, 1700-1789*

During the 18th century, İzmir became the most important port of the Ottoman Empire. It traded with Western Europe to the West and with Iran, India and China to the East. In many ways İzmir was an entrepot linking the East with the West. European cloth was shipped to İzmir and taken by a long caravan route to the East to be exchanged with Iranian silk. The latter was used as a raw material in the luxury industries of the West.

Trade between the Ottoman Empire and the West began to grow from the end of the 17th century. The growing need of the West for raw materials of the Empire, continuous technological innovations which made transportation by sea more secure and economical and the export of an increasingly improved and competitively priced European manufactured cloth are factors which contributed to such developments. İzmir took an increasingly larger share in this trade of the Empire with the West.

All major European nations traded with İzmir in the 18th century. Holland and Britain had their period of peak trade activity in the beginning of the 18th century, whilst France dominated the Levant including İzmir from the 1740's onwards. This was also the period of ascendancy for the trade in İzmir. At the end of the century, there was a decline in the trade of France with İzmir due to the French Revolution. There was a brief period of ascendancy for the Italian ports during the Napoleonic Wars, as the major European powers fought each other, and trade between İzmir and the West was directed to these ports.

> «Il en résulte de ce qui vient d'être des directions que le commerce du Levant a prise pendant la guerre que depuis 1793 jusqu'en 1814, Gênes, Livourne ou Trieste ont été ou sont encore à l'égard de la France, de l'Allemagne, de la Belgique et de la Suisse, ce que Livourne était auparavant à l'égard de l'Angleterre; de son côté l'Angleterre s'est mise pour ce qui concerne l'importation dans le Levant des denrées coloniales et des produits de son industrie, à la place de la France...»[1].

---

* There has been a change in the title, from its original publication in 1985, whereby [France] has been changed to [Marseilles].

[1] Archives Nationales de France, Paris, AE Biii 243, O. Miège, Renseignements sur le commerce du Levant, Livorno, 13 May 1825. Hereafter this archive will be cited as ANF.

In the beginning of the 19th century, Britain emerged as the dominant power in the Levant, including İzmir. Throughout the 18th century, the Ottoman Empire exported more to Western Europe than it imported from the West and İzmir was no exception. France was its main trading partner and accounted for over 50% of the port's trade with Western Europe. It was also the main partner in the Empire's trade with the West. From the 1740's, the predominance of İzmir over the other Ottoman ports was apparent. From 1754, trade between İzmir and France grew faster than of any other Ottoman port. The last quarter of the 18th century was the period for the 'taking off' of the economy of İzmir and there was quantitative as well as qualitative growth. Its commercial predominance continued into the early 19th century.

The following tables, 1 and 2, show the fluctuations of the trade of İzmir throughout the 18th century and the share of the Western Anatolian port in the total trade of the Ottoman Empire with France. By France we mean Marseilles, as all French trade to the Levant was centered on Marseilles. The value of trade is depicted in livres tournois which was the monetary term used in the records of the French Consuls and of the Chamber of Commerce of Marseilles. Its rate of exchange with the Ottoman piastre was 3 livres tournois to 1 piastre.

In the second half of the 18th century the index for the exports of İzmir to France (table 1) was higher than the index for total Ottoman exports which meant that the port of İzmir took an increasingly higher share of the total

TABLE 1. Exports of İzmir Compared to Total Ottoman Exports to Marseilles, 1700-1789, in livres tournois[1]

Year	*Ottoman Exports* *Index*	*İzmir Exports* *Index*	*% Share*
1700	51.6	45.2	20.5
1701	74	84	27
1702	38	28.1	17.4
1703	21.2	28	31
1704	48	37.2	18.1
1705	42.2	30.5	17
1706	35.1	34	22.4
1707	34.3	24	16.4
1708	31	18	14
1709	30	18.2	14.2
1710	30.5	16	16
1711	40.5	20.1	12
1712	67.3	58	21
1713	59	39.1	16
1714	115	96.2	19.5
1715	75.4	22.4	7
1716	120.1	18	22
1717	24	14	17.2
1718	67.5	67	5
1719	87.6	111	18
1720	100.1	52	12.2
1721	32.5	10.2	7.4
1722	18	4	5.5
1723	62	31.5	12
1724	66.4	52	18.3
1725	78	42.3	13
1726	64	21.1	8
1727	76.5	54.3	17
1728	70.4	29.4	10
1729	78.2	33.4	10
1730	56	17	7
1731	62.5	44	16.4

[1]These figures are based on Consular Correspondance ANF, AE Bi and Biii and the Archives of the Chamber of Commerce of Marseilles, ACCM, I/19-20 and I/26-8; for more specific references see author's PhD thesis, "The Commerce of İzmir in the 18th century, 1695-1820", London University, UK, 1985, pp. 130-168.

Year	Ottoman Exports Index	İzmir Exports Index	% Share
1732	67	52	18
1733	74.1	41.4	13
1734	107	27	12
1735	47	27	13.4
1736	61.5	50.4	19.2
1737	72	44.3	14.4
1738	78	40.3	12
1739	83	35	10
1740	78.3	44.3	13.3
1741	71.5	59	19.3
1742	74	54.2	17.2
1743	92.5	74	19
1744	45	42.4	22
1745	55.4	40.3	17
1746	51	61	20.1
1747	73	71.2	23
1748	40.4	45.2	26.2
1749	100	100	23.4
1750	109	124.2	27
1751	113	83.3	17.3
1752	115	94.5	19.3
1753	122.4	115	22
1754	117.3	145	29
1755	121	159	31
1756	79	149	44.2
1757	73	126.4	41
1758	35	60	40.3
1759	29.2	59.1	47.5
1760	47	78.5	39.3
1762	54	79.5	35
1763	109	172	37
1764	114	190.1	39.1
1766	129	234.2	42.5
1767	135.5	221.2	38.2
1768	144	237	38.5
1769	140.1	169.2	28.3
1770	127.5	171.5	31.5

Year	Ottoman Exports Index	İzmir Exports Index	% Share
1771	154.2	149	23
1772	135.1	151.1	26.2
1774	142	186	31
1776	128	220	40.3
1777	158	280	41.4
1778	111	150.1	32
1779	55	98.4	42
1786	201	312	36
1787	191.5	336.3	41.1
1788	221	364.1	39
1789	166.5	262	37

Ottoman Exports to Marseilles, 1749 = 19,348,040 lt. = 100
İzmir Exports to Marseilles, 1749 = 4,531,162 lt. = 100

TABLE 2. Exports of İzmir Compared to Total Ottoman Imports from Marseilles, 1700-1789, in livres tournois[1]

Year	Ottoman Exports Index	İzmir Exports Index	% Share
1749	100	100	24
1750	85	101.1	28.3
1751	79	60	18.1
1752	83	98	28.2
1753	92.4	129	33.2
1754	90	97	26
1755	83	101	29
1763	95	124	32
1764	115	141.2	29.2
1765	101.2	135	62
1766	111	195.5	41.1
1767	117.4	168	34
1768	107	122.2	17.2
1769	103	110.4	25.5
1776	118.2	156	31.4
1777	82	121.3	28.4
1778	86	128	36
1779	94	168	43
1786	102	130	30.4
1787	99.4	131	31.3

Ottoman Imports from Marseilles, 1749 = 17,734,169 lt. = 100
İzmir Imports from Marseilles, 1749 = 4,222,984 lt. = 100

[1] *Ibid.*

Ottoman trade. This was not the case in the first half of the century when there was a great deal of parity between the two indices. The index for the imports of İzmir (table 2) did not rise as fast as for the exports, but here too it was higher than the index for the entire Ottoman imports to France. İzmir continued to hold this position of dominance in both the imports and exports of the Ottoman Empire to France in the early 19th century[1].

At the beginning of the century, imports balanced exports. From the 1750's onwards as the needs of French manufacture for raw materials from İzmir increased, trade deficit with the Ottoman Empire grew for France. In the period that corresponds broadly with the Seven Years War (1756-1763), an equilibrium was established between imports and exports; the deficit for France was small. This was also a time when the volume of trade fell. Ottoman exports in particular were hit as the trade route between İzmir and Marseilles was badly affected by British privateers. French and other European merchants preferred to send their goods to Livorno and receive European manufactured cloth from there[2]. At the end of the War, Ottoman exports to Marseilles began to surpass French imports once more. This time, however, the margin was smaller. Trade surplus for İzmir was 27.5% on an annual average for 1749-1756 and 12% for 1761-1770.

The only period with a passive balance of trade for İzmir was in 1771-1776, with an annual average deficit of 10%. This was also the period when the economy of İzmir began to 'take off' and its internal market started to expand. If we except certain years, exports exceeded imports with an annual surplus for İzmir of 25.6% on average for 1777-1789 and 32% for 1803-1820. The tendency for exports to surpass imports was marked throughout the Levant in the last quarter of the 18th century. As the prices for European goods had fallen considerably at that time, the volume of Western imports had actually increased. The inelasticity of the Ottoman market to absorb an ever-increasing amount of European imports was being reversed.[3] During the first quarter of the 18th century, the value of exports fell. As this was a period of a sharp rise in the prices of all raw materials in the market of İzmir (particularly in the years 1719-22) there was a net decrease in the volume of goods exported. In the second quarter of the century exports rose slightly. The rate of

---

[1] Archives du Ministère des Affaires Étrangères, CCC, Vol. 42.

[2] C. Carrière, & M. Courdurié, «Grandes heures de Livourne au XVIIIe siècle», *Revue Historique*, CCLIV, pt 1, pp 40-1.

[3] Archives de la Chambre de Commerce de Marseille, I/19-20 and 26-28, 1/19-20 and 26-28.

depreciation for the Ottoman coin was 9% for the years 1715-1749[1]. Prices for the principal goods rose at rates which were substantially higher than the depreciation rate *vis-à-vis* foreign currencies. Despite the increase in price these goods were very competitive in the European markets.

During the third quarter of the century, exports doubled in value. In relation to the first half of the century, they rose three times. Prices rose at a slower rate than previously. The rate of depreciation for the Ottoman piastre increased to 32% and went on increasing as the century drew to a close. In some cases, the rise in price was eliminated by the rate of devaluation which made Ottoman exports even more competitive abroad. In the last quarter of the century (1775-1789) the value of exports continued to rise. In relation to the previous quarter they almost doubled. Compared to the first half of the century they increased six fold. The rate of depreciation for 1774-1789 was 47.5%. There were small price increases and for some of the goods a decrease in price. Therefore there was an increase in both volume and value in the exports for this period.

In the years 1749-1775, imports doubled in value whilst in the years 1776-1789 they fell slightly. As prices fell quite considerably in this period, despite the depreciation of the Ottoman coin which must have made European goods dearer, imports may have increased in volume more than exports. In the early 19th century (1802-3 and 1817-20) imports were maintained at the same level; in relation to 1749-1789 they had doubled. This followed the general trend of an increase in the level of economic activity in the Levant in the 19th century. It was the same for the exports which continued to rise and doubled in relation to 1749-1789.

The excess in value of exports over imports in the last quarter of the century appears even greater if we take into consideration only the movement of goods and not that of money, imported and exported from İzmir, in specie (Sevillian piastres or Austrian thalers) and in bills of exchange. In table number 3, exports and imports of money, or transfers of funds, are depicted annually — where data permits it — and their share in the total value of trade for that year. No comparable data exists for any other Western port actively engaged in trade with İzmir, as for instance, London or Amsterdam.

[1] V. Kremmydas, *Τὸ ἐμπόριο τῆς Πελοποννήσου στὸ 18° αἰῶνα, (1715-1792)*, (*The Commerce of the Peloponnese in the 18th century (1715-1792)*, Athens, 1972, pp. 116-7.

The French transferred more money to İzmir at the end of the century than they did at the beginning. At first they transferred very little money. They started to increase the amounts sent, from 1760 onwards, although for two decades, 1760-1779, they transferred more money from İzmir than to the port. It was only in the final decade prior to the Revolution that they started to transfer greater amounts than they were getting out. It is clear that in the 1780's money was sent to İzmir to cover the trade deficit and make up for the inability of French manufacture to export cloth at competitive prices and quality. French manufacture was then in great difficulties. Flow of money, however, did not always coincide with the balance of trade.

In 1721 and 1734, when the balance of trade was favorable to France, most of the exports in value were made up in specie — that is, in foreign currency.[1] Large amounts of Spanish piastres and Venetian sequins were sent from İzmir in those two years (table 3). Both years were times of crisis for the economy in Marseilles during which the need for specie was particularly acute[2]. Very few raw materials were as yet being exported to Marseilles: French manufacture had not yet developed sufficiently to absorb large quantities of raw materials.

TABLE 3. Transfers of Specie and Bills of Exchange Into and Out of İzmir and Share to Total Trade with Marseilles, 1721-1789, in livres tournois

Year	*Money Into İzmir*	*% Share*	*Money Out of İzmir*	*% Share*
1721	57,408	3	1,933,770	96.4
1734	96,042	3	2,295,498	70.1
1750	821,829	17.5	953,985	18
1751	105,082	4.1	—	
1752	938	—	—	
1753	5,544	0.1	—	
1755	1,316	—	—	
1756	441,015	7	1,624,953	28.1
1759	85,800	2.3	1,059,162	35
1760	—		1,296,057	40.4
1761	202,500	5	577,077	15.3
1762	32,100	1	429,636	10.5
1763	996,945	13.5	779,157	10.1
1764	1,398,714	16	1,068,531	14
1765	1,393,971	20.4	1.007,082	13
1766	2,096,943	22	1,311,153	14

[1]ANF, AE Bi 1045, for Consul's report, 1721 and ANF, AE Bi 1046, for Consul's report, 1734.
[2]For the 1721 crisis see C. Carrière, M. Courdurié, & F. Rebuffat, *Marseille, ville morte. La peste de 1720*, Marseilles, 1968; for the 1734 crisis see R. Paris, *Le Levant de 1660 à 1789*, in *Histoire du commerce de Marseille*, eds L. Bergasse & G. Rambert, vol IV, Paris, 1957, pp. 574-5.

Year	Money Into İzmir	% Share	Money Out of İzmir	% Share
1767	2,749,428	24	1,454,820	15.1
1768	2,180,076	22.4	1,604,331	15.5
1769	1,815,021	25.5	1,590,717	22
1770	1,384,576	19	884,571	11
1771	1,227,333	16	1,922,112	27
1772	1,622,448	16.3	3,403,468	39.2
1773	1,347,324	13	2,647,863	27.4
1774	1,486,911	15	1,407,702	14
1775	2,046,657	15.4	528,336	4.1
1776	1,637,322	12.2	835,415	8.5
1777	394,002	5.4	679,000	5.1
1778	450,000	6.4	524,000	5.5
1779	—		986,904	12.1
1780	801,909	7.3	558,876	5
1781	612,399	7	629,412	7
1782	23,940	0.2	44,100	0.4
1783	371,317	4	363,600	5
1784	435,940	5	165,555	2
1785	1,860,272	16	378,220	3
1786	4,105,982	31.4	863,189	6.2
1787	5,393,574	40	960,195	14
1788	7,261,786	55	—	
1789	1,151,195	12	2,020,026	16

By the middle of the 18th century, the French, despite physiocratic principles regarding bullion as precious metal, were aware that it was better to import goods from the Levant than money. For when they sent money to Marseilles, which they made selling goods in İzmir or from other profitable activities, they lost on the rate of exchange converting Ottoman piastres into *écus*[1]. At other times, they found that it was better to convert piastres into a European currency in circulation in the Levant and then send that money to Marseilles[2].

In the 1750's as French manufacture (the biggest single purchaser of raw materials in the market of İzmir) had sufficiently developed, transfers of money from İzmir were diminished substantially. Nevertheless, amounts of money were still transferred from the Ottoman port in excess to the balance of trade. In 1761, exports in value from the W. Anatolian port exceeded imports by the amount of money transferred.

[1]ANF, AE Bi 1053, Peyssonnel, Mémoire, İzmir 22 Nov 1751.
[2]ANF, AE Bi 1046.

The flow of money between İzmir and Western Europe or between İzmir and the rest of the Ottoman Empire must be seen in terms of the banking activities that went on in İzmir.

> «Les fonds nécessaires pour l'achat des huiles de l'isle de Crète sont tirés en bonne partie de Smyrne par la voie des lettres de change et par les expéditions en espèces. Assez souvent, nous fournissons aussi de quoi subvenir l'achat des soies de Tripoli et des marchandises de quelques autres échelles ce qui dépend des projets qui forment les négociants de Marseille qui ont commerce à Smyrne»[1].

Long established trade links of İzmir with the European markets abroad and with the rest of the Ottoman market internally and European and local capital and expertise contributed to the development of banking in İzmir. Banking was still informal and complimentary to trade. It was carried out by individuals, merchants-cum-bankers, who invested in trade, dealt in bills of exchange, controlled capital liquidity in the market of İzmir and speculated in the international money market. Money in specie or bills of exchange that were sent to İzmir from Marseilles found their way back through bills of exchange drawn upon Marseilles to cover purchases made in the interior of Anatolia, Bursa or Ankara. Money was also sent for purchases of olive oil and wheat from the islands of the Archipelago and Crete[2]. Finally, money transferred to other parts of the Ottoman Empire found their way back to Western Europe largely through İzmir for the latter was the nucleus of all trade to the West[3].

Despite the passive balance of trade of the French in İzmir, the profits and by consequence the surplus money did not stay in the Levantine port[4]. There are a number of reasons for this. In order to carry out trade in İzmir French merchants had established themselves there. In this way they held their entire trade circuit in their hands. They were thus able to accumulate profits from trade, investment, insurance, usury, monetary speculation, shipping. Until the early 19th century, all carrying trade was in the hands of Western Europeans and in particular the French[5]. The stronger currency of the French economy, part of the Western economy, when compared to the Ottoman currency, gave additional profits to the French.

---

[1]ANF, AE Bi 1053, Peyssonnel, Mémoire, İzmir 22 Nov 1751.
[2]R. Paris, *Le Levant,* 1957, p. 453.
[3]ANF, AE Biii 414, Amoureux, Mémoire sur le commerce d'importation à Smirne, İzmir, 7 May 1781.
[4]C. Carrière & M. Courdurié, «Un sophisme économique», *Histoire, économie et société*, 1er trim, 1984, pp. 7-51; p. 23.
[5]ANF, AE Biii 242, B. Jumelin, Mémoire sur le commerce de Levant, 1812.

To these profits must be added the profits inherent in the nature of the relation between İzmir and France. The latter imported raw materials and exported manufactured goods. It this way the long term benefits stayed with the French economy. Its manufacturing sector grew. For its economy was able to exploit productively the raw materials that İzmir exported to France. Cotton, which remained in the sector of merchant capital in İzmir, entered the sector of industrial capital in France.

In the final analysis, profits from all these trade activities may have left Marseilles with a surplus in its balance of payments that was greater than the deficit in its balance of trade with İzmir. For İzmir the opposite was potentially true. «Le Levant reçoit 1,000 livres mais doit payer 1,500. C'est une fonction permanente, une perte de substance: le type des échanges inégaux»[1]. In its passive balance of trade Marseilles was not losing and the gains of İzmir may have been more apparent than real. Lack of documentation on all profit making activities in İzmir makes it impossible to analyze in detail its balance of payments, however.

Local capital accumulation among the Ottoman merchants and growth of their economic activities at the end of the 18th century, shows that part of the profits of this trade did stay in İzmir. Nevertheless, the profits that accrued to the French, both in the nature of the trade relation and from the organization of trade, were quantitatively and qualitatively greater. Trade with the West created wealth and helped the growth of the forces of production but not the relations of production. In İzmir, merchant capital did not develop into industrial, productive capital. Nevertheless, by the end of the eighteenth century, the city-port's commercial and merchant banking sectors as well as its money market grew and became more complex as well as better capitalized in relation to earlier times. For İzmir, part of the Ottoman economy, both participated in and benefited from the growth of the eighteenth-century world economy overall and from the growing economic prosperity of the Mediterranean in particular.

[1]C. Carrière, «Un sophisme économique», *CNRS Paper*, 1973, p. 4.

THE COASTAL TRADE OF THE OTTOMAN EMPIRE, FROM THE MID-EIGHTEENTH TO THE EARLY NINETEENTH CENTURIES

This chapter analyses the Ottoman coastal trade, also referred to as internal maritime trade, from the second half of the eighteenth to the early nineteenth centuries. At the time, the Ottoman Empire was immense, spread over three continents — Europe, Asia and Africa — and bordering parts of the Mediterranean, Black and Red Seas. Its economy was basically merchant capitalist with a high degree of monetization in its urban areas and in particular in the western parts of the Empire which bordered the Mediterranean. This was also the region that included the biggest urban centers of the Empire at that time: Istanbul, İzmir, Alexandria, Salonica. In the eighteenth century, internal maritime trade served to connect such urban centers and their hinterland more efficiently and cost-effectively than any other means.

In such an economy, coastal trade served an important function primarily in contributing to the commercialization of agriculture, the monetization of the economy and to the further growth and greater unification of the domestic market. Through coastal trade, goods, people, capital and information were moved more efficiently and cost-effectively than would have been possible through land transport. It was the maritime regions of the Empire that were most affected. For the land mass that made up a large part of the Empire, caravan routes, despite their shortcomings, were still the most frequent means of communication. Moreover, established fairs and caravan routes linking inland markets helped create internal commercial zones which contributed to not only the external trade of the Empire but also the coastal trade of its maritime regions[1].

[1]Archives Nationales de France, Paris, AE Biii 243, Inspection générale du Levant, 1817. Hereafter, these archives will be cited as ANF. See also E. Wirth, "Alep dans la première moitié du XIXe siècle: un exemple de stabilité et de dynamique dans l'économie ottomane tardive," in: *Revue du Monde Musulman et de la Méditerranée*, 62/4 (1991), pp. 137-49.

The second half of the eighteenth century was a period of considerable economic growth for the Ottoman Empire.[1] It was part of the general growth of the Mediterranean which affected primarily the Empire's maritime regions. Within the Ottoman economy the internal and external commercial sectors and other associated sectors such as shipping, experienced particular growth. Within the commercial sector, coastal trade played a major role in this economic development, linked as it was with external trade. For the external trade of the Ottoman Empire with western Europe, reflecting the expansionist phase of international trade at the time, grew very considerably in this period contributing in part also to the growth of internal trade.

In the Ottoman Empire, as elsewhere, coastal shipping was synonymous with *cabotage* or internal trade. In essence, it included all maritime trade that was carried out within its territorial boundaries. It was distinct from, although closely related to, the external maritime trade of the Empire. The latter was carried out primarily with Europe through the Mediterranean to the west and with the Far East through the Red Sea and the Indian Ocean to the east. Due to the considerable distances involved, even when taking into account only the Mediterranean — given that the Empire covered nearly two thirds of the Mediterranean coastline — Ottoman coastal trade, by necessity, included some deep-sea navigation. This was the case for ships that crossed the Mediterranean but still remained within home waters. Thus the definition of coastal trade as internal maritime trade was the most apt for the Ottoman case. The term most used in the primary sources at the time to denote Ottoman coastal trade, particularly in the Mediterranean, was *caravane maritime*.[2] In secondary literature, which is often francophone, both the terms *grand* and *petit cabotage* are used to denote longer and shorter distance coastal trade although here, too, *caravane maritime* is the term most used to define Ottoman coastal shipping.

Given the geographical expanse of the maritime regions of the Empire, and the considerable body of water thus covered, there was bound to be a proliferation of traffic patterns and ports of call if one were to include all the

[1]Given the paucity of direct data, one way of measuring the rate of economic growth is through the trading activity of the great port-cities of the Empire with France, its most important trading partner. From the middle of the eighteenth century to the eve of the French Revolution imports to İzmir, Istanbul and Salonica increased by well over 30 per cent, while their exports to France grew over 100 per cent, led by İzmir which registered almost double this growth rate: Elena Frangakis-Syrett, *The Commerce of Smyrna in the Eighteenth Century, 1700-1820,* Athens, 1992, pp. 259-60.

[2]E.g., ANF, AE Biii 271-277, États des bâtiments (1756-1787). Moreover, French sources constitute some of the most important archives on the subject, given the dominant role of French shipping in Ottoman coastal trade at the time.

minor markets, in islands or coastal towns, that coasters could have stopped at, in any given voyage. In actual fact, however, the principal routes and the ones most used in coastal trade were fewer in number and mostly reflected the size and economic importance of the centers they linked. Despite the problems of transport and communication the internal Ottoman maritime world was quite well-connected. Given its size, it also tended to be divided into a number of regions, each region dominated by one or more economic centers, which were also city-ports and linked the regions with each other. In this respect, three city-ports, rising to an importance which went well beyond their regions, contributed greatly to linking the Empire together: Istanbul, whose political importance and demographic size made it the biggest consumer in the Empire[1]; İzmir, whose pivotal role in the Ottoman external as well as internal trade allowed it to dominate both the Empire's internal and external commercial networks; Alexandria, because it played a crucial role in the trade in certain commodities within the Empire.

The Black Sea formed an important maritime region of the Empire. Since the creation of the Empire, the Ottoman government, conscious of the need to supply the capital[2], had rerouted trade in this region to benefit Istanbul. Indeed until 1774 the Black Sea was closed to all non-Ottoman maritime traffic[3]. Even after 1774 Istanbul remained the most important purchaser and consumer of goods in the region. Given the size of the capital in the eighteenth century, the coastal trade that was centered around supplying Istanbul with grain was a complex operation, mostly undertaken or at least directed by the state. It was also an important part of Ottoman internal trade. Furthermore, given the perishable nature of this type of cargo and the shortness of the season for optimum weather conditions as well as the political pressures likely to arise from grain shortages in the capital, the state devoted considerable resources and organizational effort to this sector of the coastal trade. This included the hiring of private — Ottoman and European — merchant ships with an official shipping broker acting as a middleman between the state and the shipowners. It also necessitated the creation, as far as possible, of an infrastructure that could ensure regular and timely unloading of

[1]Istanbul was by far the biggest city in the Empire. In the eighteenth century the population of the city was thought to be between 300,000 and 350,000, while Greater Istanbul, which included the surrounding regions, was estimated at 600,000 to 700,000: R. Mantran, *Histoire d'Istanbul*, Paris 1996, pp. 253-4; W. Eton, *A survey of the Turkish Empire*, London, 1799, p. 287; J. McCarthy, *The Ottoman Turks*, London, 1997, p. 257.

[2]Mehmet Genç, "Osmanlı İmparatorluğu'nda Devlet ve Ekonomi", in: *Beşinci Milletlerarası Türkiye Sosyal ve İktisat Tarihi Kongresi Tebliğler*, Ankara 1990, pp. 13-25.

[3]The treaty of Küçük-Kainarci in 1774 gave merchant ships under a Russian flag the right of passage through the Straits.

the grain once the ships reached Istanbul.[1] In view of the overall consumption needs of the capital, the entire maritime trade of Istanbul, which included both internal and overseas trade, carried a negative balance. Istanbul was able to cover such deficit by being the recipient of the Empire's tax revenues as well as of some of the trade surplus registered by important commercial centers such as İzmir. An elaborate system of bills of exchange transferred such funds to the capital from such economic centers as İzmir, Aleppo or Salonica.[2]

At the other end of the Empire, the city-port of Alexandria and the port of Suez, in Egypt, as well as the port of Djedda, in Arabia, dominated the internal trade of the Red Sea. Goods went along the coast from Djedda to Suez. After a short land journey by caravan to Cairo they were then sent to the main ports in the mouth of the Nile to be subsequently transported to directions east and west. Cargoes were sent to Rosetta and Alexandria where ships could either take them north-west to the island of Crete in the eastern Mediterranean and/or proceed with the merchandise further north to ports in the Greek mainland and the Aegean and/or the Black Sea. Alternatively, commodities could be sent from Alexandria west along the North African coast to major and minor ports in that region. Goods could also be taken in an easterly and north-easterly direction from the port of Damietta on the mouth of the river Nile to ports along the Syrian and Palestinian coasts, including the port of Alexandretta, Cyprus and/or along the Caramanian coast (south western Turkey).

In-between the Red and Black Sea maritime regions, there was the Mediterranean which linked both regions, and thus the entire Ottoman maritime internal trade. Within the Mediterranean, the most frequented axis was the Istanbul-İzmir-Alexandria route. Within this axis İzmir was the most important link. This was because İzmir not only united the various Ottoman maritime regions, from Istanbul to North Africa, with each other, but also a great part of the interior with the maritime regions of the Empire. At the same time, İzmir also linked large parts of the Empire with Europe.[3] In the course of the second half of the eighteenth and early nineteenth centuries, İzmir

---

[1]The complexity and size of such operations can be gauged from the following example: in 1748, a convoy was organized by the head of the Istanbul customs, on behalf of the state, of sixty ships from various Aegean ports to carry grain to Istanbul from Alexandria. The convoy included some triple masted ships of c. 300 tons capacity. Rhoads Murphey, "Provisioning Istanbul: the state and subsistence in the early modern Middle East", in: *Food and Foodways* 2 (1988), p. 253.

[2]Frangakis-Syrett, *The Commerce of Smyrna,* pp. 147-54; see also, Edhem Eldem, "Le commerce français d'Istanbul au XVIIIe siècle", unpublished Université de Provence, Ph.D. thesis, 1988.

[3]ANF, AE Bi 1053, Consul Charles de Peyssonnel, Mémoire, İzmir, 22 Nov. 1751.

emerged as the biggest importer and exporter of goods in the trade of the Ottoman Empire with Europe surpassing by far even the larger Ottoman ports.[1] In the process, İzmir drew goods from, as well as distributed goods to, a vast hinterland which included the interior of Anatolia (Turkey) and parts of the Greek mainland and stretched into Syria, Palestine, Iraq and Iran. It also included the western Anatolian coastline and islands in the Aegean and the Mediterranean, from Chios to Crete, while its extensive commercial networks brought it into constant communication with Istanbul, Salonica, Alexandria and the principal ports in the Maghrib.[2] Thus İzmir was not only the port with the most extensive contacts with Europe but also the port with the largest network of commercial contacts within the Ottoman world, including the maritime world.[3] By the early nineteenth century, given its spectacular commercial growth, İzmir dominated absolutely both the internal and the external Ottoman commercial networks.[4]

Notwithstanding the role of İzmir as a central, pivotal pole for the Empire, a sort of *plaque tournante,* Alexandria also dominated a number of maritime routes within the Ottoman world. To start with, a cluster of traffic patterns was formed around Alexandria and the island of Rhodes, and its near-by Caramanian region, in the southern part of the eastern Mediterranean, with a number of axis emanating as a result: namely, Rhodes-Alexandria; the Caramanian coast-Cos-Alexandria and the reverse. Another important cluster of coastal trade activity was formed between Alexandria and Crete. Then there were the routes leading mostly to major port cities. To the east there was an active coastal trade route between Alexandria and the Syro-Palestinian coast, which included also the Alexandria-Cyprus route, while another route, to the west, linked Alexandria with the North African ports. Going north there was an active route leading to Istanbul primarily, as well as to ports along the

[1]France was the biggest European trading partner of the Ottoman Empire in the second half of the eighteenth century. An average of 35 per cent of all Ottoman exports were annually sent to Marseilles from İzmir, while the ports of Salonica, Alexandria and Istanbul averaged annually 10, 9.3 and 5 per cent respectively of Ottoman exports. Archives de la Chambre de Commerce de Marseille, I, 26 & 28, États des marchandises venant du Levant et de Barbarie (1750-1789). Hereafter, these archives will be cited as ACCM. As far as the import trade was concerned, an average of 30 per cent of all goods coming into the Empire from Marseilles went through İzmir, while the annual share of the other ports was for Istanbul 20.8 per cent, for Alexandria 10.5 per cent and for Salonica 8.7 per cent. ACCM, I, 19-20, États des marchandises envoyées en Levant et Barbarie (1750-1789). See also Frangakis-Syrett, *The Commerce of Smyrna,* pp. 257-60.

[2]ANF, AE Biii 242, Consul Fourcade, Mémoire sur le commerce de Smyrne, c. 1812.

[3]For a commercial history of İzmir in the eighteenth century, see Frangakis-Syrett, *The Commerce of Smyrna, passim;* see also *idem.* "Trade between the Ottoman Empire and Western Europe: The case of İzmir in the eighteenth century", in: *New Pespectives on Turkey,* 2 (1988), pp. 1-18.

[4]ANF, AE Biii 243, Félix de Beaujour, Inspection générale du Levant, İzmir, 5 July 1817.

Macedonian and Thracian coastline, (in northern Greece), to ports such as Salonica or Cavalla, although the former took the greatest share of that region's coastal trade. The single most frequented route, however, was the one between Alexandria and İzmir which included İzmir's feeder ports on the western Anatolian coast and the Aegean islands.[1]

The port of Alexandria was of paramount importance for the internal maritime trade of the Empire and complemented that of İzmir in a number of ways. The difference between İzmir and Alexandria was, primarily, in the type of goods they moved and the geographical areas they took goods from or sent goods to. In other words, İzmir mainly brought in western and colonial goods and collected goods for the external market from practically the whole of the Ottoman Empire. Alexandria took goods that originated in certain regions and sent them to the appropriate markets within the Empire and vice-versa. For instance, Alexandria took coffee from Yemen, Indian textiles, and herbs. It sent these valuable and popular commodities, together with its own rice, to major markets such as İzmir, Istanbul and Salonica partly for local consumption and partly for further distribution.[2] As a result, Alexandria had a deficit in its trading relations with some regions of the Empire and a surplus with others. For instance, it sent more goods from its own and Red Sea areas to the markets in the Balkans and Asia Minor (Anatolia) as well as to North Africa than it received from them. At the same time Alexandria received more goods, important raw materials that originated in the Syrian and Palestinian regions necessary for Egyptian manufacture, than it sent to those regions, since the latter could also get goods from the Red Sea region by land. Its deficit with the Red Sea region and Syria was thus covered by the surplus Alexandria registered with the other regions of the Empire.[3]

The fact the Ottoman Empire had a surplus in its trade with Europe in the eighteenth and early nineteenth centuries meant that at least some of this surplus was used in its trade with India and the Far East with which the Empire had a deficit. İzmir regularly used at least some of its surplus from its trade with Europe to buy goods from Alexandria;[4] the latter port, in turn, used

---

[1]Daniel Panzac, "Affréteurs ottomans et capitaines français à Alexandrie: la caravane maritime en Méditerranée au milieu du XVIIIe siècle", in: *Revue de l'Occident Musulman et de la Méditerranée* 34 (1982), pp. 23-38.

[2]Michel Tuchscherer, "Activités des Turcs dans le commerce de la mer Rouge au XVIIIe siècle", in: D. Panzac (ed.), *Les villes dans l'Empire ottoman: activités et sociétés,* Paris, 1991, vol. 1, pp. 322-4, 327.

[3]André Raymond, *Artisans et Commerçants au Caire au XVIIIe siècle,* Damas 1974, vol. 2, pp. 184-92.

[4]ANF, AE Biii 243, Beaujour, Inspection, 1817.

its surplus with İzmir to buy goods from India and the Far East. Through the Empire's internal and external trade, İzmir and Alexandria became important links in the flow of silver going east to India and, finally, to China.

Apart from the principal axis centered around major markets, and in particular emanating from, and centered around, Istanbul, İzmir or Alexandria, there were a number of other smaller traffic routes among coastal ports or islands.[1] The latter, in particular, being scattered in the eastern Mediterranean, were natural stopping places for coastal trade. For instance ships frequently stopped at islands such as Cos (on the Alexandria-Rhodes route), Lesbos or Samos (on the Alexandria-İzmir or İzmir-Istanbul-Salonica routes). The surplus production, often in foodstuffs or in other goods particular to an island, were usually sent to the large urban centers, as were some of the more expensive manufactured goods, such as silk stuffs from the island of Chios, for these were the markets that could best absorb such goods. Goods were also traded locally within the smaller markets of the region especially among the bigger islands. Among them, Chios was an important port of call for most ships crossing the eastern Mediterranean on the north-south axis. The particular prominence of the island of Chios as a stopping place in the coastal trade of the eastern Mediterranean was primarily because of its good location rather than its potential as a major market.[2] Situated in the middle of the Aegean sea, ships tended to stop there to get provisions, fresh water, the current news concerning piratical activity or the outbreak of plague in near-by ports.[3] As one of the more prosperous islands in the region, it also traded with other Ottoman markets, both major and minor ones. Its own market was mostly, although not exclusively, supplied from İzmir with goods that included some of the city-port's more up-market western manufactured imports.[4] Another prosperous island economy was that of Crete. Olive oil, wine and currants were some of the goods that Crete sent to other markets in the Empire. The existence of a local industry, soap-making, coupled with an active overseas trade, based primarily on the export of olive oil[5], meant that

---

[1]Olga Katsiardi-Hering, *Η Ελληνική παροικία της Τεργέστης (1751-1830)*, (*The Greek Community of Trieste (1751-1830)*, Athens, 1986, vol. 2, pp. 547-8.

[2]ANF, AE Bi 1013, Consul Jouvin, Chios, 15 May 1763 to Minister, Paris.

[3]Daniel Panzac, "L'escale de Chio: un observatoire privilégié de l'activité maritime en mer Égée au XVIIIe siècle", in: *Annales* 4 (1985), p. 541-61. This study, while interesting, tends to exaggerate the importance of Chios since no distinction is made between ships stopping there to trade or simply to get provisions or information.

[4]For a commercial history of the island of Chios in this period and of the international trading activities of its merchants, see Elena Frangakis-Syrett, *Οι Χιώτες έμποροι στις διεθνείς συναλλαγές 1750-1850*, (*Chiot Merchants in International Trade, 1750-1850*) Athens, 1995.

[5]Yolande Triantafyllidou-Baladié, *Το εμπόριο και η οικονομία της Κρήτης (1669-1795)*, (*The Commerce and Economy of Crete, 1669-1795*), Iraklion, 1988, p. 62.

despite its size, Crete had a local market that enabled it to purchase from major markets, such as İzmir and Alexandria, apart from potash for its soap-making industry, other goods such as rice, coffee, tobacco or western manufactures. Crete was also an important link in the trading routes between Alexandria and İzmir or Istanbul.

The specific needs of the various regional markets for certain commodities and the goods that the various regions produced for the internal and external trade of the Empire greatly affected the pattern and type of coastal trade activity. For instance, Rhodes had contacts, through the coastal trade, with a number of small regional markets such as Cos, Cyprus, Chios, Crete, ports in the Peloponnese and the Syrian coast. However the principal markets with which it carried out most of its trade were fewer: Alexandria, İzmir and, to a lesser extent, Istanbul. Moreover, there was a distinct pattern of trade between the island and these markets: Alexandria received more goods from Rhodes than it sent to it, and more ships from Alexandria, while on their coastal trade voyage, made a stop at the island, than ships left Rhodes for Alexandria. The goods that were sent to the Alexandrine market were mostly foodstuffs, such as, citrus fruits, raisins, figs, honey, wine as well as other goods, such as, tobacco or wood from the forests of the region. Alexandria sent to Rhodes some of its principal staple goods, such as, coffee, for which there was a mass market in the eighteenth-century Ottoman Empire, rice as well as salt and, in limited qualities, flax seed.[1] As far as the Caramanian region, as a whole, was concerned, İzmir supplied it, primarily through Rhodes and secondarily through Cos, with European goods, such as cotton cloth, thus competing with local manufacture.[2] It was to İzmir also that coasters carried the region's lucrative cargo of sponges where it was bought by Europeans and exported to major western markets.[3] Some foodstuffs, such as fruit, were also sent primarily from Rhodes both to İzmir and Istanbul, for local consumption while certain other goods, such as wine, were sent to the Ottoman capital for export to Russia.[4]

---

[1] Maria Efthymiou-Hadzilacou, *Rhodes et sa région élargie au 18ème siècle: les activités portuaires*, Athens, 1988, pp. 193-228.

[2] ANF, AE Biii 242, Fourcade, Mémoire, 1812; see also AE Biii 415, Picard, Notice sur l'île de Stancho (Cos), c. 1801.

[3] ANF, AE Bi 1068, Consul Amoureux, İzmir, 3 June 1778 to Minister, Paris.

[4] ANF, AE Biii 242, Fourcade, Mémoire, 1812.

Given the demographic growth experienced in the Ottoman Empire in the eighteenth century, one of the most important commodities in the internal maritime trade, were foodstuffs and, in particular, cereals and grain.[1] At times of bad harvests and famine, which could hit any part of the Empire at any time, wheat and cereals had to be sent to the affected area by sea while the large urban centers, led by Istanbul, had an on-going need for foodstuffs, including cereals. It was such needs that were being met by the coastal trade that carried, for instance, cereals for local consumption from ports in Syria or Anatolia to the ports of North Africa. While rice was a staple commodity in the trade of Alexandria with all the principal Ottoman markets, olive oil, often sold for ready cash as opposed to barter or on credit[2], was another valuable foodstuff, both for the external and the internal trade of the Empire. Areas that produced olive oil, such as Crete or Mitylene, were integrated into some of the most active coastal trade routes.

Ottoman coastal trade was also important in the supplying of local industries with raw materials as well as in distributing finished products. A case in point was the soap industry of Crete.[3] Potash was sent to Crete from Tripoli in Libya, the Syrian ports, Alexandria, İzmir and Salonica.[4] The most important finished goods carried in the coastal trade were local and western textiles. Western textiles were sent principally from İzmir to a number of markets within the Empire. There was also an active internal trade in local textiles. For instance, although North Africa had well-established commercial links with Europe by then, and could thus be easily supplied with western cloth, there was still demand in the region for locally produced textiles which were sent there principally from İzmir and Alexandria.[5] This is not as contradictory as it may first appear. Certainly the trade of the Empire with Europe, based mainly on the exchange of Ottoman raw materials and foodstuffs for western textiles, was growing at the time. However, given the territorial expanse of the Empire there were many Ottoman regions, as well as sectors of regional markets, that the international market could not yet reach and which were still being supplied through the internal market. Moreover, given that we are still dealing with pre-Industrial-Revolution Europe, certain types of Ottoman textiles were still able to compete, under certain market conditions, with western manufactures.

---

[1]Murphey, "Provisioning Istanbul", p. 220.
[2]ANF, AE Bi 1052, Consul Charles de Peyssonnel, İzmir, 29 Jan. 1749 to Minister, Paris.
[3]Yolande Triantafyllidou-Baladié, "L'industrie du savon en Crète au XVIIIe siècle: aspects économiques et sociaux", in: *Revue des études balkaniques* 4 (1975), pp. 75-87.
[4]N. Svoronos, Le *Commerce de Salonique au XVIIIe siècle*, Paris, 1956, pp. 270-1.
[5]Daniel Panzac, "Le commerce maritime de Tripoli de Barbarie dans la seconde moitié du XVIIIe siècle", in: *Revue d'Histoire maghrebine*, 69-70 (1993), pp. 149-50, 153-4; see also Raymond, *Artisans*, pp. 191-2.

Although Ottoman coastal trade was *de facto* open to all nationalities, in theory the situation was more complicated. Based on the Capitulations, the European states claimed the right to participate in the Ottoman coastal trade.[1] They cited, for instance, article 75 of the Capitulations signed in 1740 between the Ottoman Empire and France which gave, quite clearly, the right to the French to participate in the Ottoman coastal trade:

> Lorsque les musulmans ou les rayahs, sujets de ma Sublime Porte, chargeront des marchandises sur des bâtiments français pour les transporter d'une échelle de mon empire à une autre ; il n'y sera porté aucun empêchement.[2]

Throughout the eighteenth century, internal Ottoman government decrees tried to secure coastal trade either in Ottoman hands only or, at least, have Ottoman ships be given priority in coastal trade. Such decrees could not be enforced either because local authorities, such as customs officials, had an interest, due to the revenues that would thus be accrued, in allowing an active coasting trade to go through their offices, or because local brokers, who chartered the ships, or local merchants, whose goods were thus being transported, were reluctant to follow such decrees. This was either because the European ships were the only ones available or because, compared to Ottoman ships, they were considered safer for the transport of the merchants' goods.[3] The superior design and construction of European ships was accepted by the Ottomans.[4] They were also aware that there were not enough Ottoman carriers, especially in view of the growth of the internal maritime trade at the time. So that, although there were specific sectors where local — Arab, Greek or Turkish — carriers predominated, within the coastal trade of the Empire, overall, European ships filled the existing and growing needs. The result was not only the active participation of a number of European flags in Ottoman internal trade, but the dominance of this coastal trade by European captains and ships and, in particular, by the French.[5] They were the single most important group, especially in the earlier part of our period, in all routes — except for

---

[1]The Capitulations were legal agreements made between the Ottoman government and a number of European powers granting non-reciprocal trading privileges to the Europeans in the Ottoman Empire; these agreements also regulated all aspects of the economic activities of the Europeans in the Empire.

[2]George Young, *Corps du droit ottoman,* Oxford, 1905, vol. 3, p. 63.

[3]Raymond, *Artisans,* pp. 170-1.

[4]Murphey, "Provisioning Istanbul", p. 223.

[5]Although the coastal trade related primarily to the transport of goods, European ships also carried passengers. This included merchants and local officials, pilgrims and Ottoman troops.

the Red Sea, in Ottoman coastal trade[1]. There was a tendency for French and other European carriers to be primarily active in the longer routes, or *grand cabotage*, while Ottoman carriers tended to be active in the shorter coastal routes, or *petit cabotage*. Ottoman small craft also dominated the lighterage sector of the coastal trade.

There were a number of advantages that European ships enjoyed in the coastal trade which helped them acquire and maintain their dominance. These were an advantageous position, based on the Capitulations, as far as customs dues were concerned: for instance, on entering and leaving ports in the Empire they paid lower dues than Ottoman ships. European captains were also less likely to be harassed by demands for extraordinary payments, called *avanias*, by local port authorities, than local captains were, for the Europeans always enjoyed the protection of a western consular authority. This authority was based on and reflected not only the prestige of the European country in question but also the terms of the Capitulations signed between that country and the Porte. Indeed, as we saw above, it was the Capitulations that gave the European powers the right to claim participation in the internal Ottoman maritime trade for their nationals.[2] The Capitulations, together with a vigorous exercise of consular authority, resulted in greater security and protection for the European captains in the eastern Mediterranean and hence in greater safety for the cargoes they carried. This factor, coupled with the superior construction and bigger size of the European ships, cited above, which allowed them to withstand the weather better, made them preferable to Ottoman ships. Finally, another asset that the Europeans enjoyed, and which should not be underestimated, was their immunity from the Maltese corsairs which their Ottoman rivals, to their detriment, did not have. Periodic attacks on Ottoman shipping from Maltese corsairs, throughout the period under study, made local merchants and brokers turn even more to European captains.[3]

For the French, the Ottoman coastal trade was considered a lucrative occupation.[4] Compared to the overseas trade of the French with the Ottoman Empire, considerable resources, in terms of ships, were put into the Ottoman

[1]ANF, AE Bi 1062, Consul Charles-Claude de Peyssonnel, İzmir, 22 July 1775 to Minister, Paris.

[2]Young, *Corps du droit*, p. 63.

[3]Peter Earle, *Corsairs of Malta and Barbary*, London, 1970, pp. 141-67.

[4]E.g., ANF, AE Bi 1012 in Hélène Pegnié, "*Εξωτερικό και διανησιώτικο εμπόριο στη Χίο του 18° αιώνα*", ("External and inter-island trade in Chios in the 18th century") in: *Ta Historika*, vol. 5, no. 8 (1988), p. 117; see also report of the Chamber of Commerce of Marseilles in H.A.R. Gibb/Harold Bowen, *Islamic Society and the West*, Oxford, 1950, vol. 1, pt. I, p. 309.

coastal trade. Almost three-quarters of the French ships in the eastern Mediterranean at that time were engaged in the coastal trade. Moreover, coastal trade was as important to Ottoman ports as blue water. For instance, in the 1750s and 1760s, almost half of the French ships that arrived in İzmir had originated from other Ottoman ports, while the rest came from Marseilles. The ratio was lower for the departures, with more French ships leaving for Marseilles than for other Ottoman ports,[1] although the proportion of French captains having another Ottoman port as their destination was still more than a third in overall departures.[2] As for Alexandria, the share of ships active in coastal trade within its total port activity was even higher.[3]

There were a number of reasons why the French merchant marine preferred the coastal trade to the set routes of Marseilles-İzmir or Marseilles to Italian ports and then onto İzmir and the reverse. Participation in the coastal trade gave them the opportunity to be at sea for at least two years, with a single quarantine at the end of the voyage. In contrast, a normal voyage between Marseilles and İzmir took six months, including a quarantine of up to ninety days, but the sailors were paid for only the four and a half months they were at sea. In the coastal trade even the longest voyages, that is when ships went directly from Salonica or Istanbul to Alexandria or from Alexandria to Tunis, which was rare for ships usually stopped at other ports along the way, only lasted between fifteen and twenty-five days. The coastal trade was also relatively inexpensive to run. On leaving Marseilles, the captain was given two months' provisions and a relatively modest sum (100 piastres) in cash.[4] As an additional recompense, the captain was allowed to keep his return cargo, of wheat or even better of rice, which he had acquired from the profits made on the freight he had carried during his voyage(s) and from monetary transactions, usually changing different currencies, western or local, that he invariably dealt in along the way[5].

---

[1]ANF, AE Biii 271-274; see also Elena Frangakis-Syrett, "İzmir — An international port in the eastern Mediterranean in the eighteenth century (1695-1820)", in: *Actes du IIe colloque international d'histoire,* Athens, 1985, vol. 1, pp. 124-8.

[2]Captains who had no specific Ottoman port as their destination left İzmir to look for cargo along the way among ports in the eastern Mediterranean.

[3]Raymond, *Artisans,* pp. 168-9.

[4]By contrast, the master of a British ship carrying goods from London to İzmir, for instance, was paid £100 worth of foreign currency or bullion, nearly ten times more than his French counterpart and given, as part of his salary, trading privileges that were allocated at a rate of 40 shillings per ton of the ship's burden. Public Record Office, London, SP 105/211, The Printed Orders of the Levant Company, 1744. Hereafter these archives will be cited as PRO. However, captains of French ships were compensated almost entirely by trading privileges. This was considered fair pay since these ships, most frequently engaged in the coastal trade too, were smaller than those used by the British and their journey was much shorter. ANF, AE Bi 1013, Consul Jouvin, Chios, 15 May 1763.

[5]Frangakis-Syrett, *The Commerce of Smyrna,* p. 91.

The participation of the French in the Ottoman coastal trade was closely related to their overseas trade with the Empire. For French ships coming from Europe, from Marseilles or an Italian port, usually stayed for a period of up to two years in Ottoman home waters, carrying goods from port to port, before picking up cargo for the return journey to Europe. Usually the return cargo to Europe was provided by the French merchants who had freighted the ship for the initial journey to the Ottoman Empire. In the case of a major port, such as İzmir, the loading could be done on the spot with, at most, the possibility that certain goods, such as olive oil or wheat, might be loaded from a near-by port. However, in the case of smaller ports, such as those in the Peloponnese or Syria, the captain might have to go to a number of ports where, with the cooperation of the French merchants established in those ports, he collected cargo for his return journey to Europe. As far as the coastal trade was concerned, however, the captain had to find freight himself.

Ships active in the Ottoman coastal trade did not belong to shipping companies, nor did they sail up and down specific routes. Instead French captains, like their rivals in the Levant, had to be prepared to change ports and routes frequently according to the charter they could secure, or even to call in ports in the hope of finding cargo. This was due to the uncertainty of the market as well as to the strong competition among carriers. In reality, most captains tended to repeat a number of ports and routes for this was where they had established contacts with charterers or local merchants. This did not mean that ships could not potentially undertake a number of voyages in any given year. Voyages lasted quite a while, with safety being more important than speed. For navigating Ottoman coastal waters was not particularly easy while bad weather and insecurity at sea, due to pirates or privateers, could force them to make additional stops for refuge, thus delaying their journey even more. Moreover, loading and unloading were done at a rather leisurely pace with the ship staying in port for a long time. For instance, in the 1760, the average time that a ship stayed in the two main ports of the island of Crete, for unloading or loading of merchandise, was two and four weeks respectively. In fact the smaller the port the longer the ship might be obliged to stay. Other times, the stay of a ship was influenced by the captain's efforts to get more or new freight.[1] Indeed, time taken up with loading and unloading, as well as with stopping at various ports on the way to the final destination, accounted for a considerable amount of the overall length of the voyage. Actual time at sea was relatively short since distances were not great. Nevertheless demarrage

[1]Robert Paris, *Histoire du Commerce de Marseille*, vol. 5: *Le Levant de 1660 à 1789*, Paris 1957, pp. 168-79.

clauses did seem to be part of such charters, and in particular, of ships hired for the transport of grain for Istanbul, or of a region affected by famine. Here tight schedules had to be met and demurrage clauses were part of the contract.[1]

In chartering ships, single voyages predominated by far while return voyages, or what the sources call *fermés*, were much less frequent. Indeed the lack of charters at any given point in time, due to the volatility of the market, led to the widespread practice of coasters setting out from a port, as we saw earlier in the example of İzmir, with no fixed destination, in search of cargo, or what the sources call en *aventure*.[2] Ships were chartered either for a period of time, often four to six months, or for a specific, mostly single, journey. Although ships were usually chartered for their entire cargo capacity, there were also space charters. In the mid-eighteenth century, a ship going to İzmir from Alexandria could be freighted in its entirety for a sum from 400 to 1,500 piastres, according to the dimensions of the ship.[3] Sometimes the freight rate was arrived at by an itemized rate for each type of good loaded on a ship. For instance, 100 *ardeb*s (18.6 tons) of rice were carried from Alexandria to İzmir for 90 piastres, to Salonica for 100 piastres and to Istanbul for 120 piastres.[4] In the grain carrying trade, the freight rate could also be arrived at by taking a fixed percentage of the value of the cargo and adjusting it according to the length of the voyage.[5] Often, the captain was paid part of his freight money at the beginning of the journey receiving the balance after the safe delivery of his cargo. Normally the freight was paid, or ultimately settled, mostly in silver specie of either Ottoman or European currencies for both types of coinage circulated in the Ottoman Empire at the time.[6] The latter coins, mostly Dutch

[1]Murphey, "Provisioning, Istanbul", p. 225.

[2]ANF, AE Biii 271-277, États des bâtiments (1756-1787).

[3]Throughout the eighteenth century, the basic Ottoman silver currency, called piastre or guruş, stayed at a fixed rate of 3 livres tournois per piastre for the French currency. However, this rate had to be further adjusted when calculating the exchange rate vis-à-vis the French currency in order to reflect the loss in value that the Ottoman currency underwent in the latter part of the eighteenth and in the early-nineteenth centuries. This becomes more evident in the exchange rate vis-à-vis the British currency which ranged from c. 7 piastres per £ in mid-century to 11 piastres per £ by 1790 and to 20 piastres per £ by the end of the Napoleonic Wars. Elena Frangakis-Syrett, "The Ottoman Monetary System in the Long Eighteenth Century', paper delivered at the colloquium on Money and Mints in the Ottoman Empire, 1680-1850, held at the French Institute of Anatolian Studies, Istanbul, Turkey, 28-30 Nov. 1997.

[4]Daniel Panzac, "Négociants, ottomans et capitaines français: la caravane maritime en Crète au XVIIIe siècle," in: H. Batu/J.-L. Bacqué-Grammont (eds.) *L'Empire ottoman, la République de Turquie et la France*, Istanbul/Paris, 1986, pp. 78-9, 82-5 and *idem*, "Affréteurs ottomans", pp. 65-6.

[5]Murphey, "Provisioning Istanbul", pp. 226-8.

[6]For reasons for such practices, see Frangakis-Syrett, *The Commerce of Smyrna*, pp. 139-54; see also Edhem Eldem, "La circulation de la lettre de change entre la France et Constantinople au XVIIIe siècle," in: H. Batu/J.-L. Bacqué-Grammont (eds.), *L'Empire ottoman, la République de Turquie et la France*, Istanbul/Paris 1986, pp. 87-97.

dollars or Maria-Theresa thalers, were often preferred. In this respect, the coastal trade was in line with other sectors of the Ottoman economy.

Not everything went smoothly between the European captain and the local merchant or shipbroker when freighting a ship and problems often arose. A reason for this was the endemic monetary scarcity which was a feature of the Ottoman economy even in the prosperous maritime regions. This made it, at times, difficult for the shipbroker to pay all the expenses, such as part of the freight, port dues and other expenses, before the goods had reached their destination and the proceeds from their sale had been realized. As a result, credit, which featured very strongly in all commercial transactions in the Empire at the time, was used in the coastal trade. It was also often the cause of subsequent disputes between the captain and the broker.[1] At the same time, the strong competition that existed in the coastal trade between various shippers made European captains willing to enter into, at times, even dubious freight contracts.[2]

Information concerning the total tonnage of the merchant fleets involved, or the tonnage of types of ships, or of individual ships active in the coastal trade is either incomplete or lacking. It is thus impossible to tell the overall tonnage of these fleets. There is also no complete data concerning the movement of ships, European or Ottoman, leaving or entering Ottoman ports that would allow us to quantify the number of ships involved in the coastal trade. It is equally impossible to tell the global amount of goods carried, even on the principal routes, by either the French or any other group of shippers, within the period under study. For even when the type of ship is given, there is no certainty as to its tonnage. Differing tonnage figures are given in the sources for the same types of ships.[3] Nevertheless, from data on the types of ships involved, we can draw some overall conclusions as to the range of their tonnage. Some of the most popular types of merchant ships used in the Ottoman coastal trade had the following range of tonnage: *tartanes* 30-125 tons; *barques* 90-150 tons; *brigantins* 60-190 tons; *pinques* 60-150 tons; *senau*(lts) 60-170 tons; *corvettes* 140-235 tons; *polacres* 60-200 tons; *bombardes* 100-145 tons.[4] We also have some indications concerning the

---

[1] ANF, AE Bi 1060, Extraits des minutes de la Chancellerie, İzmir, 12 April 1772 to Minister, Paris.

[2] ANF, AE Bi 1052, Consul Charles de Peyssonnel, İzmir, 5 March 1749 to Minister, Paris.

[3] Yolande Triantafyllidou-Baladié, "Transports maritimes et concurrence en Méditerranée orientale au XVIIIe siècle: L'exemple de la Crète", in: *Actes du IIe colloque international d'histoire*, Athens 1985, vol. 1, p. 24.

[4] The data has been taken from a number of sources, namely: Triantafyllidou-Baladié, "Transports maritimes," pp. 23-4; Charles Carrière, *Négociants marseillais au XVIIIe siècle*, Aix-en-Provence, 1973, vol. 2, pp. 594-9; Vasilis Kremmydas, *Το εμπόριο της Πελοποννήσου στο 18ο αίωνα,* (1715-1792), (*The Commerce of the Peloponnese in the 18th century, 1715-1792)*, Athens, 1972, p. 254.

productivity of Ottoman coastal trade, that is, the number of men per ship. Here, there is concurrence in the sources for the French, for whom the data is more complete, that indicates that the man-to-ton ratio was just over ten tons per man.[1] Other nationalities, such as the Venetians, Ragusans or Russians, seem to have had a higher ratio of men per ton than the French. Given the limited data, these figures can only be indicative. Productivity was also affected by other factors as the case of the Ottoman Greeks makes clear. Despite their much lower man-to-ton ratio, which averaged about six tons per man, they were nevertheless very competitive, a fact reflected in the growth of the Ottoman Greek merchant marine in this period. Lower wages and cheaper provisions for the crew contributed to lower overall costs, despite the larger crew sizes.[2]

Despite the stiff competition that the French faced from other European and Ottoman carriers, lucrative freight rates made up, as far as the French captains were concerned, for the infrequency and length of charter. This was probably true for other European captains. Moreover, European ships tended to carry more expensive goods, making their freight rates more worthwhile. So that even when the number of European ships involved in a certain route were small, the tonnage thus represented, and even more the value of the cargo carried, were higher. By contrast, in the transport of less expensive bulkier goods, covering shorter distances, smaller local, Turkish, Greek or Arab, ships were preferred. For instance, Ottoman shipowners predominated in the coastal trade between Alexandria and the Caramanian coast, including Rhodes, as they did in the trade between the Ionian islands and the western coast of Greece while the lighterage sector was also in Ottoman hands. Small craft under the Ottoman flag were used for the local traffic connecting Istanbul and Galata (the Asiatic and European shores of the Ottoman capital).[3] At the same time, the coastal traffic of small ports, situated near a major port, such as those in the gulf of Salonica or along the Syrian coast, which acted as feeder ports for the external trade of the major port in the area, was also in the hands of Ottoman

[1]E.g., Murat Cizakça, *A Comparative Evolution of Business Partnerships. The Islamic World and Europe*, Leiden, 1996, p. 129; Kremmydas, *Το εμπόριο της Πελοποννησου*, p. 254; Triantafyllidou-Baladié, "Transports maritimes", p. 29.

[2]Kremmydas, *Το εμπόριο της Πελοποννησου*, pp. 254-6; Triantafyyllidou-Baladié, "Transports maritimes", pp. 27-9.

[3]E.g. Raymond, *Artisans*, p. 168; Efthymiou-Hadzilacou, "Rhodes", pp. 282-6; George B. Leon, "The Greek merchant marine (1453-1850)," in: S. A. Papadopoulos (ed.), *The Greek Merchant Marine*, Athens, 1972, pp. 20, 27, 29, 31.

shippers.[1] Equally the coastal trade between İzmir and Istanbul, closely related to the external trade, was in the hands of Turkish shipowners.[2]

Among the major European economies of the time, only the French participated so actively in the Ottoman coastal trade: the Dutch did not participate in it and the British did so only to a limited extent. The British tended to be more active at times of war, as for instance, during the Seven Years' War (1756-63) when the regulations of the Levant Company concerning the trading activities of its members as well as of non-members, were more relaxed. Although in the second half of the eighteenth century, the Levant Company was no longer able to control shipping between Britain and the Levant, as it had done earlier[3], the British did not become, even then, prominent players in the Ottoman coastal trade. Like their French counterparts, British captains were not averse to utilizing their time, while waiting for cargo to be collected by the European merchants for their journey home, to go coasting. In such a case, the captain might get the help of the British merchant(s) who had initially chartered him from London, either with some freight for near-by ports or with recommendation letters.[4] When a certain Ottoman port could not offer enough cargo for the return journey to London, like his French counterpart, the British captain continued his journey to a number of other coastal ports in the vicinity picking up cargo on the way.[5] Although these goods were destined for the external market, it was also possible for other transactions to be made and for some goods to be carried locally while the captain was undertaking such a coastal route.

Other European participants active in the Ottoman internal trade were the Danes, Swedes, Ragusans, Venetians and those of Imperial Germany. While the French faced strong competition during peacetime, it was primarily maritime wars between France and other European powers that caused them their biggest problems and led to the erosion of their dominance. During such wars, the commerce raiding activities of their enemies affected them adversely and severely compromised the safety of their cargoes. As a result, local

[1]Ammon Cohen, "Ottoman rule and the re-emergence of the coast of Palestine (17th-18th centuries)", in: *Revue de l'Occident Musulman et de la Méditerranée*, 39 (1985), p. 165.

[2]E.g. PRO, SP 105/188, Ambassador Sir Robert Ainslie, Istanbul, 11 & 16 May 1782; 3 Feb. and 2 Dec. 1783; 27 Jan. 1786.

[3]E.g., PRO, SP 105/116, Levant Company, London, 13 Aug. 1719 to Consul Cooke, İzmir; SP 105/117, Levant Company, London, 26 Sept. 1729 and 1 Sept. 1730 to Consul Boddington, İzmir; *ibid.*, Levant Company, London, 13 March 1739 to Treasurer Tooke, İzmir.

[4]Elena Frangakis-Syrett, "Trade practices in Aleppo in the middle of the eighteenth century: the case of a British merchant," in: *Revue du Monde Musulman et de la Méditerranée*, 62 (1991), p. 126.

[5]PRO, SP 110/36, Th. Landsdown, Aleppo, 17 Jan. 1760 to Captain C. Wilson, İskenderun.

merchants and charterers alike tended to avoid French ships during wartime. With business falling sharply, French captains even resorted to selling their ships on the spot to their erstwhile local or other western rivals and to temporarily withdrawing from the coastal trade.[1] Other nationalities filled the gap left by the French. During the Seven Years' War, the Ragusans became the single most important carriers of the coastal trade along the western Anatolian coast and the Aegean Sea.[2] Moreover, in the aftermath of the War, the Ragusans emerged probably as the biggest competitors to the French.[3] In the last quarter of the eighteenth century and onwards, due to a number of factors, among them being the economic prosperity cited above, Greek and Turkish shipowners were able to benefit most from the problems of the French.

The upheaval of the French Revolution, coupled with the destruction of the French merchant fleet by the British navy during the French Revolutionary and Napoleonic Wars, allowed the local shipowners, the Greek more than any other group, to make even greater inroads, in the late-eighteenth and early-nineteenth centuries, into the French carrying trade than the Ragusans ever had. A number of reasons account for such developments. The general commercial prosperity of the eastern Mediterranean was particularly evident among the Greeks of the Ottoman Empire. It was reflected in their active and increasing participation in the overseas trade of the Empire, particularly that between the eastern Mediterranean and the Italian ports, as well as in the growth experienced by the Greeks in the carrying trade.[4] In this sector they were increasingly active in both the overseas and the internal Ottoman maritime trade. Greek ships started carrying goods not only between Ottoman and Italian ports or Marseilles, but also among islands and ports in the eastern Mediterranean.[5] Thus the Greeks, from the outset, were active both in commerce and in shipping.[6]

---

[1]Panzac, "Négociants ottomans", pp. 79-80.

[2]ANF, AE Biii 271, États des bâtiments, 1756-1762. For Ragusan competition to French coastal trade following the Seven Years' War, see AE Bi 1062, Consul Charles-Claude de Peyssonnel, İzmir, 22 July 1775 to Minister, Paris.

[3]Francis W. Carter, *Dubrovnik (Ragusa). A Classic City-State,* London, 1972, pp. 421-41.

[4]ANF, AE Bi 859, Consul L'Allement, Messina, 20 March 1784, 3 Sept. 1785, 4 Feb. 1786 and 14 Jan. 1788 to Minister, Paris.

[5]ANF, AE Bi 1087, Consul Fraunnery, Trieste, 27 Jan. 1789 to Minister, Paris.

[6]Elena Frangakis-Syrett, "Greek Mercantile Activities in the eastern Mediterranean, 1780-1820," in: *Balkan Studies,* 28 (1987), pp. 73-86.

At the same time, the specialization of the Greeks in the commerce and transport of certain key products in the overseas trade of the Empire, such as Ottoman wheat and European cloth, gave them an important asset which in turn contributed to the increase of their merchant marine.[1] The Greeks also enjoyed a number of other assets which their local Turkish rivals in the coastal trade did not. They carried out privateering activities during a number of European or Ottoman wars in the second half of the eighteenth and in the early-nineteenth centuries.[2] For instance, during the Russo-Ottoman War (1768-74) Russian-protected Greek privateers were very active in the Aegean Sea to the detriment not only of their Turkish but even more of their Ragusan rivals. During this war the Ragusans were badly hit by the Russians who considered them Ottoman.[3] When there were no wars, the Greeks often reverted to piracy, which was rife in the Aegean Sea in the late-eighteenth and early-nineteenth centuries.[4] Such activities contributed to their capital accumulation and overall economic growth, including their share of the internal Ottoman maritime trade. There were certain exceptions to this. For instance, an area of coastal trade where Turkish shipowners maintained a clear dominance over their Greek and European rivals, in the late eighteenth century, was the carrying trade between İzmir and Istanbul.[5] Yet, even after a sharp decline in French trade activity in the Levant, in 1812, the coastal trade in the Aegean Sea alone was considered profitable enough to warrant the continuation of French trade in the area.[6]

---

[1]E.g., Archives du Ministère des Affaires Étrangères, Paris, CCC, Vol. 8, Vice-Consul David, Chios, 17 Oct. 1824 to Minister, Paris. Hereafter, these archives will be cited as AMAE. See also Frangakis-Syrett, *The Commerce of Smyrna*, pp. 101-2, 110-4 and Leon, "Greek Merchant Marine," pp. 30-2, 41-2.

[2]M.S. Anderson, "Russia in the Mediterranean, 1788-1791: a little-known chapter in the history of naval warfare and privateering," in: *Mariner's Mirror*, 45 (1959), pp. 25-35.

[3]However, they subsequently recovered to become once more active in the Ottoman coastal trade in the 1800's; see, Carter, *Dubrovnik (Ragusa)*, pp. 439-41.

[4]E.g., ANF, AE Bi 168, Consul Benincasa, Ancôna, 24 Feb. 1785 to Minister, Paris; PRO, SP 105/128, Consul Werry, İzmir, 1 Feb. 1802 to Levant Co., London; PRO, SP 105/129, Consul Werry, İzmir, 2 May 1803 to Levant Co., London; PRO, SP 105/132, Consul Werry, İzmir, 19 May, 9 July & 20 Nov. 1809 to Levant Co., London; PRO, SP 105/135, Consul Werry, 6 April 1815 to Levant Co., London; PRO, FO 78/136, W. Hamilton, Istanbul, 2 July 1823 to Consul General Cartwright, Istanbul; AMAE, CCC, Vol. 8, Vice-Consul David, Chios, 17 Oct. 1824 to Minister, Paris. See also, C. G. Pitcairn Jones, *Piracy in the Levant, 1827-8*, London, 1934, *passim;* D. Themeli-Katifori, *Η δίωξις της πειρατείας και το θαλάσσιον δικαστήριον κατά την πρώτην καποδιστριακήν περίοδον, 1828-1829* (*The Suppression of Piracy and the Maritime Court during the first Capodistrian period, 1828-1829*), Athens, 1973, vol. 1, pp. 47-54.

[5]Başbakanlık Osmanlı Arşivi in Mehmet Genç (forthcoming); see also PRO, SP 105/188, May 1782, Feb. & Dec. 1783.

[6]ANF, AE Biii 242, Jumelin, Commerce du Levant en général, c. Sept. 1812.

Given the pre-industrial nature of the economy, the internal maritime trade of the Ottoman Empire fulfilled an important function by circulating goods, mostly agricultural, that were necessary either for local consumption or for local industries. It also circulated, perhaps to a lesser extent, goods of local manufacturers. Coastal trade thus directed the output of a specific region to the market needs of another region, primarily maritime, within the Empire in the most cost-effective manner. In the process, it contributed to the further commercialization of the Empire's agricultural production and to the further monetization of its economy. For the Europeans, and particularly the French, it was a lucrative part of their extensive trading activities with the Ottoman Empire in the eighteenth century. Their participation in the Ottoman coastal trade, which went against the trend of protection of a country's coastal trade mostly in force in Europe at the time, was an economic necessity for the Empire given its territorial expanse, cost of land transport and inadequacy of the Ottoman merchant marine. The participation of the Europeans was also a natural extension of the growing integration of the Ottoman Empire into the international market and the growing commercial links that were being forged between the Empire and Europe. The close ties between the internal and external trade of the Empire further reflected such trends. Finally, the nature and organization of Ottoman coastal trade and of European participation in it were also the results of wider trends in economic growth that the world economy experienced, in the second half of the eighteenth and in the early-nineteenth centuries, and of which the Ottoman Empire was also part.

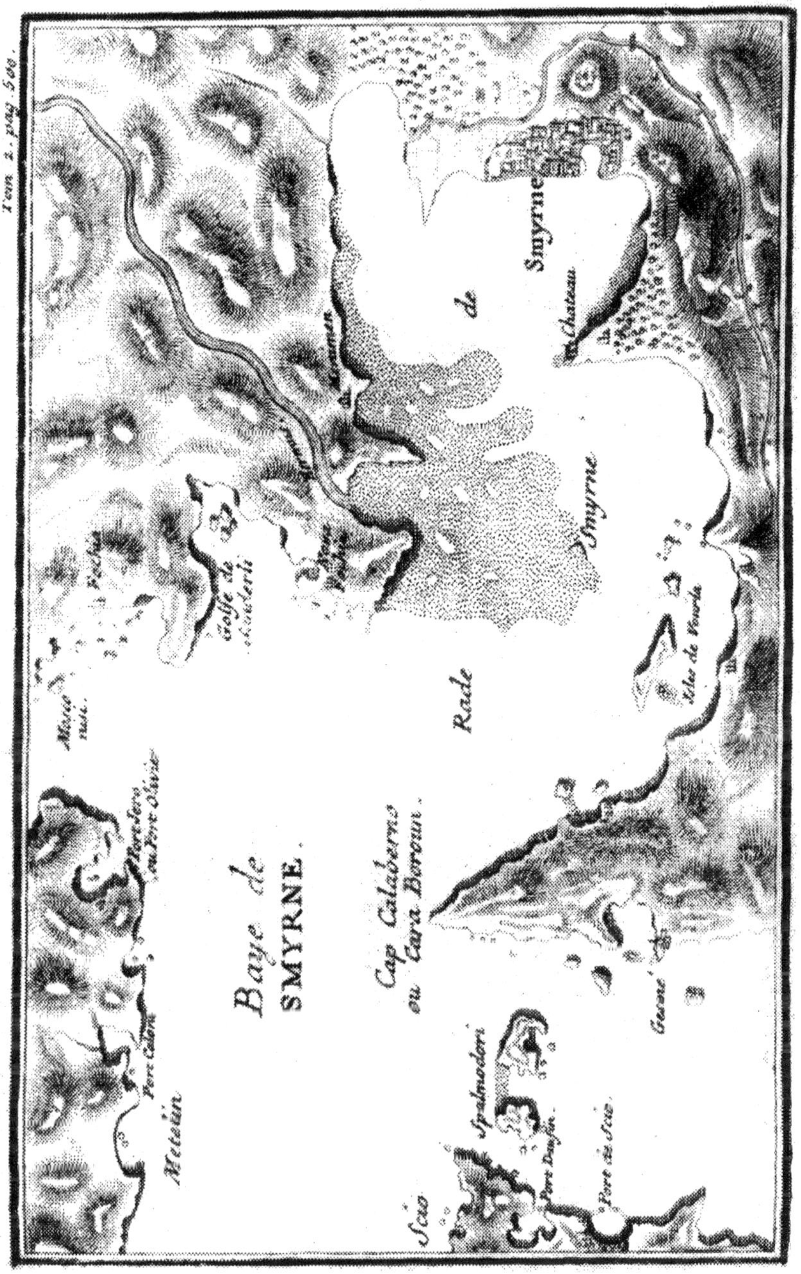

1. View of the Bay of İzmir. (From Pitton de Tournefort, *Voyage du Levant*.)

2. View of the Port and Town of Çeşme.
(Courtesy of the Centre for Asia Minor Studies).

3. View of the Port and Town of Mitylene.
(From Pitton de Tournefort, *Voyage du Levant* ...)

İZMİR AND THE OTTOMAN MARITIME WORLD OF THE EIGHTEENTH CENTURY

The sea had always played an important role in the life of the Ottoman empire: in the 18th century, coastal and blue water shipping were a vital means of communication for people, ideas and goods as well as a crucial medium for economic development and particularly for trade. It is no accident that the maritime regions of the empire included some of the biggest and most economically developed urban centers, such as İzmir. The sea was essential for the economy of İzmir too: it was one of its life-lines and defining characteristics. The other was its immense hinterland spread over a large part of the empire. The sea on the one hand, and the hinterland on the other, were fundamental parts to the equation that resulted, by the end of the 18th century, in the spectacular growth of the port of İzmir. Multiple maritime contacts with Europe, as well as with the rest of the empire, were vital in securing İzmir's spectacular economic growth.

Although İzmir had been participating in the external trade of the empire since the beginning of the 17th century, it was in the course of the 18th century, following the growth of the European economy and the revitalization of the Mediterranean basin, that İzmir rose to become both the most important port of the empire, surpassing Alexandria and Istanbul, and one of the major ports of the Mediterranean, handling, both in terms of volume and value, most of the exports to the West and imports, and dominating maritime and shipping routes, both coastal and deep-sea, within the empire.[1]

While Alexandria initially rivaled İzmir in internal trade, playing a crucial role in key commodities such as rice and wheat, and was also important in the export trade with Europe, İzmir was able by the mid-18th century to dominate the commercial routes to Europe, thus overtaking Alexandria in the external trade sector.[2] In the second half of the 18th century İzmir surged ahead of Alexandria in all aspects of the empire's trade with Europe. In internal trade too, İzmir, strengthened by her commanding position in the external maritime trade with Europe, and, due in part to her geographical location, came to dominate Ottoman trade overall. Alexandria, however, continued to specialize in trade in certain commodities, particularly foodstuffs.

---

[1]Archives Nationales de France, Paris, AE Biii 243, Félix de Beaujour, Inspection générale du Levant, 1817. Hereafter these archives will be cited as ANF.

[2]Frangakis-Syrett, Elena, *The Commerce of Smyrna in the Eighteenth Century, 1700-1820*, Athens, 1992, pp. 119-137.

Yet in terms of the overall trade and economic needs of the empire, including monetary flows, İzmir and Alexandria also complimented each other. Alexandria received specialized goods of near-by regions and sent them on the other parts of the empire together with its own, locally-produced, goods. For instance, Alexandria received coffee from Yemen, through the Red Sea, Indian textiles and herbs.[1] At the same time it received raw materials from the Syrian and Palestinian regions for use in Egyptian manufacture. For these regions, and even more for regions further away, such as North Africa or Anatolia, maritime links through Alexandria were necessary to make trade in such goods viable. For instance, Alexandria sent coffee from Yemen, together with its own produce of rice, and often of wheat, by sea, to large urban centers such as Istanbul, İzmir or Salonica for local consumption and/or further distribution. In its trade overall, Alexandria ran a deficit with certain areas and with other regions a surplus. For instance, it sent more goods to the Balkans, Anatolia — primarily Istanbul — and North Africa, whilst it received more goods than it sent to Syria, Palestine and the Red Sea.[2] In its trade with the West, İzmir registered a surplus which it used, in part, to buy goods from Alexandria thus restoring some of the deficit of the Egyptian port. The latter port, in turn, used such funds to buy goods from India and the Far East. İzmir used another part of its surplus with Europe to buy goods directly from India and the Far East, too, with which areas the empire registered overall a trade deficit. İzmir sent the remaining part of its surplus to Istanbul; the government in the capital bought, with part of such remittances from İzmir, foodstuffs from Alexandria or Salonica.[3] Internal maritime trade was thus crucial in balancing out Ottoman land and maritime regions and in securing necessary flows of funds as well as of goods within and without the empire. The empire's trade with the West provided it, in large part, with funds for its trade with the East; such movement of funds became part of the global monetary flows, mainly of silver, from West to East.

As the largest urban center in the empire in the 18th century, Istanbul was another rival to İzmir, this time in the import sector of the external trade with Europe and, like Alexandria, in the internal Ottoman maritime trade, too. Indeed, its constant need for foodstuffs, such as wheat, made Istanbul one of the most important axes around which Ottoman maritime trade revolved.

---

[1] Tuchscherer, Michel, "Activités des Turcs dans le commerce de la mer Rouge au XVIIIe siècle", in: Panzac, D. (ed.), *Les villes dans l'empire ottoman: activités et sociétés*, Paris, 1991, I, pp. 322-324, 327.

[2] Raymond, André, *Les artisans et commerçants du Caire au XVIIIe siècle*, Damascus, 1973-74, II, pp. 184-192.

[3] ANF, AE Bi 1057, Consul Charles-Claude de Peyssonnel, Mémoire, İzmir, 20 April 1769.

However, as the empire's capital, its political and administrative activities left a large part of the empire's landed and maritime networks for İzmir to provision. For instance, important export trades from the vicinity of Istanbul, such as Bursa silk or Ankara mohair yarn, reached the European markets, through İzmir's commercial networks rather than those of the capital. The *raison d'être* for the commercial networks of Istanbul in the 18th century was strictly to fulfill the capital's need for goods which it received, mostly by sea, either from within the Ottoman empire or from abroad. Unlike İzmir, Istanbul neither attracted goods from the Ottoman interior for export, nor did it distribute imported goods into Anatolia. The resilience of İzmir's commercial networks in both the above trades was such, in the 18th century, that all attempts to supplant them, even by merchants based in Ankara or Bursa, failed. It was not so in the 19th century: by the 1840s, Istanbul had taken over part of the Bursa silk export trade to Britain.[1]

The prominence in Istanbul of élite consumers, amongst the well-to-do administrators and other Ottoman officials, who conglomerated in the capital, meant that its market attracted western goods usually to be found in the upper end of the market; this, in turn, restricted the potential amount of such imports.[2] Such factors contributed to İzmir becoming the outlet of the empire's large Anatolian hinterland, as well as of Persia besides the coastal regions of western and southern Anatolia, the Aegean islands, parts of the Greek mainland and areas of the Fertile Crescent. İzmir became equally the distributor to the same hinterland, inland areas as well as maritime regions, of medium quality, and hence affordable, western commodities, such as cloth, together with other western manufactured and colonial goods.[3]

Like Alexandria, Istanbul also complimented İzmir's trading activities. As we saw above İzmir sent funds to Istanbul, in the form of taxation, through the internal networks of bills of exchange, promissory notes, or even cash.[4] However, a reverse flow of funds also took place through the European monetary networks, which were well connected with the local networks and functioned through similar instruments of payment and mechanisms of credit. Given the fact that the capital was principally an importing port, the

---

[1]Public Record Office, F.O. 78/490, Consul D. Sandison, Bursa, 5 Feb. 1842 to F.O., London. Hereafter these archives will be cited as PRO.

[2]ANF, AE Bi 1054, Consul Charles de Peyssonnel, İzmir, 15 Feb. 1754 to Minister, Paris.

[3]ANF, AE Bi 1053, Peyssonnel, Mémoire, İzmir, 22 Nov. 1751.

[4]Eldem, Edhem, "La circulation de la lettre de change entre la France et Constantinople au XVIIIe siècle", in: Batu, H & J.-L. Bacqué-Grammont (eds.), *L'empire ottoman, la République de Turquie et la France*, Istanbul-Paris, 1986, p. 88.

Europeans in Istanbul registered surpluses in their trading activities;[1] conversely, their counterparts in İzmir registered deficits, given the western Anatolian port's principal function as an exporter of Ottoman goods to the West. Hence the former sent funds to the latter in İzmir, as well as to other commercial centers in the Ottoman empire, where there were European merchants. For instance, French merchants sent funds to Crete for their counterparts, there, to furnish Marseilles with olive oil, for which there was constant demand in the French market.[2] If such funds were in the form of bills of exchange, they often entered the internal financial networks of the empire; if they were in specie, they could be carried to Crete, from Istanbul, by European captains, who actively participated in the Ottoman coastal trade, especially in its more major routes, such as the Istanbul-Alexandria axis, which included Crete.[3]

An important characteristic of the Ottoman maritime world of the 18th century was a proliferation of different maritime routes that were used to connect Ottoman ports with each other or to connect the empire with Europe. From a sample of French archival data, covering the 1720s to the 1790s, and including both coastal and deep-sea shipping, one can identify literally hundreds of different routes that vessels could take when plying Ottoman coastal waters or carrying goods between Europe and the empire. İzmir dominated this network of shipping routes, both major and minor, absolutely. Fully 30 per cent of all routes either originated or terminated in İzmir, or else included it as an intermediary port of call. İzmir was also the most important link in the most frequented axis of Ottoman internal maritime trade: the Istanbul-İzmir-Alexandria route.[4] In deep-sea shipping İzmir received over one-quarter of all French ships that called on Ottoman ports from Marseilles in the third quarter of the century,[5] at a time when Marseilles was the most important western trading partner, accounting for well over half of the empire's trade with Europe. In terms of value of the goods carried by these

---

[1]Eldem, Edhem, "Structure et acteurs du commerce international d'Istanbul au XVIIIe siècle", in: Panzac, *Villes, cit.*, I, pp. 244-245.

[2]Triantafyllidou-Baladié, Yolande, "Le marché des produits agricoles de la Canée aux XVIIe et XVIIIe siècles. Le mécanisme des échanges et les pratiques du crédit", in: Panzac, *Villes, cit.*, I, p. 311.

[3]Triantafyllidou-Baladié, Yolande, "Transports maritimes et concurrence en Méditerranée orientale au XVIIIe siècle: L'exemple de la Crète", in: *Actes du IIe colloque international d'histoire,* Athens, 1985, vol. I, p. 24; see also, Panzac, Daniel, "Affréteurs ottomans et capitaines français à Alexandrie: la caravane maritime en Méditerranée au milieu du XVIIIe siècle", in: *Revue de l'Occident Musulman et de la Méditerranée*, XXXIV (1982), pp. 23-38.

[4]ANF, AE Biii 271-274; see also, AE Bi 1011, 1014.

[5]İzmir's share would have been even larger were shipping figures available for the last quarter of the century when its dominance of Ottoman-French trade was even stronger.

ships, İzmir's average annual share was even higher — namely, nearly 40 per cent in the export trade and over 30 per cent in the import trade.[1]

Whilst no other port seriously rivaled İzmir's dominance in Ottoman trade in the second half of the century, yet a number of the Ottoman ports carried on an active trade with Europe as well as with other ports within the empire as we saw above. Given the size of the empire, İzmir could not respond to all commercial needs or cover all the routes. This was particularly evident in the case of the other major ports in the empire. Even at the height of İzmir's commercial dominance, in the last quarter of the 18th and in the early 19th centuries, the port did not control all of the empire's trade or maritime routes. That this was so was also part of the general economic growth that the empire's maritime regions, in particular, experienced in the 18th century — especially in the latter part of the century — as well as of the growth and vitality of Ottoman trade in this period.

Alexandria dominated a number of maritime routes within the Ottoman world. For instance, a cluster of traffic patterns and routes was formed around Alexandria and the island of Rhodes and its near-by Caramanian region, in the southern part of the eastern Mediterranean, such as the Alexandria-Rhodes-Alexandria route or the Caramanian coast-Cos-Alexandria route and the reverse.[2] Another important maritime route was formed between Alexandria and Crete. Then there were the sea lanes leading mostly to important ports in the empire. To the East, there was an active coastal trade between Alexandria and the Syro-Palestinian coast, which included also the Alexandria-Cyprus-Alexandria route; another route, to the West, linked Alexandria with the North African ports. Going North, there was an extremely active and frequented trade route leading to Istanbul, often with a stop-over at Chios,[3] mainly for the supply of the capital with foodstuffs.[4] Given the *de facto*, if not *de jure*, freedom for non-Ottomans to navigate the Ottoman coastal waters that existed in the 18th century,[5] this route was very popular for western captains.[6] For a number of reasons, including cost-effectiveness and security of transport,

---

[1]Archives de la Chambre de Commerce de Marseille, Marseilles, I. 19-20 and 26-28. Hereafter these archives will be cited as ACCM.

[2]Efthymiou-Hadjilakou, Maria, *Rhodes et sa région élargie au XVIIIe siècle: les activités portuaires*, Athens, 1988, pp. 193-228.

[3]Pegnié, Hélène, "*Εξωτερικό και διανησιώτικο εμπόριο στη Χίο τον 18° αιώνα*" ["External and intra-island trade in Chios in the 18th century"], in: *Historica*, V/8 (1988), p. 117.

[4]Murphey, Rhoads, "Provisioning Istanbul: the state and subsistence in the early modern Middle East", in: *Food and Foodways*, II (1988), *passim*.

[5]Young, George, *Corps du droit ottoman*, Oxford, 1905, III, p. 63.

[6]ANF, AE Biii 271-274; AE Bi 1011, 1014.

western ships were often preferred by Ottoman merchants and charterers to local ships on the longer routes, such as Alexandria-Istanbul, of Ottoman domestic maritime trade.[1] Muslim merchants, who were particularly active in the internal trade of the empire, were amongst the biggest clients of the European captains, whose carrying trade activities were thus an integral part of the domestic Ottoman economy. The French, more than any other major European nationality trading in the Ottoman empire in the 18th century, participated in this sector and, at times, even dominated the carrying trade in some of the major routes of Ottoman coastal trade.

Another pattern of routes had developed between Alexandria and the Macedonian and Thracian coastline, in northern Greece, leading mainly to the ports of Salonica and Cavalla. Besides its active trade with a number of European ports, Salonica was itself the focal point of a whole set of maritime routes and commercial networks that linked the Macedonian port with its coastal region, as well as with Istanbul, İzmir, the Aegean islands, Crete or the Peloponnesian ports and going as far south as Alexandria.[2] The single most frequented route for Alexandria was also the one between the Egyptian port and İzmir; this route also included İzmir's feeder ports on the western Anatolian coast and the near-by Aegean islands for these were, in essence, part of the Greater İzmir commercial and maritime region.

Apart from the major maritime routes centered around and emanating from major city-ports, there were also smaller patterns of shipping routes and commercial networks that connected together coastal ports or islands. They led to a proliferation of maritime routes which was one of the main characteristics of the Ottoman maritime world. They also testified to the existence of vibrant, although often small, local markets. A good part of the trading activities of such markets were certainly oriented towards near-by major city-ports, which naturally absorbed part of their surplus production in foodstuffs. Nevertheless, goods were also traded locally, within the smaller markets of the region, especially among the bigger islands in the Aegean Archipelago. Such islands were Chios or Mytilene, and further south, Rhodes or Crete. Sales of their surplus production of foodstuffs or of their specialized goods, such as olive oil, allowed the Aegean islands to enter, as producers and consumers, directly or indirectly, both the internal, Ottoman, and the external, western, markets.

---

[1]Murphey, "Provisioning Istanbul", cit., p. 223; see also, Panzac, Daniel, "Négociants ottomans et capitaines français: le caravane maritime en Crète au XVIIIe siècle", in: Batu & Bacqué-Grammont, *L'empire ottoman, cit.*, pp. 78-79, 82-85.

[2]Svoronos, N., *Le commerce de Salonique au XVIIIe siècle*, Paris, 1956, p. 401.

The second biggest island in the eastern Mediterranean, Crete, had a lively export trade of olive oil not only to other markets in the empire but also to Europe. It was a very sought-after commodity and one which, in a barter economy where Ottoman exports were often exchanged for western manufactured goods, olive oil was usually sold to the Europeans for cash. As a result, the commercial networks that had developed in the olive oil export trade — purchase from the producer, transport to the market, sale to the exporter and, in the case of the Europeans, shipping the produce abroad — were fiercely competitive. This was particularly so since, at all stages of the marketing process, a number of different groups were involved: Ottoman — Muslim and non-Muslim — producers, petty bankers and merchants, as well as the Europeans.[1] Crete also participated in the empire's internal trade: for instance, it sent wine and currants to other neighboring markets. Moreover, the existence of a soap-making industry on the island, from the early 18th century, led Crete buying potash for this industry from İzmir and Alexandria.[2] As a result of all these trade activities Crete had also become an important link in the trading routes between Alexandria and İzmir, Istanbul or even Salonica. However, Crete's direct links with the international market throughout the 18th century were the exception rather than the rule. For as far as most of the Aegean islands, most of the time, were concerned, it was the major Ottoman ports — and İzmir most of all — that acted as their intermediaries with the western markets. A prosperous island in the region, Chios, traded its silk stuffs to neighboring markets. However, mastic, a produce par excellence of Chios, at least those quantities of mastic which were allowed to be exported or were smuggled out of the island, reached the western markets through İzmir.[3] It was also through İzmir that Chios received its European goods: these included some of the better-quality western cloth that İzmir imported.[4] All this testified to the prosperity of the island's economy but also to the way İzmir was able to dominate it. As for the Chiots, they did trade with the international market. They did so, not from Chios however, but from merchant houses that they established in İzmir, where they migrated in the course of the 18th century.[5] As for Rhodes, it was to the major markets of Alexandria, İzmir and Istanbul that it sent its goods as well as received from

[1] Triantafyllidou-Baladie, Yolande, *Το εμπόριο και η οικονομία της Κρήτης (1669-1795)* (*The Commerce and Economy of Crete, 1669-1795*), Iraklion, 1988, p. 62.

[2] Triantafyllidou-Baladie, Yolande, "L'industrie du savon en Crète au XVIIIe siècle: aspects économiques et sociaux", in: *Revue des études balkaniques*, IV (1975), pp. 75-87.

[3] ACCM, I, 26-28.

[4] ANF, AE Bi 1013, Consul Jouvin, Chios, 15 May 1763 to Minister, Paris.

[5] On the trading activities of the Chiots in this period see Frangakis-Syrett, Elena, *Οι Χιώτες έμποροι στις διεθνείς συναλλαγές, 1750-1850* [*Chiot Merchants in International Trade, 1750-1850*], Athens, 1995.

them local or western goods for distribution to its regional market. Rhodes thus acted as an intermediary for its region, vis-à-vis the bigger Ottoman urban markets, whilst İzmir acted as an intermediary between Rhodes and the western markets. For instance, İzmir received through Rhodes, for the Caramanian coast as a whole, sought-after sponges for export to the European markets and sent to Rhodes, for transshipment to its region, European goods, such as cloth. Rhodes sent to Alexandria, mostly for local consumption, foodstuffs such as citrus fruits, raisins, figs, honey, wine, together with tobacco and wood from the forests of the region. Alexandria sent to Rhodes some of its principal staple goods, such as coffee, rice, salt and, in more limited quantities, flax seed.[1] Rhodes also sent foodstuffs to Istanbul to be consumed locally and certain other goods for export, to the Black Sea region, such as wine.[2]

The export trade in olive oil of Mitylene is another case in point. It was French merchants in İzmir who actually disposed of the funds — at times in gold or silver coins if demand for olive oil was such that purchases had to be made in cash — and who gave it to the French captains who effected purchases on their behalf. European merchant houses based in İzmir also sent their agents to buy the produce, or even went there themselves, in order to complete their exports to Marseilles with a lucrative produce.[3] With İzmir acting as a banking center for the western Anatolian-cum-Aegean islands region, purchases made in Mytilene were often cleared in the city-port. Thus, even when funds were procured from a surplus among the French merchants in Istanbul, it was through the commercial networks of İzmir that these funds made their way to Mitylene. By the middle of the 18th century, the vested interests of İzmir-based French exporters became so entrenched that any Frenchman trying to establish himself in Mitylene, in order to trade directly with the French market, was met with strong opposition from them as well as their allies in the Chamber of Commerce in Marseilles.[4]

The tendency for centralization of the external trade in the eastern Mediterranean towards larger markets and, in particular, towards İzmir, became more pronounced in the second half of the 18th century. In the earlier part of the century, the Aegean islands had an active trade with the European market.

[1]Efthymiou-Hadjilakou, *Rhodes, cit.*, pp. 193-228.
[2]ANF, AE Bi 1068, Consul Amoureux, İzmir, 3 June 1778 to Minister, Paris and AE Biii 242, Consul Fourcade, Mémoire sur le commerce de Smyrne, c. 1812.
[3]Boulanger, Patrick, "L'île de Mytilène et le négoce français au XVIIIe siècle", in: Panzac, *Villes, cit.* I, pp. 278-279.
[4]*Ibid*, pp. 280-281.

Trade figures from the French archives concerning exports from the islands to Marseilles, for the first half of the century, gave them an annual share of 12 per cent on average of the Ottoman export trade to the French port. However, in the period 1755-1759 this figure decreased considerably, resulting in a 4.5 per cent share for the Aegean islands.[1] Furthermore, after 1759, the Aegean islands no longer figure on their own in the export lists but are included together with the exports to Marseilles from other ports in the eastern Mediterranean. This is probably not incidental but an indication of the reduced significance of direct trade between these islands and the French market due, at least in part, to a channeling of this trading activity to İzmir, for these years also coincide with the emergence of İzmir as the first port in the Ottoman export trade. The share of the western Anatolian port in Ottoman-French export trade in the years 1750-54 was 23 per cent whilst in the next five years it increased sharply to 38 per cent. Furthermore, from 1754 to the end of the century, İzmir *annually* topped the lists in the value of goods exported from the empire to Marseilles: no other Ottoman port was able to rival İzmir.

In the Ottoman import trade from Marseilles, for which figures exist, with gaps, only for the second half of the 18th century, the Aegean islands do not figure at all as *direct* recipients of French goods. This does not mean that *indirect* trade with France did not continue or indeed increase in this period of growth in Ottoman-European trade. What it means however, is that such trade was directed to and channeled through the major Ottoman maritime markets and in particular through İzmir.[2]

An important factor that contributed to the economic prosperity of the Ottoman maritime world of the 18th century was the growth and vibrancy of Ottoman-European trade where the westerners predominated and which was conducted both within and without the empire through a series of inter-connected maritime routes and commercial networks. For it was through the efficient formation and functioning of such shipping routes and commercial networks, namely, through the ports that these merchants were established at and traded with; the routes they used to carry their goods and funds and the inter-personal relationships they formed, that Ottoman-European trade grew and flourished in the eastern Mediterranean.

---

[1]Frangakis-Syrett, *The Commerce of Smyrna, cit.*, pp. 257-259.
[2]E.g., ANF, AE Biii 242, Fourcade, Mémoire, *cit.*, see also, Efthymiou-Hadjilakou, *Rhodes, cit.*, pp. 230-231, 249. Similar trends are evident in the trade of the islands in the northern part of the Aegean Archipelago, such as Thasos, which were close to the major Ottoman port of Salonica. Merchants in the Macedonian port, with the participation of Turkish landowners and officials, arranged for and financed the export trade of these islands. See Svoronos, *Le Commerce de Salonique, cit.*, pp. 272-280.

Perhaps the most frequented shipping routes in the Ottoman-European trade of the 18th century were those linking the Ottoman ports, and particularly İzmir, with the Italian ports of Livorno, Trieste, Ancona, Genoa, Messina and Venice. Amongst them Livorno, at least until the late 18th century, in its capacity as an entrepôt, has perhaps the pride of place, for it was constantly used, either in peacetime or in wartime, by all the participants in Ottoman-European trade — Europeans and Ottomans. For instance, in the early 18th century the British, as merchants of the Levant Company and hence as "official" participants in the British Levant trade, faced competition from other British merchants, who were not members of the company and who were thus trading illicitly with İzmir from their bases in Livorno. These "Italian" merchants, as the Levant Company called them, exported British and even French cloth to İzmir and from there imported Ottoman silk and mohair yarn destined for the British market. Such activities may have damaged the vested interests of one group of merchants, the British in İzmir, but strengthened the position of the Ottomans, who were established in the Italian port and traded with the western Anatolian port. It also made British Levant trade more competitive which helped both the British and the Ottoman markets.[1] By the middle of the 18th century, the Levant Company unable to control the routes through which British Levant trade was conducted, tried to benefit from the *status quo* and allowed its members in İzmir to act as agents. They could receive goods from Livorno on behalf of Ottoman as well as of other European merchants, sent there by other Ottoman or European merchants, and transported to the western Anatolian port in both British and non-British ships. Eager to participate in the trading activity carried out on the routes between Ottoman and Italian or Dutch ports, the Levant Company also sanctioned their merchants receiving goods coming from those ports.[2]

Trade was also lively in the routes between İzmir and other Italian ports and ships of all nationalities plied them: apart from Italian, there were British, French and Dutch ships and, in the last two decades of the 18th and in the early 19th centuries, there were also ships flying the Ottoman flag.[3] Whilst trade was going on at all times on these routes, it was in wartime and especially during maritime conflicts between Britain and France that the "Italian routes", if one can call them thus, acquired special significance. It was

[1] Matterson, Clarence, "English Trade in the Levant, 1693-1753," unpublished Harvard University PhD dissertation, 1936, pp. 196, 295.

[2] PRO, SP 105/211, Printed Orders of the Levant Company, October 1741.

[3] ANF, AE Bi 859, Consul l'Allement, Messina, 4 Feb. 1786 to Minister, Paris; see also Frangakis-Syrett, Elena, "Greek mercantile activities in the Eastern Mediterranean, 1780-1820", in: *Balkan Studies*, XXVIII/1 (1987), pp. 75-77, 82-84.

during such times that the networks and shipping routes of these two protectionist powers could be most disrupted. For instance, during the Seven Years' War (1756-1763), with the blockade by the British Navy of the port of Marseilles, Livorno largely took over the role of the French port in French Levant trade. French, and other merchants established in Livorno, exported French goods and in particular cloth to İzmir and imported from there, for the French market, cotton and cotton yarn.[1] Apart from Livorno, the Dutch ports also gained from this maritime conflict. Dutch ships, as neutral and following a non-protectionist policy, carried goods of British, French as well as Ottoman merchants, mostly non-Muslims and in particular Armenians, Jews and Greeks, from the ports of Amsterdam and Rotterdam to İzmir and vice-versa.[2] Indeed the Seven Years' War was a formative period for Ottoman merchants, for this is when they started establishing themselves in the commercial networks of the Dutch Levant trade.

The American War of Independence, (1776-1782), which led to the Dutch ports being blockaded by the British Navy in 1780-1782, led also to the Dutch Levant trade being re-directed, through an overland route, to Trieste and then on to İzmir by sea. As a result, the İzmir-Trieste-İzmir route flourished in this period. (Appendix C). After the war, the Italian port continued a lively trade with İzmir, for Ottoman merchants, and Greeks especially, had by then successfully penetrated the commercial networks in the Levant trade of Trieste and particularly in the Dutch Levant trade.[3] Perhaps the greatest disruption to major shipping routes in Ottoman-European trade was caused by the French Revolutionary (1729-1801) and Napoleonic Wars (1803-1815) which led both to trade between the Levant and Europe being re-directed to the Italian ports and to an increase in piratical and privateering activities in the eastern Mediterranean. With the port of Marseilles once more blockaded by the British Navy, trade on the İzmir-Marseilles-İzmir route was re-directed to the Italian ports and particularly to the ports of Ancona and Trieste. In 1801, for example, the share of Marseilles in the exports of İzmir to Europe was a mere one per cent, whilst the share of Trieste and Ancona was 70 per cent. Whilst

---

[1]Carrière, C. & M. Courdurié, "Les grandes heures de Livourne au XVIIIe siècle", in: *Revue Historique* CCLIV/1 (1975), pp. 40-41.

[2]Algemeen Rijksarschief, Consulaatarschief Smirna, De Invoer en de Uitvoer met Nederlandschen Scheppen te Smirna, 22 Feb. 1762 to 22 Aug. 1762 in Nanninga, J.G. (ed.), *Bronnen tot de Geschiedenis van den Levantschen Handel. Derde deel: 1726-1765*, 'S-Gravenhage, 1952, pp. 715-763. Hereafter these archives will be cited as ARA; see also Frangakis-Syrett, Elena, "Commercial practices and competition in the Levant: the British and the Dutch in eighteenth-century İzmir", in: A. Hamilton, A. de Groot and M. van den Boogert (eds.) *Friends and Rivals in the East*, Leiden, 2000, pp. 150-153.

[3]ANF, Marine B/7, 446, Consul Bertrand, 19 Oct. 1782 in Commerce des ports de l'Europe, 1 Feb. 1783.

Marseilles would have ordinarily accounted for as much as 40 per cent of İzmir's trade, the high figure shows that Trieste and Ancona were absorbing the trade of other networks, too, not only of the French Levant trade. Indeed, the maritime routes for the British Levant trade had shifted by then to include, besides London, the Italian ports and Malta. (See Appendix C). By the early 19th century the very considerable expansion in the British economy, and of its textile sector in particular, meant that Britain was starting to abandon its protectionist policies and actively sought markets for its exports. Given also the on-going disruption at sea due to the Napoleonic Wars, Malta became an important *entrepôt* for British goods in the Mediterranean. British, American and Ottoman ships — the latter two were neutral countries during the Napoleonic Wars — carried British goods, particularly textiles, to İzmir and took Ottoman goods for distribution to Britain, although the Ottoman port received more goods than it sent to the British market. The Italian ports were also part of the İzmir-Malta route: Ottoman Greek ships took Ottoman goods to the Italian ports, which they sold for cash, picked up provisions for their return voyage and proceeded to Malta where they bought British textiles with the funds they had already procured.[1]

Piracy and privateering were two other activities that flourished in wartime affecting, in the process, established Ottoman-European trading routes. For instance, in 1779, during the late phase of the American War of Independence, when the British Navy in essence withdrew from the Mediterranean, British ships did not risk the Levant. No ships reached İzmir in 1781 whilst no British ships left İzmir for London in 1779. As for the rest of the period, the share of Britain in İzmir's trade with Europe fell sharply.[2] However, as far as the Ottoman maritime world was concerned, privateering and piracy were very positive for they led to an increase in the level of capital accumulation for those who participated in them. Such activities, particularly privateering, although dangerous and risky, could also be very lucrative.[3] Further, once peace had been reestablished, the transition from privateer to legitimate ship owner was not a difficult one.[4] Indeed one of the most important economic activities for the Ottoman Greeks in the last decades of the 18th century was the carrying trade in Ottoman coastal waters and in the routes linking the Ottoman empire with the Italian ports.

---

[1]ANF, AE Biii 242, Consul Jumelin, Commerce du Levant en général, c. Sept. 1812.

[2]Frangakis-Syrett, *The Commerce of Smyrna*, *cit.*, p. 274.

[3]Archives du Ministère des Affaires Étrangères, Paris, CCC, VIII, Consul Étienne David, Mémoire sur Scio, Chios, 1823.

[4]ANF, AE Bi 168, Consul Benincasa, Ancona, 19 Aug. 1785 to Minister, Paris.

The routes between the Ottoman ports, again led by İzmir, and the major European ports of Amsterdam and Rotterdam, as far as the Netherlands were concerned, and London and Marseilles, as far as Britain and France were concerned, though not as frequented even in peacetime, were nevertheless as important as the "Italian" routes, if not more so, for Ottoman-European trade. Although fewer numbers of ships overall plied these routes, the ships used were larger in tonnage, thus representing a larger amount of trade both in terms of value and volume of goods carried. Overall, Dutch ships were the largest of those used in Ottoman-European trade. British ships were smaller than the Dutch but larger than the French, being almost twice the tonnage of the latter. Although bigger than Ottoman ships, (at just over 100 tons per ship), the French were amongst the smallest of the major European flags in the eastern Mediterranean.[1]

There was a definite advantage in the French usage of smaller ships: they could use them in the Ottoman coastal trade, a sector where they predominated over all other Europeans and even, at times, over local shippers. There was in many respects considerable fluidity and complimentarity between the Marseilles-İzmir-Marseilles route and Ottoman coastal trade. Over approximately a two-year period, French captains calculated in their profits not only freight from the Marseilles-İzmir route but also the freight of the goods they carried on Ottoman coastal routes, besides profits from trade in goods and money that they dealt in along the way whilst coasting in the Aegean sea. Besides carrying both goods and money the French, along with other European or Ottoman captains, often carried information that was valuable to commerce on such matters as market opportunities, political and military developments and on hazards to trade from such disasters as plague or war.

The commercial networks that functioned in the maritime routes through which Ottoman-European trade was conducted had a series of important characteristics. Europeans dominated them, especially in the earlier part of the century, while Ottoman merchants also participated in them, particularly in the latter part of the century. The Europeans, and later on the Ottomans too, even when catering for the external western market, for which purpose the westerners were established in the Ottoman empire, traded through a number of ports and markets both in the empire and in Europe. Underpinning the external trade networks of the Europeans that linked the

[1]E.g., Kremmydas, Vasilis, *Το εμπόριο της Πελοποννήσου στο* 18ο *αιώνα, 1715-1792* [*The Commerce of the Peloponnese in the 18th century, 1715-1792*], Athens, 1972, p. 254; Çizakça, Murat, *A Comparative Evolution of Business Partnerships. The Islamic World and Europe,* Leiden, 1996, p. 254; Triantafyllidou-Baladié, "Transports maritimes", *cit.*, p. 29.

Ottoman ports with the western markets, there were the networks that linked the ports with their hinterland. Such networks remained dominated by Ottoman merchants with the Europeans making occasional forays into the interior mostly through Ottoman merchants who acted as their agents.[1] As a result the networks that were formed served three functions respectively: they connected an Ottoman port to the external (European) market; to the internal (Ottoman) maritime market and the Ottoman interior. All three sets of networks, but especially the first two were widespread, complex, fiercely competitive and, to a great extent, open to all. They linked Ottoman ports with each other and with European ports and in the process increasingly integrated the Ottoman maritime regions into the international market.

The need to overcome the vagaries, uncertainties and expense of long-distance trade, at a time when regular communications were not yet established nor could demand or supply be guaranteed, led to these networks being characterized by ties of family and kinship, by a constant and close supervision of the merchants in the Levant by their associates in Europe as well as by a great fluidity in the type of partnerships that were formed between the merchants in the Levant and their associates in Europe. The Europeans trading in the Levant, displayed not unlike their Ottoman counterparts, considerable know-how, family contacts, credit-worthiness, an ability to communicate information concerning goods, prices and market projections and ways to monitor each other's activities and business decisions, all of which was as important as capital and allowed them to overcome at times even limited capital resources.

Family relationships and networks of kinship, often associated with the Jewish, Greek or Armenian merchants were also important for the Europeans in the Ottoman empire. From the beginning of the 18th century different members of the same European family established themselves in different city-ports of the Ottoman empire in order to trade with London as well as with other European ports. Such an example was the Barker family. By the middle of the 18th century, various members of the family were established in several Ottoman cities and ports. Moreover, the Barkers were a merchant banking house, which for several generations carried out trading as well as merchant banking operations. The demarcations between trading and merchant banking were very unclear in the 18th century and overlapped with entrepreneurs, both Ottoman and European, often acting as merchant-cum-

[1]ARA, De Vogel, 19 Nov. 1762 to Bartholo Cardamici, İzmir in Nanninga, *Bronnen... 1726-1765, cit.*, p. 475.

bankers. The Barkers were thus no exception. Their merchant banking operations included buying and selling bills of exchange, discounting bills of exchange or facilitating other British merchants in the empire in receiving funds which their employers in London had remitted to them. They did so either through credit networks of other Europeans who might be the Barkers' business associates or "friends", or through internal Ottoman networks of bills of exchange. The Barkers had usually a presence in Istanbul, given the pivotal role that the empire's capital played in any credit and other financial networks in the eastern Mediterranean, either on their own or in partnership with other houses. For instance, in mid-18th century Istanbul there were the houses of Benjamin & George Barker and of Humphreys & Barker, both active in merchant banking operations. Given the limited capital resources of both local and western merchants, since both the Ottoman and European economies were essentially pre-industrial economies, and given also the absence of institutionalized banking in the Ottoman empire, a merchant banker often relied on the credit of other merchants, too, for additional funds for his operations. In the 1760s for example, Humphreys & Barker had a correspondent in İzmir and an agreement with a British merchant established in Aleppo,[1] Thomas Landsdown, for the İzmir house to draw on Landsdown whenever necessary whilst they, in Istanbul, acted in turn as a clearing house for Landsdown in Aleppo.[2]

Although the Europeans did not stay *en famille* in the Levant in the 18th century and had, unlike the Ottomans, no opportunities for inter-marrying, they nevertheless, like the Ottomans, formed inter-family commercial partnerships together. Thus the intimacy, trust-worthiness, know-how, circle of contacts and capital resources of one family was extended over a larger network based on kinship. For example in the second quarter of the 18th century, there were in İzmir the partnerships of Shaw & D'Atch, D'Atch & Lee[3] as well as Barker & D'Atch, which was also active in Istanbul. They were all trading with London houses in the same manner and in similar goods.

Similarly the Chiots, Ottoman Greeks who came from the island of Chios, laid the foundations, in the 18th and early 19th centuries, of an international network of trading companies closely linked together with the ties and loyalty of kinship. For instance, in the 1760s, several members of the

---

[1]Aleppo, although an inland economic center, was linked to the maritime networks through the port of İskenderun.

[2]PRO, SP 110/37, Landsdown, Aleppo, 5 Feb. 1762 to Humphreys & Barker, Istanbul.

[3]PRO, SP 105/118, Levant Company, London, 27 April 1750 to Treasurer, İzmir.

Mavrogordato family were trading with the Netherlands from their bases in İzmir, on their own or in partnerships, as for example G. Mavrogordato, G. Anastas & Co. This was also the case with the Petrocochino and Petrici families.[1] Twenty-five years later, given the growing prominence of the Chiots in the trade of İzmir with the Dutch ports, the Mavrogordato family had been joined by others who were trading in İzmir on their own or in partnerships: namely, S. Mavrogordato & D. Petrici, S. Mavrogordato & A. Kappari, Mavrogordato d'Issay & Co., Ralli Petrocochino & Co., Mavrogordato & Petrocochino, and others.[2] By then new partnerships were being formed amongst these families, reflecting the expansion of their trading activities in a number of European ports, besides the Ottoman empire and the Netherlands, whilst old-established firms, such as G. Mavrogordato, G. Anastas & Co., were still carrying on trade between İzmir and the Netherlands.[3] Like the Barkers, the firm of d'Issay, established in Amsterdam in the second half of the 18th century, acted as a merchant banking house. Again like the Barkers, the Mavrogordato family was also trading in Istanbul, whilst by the latter part of the century it was also present in a number of other ports such as Livorno, Trieste,[4] Ancona, Marseilles and Odessa;[5] by the early 19th century, they had reached London, too.[6]

The European merchant, or factor as he was called, whilst in the Ottoman empire usually traded for a number of employers, or principals, in Europe. As for the merchant houses in Europe, they also employed several factors, established in the same or in different ports in the Ottoman empire. In İzmir, in the 1720s, Thomas Allen of the house of Allen & Shaw had a number of London houses it traded for and sent Ottoman goods to, namely, Sir John Williams, Charles Phillips, Messrs. Lockwood & Phillips, William

---

[1]ARA, Consulaatarchief Smirna, De Invoer en de Uitvoer met Nederlandschen Scheppen te Smirna, in Nanninga, *Bronnen... 1726-1765, cit.*, pp. 715-763.

[2]ARA, Consulaatarschief, De Invoer en te Uitvoer met Nederlandschen Scheppen te Smirna, 22 Aug. 1876 to 22 Feb. 1787, in: Nanninga, J.G., (ed.), *Bronnen tot de Geschiedenis van den Levantschen Handel. Vierde deel 1765-1826*, 'S-Gravenhage, 1966, pp. 1428-1466.

[3]Frangakis-Syrett, *Χιώτες έμποροι, cit.*, p. 43; see also, *idem The Commerce of Smyrna, cit.*, pp. 110-111 and *idem*, "The Greek mercantile community of İzmir in the first half of the nineteenth century", in: Panzac, *Villes, cit.*, I, pp. 393-402.

[4]Katsiardi-Hering, Olga, *Η ελληνική παροικία της Τεργέστης, 1751-1830 [The Greek community of Trieste, 1751-1830]*, Athens, 1986, II, pp. 547-558.

[5]Herlihy, Patricia, "Greek merchants in Odessa in the nineteenth century", in: *Harvard Ukrainian Studies* III-IV (1979-1980), pp. 399-420; Pepelasis-Minoglou, Ioanna, "The Greek merchant house of the Russian Black Sea: a nineteenth-century example of a traders' coalition", in: *International Journal of Maritime History*, X/1 (June, 1998), pp. 85-90.

[6]Chapman, S. D., "The international contribution to British commerce, 1800-1860", in: *Journal of European Economic History*, VI (Spring, 1977), pp. 36-39; see also, Mangriotis, D., "*Η Παροικία του Λονδίνου*" ["The (Greek) community of London"], *Historica*, III/6 (December 1986), pp. 350-352 and Frangakis-Syrett, *Χιώτες έμποροι, cit.*, pp. 22-25, 31-40, 57-60.

Snelling, Francis Townley, Edward Harley, Nathaniel Cambridge and Edward Gouge. Conversely, the merchant houses in London traded with more than one factor in İzmir: William Snelling received different consignments, in the same ship, of similar goods from two houses in İzmir, Allen & Shaw and Mitford, Winton & Frye.[1] Another example is Edward Barker who traded from London in the 1720s with several factors, including the factorages of Chadwick & Uvedale and Arthur Bernadiston, in İzmir. Bernadiston himself, in turn, traded with more than one house in London sending goods to Messrs. Ralph & Edward Radcliffe too, whilst Chadwick & Uvedale traded with several members of the Eyles family also in London.[2]

There was considerable fluidity, especially amongst the British and the Dutch, in the relationship between principal and factor, for although the Europeans were primarily factors in the Levant they could also work on their own behalf. Indeed, in long-distance trade, such as the Ottoman, if a merchant concluded a purchase on commission in part for his principal and in part for himself, his employer could then feel that the factor had given him the best terms possible.[3] The factors also cooperated with each other and exchanged information thus participating, for mutual benefit, in each other's networks.

The fiercely competitive climate in which trade with Europe was carried out in the empire, with İzmir being a competitive market *par excellence*, pitted one group of merchants against another and often followed national and confessional lines. There were nonetheless commercial interactions and other associations, even partnerships that cut across national lines as well as cooperation amongst merchants in different Ottoman ports. More than any other group, the Dutch, with their liberal policies, championed such cooperation. As a result British merchants established in İzmir had commercial relations with Dutch firms in Amsterdam and Rotterdam with whom they traded regularly. For instance, the İzmir house of Henry, John & Thomas March had a lively export trade with Muilman & Meulenaar of Amsterdam sending them, in Dutch ships, mohair yarn, sherbassi silk and carpets,[4] whilst the İzmir house of Allen & Shaw, cited above, traded with Pietro Antonio De Leopaul who were its correspondents in Amsterdam. The Dutch merchants,

---

[1]PRO, SP 105/207, *The Asia*, bound for London, İzmir, 28 Oct. 1721.

[2]*Ibid.*

[3]For more information on the factor/principal relationship, see Frangakis-Syrett, Elena, "Trading practices in Aleppo in the middle of the eighteenth century. The case of a British merchant", in: *Revue de Monde Musulman et de la Méditerranée*, LXII/4 (1991), pp. 123-124; see also, Davis, Ralph, *Aleppo and Devonshire Square. English Traders in the Levant in the Eighteenth Century*, London, 1976, *passim*.

[4]PRO, SP 105/207, The Dutch *Wendale*, bound for Amsterdam, İzmir, c. 1723.

too, as did the French, had extensive and interlocking commercial networks. For instance, de Vogel in Amsterdam was trading with İzmir through David van Lennep & Enslie, Clement van Saan and Fremeaux & Hopker.[1] David van Lennep also traded on his own account with the Netherlands. Van Lennep also acted as an agent in İzmir for a British house in Istanbul for whose account he sent to Amsterdam and Rotterdam goods, which were consigned to another British house there.[2] Moreover, Dutch merchant houses in Amsterdam or Rotterdam used British merchants in Ottoman ports as correspondents thus benefiting from the networks that the latter had established within the empire, in much the same way as merchant houses in London did when they traded with a number of factors in the Levant. At the same time, Dutch companies trading with the Levant had agents in several Dutch ports, thus multiplying their commercial contacts.[3]

Besides the Dutch, the liberal policies of the Italian ports also meant that all nationalities, including Ottoman merchants, could participate in their commercial networks. British houses in İzmir often had correspondents in the Italian ports. For example, Allen & Shaw of İzmir traded with the house of Marshall & Whitchurch in Livorno. Dutch houses also traded extensively with the Italian ports. For instance, the house of David van Lennep & Willem Enslie, which carried out a considerable part of the trade of İzmir with the Dutch market, also carried out a lively trade with Livorno, Venice and Marseilles; in the tradition of the Barkers, the house was also a merchant banker in İzmir of considerable scale.

The Dutch established long term associations not only with other Europeans but also with Ottoman merchants. This was an important factor for the participation of the latter in Ottoman-European external trade networks. For instance, in the 1760s, a member of the Ottoman Greek Cardamici family acted as agent in İzmir for the Amsterdam-based de Vogel house.[4] By the 1780s, there was the Istanbul-based commercial house of Raphael Cardamici & Son which was trading through a Dutch agent in Amsterdam. The Ottoman house was now directly participating in the external trade networks. The Istanbul house had also an agent in İzmir, Paolo Cardamici, who as part of his activities sent goods to Amsterdam on Dutch ships to the Dutch agent of his

---

[1]ARA, De Vogel, 21 Dec. 1762 to Jean Boilley in Nanninga, *Bronnen... 1726-1765, cit.*, pp. 477-478.
[2]PRO, SP 105/187, British Chancery, Istanbul, 30 April 1781.
[3]PRO, SP 105/187, British Chancery, Istanbul, 15 Feb. 1781.
[4]ARA, De Vogel, 19 Nov. 1762 to Bartholo Cardamici, İzmir, in: Nanninga, *Bronnen*... 1726-1765, *cit.*, p. 475.

employer, on account in part of the Istanbul house and in part of another house, the Brussels-based German house of Michel von Schoor & Fils.[1]

Moreover the Dutch, gave Ottoman merchants access not only to a major European commodities market but also to a financial one. Given the high degree of speculative monetary activities, that accompanied trading in commodities, this was important for many merchants-cum-bankers in the Levant, European and Ottoman, in the latter part of the 18th century. One of the reasons for the development of the Ottoman financial networks, which were in essence sophisticated networks of various forms of credit, including bills of exchange, was specie scarcity, which was a chronic phenomenon in the Ottoman economy. Specie scarcity, coupled with an open monetary system, where foreign currencies circulated side by side with Ottoman currency, led to an active trade in money — where money was treated as a commodity, and to extensive monetary speculative activities by all merchants in the Ottoman empire in the 18th century.[2]

As *entrepôts*, one of the functions of the Italian ports was to move money not only commodities in the Levant-western networks: they imported Ottoman goods for distribution to other European markets and sent to Ottoman ports, and particularly to İzmir, money.[3] For a number of reasons, such as the need for specie in an active commercial center, like İzmir, or the existence of efficient and competitive networks to move imported specie from the western Anatolian port to other Ottoman markets, at the height of the trade in money in the empire in the last decades of the 18th century, İzmir became the port of entry *par excellence*, attracting even more foreign specie than Istanbul. Although the Dutch were well represented in such activities,[4] the merchants who personified monetary speculative activities most are perhaps those of the merchant banking house of Roux Frères, owned by three generations of Roux family members. By the end of the 18th century, it was one of the most important commercial businesses in Marseilles. It had a truly global network of correspondents and agents that encompassed a large number of Ottoman and Italian ports, as well as Dutch ports, with İzmir being an important center of their operations which included, besides trading in commodities, speculating in the currency markets and in bills of exchange. Its

[1]PRO, SP 105/187, British Chancery, Istanbul, 1 June 1781. I would like to thank Mr. Maurits van den Boogert for drawing my attention to this reference.

[2]ACCM, LIX/741, Garavaque et Cusson, İzmir, 20 March 1767 to Roux-Frères, Marseilles.

[3]ANF, Marine B/7, French Consul Benincasa, 30 July 1782 in Commerce des ports de l'Europe, 1 Feb. 1783; see also, ANF, AE Biii 241, Observations sur l'échelle de Smyrne, 1779.

[4]ANF F/12 549-550, Mémoire sur le commerce du Levant, 1777.

correspondents in Trieste, Ancona or Amsterdam often bought bills of exchange underwritten by Ottoman merchants with whom they cooperated in other ways in the course of their speculative monetary activities, in the process linking İzmir with a number of financial markets in Europe and within the empire.[1]

From the above, it thus becomes apparent how the commercial networks were able to make effective use of maritime routes and link Ottoman and European markets together, as well as Ottoman markets with each other, for the successful flow of goods, money and ideas, in the process creating an open, competitive and economically vibrant Ottoman maritime world. It was a world where Ottoman charterers and European captains, Ottoman producers and European exporters, Ottoman and European merchant bankers, all came into contact with each other for the purposes of trade either in complimentary business transactions or in partnerships or in bitter rivalry. Whilst individually they may have competed with each other, as groups, both the Europeans and the Ottomans, formed elaborate and strikingly similar commercial networks of kinship and interlocking partnerships. Not surprisingly such networks also cut across national and confessional lines bringing Ottomans and Europeans together, bound by the common objective of profit.

What led to the formation of these networks and made the maritime routes flourish was the considerable growth of Ottoman-European trade in the 18th century and the way that such growth not only linked Ottoman and European markets together, but also strengthened existing links amongst Ottoman maritime markets. When İzmir emerged as the most important port in the trade of the Ottoman empire with Europe, it did so as a *plaque tournante* within the Ottoman-European commercial world, able not only to attract the most extensive commercial networks from the West but also to command those within the empire. Moreover, İzmir's position within the commercial networks was complimented by its command of the maritime routes both within the Ottoman and the Ottoman-European commercial world. At the same time, the emergence of İzmir did not stifle the rest of the Ottoman maritime world, but rather added to its vibrancy. İzmir contributed to the trading activity and importance of the Istanbul-İzmir-Alexandria route, the principal route and hub of the Ottoman maritime world through which so many other markets and routes were connected. By distributing its monetary surplus from Europe to these two cities, İzmir also responded to the economic needs of the empire.

---

[1] *E.g.*, ACCM, LIX/750, Denis Rolland & Cie, İzmir, 19 March 1790 to Roux Frères, Marseilles.

TRADE BETWEEN THE OTTOMAN EMPIRE AND WESTERN EUROPE: THE CASE OF İZMİR IN THE EIGHTEENTH CENTURY

The main objectives of this article are to delineate the economic activities of the port of İzmir in the eighteenth century and to show that İzmir, during the course of the century, developed into the most important port in the import and export trade of the Ottoman Empire with western Europe. The French, operating out of Marseilles, were the principal trading partners of both İzmir and the Ottoman Empire at the time.[1] Among the other most important western European communities that did business in İzmir were the British and the Dutch.[2] İzmir was also the center of complex and diverse financial transactions that were as important as trade and sometimes even more. Furthermore, this study shows the key role that non-Muslims played in the economic activities of the city-port. İzmir's close commercial relations with major western European economic centers makes the city-port of great importance for the study of Ottoman economic history in the eighteenth century.

Since the early seventeenth century, İzmir emerged as an international port in the trade of the Ottoman Empire with western Europe. The discovery of the new trade routes, which led, among other things, to the decline of its erstwhile rival, the island of Chios, and the establishment of western European mercantile communities in İzmir at the same time helped the city-port establish its international trading links (Goffman, 1985, pp. 177-204). The taking over of the Persian silk trade from Aleppo was also important for the port's commercial growth, for high quality Persian silk was greatly sought after in the luxury silk industries of western Europe (D'Arvieux, 1735, vol. 1, pp. 307-308). Also the Persian market absorbed a fair amount of western European cloth and other manufactured goods. Finally, the availability of good quality cotton in İzmir's immediate hinterland (Goffman, 1985, pp. 205-301) and the port's proximity to an important mohair yarn producing area, Ankara

---

[1]For relevant data, see Archives du Chambre du Commerce de Marseille, Marseilles; Archives Nationales de France, Paris and Archives du Ministère des Affaires Étrangères, Paris.
[2]For relevant data for the British, see the Archives of the Levant Company, Public Record Office, London; for the Dutch, see Nanninga (1952, 1966).

(Tancoigne, 1820, p. 19), gave the city-port two other highly-marketable commodities with which to attract Western merchants.

As trade increased between the Ottoman Empire and the West, during the course of the eighteenth century, and particularly in the second half of the century, İzmir emerged as the biggest and most important port of the empire in its European trade. The ports of Egypt, Syria, and the islands of the Aegean Archipelago, which had an active trade with the West in the beginning of the eighteenth century, were surpassed by İzmir during the course of the century. In the case of the Egyptian and Syrian ports, lack of security in their hinterland greatly hampered their ability to collect goods for export to Europe. In the case of the Aegean Islands, the limited amount of wheat and olive oil that they produced[1] could not meet the increase in volume and diversity that developed in the trade between the empire and the West. The growth in the manufacturing sector in western Europe called for raw materials used in the production of textiles and for a market to sell its finished produce; it was on this need, mainly, that trade between western Europe and the Ottoman Empire developed.[2]

İzmir was able to export such raw materials in sufficient quantities and varieties to meet demand in the international market. Between 1700 and 1745, İzmir exported 20 percent of all Ottoman exports to France, which was the biggest trading partner of the empire, and between 1745 and 1789, 34 percent.[3] No other port in the empire was able to rival it. For instance, from 1776 to 1779 and from 1786 to 1789, Salonica exported 14 and 7.6 percent of all Ottoman exports to France, whilst İzmir exported 40 and 38.3 percent, respectively (Frangakis, 1985a, p. 311). At the same time, the largest share — 30 percent — of Ottoman imports from France were shipped to İzmir.[4] For instance, from 1776 to 1779 and from 1786 to 1789, Istanbul, its principal rival, imported 19.8 and 26 percent of all Ottoman imports from France, whilst İzmir imported 34.2 and 31 percent, respectively (Frangakis, 1985a, p. 312). From the mid-1740s onwards, İzmir exported to the West and imported into the empire the greatest amount of goods, in value. In fact, the

[1]Archives Nationales de France, Paris, Série AE Bi 1043, Tableau des marchandises qui ont été importéess et exportées de Smyrne à Marseille pendant l'année 1734. Hereafter this archive will be cited as ANF.

[2]Cloth represented almost half of İzmir's imports from western Europe, sometimes more, whilst raw materials for the textile industry made up three quarters of the port's exports to the West.

[3]Archives de la Chambre de Commerce de Marseille, Marseilles, Série I, 26-28, États des marchandises venant du Levant et de Barbarie, 1700-1789. Hereafter this archive will be cited as ACCM.

[4]ACCM, I, 19-20, États des marchandises envoyées en Levant et Barbarie, 1749-1789. No comparable data exists for the years 1700 to 1748.

ability of İzmir to become the outlet of a large proportion of Ottoman agricultural production, and of Persian goods, and to distribute deep into Anatolia, and further East, its western European imports made it into not only the port with the most extensive trade with Europe but also with the biggest trade network inside the empire.[1] Despite a record of peaceful co-existence between western Europeans, non-Muslims,[2] and Muslims İzmir fell prey to the wave of anti-Christian feeling that swept the empire during the closing decades of the eighteenth century. Twice, in 1774 and in 1797, the non-Muslim population of İzmir, as well as the European population, were subject to attack.[3] (Peyssonnel, 1785, pp. 78-80). For the rest of the time, however, there existed a tolerance and a working relationship between the local inhabitants, the city authorities, and the European merchants which contributed to the growth of the European community in the city and led to the cosmopolitan flavor that characterized İzmir, and earned it, in the nineteenth century, the name of gavur İzmir (Deschamps, 1894, p. 115).

İzmir's extensive hinterland and good trade network assured the European merchants of a return cargo in a relatively short time which was one reason why merchants in Marseilles often sent their goods to İzmir.[4] Also, shippers, who could be guaranteed a return cargo to Europe, charged less for carrying goods to the Levant.[5] Nevertheless, environmental hazards, such as epidemics, and in particular plague, either in the city or in its hinterland, earthquakes and fires disrupted the flow of goods in and out of the city and contributed to the, at times, volatile nature of the market of İzmir. (Tavernier, 1712, vol. I, p. 107; Sonnini, 1811, vol. II, p. 338; Comte de Choiseul Gouffier, 1842, vol. II, p. 342).[6]

---

[1]ANF, AE Biii 243, Félix de Beaujour, Inspection générale du Levant, İzmir, 5 June 1817.

[2]The principal non-Muslim communities of İzmir were the Jewish, Armenian, and Greek communities.

[3]Public Record Office, London, Series SP 105/126, Consul Werry, İzmir, 17 March 1797 to Levant Company, London. Hereafter this archive will be cited as PRO.

[4]ANF, AE Bi 1052, Consul Peyssonnel, İzmir, 29 January 1749 to Minister, Paris.

[5]There were always ships that left İzmir empty and cruised along the western Anatolian coast picking up cargo along the route and carrying it to ports in the eastern Mediterranean. Yet, it may well have been the lucrative nature of such an enterprise that prompted French captains, in particular, to such a venture. See ANF, AE Bi 1013, Consul Jouvin, Chios, 15 May 1763 to Minister, Paris.

[6]ANF, AE Bi 1061, Consul Peyssonnel, İzmir, 12 December 1772 to Minister, Paris.

Ottoman and European Merchants

From the beginning of the century and until the 1780s Western merchants, established in İzmir, imported European and colonial goods and sold them in the city's market; they also bought and sent to Europe Ottoman goods. Transfer of goods to and from İzmir was done in Western ships; goods were insured by Western capital. (Nanninga, 1952, pp. 477-478). These merchants, armed with the Capitulations,[1] had both the right to trade in the Ottoman dominions and certain privileges over and above the local merchants. These rights were not always extended to the Ottoman merchants, who could not trade with Britain or France in a reciprocal manner until the 1780s. Exceptions to this were times of war or a clandestine co-operation between a western European and an Ottoman merchant. At the same time Ottoman merchants in İzmir, and particularly the non-Muslim merchants, became the middlemen through whose hands most of the trade transactions between Western merchants and Ottoman producers passed. This was not the rule everywhere in the eastern Mediterranean, at the time, but only in large urban cities such as İzmir, Aleppo or Istanbul.[2] It had not been so in İzmir either, before the eighteenth century (Goffman, 1985), pp. 205, 304). So if the Western merchants, largely, dominated İzmir's trade with western Europe, the non-Muslim merchants, on the whole, dominated the trade between the Western merchants and the Ottoman, Muslim and non-Muslim, purchasers, sellers, and producers. Ottoman merchants also conducted İzmir's trade with the rest of the Ottoman Empire and the East, carrying goods on caravan routes overland. Until the 1780s European merchants virtually controlled all carrying trade by sea both between İzmir and eastern Mediterranean ports, and İzmir and western European ports. Yet it would be misleading to see the Western merchants, despite their favorable legal position and, on the whole, stronger economies and currencies, as all-powerful in their trade transactions with the Ottoman merchants. One of the problems that the French merchants faced was their frequent shortage of cash and the fact that they could not afford to wait for the prices to drop or for other favorable conditions to appear in the market of İzmir.[3] Ottoman merchants, and non-Muslims in particular, were able to turn these factors to their advantage, extending credit in money or in kind to the French, and in using their knowledge of the market and expertise to act as the Westerners' brokers. The strong competition that existed, not only

---

[1]These were trade agreements made between the Sultan and a western European power which discriminated in favour of the Western marchants. Sometimes they were an 'exchange' for diplomatic or political support given to the Sultan by the European power concerned.

[2]ANF, AE Biii 242, Jumelin, Commerce du Levant en général, 16 December 1812.

[3]ANF, AE Bi 1052, Consul Peyssonnel, İzmir, 29 January 1749 to Minister, Paris.

amongst the various European mercantile communities but within a mercantile community itself often led to the merchants underselling each other. They thus suffered considerable losses and even undermined their position vis-à-vis the Ottoman merchants.[1] Of course competition, at times detrimental, also existed for the Ottomans, either as merchants or as brokers. Usury was rife, but borrowing at extremely usurious rates could be very risky for small European and Ottoman commercial houses. If a European merchant defaulted on his loans, his creditors might be unable to pay their debts which would result in still more defaults.[2] Bankruptcy could also be practically forced upon a European merchant through the bankruptcy of his Ottoman broker, who most likely had not only speculated his own assets but a large part of his principal's assets, too.[3] Equally a chain of bankruptcies among Ottoman brokers, who were usually Jewish, Armenian or Greek, could adversely affect the Europeans' trade (Panzac, 1985, p. 396). Economic crises in the European markets could cause defaults in İzmir, too.

The Trade of İzmir and Marseilles

Throughout the eighteenth century, Marseilles suffered from such a series of economic crises: its economy, interrupted by war, usually over-expanded at the end of it, and had thereafter to re-contract in order to adjust itself to a more realistic level of economic activity. Such was the crisis of 1715, at the aftermath of the War of the Spanish Succession, (1701-1714), with defaults in both Marseilles and İzmir (Carrière, 1973, vol. I, pp. 432-440). When such difficulties were compounded by adverse conditions in İzmir, such as those caused by a plague epidemic, the effects on the İzmir-Marseilles trade were quite disastrous. From 1758 to 1762, the trade between Marseilles and the Ottoman Empire as a whole, though to a lesser extent between Marseilles and İzmir, took a plunge as a result of a serious two-year plague epidemic and the continuing Seven Years' War (1756-1763). During that conflict, the British had wiped out the French navy and its merchant marine and deprived it of its colonies, thus forcing an almost complete halt to French trade in the Mediterranean. Not surprisingly, no exports from İzmir reached Marseilles by sea in 1757 and in 1758 French imports from İzmir and exports to the Ottoman port had reached an all-time low.[4] Yet trade between the two

[1]ANF, AE Bi 1045, Consul Peleran, İzmir, 28 February 1732 to Minister, Paris.
[2]ANF, AE Bi 1063, Consul Peyssonnel, İzmir, 9 June 1777 to Minister, Paris.
[3]ANF, AE Bi 1052, Consul Peyssonnel, İzmir, 5 March 1749 to Minister, Paris.
[4]ANF, AE Biii 271, Tableau des marchandises qui ont été importées et exportées de Smyrne à Marseille pendant l'année 1758.

ports quickly recovered and actually increased between 1759 and 1763. One possible explanation was the rapid growth of the two economies at the time. Restricted monetary supply resulted in the acute economic crisis in 1774 that affected not only Marseilles but the rest of Europe, too, and caused the considerable drop in the exports of İzmir in 1775.[1] The shortage of specie in Marseilles had led brokers (who were also lending to merchants as unofficial bankers), to speculate on bills of exchange and other monetary instruments since the 1760s. By 1774, the brokers had been issuing more bills than they could cover, so the crisis erupted.

Wars affected adversely the trade of İzmir. Ottoman-Persian wars in the East, in the first half of the eighteenth century, affected its caravan trade negatively and Ottoman-European or inter-European wars, throughout the century, affected its shipping routes equally negatively. The high costs and risks in transporting goods between İzmir and western Europe during wartime contributed, to a large extent, to the fluctuations in the imports and exports of İzmir. Some of the wars, as for instance the recurring wars that the Ottoman Empire fought against Russia and Austria, in 1768 to 1774 and in 1787 to 1792, were particularly strenuous to the Ottoman economy resulting in fiscal crises and depressing the purchasing power of the peasants through overtaxation and inflation.

Some wars, however, were beneficial for the growth of the city's economy. Wars such as the Seven Years' War (1756-1763) or the long sequence of the French Revolutionary (1792-1801) and Napoleonic Wars (1803-1815) were more strenuous to France than they were to İzmir.[2] The Seven Years' War resulted in the first serious challenge by other trading nations to French supremacy in İzmir's trade with the West.[3] After 1763, partly as a result of the war, French cloth no longer dominated the cloth trade in İzmir. Even more detrimental to the French economy were the later wars.

Nevertheless the French dominated the Ottoman Empire's trade with western Europe from the second decade in the eighteenth century right until the French Revolution. Whilst İzmir became the most important port in the trade of the empire with western Europe, the French became the most important European mercantile community in İzmir. In fact, the growth of

---

[1]ANF, AE Biii 241, Mémoire sur l'argent, Marseilles, 1775.
[2]ANF, AE Biii 243, Miège, Renseignements sur le commerce du Levant, Livorno, 13 May, 1825.
[3]ANF, AE Biii 271, États des batiments, 1756-1763.

Ottoman-French trade in the eighteenth century broadly reflects the rise of İzmir commercially. However, when French trade started to decline, with the outbreak of the French Revolution and the events that followed it, İzmir continued to grow commercially and to dominate the Ottoman Empire's trade with the West during the early decades of the nineteenth century.[1]

The British and Dutch Merchants; the Italian Ports

Although in the first decades of the eighteenth century the British had a better organized trade than the French in İzmir, thereafter they became more interested in their colonies, both as sources for raw materials and as markets for their goods. As a result, British trading activities in İzmir were second to the French. This changed in the last quarter of the eighteenth century. British cloth started to compete with French cloth successfully since the 1770s,[2] and replaced French cloth altogether a decade or so later.[3] By early nineteenth century, Britain became İzmir's principal trading partner and British cloth filled the Ottoman port's market (Cunningham, 1983, p. 21).

The Dutch were the third major western European trading community in İzmir in the eighteenth century. Contrary to the strongly protectionist policies of their British and French rivals, the Dutch were the first to put into practice a liberal state policy that allowed Ottoman merchants in İzmir to trade with Holland directly or to establish their own commercial houses in the Dutch ports. This was important for the process of capital accumulation of the non-Muslim mercantile communities, in particular, who took advantage of the opportunities offered to participate in the Dutch Levant trade during the second half of the eighteenth century. (Nanninga, 1952, pp. 715-763; *ibid.*, 1966, pp. 339-341, 1428-1466).

Equally important in this respect, and perhaps even more so for the late eighteenth century, were the Italian ports of Livorno, Messina, Trieste, Ancôna, and Venice. These ports had been trading outposts for non-Muslim merchants trading with the Levant since the seventeenth century or even earlier. (Macler, 1904, pp. 8-16).[4] Unlike London or Marseilles, the Italian ports had no regulations prohibiting foreigners from trading in their ports. In

[1]ANF, AE Biii 243, Félix de Beaujour, Inspection générale du Levant, İzmir, 5 June 1817.
[2]ANF, AE Biii 415, Amoureux, Mémoire sur le commerce d'importation à Smirne du produit des manufactures de plusieures nations étrangères, İzmir, 7 May 1781.
[3]ANF, AE Biii 242, Fourcade, Mémoire sur le commerce de Smyrne, c. 1820.
[4]ANF, AE Biii 235, Commerce de Levant, 1693.

fact, they actively encouraged it.[1] Moreover, during peacetime these ports, and particularly Livorno, became the centers of clandestine trade from British and French merchants who, ignoring their countries' monopolistic policies, co-operated with Jewish, Armenian or Greek merchants in order to carry out profitably a trade with the Levant. From there, they either sent goods to non-Muslims and Muslims in İzmir,[2] or used the Italian ports as entrepots in order to send goods from western Europe to non-Muslims established there.

At times of war amongst the major European Powers, the Italian ports became the main entrepots in İzmir's trade with western Europe. For instance, when the Dutch ports were closed by the British navy in 1781-1782, during the final years of the American War for Independence, Dutch trade had to follow an overland route to Trieste, only thereafter reaching İzmir by sea. Conversely, İzmir sent goods to Trieste by sea, and thereafter to Holland, the Holy Roman Empire or Switzerland by land (the latter two were supplied with Levantine goods by the Dutch). In this instance Greek merchants, established in Trieste, and active in the Dutch trade also, were the principal beneficiaries of this re-direction of the Dutch Levant trade.[3] It was during the period of the French Revolutionary (1792-1801) and Napoleonic wars (1803-1815), when the Italian ports acquired their greatest significance in İzmir's Western trade, that they contributed most towards the economic growth of the city-port's non-Muslim communities.

The period from the American War for Independence to the end of the Napoleonic Wars, which coincided with an expansionary phase in the world economy and the beginnings of the Industrial Revolution in Britain, was particularly significant for İzmir's economic growth. The growing needs of western Europe, and particularly of Britain, for raw materials and markets for their finished products led to the spectacular growth in İzmir's trade with the West. At the same time, the French Revolution of 1789, and the events that followed, broke the dominance of the French in İzmir leaving a gap in the city-port's trade with the West, which could not be filled by the British until the end of the Napoleonic Wars, thus allowing the non-Muslim merchants, in particular, to step in. Furthermore, their military confrontation forced Britain and France to open up their İzmir trade to non-nationals at a time when free

[1]ANF, AE Bi 859, Consul l'Allement, Messina, 22 May 1784 to Minister, Paris.
[2]PRO, SP 105/115, Levant Company, London, 21 June 1699 to Consul Raye, İzmir.
[3]ANF, Série Marine B/7, 446 Bertrand, 19 Oct 1782 in Commerce des ports de l'Europe.

trade was increasingly becoming an economic need but was not yet an established state policy.[1]

Between 1792 and 1815, whilst Marseilles was, for most of the time, blockaded by the British navy, Livorno, Genoa, Trieste, and Ancôna became the principal entrepots for İzmir's trade with France, the Holy Roman Empire,[2] Flanders, Switzerland, and Holland.[3] The principal loser was Marseilles whose considerable trade with İzmir was taken over by the Italian ports and the French merchants who saw this trade pass into the hands of non-Muslims, mainly, as well as of the British and, as far as the maritime carrying trade was concerned, of the Americans also (Perkins, 1969, pp. 70-79). British naval presence in the Mediterranean during this period, and particularly during the Continental System (1806-1814), ensured that French goods or the goods of France's allies carried anywhere in the Mediterranean would probably be seized. So that any trade that took place between İzmir and the Italian ports or any French, French-allied, or French-controlled ports was either over a land route or, if by sea, at the sufferance of the British. This, of course, helped enormously the neutral Ottoman non-Muslim merchants, who started carrying goods between İzmir and the Italian ports, or even between the Italian ports and Marseilles,[4] armed with licenses, issued by the British, that covered them from capture by either side of the conflict. It was either as privateers, or even as pirates, that these merchants, who were usually Greek, raised the initial capital for legitimate, even though risky, ventures into the carrying trade. These ventures, when successful, were particularly lucrative — due to the exorbitant wartime freight rates charged — allowing progress to be made to the next stage of operation, the setting-up of commercial houses not only in the Italian ports,[5] but also in Marseilles, Vienna, Odessa, and finally London, from where they took an active part in the international trade of İzmir (Herlihy, 1979-1980, pp. 399-420; Échinard, 1973, pp. 62-69; Robson, 1841, p. 825; Katsiardi-Hering, 1986).

[1]ANF, AE Biii 242, Sur l'article de l'ordonnance du 20 Sept. 1810, Commerce du Levant, 28 Sept. 1814; and, PRO, SP 105/121, Consul Werry, İzmir, 30 June 1797 to Levant Company, London.

[2]The Holy Roman Empire formally ceased to exist on 12 July 1806 and on 25 July 1806 the Confederation of the Rhine was declared (Chandler, 1966, p. 449).

[3]ANF, AE Biii 242, Miège, Renseignements sur le commerce du Levant, Livorno, 13 May 1825.

[4]ANF, AE Bi 859, Consul l'Allement, Messina, 9 February 1782 to Minister, Paris.

[5]ANF, AE Bi 859, Consul l'Allement, Messina, 20 March 1784 to Minister, Paris.

Exports and Imports

Throughout the eighteenth century, all the principal exports and imports of İzmir were linked to the western European textile industry, and developments in the latter affected the city's economy greatly. Silk, mohair yarn, and wool were the principal exports of İzmir in the first half of the eighteenth century with cotton exports picking up in the second quarter. The first two goods were produced outside the immediate hinterland of İzmir and had to be brought into the city with all the risks and additional costs that caravan transportation entailed at that time. As a result, only a certain amount of produce could be sold in the market of İzmir. Both silk and mohair industries were luxury textile industries in the West at the time and, thus, needed limited amounts of raw materials.

This was not the case with the cotton textile industry and demand for cotton grew increasingly, especially in the second half of the eighteenth century, following the expansion of the world economy. İzmir was able to meet this growing demand for cotton (Bowring, 1810) with increasingly greater exports. For instance, the index in the volume of cotton exports from İzmir to Marseilles rose from 100 in 1700, to 1,041 percent in 1760 and to 12,400 percent in 1788 (Frangakis, 1985a, p. 264). As cotton was the principal export of İzmir at the time and as this coincided with a period of spectacular growth in İzmir's trade with western Europe, leading to a take off in the city's economy, cotton was an important factor in this growth. Only a severe attack of plague in the environs of İzmir, or a prolonged armed conflict in the outskirts of the city, such as the Sarıbeyoğlu incident in 1738, could severely affect the transportation of cotton to the city (Pococke, 1772, vol. 5, p. 19). Although severe plagues were more frequent than social disturbances (Panzac, 1985),[1] exports increased in response to the increase in international demand. French merchants, in fact, used cotton as a staple which they could exchange for the cloth.[2] Specie was scarce in both the Ottoman and the French economies throughout the eighteenth century and barter was a popular medium

[1]On the short-term, plague constituted a menace to the smooth running of the city's economic activities thus making an already fragile economic situation worse. It took as much as two years sometimes for the full effect of a disruption, due to plague, to be felt on the export of cotton and on the import of cloth as these two sectors were interlinked. On the long-term, plague was most devastating on the demography of the city which fluctuated throughout the century but never surpassed the level of 100,000 despite the fact that İzmir, as a large and prosperous urban center, continuously attracted people from the countryside.

[2]ACCM, MQ, 5.1, Mémoire presenté à Monsieur le Consul général de France à Smyrne par les députés du commerce français, İzmir, 22 July 1820.

of exchange of the Ottoman Empire.[1] Wool maintained a prominent position among İzmir's exports, though usually coming after silk and mohair yarn in the first half of the century, and after cotton and cotton yarn in the second half. İzmir exported both dyed and natural cotton yarn. Although exports of cotton far exceeded those of cotton yarn, the latter was particularly popular in the last decades of the century as shown by the increase in its price.

Concerning price changes[2] the following points should be made. Firstly, similar price patterns existed in other major Ottoman ports that traded with western Europe, such as Salonica (Svoronos, 1956, pp. 75-91). Secondly, these price changes may well have corresponded to the high rate of depreciation of the Ottoman coin *vis-à-vis* the European currencies at the time.[3] Also, price increases in Ottoman currency were often substantially reduced in the international market, due to the high rate of depreciation of the Ottoman coin vis-à-vis the European currencies (Frangakis, 1985a, pp. 267-269, 273-274, 279-280). Prices were of course affected by supply and demand in the market of İzmir as well as by other incidental factors such as plague or war. Thirdly, developments in world prices may well account for some of these price variations. However, with the information available at present, it is difficult, if not impossible, to ascertain this.

The growth of trade of İzmir can best be seen from the trade between İzmir and Marseilles, which accounted for more than half of the trade of the Levantine port with western Europe, and for which we have the most complete data. Exports to Marseilles, in French currency, for the period 1700-1750, did not increase much, although actual trade figures in 1750 were double those in 1700. In fact, during the first quarter of the century, exports fell in value, whilst in the second quarter, they rose slightly. In the third quarter of the century, however, trade trebled in relation to the previous twenty-five years. During the closing decades of the century, 1775-1789, trade rose one and-a-half times in relation to the previous quarter. In the second half of the century, 1750-1789, trade for the average year was four times that in the first half of the century. However, part of the increase in the value of exports in the second half of the century was due to increasing prices at least for certain goods. The biggest increase in a price index in French currency for Ottoman exports occurred from the 1750s to the 1770s.

[1]Such practices survived well into the nineteenth century, see, *Parliamentary Papers, Tariffs*, vol. 2 (London, 1843), p. 98.

[2]ACCM, I, 28; ANF, AE Bi 1065-1066; AE Biii 269-277, États des merchandises qui ont été transportées de Smyrne à Marseille, 1776-1789.

[3]For data on the rate of depreciation of the Ottoman coin, see N. Svoronos, 1956, p. 82 and V. Kremmydas, 1972, pp. 116-117.

Between 1749 and 1775, imports in French currency, from Marseilles into İzmir rose in value by more than one and-a-half times and again at the same rate in the years 1776 to 1789, though falling slightly in the final years before the French Revolution. As the prices of imports increased, on the whole, less than did those of exports, the rise in the value of imported goods also signified a corresponding rise in the volume, and although İzmir's favorable balance of trade may seem to belie it, imports may have increased more than exports (Frangakis, 1985b, pp. 155-157). Prices of imports remained constant in the decades 1749 to 1769 increasing, on the whole, thereafter.

Speculation

Other factors as important for the economic growth of İzmir as the trade in goods were activities such as banking and monetary speculation that took place in the city-port, particularly in the second half of the eighteenth century, following increasing inflation and depreciation of the Ottoman coin. Profits derived from such activities, including usury, were sometimes extremely lucrative and contributed to local capital accumulation.

In the first half of the eighteenth century, the rate of depreciation of the Ottoman piastre vis-à-vis the European currencies was limited and smaller than the rise in the prices of İzmir's exports. In the second half of the century, an increasing technological gap with the West in a number of spheres, political instability, continuous and unsuccessful wars, and a chronic monetary shortage, coupled with an at times arbitrary fiscal policy on the part of the Sultan, contributed to a rapid rate of depreciation of the Ottoman coin (Kremmydas, 1972, p. 116). This increased further as the century drew to a close. There was also considerable inflation: in the last decade of the century, in fact, there was an estimated seven-fold increase in the prices of necessities of life such as food and rent.[1] Market mechanisms that aimed at discounting prices,[2] such as *agio*,[3] extended credit,[4] or barter[5] were continuously imposed

[1]PRO, SP 105/126, British Factory, İzmir, 15 January 1798 to Levant Company, London; see also, SP 105/127, British Factory and Consul Werry, İzmir, 17 September 1799 to Levant Company, London. The term 'factory', current at the time, denotes the British mercantile community in İzmir.

[2]ACCM, I, 19-20, 26-28; ANF, AE Bi 1065-1066; AE Biii 269-277, États des merchandises qui ont été transportées de Smyrne à Marseille, 1700-1789; and États des marchandises qui ont été transportées de Marseille à Smyrne.

[3]ANF, AE Bi 1058, Consul Peyssonnel, Éclaircissements sur la supputation qui a été faite du prix des Londrins Seconds de Carcassonne à Smyrne, İzmir, 20 November 1767.

[4]ACCM, MQ, 5.1, Agreement proposed by the deputies of the western European and Greek cloth importers to the union of Greek and Armenian shopkeepers and to the Jewish community, İzmir, 5 September 1820 (in French).

[5]PRO, SP 105/336, British Factory, İzmir, 16 September 1754 to Levant Company, London.

on the prices of imported goods. Although they reduced the Europeans' profits, at times they constituted the only way to do trading in İzmir.

An unstable economic condition and a weak currency led to endless speculation with lucrative results for those practicing it, though potentially bad for the economy itself. In fact, throughout the eighteenth century, trade in money and monetary speculation went hand in hand with trade in goods. Until the 1780s, trade in money, either specie or bullion, and treated as merchandise, was, on the whole, in the hands of the European merchants, who brought it into İzmir on board their own ships.[1] When there was an acute shortage of specie in Marseilles, the French merchants there imported money from İzmir (Frangakis, 1985a, pp. 134-135). When money was in short supply in İzmir (which, towards the end of the century, was usually the case) the French, and other Europeans, exported specie there. Both European and Ottoman merchants dealt in bills of exchange remitting to and drawing money from the market of İzmir — Ottoman participation in this sector was estimated to be as much as 50 percent (Eldem, 1986, p. 97).

İzmir was also the center of banking activities for a large area of Anatolia including Bursa, Ankara, the Aegean Islands, and Crete. For example, olive oil and wheat were ordinarily purchased in the Aegean Islands but were paid for with bills of exchange drawn upon Marseilles, London, Amsterdam and other financial centers (Paris, 1957, p. 453).[2] There was nothing innovative in using bills of exchange which had been thus used since the seventeenth century (Eldem, 1986, p. 87). From the second half of the eighteenth century, however, merchants widely used bills of exchange for speculation: that is, moving bills of exchange from one place to another, within Europe and the eastern Mediterranean, including İzmir, in order to profit from the differences in the rates of exchange. Besides, the number of circulating bills of exchange in a given economic market, which *arbitrageurs* carefully manipulated, affected the rate of exchange. Furthermore, a merchant in İzmir did not buy a bill of exchange unless it was discounted, so that by selling it either at face value or above the discount level he realized a profit. Conversely, the seller did not give a discount unless it was less than the cost of transferring specie to that place. Profitability of a bill of exchange issued in a certain specie, varied according to the relative scarcity or abundance of that specie in the market of İzmir (Carrière, et al., 1976, pp. 107-109, 137-139). Certain market mechanisms developed to bring some order to the market in

[1]ANF, F/12, 549-550, Mémoire sur le commerce du Levant, 1777.
[2]ANF, AE Bi 1053, Consul Peyssonnel, Mémoire, İzmir, 22 Nov. 1751.

İzmir, for speculation feeding on political instability and fiscal crises could, at times, render the financial situation in the city-port, chaotic. Such a mechanism was the *agio* (also called a discount or un *bénéfice*) which was used to avoid losses on the continuously variable exchange rates between the Ottoman piastre and the European currencies. The *agio* was calculated on the basis of the real, not the nominal, rate of exchange between the Ottoman piastre and Venetian sequin and was then applied to the rate of exchange between the Ottoman coin and other European currencies (Svoronos, 1956, pp. 82-83). For instance, the French kept the same rate of exchange between the livre tournois and the Ottoman piastre despite the fact that the latter had depreciated considerably in value. They were able to do this because the *agio* adjusted the difference in the exchange rate between the two by adding or subtracting an amount equivalent to the fluctuations in the real value of the Ottoman currency (Rebuffat and Courdurié, 1966, p. 150). Applying the *agio* to the rate of exchange in such a way as to favor the Ottoman currency vis-à-vis the foreign currencies, by as much as 10 percent, was one way of attracting business to İzmir. Whenever the *agio* was totally suspended — as it happened in 1758 when European merchants considered it too onerous for their business and hence suspended it — Ottoman merchants moved to another Ottoman city to trade and İzmir lost capital and business.[1]

There were many reasons, other than lack of *agio,* which led to monetary shortages in the market of İzmir and hence to speculation. One such reason was the plague which sometimes forced European and Ottoman moneylenders and money changers to flee the city or to stay at home for as much as a month or more, which paralyzed business and stopped all capital from circulating[2] (Panzac, 1985, pp. 396-397). Other reasons were continuous remittances to Istanbul for the needs of the Treasury; direct over-taxation by the state for extraordinary military expenditure; remittances to the East for Indian cloth and spices and, at the end of the century, to the west, Malta in particular, for British cloth. When the money supply was particularly low and increases in the rates of exchange for foreign currencies were not attracting money to İzmir fast enough, trade relied heavily on barter and credit. The disadvantages of barter, which revealed the need for banking institutions, were evident but extending credit was even more risky. Lack of specie could also lead to frantic, and sometimes uncontrolled or speculative, use of promissory notes. Finally, any worsening of the supply and circulation of capital in the

---

[1]ANF, AE Bi 1057, Consul Peyssonnel, Précis du mémoire que la nation a envoyé à la Chambre de Commerce pour servir d'éclaircissement au système qu'elle a adopté en faveur de l'agio sur les éspèces, İzmir, 29 April 1769.

[2]PRO, SP 105/127, Consul Werry, İzmir, 17 June 1800 to Levant Company, London.

market of İzmir had as result the increase in usury, which added more hardship to the ordinary man and petty producer.

Conclusion

As a postscript to an eighteenth century study of İzmir's commercial relations with western Europe it would be worthwhile to look, briefly, at the early decades of the nineteenth century, which was an important period in İzmir's further economic development. Apart from the rise to commercial prominence of the non-Muslim communities (though, of course, Muslim merchants and landowners also prospered), certain other changes took place in the city's economy at that time. The invention of the cotton gin by Eli Whitney in 1793 increased cotton production in the United States spectacularly, which cut very deeply into İzmir's share of the European cotton market. By 1820, French merchants unable to import considerable amounts of western Anatolian cotton into Marseilles, as before, were left without an important product to barter for their cloth within İzmir.[1] Furthermore, instead of exporting cotton yarn, İzmir started to import it.[2] Its principal exports, on the whole, changed: foodstuffs became its primary exports (raisins, figs, dried fruit, and wheat). By the 1830s, İzmir was also importing a whole new array of goods, mainly consumer goods,[3] indicating a considerable expansion in its internal market, itself a result of the tremendous growth of its urban sector. It also started to grow demographically as plague epidemics ceased after 1837 (Biraben, 1975, vol. 2, pp. 430-449; Iconomos, 1868, p. 138). British capital, its principal trading partner in the first decades of the nineteenth century, penetrated into western Anatolia in ways that French capital, less dynamic and enveloping than the British, had never done. In so doing British capital helped integrate İzmir's economy further into the international market and the world economy (Kasaba, 1987).

---

[1]ACCM, MQ, 5.1, Mémoire presenté à Monsieur le Consul Général de France à Smyrne par les députés du commerce français, İzmir, 22 July 1820.

[2]Archives du Ministère des Affaires Étrangères, Paris, Série CCC, Vol. 35, Tableau des marchandises qui ont été exportées et importées de Smyrne en Europe, 1819. Hereafter this archive will be cited as AMAE.

[3]AMAE, CCC, Vols. 42-43, Tableau des marchandises qui ont été exportées et importées de Smyrne en Europe, 1826 and 1832.

REFERENCES

Arvieux, Laurent de, Chevalier. 1735. *Mémoires de Chevalier d'Arvieux, 1653-1657.* 6 vols. Paris: C.J.B. Delespine.

Biraben, Jean-Noel. 1975. *Les Hommes et la Peste en France et dans les Pays méditerranéens.* 2 vols. Paris: Mouton.

Bowring, John. 1840. *Report on the Commercial Statistics of Syria.* London: W. Clowes and Sons for HMSO.

Carrière, Charles. 1973. *Négociants Marseillais au XVIIIe siècle.* 2 vols. Marseilles: Institut Historique de Provence.

Carrière, C., Courdurié, M., Gusatz, M., Squarzoni, R. 1976. *Banque et capitalisme commercial (La lettre de change au XVIIIe siècle).* Marseilles: Institut Historique de Provence.

Chandler, David G. 1966. *The Campaigns of Napoleon.* New York: MacMillan.

Choiseul-Gouffier, Marie Gabriel Florent Auguste de, Comte. 1842. *Voyage pittorresque dans l'Empire Ottoman* ... 2 vols. Paris: Libr. J. P. Aillaud.

Cunningham, A.B. 1983. "The Journal of Christophe Aubin: A Report on the Levant Trade in 1812," *Archivum Ottomanicum,* 8, pp. 5-131.

Deschamps, Gaston. 1894. *Sur les routes d'Asie.* Paris: A. Colin & Cie.

Échinard, Pierre, 1973. *Grecs et Philhellènes à Marseille de la révolution française à l'indepéndance de la Grèce.* Marseilles: Institut Historique de Provence.

Eldem, Edhem. 1986. "La circulation de la lettre de change entre la France et Constantinople au XVIIIe siècle," in Batu, H. and Bacqué-Grammont, J. L. (eds.), *L'Empire Ottoman, la République de Turquie et la France.* Istanbul-Paris: Éditions Isis, pp. 87-97.

Eldem, Edhem, 1999. *The Commerce of Istanbul in the Eighteenth Century.* Leiden: Brill.

Eldem, Edhem, Goffman, Daniel, and Masters, Bruce, 1999. *The Ottoman City between East and West. Aleppo, İzmir, and Istanbul.* Cambridge: Cambridge University Press.

Frangakis, Elena. 1985a. "The Commerce of İzmir in the Eighteenth Century, 1695-1820," Ph.D. Thesis, University of London.

Frangakis, Elena. 1985b. "The Ottoman Port of İzmir in the Eighteenth and Early Nineteenth Centuries, 1695-1820," *Revue de l'Occident Musulman et de la Méditerranée,* 39 (1), pp. 149-162.

Frangakis, Elena. 1985c. "The Balance of Trade and the Balance of Payments Between İzmir and France, 1700-1789," *Communications grecques presentées au Ve Congrès International des Études du sudest-Européen.* (Athens) pp. 127-138.

Frangakis-Syrett, Elena, 1992. *The Commerce of Smyrna in the Eighteenth Century, 1700-1820.* Athens: Centre for Asia Minor Studies.

Frangakis-Syrett, Elena, 2001. "18. Yüzyıldan 20. Yüzyılına kadar İzmir Ekonomisine Bir Bakış", *21. Yüzyıl Eşiğinden İzmir Uluslararası Sempozyumu* (İzmir: İzmir Büyükşehir Belediyesi Kültür Yayını), pp. 71-89.

Goffman, Daniel. 1985. "İzmir as a Commercial Center. The Impact of Western Trade on an Ottoman Port, 1570-1650," Ph.D. Dissertation, University of Chicago.

Goffman, Daniel, 1990. *İzmir and the Levantine World, 1550-1650.* Seattle: University of Washington Press.

Herlihy, Patricia. 1979-1980. "Greek Merchants in Odessa in the Nineteenth-Century", *Harvard Ukrainian Studies*, III/IV, pp. 399-420.

Herlihy, Patricia, 1986. *Odessa. A History 1794-1914.* Cambridge, Mass.: Harvard University Press.

Iconomos, C. 1868. *Étude sur Smyrne.* (Slaars, B. trans.) İzmir: B. Tatikian.

Kasaba, Reşat. 1987. "Incorporation of the Ottoman Empire, 1750-1820," *Review,* 10(5/6), Summer/Fall, pp. 805-847.

Katsiardi-Hering, Olga. 1986. *Η παροικία της Τεργέστης, 1751-1830. (The Greek Community of Trieste 1751-1830)*, 2 vols. Athens: University of Athens.

Kremmydas, Vasilis. 1972. *Το εμπόριο της Πελοποννήσου στο 18° αιώνα, 1715-1792. (The Commerce of the Peloponnese in the Eighteenth Century, 1715-1792)*, Athens.

Macler, Frederick. 1904. "Notes de Chahan de Cirbied sur les Arméniens d'Amsterdam et de Livourne," *Annahir*, 1, pp. 8-16.

Nanninga, J.G. (ed.) 1952. *Bronnen tot de Geschiedenis van den Levantschen Handel, Derde deel: 1727-1765.* 'S-Gravenhage: M. Nijhoff.

Nanninga, J. G. (ed.) 1966. *Bronnen tot de Geschiedenis van den Levantschen Handel. Vierde deel: 1765-1826.* 'S-Gravenhage: M. Nijhoff.

Panzac, Daniel. 1985. *La Peste dans l'Empire Ottoman, 1700-1850.* Louvain, Belgium: Éditions Peeters.

Paris, Robert. 1957. *Le Levant de 1660 à 1789,* vol. V, Bergasse, L. and Rambert, G. (eds.), *Histoire du Commerce de Marseille.* Paris: Chambre de Commerce de Marseille.

Perkins, Bradford. 1967. *The First Rapprochement: England and the United States, 1795-1805.* Berkeley and Los Angeles, California: University of California Press.

Peyssonnel, Charles Claude de. 1785. *Lettre de M de Peyssonnel, ancien consul-général à Smyrne, contenant quelques obsérvations rélatives aux mémoires qui ont paru sous le nom de Baron de Tott.* Amsterdam.

Pococke, Richard. 1772. *Voyages de Richard Pococke, 1739*. 5 vols. Paris: J. L. Costard.

Rebuffat, F. and Courdurié, M. 1966. *Marseille et le négoce monétaire international, 1785-1790*. Marseilles: Chambre de Commerc et Industrie de Marseille.

Robson's. 1841. *Robson's Commercial Directory of London…for 1841*. London: W. Robson: W. Robson.

Sonnini de Manoncourt, Charles N.S. 1801. *Voyage en Grèce et en Turquie*, 2 vols. Paris : F. Buisson.

Svoronos, Nicolas. 1956, *Le Commerce de Salonique au XVIIIe siècle*. Paris: Presses Universitaires de France.

Tancoigne, M. J. 1820. *A Narrative of a Journey into Persia from Constantinople*. London: W. Wright.

Tavernier, Jean-Baptiste. 1713. *Les six Voyages de J. B. Tavernier… en Turquie, en Perse et aux Indes*. 2 vols. Paris: Pierre Ribon,

Vlami, Despina. 2000, *Το φιορίνι, το σιτάρι και η οδός του κήπου. Ελληνες εμποροι στο Λιβόρνο, 1750-1868 (Florin, wheat and Garden Street. Greek Merchants in Livorno, 1750-1868)* Athens: Themelio.

4. General view of the Fort of İzmir. (From P. Schenk, *Hecatompolis* ...)

5. View of İzmir from the Harbor. (Author's collection)

6. View of İzmir and the Citadel. (Author's collection)

THE TRADE OF COTTON AND CLOTH IN İZMİR: FROM THE SECOND HALF OF THE EIGHTEENTH CENTURY TO THE EARLY NINETEENTH CENTURY

Cotton

In the second half of the eighteenth century, İzmir experienced an unprecedented economic growth that made it the most important port in the Ottoman Empire's trade with the West. During that time France was the dominant economic power in the Levant, and, through its port of Marseilles, the principal trading partner of İzmir. By then the Egyptian and Syrian ports had fallen behind. Salonica and Istanbul, although major ports, could no longer compete with İzmir, which kept its position until the early nineteenth century. The predominance of cotton among the exports of İzmir coincides almost to the year with the predominance of İzmir as the biggest exporting port of the Empire. Cotton remained the principal export of İzmir until the beginning of the nineteenth century, after which it declined.[1] Extensive exports of cotton reflected the further orientation of İzmir's agricultural production to external commerce and its integration in the world-economy.

Unlike mohair yarn or Ottoman silk, which were transported to İzmir from Ankara and Bursa, cotton was produced in the immediate vicinity of the port-city. It was cultivated in the plains of Bakır, Gediz, Kırkağaç, Akhisar, Bergama, Kasaba, and Manisa, along the valleys of the rivers Küçük and Büyük Menderes, and in the neighborhood of the cities of Bayındır, Tire, Ödemiş, Aydın, and Denizli. Cotton from those areas was considered by European merchants to be better than that of Adana or Syria. There were eight types of cotton varying in quality and taking their names according to the place of production. Top quality cotton was produced in Aydın and Subatça.

Due to a lack of data, it is impossible to quantify total production of cotton and the proportion exported to the West, but it is possible to calculate the exports of cotton to Marseilles, the principal trading port of İzmir. Taking

---

[1]Elena Frangakis, "The Ottoman City-Port of İzmir in the Eighteenth and Early Nineteenth Centuries, 1695-1820", *Revue de l'Occident Musulman et de la Méditerranée*, Vol. 39/1 (1985), p. 162.

the average for every decade in the second half of the eighteenth century, we have the following figures: in the 1750s, 8,270 bales[1] were exported annually; in the 1760s this increased to 12,285 bales annually — an increase of 48.5 percent; in the 1770s, the annual average dropped slightly to 12,235 bales and in the 1780s it rose to 20,279 bales — an increase of 66 percent.[2] In 1750 alone exports amounted to 7,319 bales; in 1788, a peak export year, they more than trebled, reaching 26,402 bales.[3]

There was a substantial increase in the export of cotton at the end of the eighteenth century which carried over into the nineteenth century. From 1788 to 1820, cotton exports trebled to almost 70,000 bales.[4] The considerable growth of cotton exports, at least until 1820, reflects the dimensions of commercial growth of İzmir. In the early nineteenth century we have the following breakdown of the export figures: Güzelhisar and Subatça sent for export to the market of İzmir 8,000 bales; Kırkağaç, a seat of Kara Osmanoğlu, the biggest cotton producer and local administrator, sent 25,000 bales of second quality cotton to İzmir annually. Akhisar, Bergama, and Kınık furnished İzmir with another 25,000 bales of third quality cotton. Kasaba furnished the city with 10,000 bales of lesser quality cotton annually and Manisa with 4,000 bales.[5] Manisa cotton was also of low quality and was used mainly in local production of cloth; very little was exported to the West.[6]

In the second half of the eighteenth century, the share of cotton in the overall value of exports of İzmir to France varied from 30 to 59 percent. A peak year for cotton exports was 1788 with a share of 72 percent of total exports. In the 1780s, although cotton exports continued to grow in absolute value, their share in relation to the exports of İzmir averaged 49 percent annually. In 1782 İzmir's cotton exports represented 60 percent of all Ottoman cotton exported to France; this share dropped in the next two years, but in

[1]Each bale is calculated at 300 lbs. Elena Frangakis-Syrett, *The Commerce of Smyrna in the Eighteenth Century, 1700-1820* (Centre for Asia Minor Studies: Athens, 1992), p. 232.

[2]Archives de la Chambre de Commerce de Marseille, Marseilles (hereafter ACCM), I: 26-28.

[3]ACCM, I: 26-28.

[4]Archives du Ministère des Affaires Étrangères, Paris (hereafter AMAE), Correspondance Consulaire et Commerciale (hereafter CCC), Vol. 50, Consul Bentivoglio, İzmir, 26 March 1863 to Minister, Paris.

[5]Archives Nationales de France, Paris (hereafter AN), Série Affaires Étrangères (hereafter AE), sous-Série Biii 242, Consul Fourcade, Mémoire, İzmir, c. 1812.

[6]Along with cotton, plague was also transmitted to İzmir from these centers. When an attack was particularly heavy, such as the plague epidemic brought to İzmir from Aydın and Manisa in 1835, there were not only population losses but a temporary paralysis of all economic activities, too. Daniel Panzac, *La Peste dans l'Empire Ottoman, 1700-1850* (Peeters: Louvain, 1985), p. 156.

1785 it rose to 65 percent. At that time its greatest rival, Salonica, had an average share of 19 percent, with all the other Ottoman ports providing the rest.[1] Despite the absolute increase in the production of cotton, its share in total exports of the western Anatolian port dropped by the early nineteenth century. In 1820, for example, cotton represented 12 percent of İzmir's exports to France, as France was importing American cotton instead of cotton from the Levant. In 1832, cotton ranked fourth in value among İzmir's exports to Austria; it accounted for 12 percent of İzmir's exports to Russia and only 2 percent of the port's exports to Great Britain.[2]

Great Britain had been importing cotton from the United States even before American independence, and the invention of the cotton gin in 1793 resulted in greater imports of American cotton. Great Britain imported cotton from the United States even in the years 1812-13 when the two countries were at war with each other, as İzmir was cut out of the British market.[3] In 1857, according to British sources, cotton's share of İzmir's exports to the West was a mere 1 percent in value; raisins, valonia, madder, and wool represented the top export items of İzmir with shares of 14 percent, 13 percent, 12 percent and 11 percent respectively.[4] In 1858, according to French sources, cotton and wool exports together represented 8 percent of İzmir's exports to the West, with valonia and alizari topping the list with a share of 37 percent of the exports.[5]

In the second half of the eighteenth century, cotton production in İzmir mainly served the needs of the textile manufacturers in the south of France.[6] France, however, did not at any time have the monopoly of cotton purchase: the Dutch and other western Europeans in İzmir and non-Moslem Ottoman merchants — Armenians, Greeks, and Jews, who were mainly established in the Italian ports - were buying cotton and distributing it to the rest of Europe.[7] By the end of the eighteenth century and the beginning of the

[1]AN, Marine B7/452, États des cotons en laines et filés du Levant entrés à Marseilles par le lazereth pendant 1782-1785.

[2]AMAE, CCC, Vol. 43, Importation et Exportation de Smyrne, 1832.

[3]Eli Heckscher, *The Continental System* (Clarendon Press: Oxford, 1922), pp. 146-147.

[4]Lewis Farley, *The Resources of Turkey Considered with Especial Reference to the Profitable Investment of Capital in the Ottoman Empire* (Longman, Green, Longman & Roberts: London, 1862), pp. 94-95.

[5]AN, AE Biii 415, Importation et Exportation de Smyrne, 1858.

[6]AN, AE Bi 1054, État des Draps arrivés à Smyrne, janvier à juin 1755; report included in letter of Consul Peyssonnel, İzmir, 24 Aug. 1755 to Minister, Paris.

[7]AN, Marine B7/446, Castagny, 18 Aug, 1782; dispatch included in report on Commerce des ports de l'Europe avec ceux du Levant, 1 Feb. 1782.

nineteenth, Switzerland and Germany were importing cotton, either directly from İzmir, or through Holland.[1]

During the eighteenth century, the French would not permit merchants other than French nationals to import İzmir cotton into France. It was only during the Revolutionary and Napoleonic Wars that the French started to use non-Moslem Ottoman merchants as their agents or partners in İzmir.[2] By 1815, they had opened their trade in Marseilles to non-French merchants. Non-Moslem Ottoman merchants in İzmir, and in particular Greeks, started to export cotton to their compatriots who had, since the 1780s, established a commercial base in Marseilles.[3] Well into the 1820s, French merchants trading in the Levant, whose particular interests were hurt by the policy of *laissez-faire*, protested against this policy and sought its revision. Yet at the same time they were aware that British and American merchants were their biggest rivals, not the Greeks.[4] Finally, with France starting to import American cotton, French merchants in İzmir were left without an important merchandise they could purchase in exchange for the cloth they sold.

From the middle of the eighteenth century, the more liberal policy of the Dutch state allowed non-Moslem Ottoman merchants to export cotton to Holland and to set up commercial houses there. Some of the biggest names of the Greek trading community in İzmir also figured in Amsterdam — namely, Mavrogordato, d'Issay, Rodocanachi, Petrocochino, Ralli, and Vlasto.[5] In the 1780s Greek merchants taking advantage of the international economic and political situation expanded their trade activities in the Italian ports as well. As was reported:

> The trade of Trieste with the Levant is practiced mainly by Greeks whose principals are in the Ottoman Empire. Until recently their trade was limited; their capital outlays were not very considerable and their activities were limited to the Morea, Salonica, Smyrna and the Islands of the Archipelago. The growth in their trade activities that has taken place in the last two to three years is due to the Dutch who have been bringing to Trieste the silk and cotton that they had bought in the Levant. From there they take

[1]AN, F12/1850A, Consul Fourcade, İzmir, 12 July 1812 to Minister, Paris.

[2]Blow J. Williams, *British Commercial Policy and Trade Expansion, 1750-1850* (Clarendon Press: Oxford, 1972), p. 372; see also, AE Biii 242, Sur l'article 30 de l'ordonnance du 20 Sept. 1810, Commerce du Levant, 28 September 1814.

[3]Pierre Échinard, *Grecs et Philhellènes à Marseille (de la révolution française à l'indépendance de la Grèce)* (Institut Historique de Provence: Marseilles, 1973), p. 65.

[4]ACCM, MQ, 5.1, Députation des négociants français, İzmir, 22 July 1820.

[5]AN, AE Biii 242, Consul Fourcade, Mémoire, İzmir, c. 1812.

them by land to Holland, Germany and Switzerland. They use the same route for exporting cloth to the Levant from Europe.[1]

The Dutch were using a land route because the British had imposed a tight blockade of their ports in the years 1781-82.[2] In 1782, all Dutch shipping had ceased.[3]

The best time for the Western merchants to buy cotton was in December, January, and February when most of the cotton still remained in the hands of the producers. The western Europeans also sent their brokers, non-Moslem intermediaries, to the environs with money to purchase it for them. A fortnight after the money was paid, the goods were sent to the city.[4] On the eve of the French Revolution, £15,000 were sent weekly by the Europeans to the environs of İzmir for the purchase of cotton. Starting with the first week in January, this amount decreased weekly. The whole procedure went on for five months until the entire crop was sold.[5] A large part of the cotton production was bartered against goods imported from Europe and occasionally against bills of exchange at an extraordinary discount. For instance, a Western merchant would pay for cotton with a bill of exchange that he had received in lieu of payment for some coffee or indigo he had sold to an Ottoman buyer. If the Ottoman buyer were honest and paid the cotton seller by the set date, the latter not only recovered his money but made a profit too, for the western European merchant had sold him the bill at a discount. On the other hand, he ran the risk of never recovering his money.[6]

Apart from the growing demand in the international market for cotton, and competition amongst Western merchants for its purchase another factor that contributed to the rise in the price of cotton was local consumption by Ottoman manufacturers. In 1749, all the western European merchants banded together and declared a temporary boycott in the purchasing of cotton as protest against a rise in prices. The result was that Ottoman merchants bought all the best cotton for the manufacturers in the interior of Anatolia and the

[1] AN, Marine B7/446, Bertrand, 19 Oct. 1782; dispatch included in report on Commerce des ports de l'Europe avec ceux du Levant, 1 Feb. 1782.

[2] David Syrett, *Neutral Rights and the War in the Narrow Seas, 1778-1782* (Combat Studies Institute: Fort Leavenworth, Kansas, 1985), pp. 38-40.

[3] J. G. Nanninga, ed., *Bronnen tot de Geschiedenis van den Levantschen Handel. Vierde deel: 1765-1826* ('S-Gravenhage: M. Nijhoff, 1966), pp. 1468-1513.

[4] A. B. Cunningham, "The Journal of Christophe Aubin: A Report on the Levant Trade in 1812", *Archivum Ottomanicum*, Vol. VIII (1983), p. 44.

[5] Public Record Office, London (hereafter PRO), State Papers (hereafter SP) 105/337, Consul Hayes, İzmir, 15 May 1789 to Levant Company, London.

[6] Cunningham, "The Journal...", p. 44.

Europeans had, in the end, to buy what was left at a still higher price.[1] The Ottoman price of cotton continued to go up throughout the second half of the eighteenth century; but, the high rate of devaluation of the Ottoman coin, which increased as the century drew to a close, eliminated the rise in price in the international market, making cotton marketable at all times.[2]

In the 1770s, there were in İzmir factories dyeing cotton yarn and printing cloth and muslins for export to Switzerland, Germany, and Great Britain, and they also catered to an internal market.[3] Western merchants became involved in both processes. The French experimented with buying cotton yarn and having it dyed in İzmir before exporting it to Marseilles, and, in the middle of the nineteenth century, the British imported British cloth which was then printed locally and sold. But, they found that printed Swiss cloth was underselling them.[4] One reason for this was that local Ottoman officials insisted on collecting two sets of duties on the cloth — one on the import of the cloth and another on the sale of the finished product. Workshops producing coarse cloth and lesser quality silk stuffs existed in İzmir and Chios, catering mainly to the lower end of the internal Ottoman market. These low-quality products could be potentially competitive since no duties were levied.[5]

Information on the relations of production for the cultivation of cotton as well as of other goods in the hinterland of İzmir in the eighteenth century is scant.[6] From references made by European consuls, mainly British and French, on these issues, it would appear that there existed in western Anatolia both small-scale peasant proprietorship[7] and large-scale landownership,[8] both connected to the external market, either directly or indirectly. Large-scale landowners referred to in the documents as *aghas*, but in reality were lesser

[1]AN, AE Bi 1053, Consul Peyssonnel, Mémoire, İzmir, 22 Nov. 1751.

[2]ACCM, I: 26-28.

[3]AN, AE Biii 242, Consul Fourcade, Mémoire, İzmir, c. 1812.

[4]PRO, Foreign Office (hereafter FO) 195/177, Consul Brant, İzmir, 17 Sept. 1840 to British Ambassador, Istanbul.

[5]Leila Erder, "The Making of Industrial Bursa: Economic Activity and Population in a Turkish City, 1835-1975" (unpublished Ph.D. dissertation, Princeton University, 1976), p. 41.

[6]E.g., Gilles Veinstein, "'Ayan' de la région d'İzmir et commerce du Levant (deuxième moitié du XVIIIe siècle)", *Études Balkaniques*, Vol. XII/3 (1976), pp. 71-83; see also, *idem*, "'Ayan' de la région d'İzmir et commerce du Levant (deuxième moitié du XVIIIe siècle)", *Revue de l'Occident Musulman et de la Méditerranée*, Vol. 20 (1975), pp. 131-147; Yuzo Nagata, *Some Documents on the Big Farms (Çiftliks) of the Notables in Western Anatolia* (Institute for the Study of Languages and Cultures of Asia and Africa: Tokyo, 1976), *passim;* Halil İnalcik, "The Emergence of Big Farms, *Çiftliks:* State, Landlords and Tenants", in Jean-Louis Bacqué-Grammont & Paul Dumont, eds., *Contributions à l'histoire économique et sociale de l'empire ottoman* (Peeters: Louvain, 1983), pp. 105-126.

[7]PRO, SP 105/129, Consul Werry, İzmir, 31 January 1803 to Levant Company, London.

[8]AN, AE Bi 1054, Consul Peyssonnel, İzmir, 7 July 1754 to Minister, Paris.

ayans sold the produce of their land to western European merchants, sometimes through an *homme d'affaires* who was usually an Armenian.[1] The most powerful *ayans* in the area, the Kara Osmanoğlu, with their rivals the Araboğlu, were known to apply any measures possible in order to increase the price of their produce. For instance, they might not allow the peasants to use their animals to transport the crop, hoping that the delay thus incurred would force the Europeans to offer higher prices.[2]

Another favorable development, fully exploited by the *ayan*, was the increased demand from the interior for cotton,[3] usually due to a failure in the crop production either in the immediate environs of İzmir or in the interior of Anatolia.[4] Whereas lesser *ağas* seemed to be participating in the market directly, Kara Osmanoğlu and Araboğlu did so usually through their peasants. As for the small peasant producers, the question was whether they could afford the cost of transportation to İzmir's market at all. Western merchants did not yet venture inland; so, rather than waiting for cotton to be brought to the İzmir market, they preferred to send their agents inland. Non-Moslem merchants usually bought the cotton on the spot and brought it to the city's market, either independently or in order to fulfill an order placed by a Western merchant. In fact this was seen as the best way to guarantee the purchase of first quality cotton.[5] This practice, intensified in the nineteenth century, prompted the British consul to note:

> Roads should be constructed to lessen the current cost of transport which inhibits many times the grower from sending his produce to the market. Instead he sells on the spot to speculators at prices unfavorable to him.[6]

Although there were certainly large-scale landowners, *de facto* if not *de jure*, it is less clear whether they could qualify as feudal landowners.[7] As late

---

[1]AN, AE Bi 1054, Ismail Ağa Araboğlu, Governor of Bergama to Consul Peyssonnel, İzmir, included in letter of Peyssonnel, İzmir, 9 May 1754 to Minister, Paris.

[2]AN, AE Bi 1054, Consul Peyssonnel, İzmir, 7 July 1754 to Minister, Paris.

[3]AN, AE Bi 1052, Consul Peyssonnel, İzmir, 16 December 1749 to Minister, Paris.

[4]PRO, SP 105/128, Consul Werry, İzmir, 16 May 1801 to Levant Company, London.

[5]Cunningham, "The Journal...", p. 43.

[6]PRO, FO 195/241, Consul Brant, İzmir, 25 August 1845 to Levant Company, London.

[7]On Kara Osmanoğlu, one of the biggest landowners in the hinterland of İzmir, see Veinstein, "'Ayan' ..." (1975), pp. 71-83. On other large-scale landowners-cum-*ayans* in the Ottoman Empire, see e.g., Deena Sadat, "Rumeli Ayanları: The Eighteenth Century", *Journal of Modern History*, Vol. XLIV/3 (1972), pp. 346-363; Traian Stoianovich, "Balkan Peasants and Landlords and the Ottoman State: Familial Economy, Market Economy and Modernization" in N. Todorov, ed. *La révolution industrielle dans le sud-est européen. XIXe siècle* (Institut d'Études Balkaniques-Musée national polytechnique: Sofia, 1979), pp. 164-204.

as 1792, the province of Aydın is recorded to have supported 110 zaim holders, 4,235 timariots, and one *beylerbeyi* whose annual revenue was 923,000 *akçes*.[1] In other words, the classical Ottoman feudal land system was still, at least partly, in force. However, a proto-capitalist agrarian system was also in operation. Some landowners did have extensive jurisdiction over their lands, as did Kara Osmanoğlu Hacı Mustafa Ağa, who had changed the boundaries of the peasants' plots.[2] Yet "opulent landowners" in the environs of İzmir were collecting their rents in money from their peasant cultivators. In the face of rampant inflation and depreciation in the first decade of the nineteenth century, an obliging government arbitrarily adjusted the rate of exchange in favor of the Ottoman coin and of the landowners' revenue.[3] This would indicate that these peasants were either sharecroppers or tenant farmers leasing their plots of land from the landowner under various forms of tenancy. Sharecroppers were, on the whole, Greek immigrants from Morea and from the Aegean islands who came from the 1770s onwards, settled in the lands of Kara Osmanoğlu, and cultivated cotton.[4] By the beginning of the nineteenth century, 3,000 Greek cultivators were settled around Kasaba as well as in the area surrounding the city of İzmir.[5] Bringing cultivators from outside was one method used by Kara Osmanoğlu to combat scarcity of manpower and depopulation of the countryside.

Small peasant proprietorship in western Anatolia, which was prevalent in the nineteenth century, seemed also to be current in the eighteenth. The European consuls speak of great oppression being suffered by such proprietors:

> the great oppression of the aghas has determined the proprietors to cultivate their lands every third year, a period beyond which they cannot go under pain of forfeiting their lands to the aghas.[6]

These *ağas* were in a position to oppress the peasants, either in their capacity as administrators, or as tax farmers, or as providers of protection in a time of continuous anarchy created by peasants turned bandits or by feuding

---

[1]Elias Habesci, *État actuel de l'Empire ottoman* (Paris, 1792), Vol. I, p. 205; Vol. II, pp. 21-22.
[2]Veinstein, "'Ayan'..." (1976), p. 137.
[3]PRO, SP 105/128, Consul Werry, İzmir, 17 September 1801 to Levant Company, London.
[4]PRO, SP 105/337, Consul Hayes, İzmir, 15 May 1789 to Levant Company, London.
[5]Erder, "The Making of Industrial Bursa...", p. 41.
[6]PRO, SP 105/129, Consul Werry, İzmir, 31 January 1803 to Levant Company, London.

ayans.[1] At the end of the eighteenth century, and at the height of the power of the *ayans*, the British consul made the following observation of what was happening in the countryside:

> The population is reckoned to increase here [in the city of İzmir] considerably which is to be attributed in a great measure to the interior parts of the country being much depopulated by the extortions and oppressions of the numerous aghas appointed to the government of extensive districts which include many small towns and villages and who levy greater taxes on the inhabitants than are legally due.[2]

Lending to the peasants at usurious rates, so that the peasants could then meet their ever-increasing tax obligations to them and letting them slide into growing indebtedness, was another method used by these *ağas* to extract surplus and increase their power over the peasants. Inflation and depreciation, endemic in the Ottoman economy from the third quarter of the eighteenth century and continuing into the nineteenth, made usury widespread.[3] Depreciation of the Ottoman currency also took away a large part of the gain realized by the peasant in selling his produce, despite the continuous increase in international demand for cotton. Another labor relation was wage labor: either seasonal labor or laborers hired on a daily basis.[4] The scarcity of manpower increased the need for migrant/seasonal labor.

Sources refer to Kara Osmanoğlu, the most powerful *ayan* in the area, both as "a proprietor of the grounds where cotton is planted... and (where) immense riches have been accumulated by the great demand for that article"[5] and as "an extraordinarily good administrator (where) trade is flourishing."[6] Certainly Kara Osmanoğlu was a landowner of considerable scale, with lands and titles his family had amassed through service to the Sultan. He was influential in the cultivation of cotton in the area by bringing in additional

[1]AN, AE Bi 1061, Consul Peyssonnel, İzmir, 5 January 1773 to Minister, Paris; see also, Algemeen Rijksarchief (hereafter ARA), 164, European Consuls, İzmir, 15 March 1773 to their Ambassadors, Istanbul in Nanninga, *Bronnen*..., pp. 178-180.

[2]PRO, SP 105/337, Consul Hayes, İzmir, 15 May 1789 to Levant Company, London.

[3]On depreciation of the Ottoman currency and usury, see e.g., PRO, SP 105/128, Consul Werry, İzmir, 17 August 1801 to Levant Company, London; SP 105/130, Consul Werry, İzmir, 2 August 1805 to Levant Company, London; FO 78/868, Consul Brant, İzmir, 1 August 1851 to Foreign Office, London. For increase in prices of exports of İzmir in the second half of the eighteenth century, see ACCM, I: 26-28.

[4]Yuzo Nagata, "Notes on the Managerial System of a Big Farm (*Çiftlik*) in the Mid-18th Century Turkey", *Annals of the Japan Association for Middle East Studies*, Vol. 2 (1987), pp. 319-341.

[5]PRO, SP 105/337, Consul Hayes, İzmir, 15 May 1789 to Levant Company, London.

[6]Frederick Hasselquist, *Voyages and Travels in the Levant in the years 1749, 1750, 1751 and Containing Observations in Natural History, Physick, Agriculture and Commerce* (London, 1766), p. 30).

labor, owning the means of transportation, not being overtly extortionist, and protecting all peasants.[1] He owned the largest number of camels in the caravan trade between İzmir and western as well as eastern Anatolia.[2] He was also involved in large-scale international commerce. Western merchants were, at times, duly appreciative of his actions.[3] Although he was all-powerful in his own region, his position was still precarious. He had to fight palace intrigues that aimed to undermine his position, or that of his supporters.[4] This precariousness made him vulnerable as a landowner. Ultimately, perhaps, it was as administrator and tax collector that he was most influential in the area.[5]

In the nineteenth century, following the destruction of the power of the *ayans* and the abolition of the *corvée*, small-scale peasant proprietorship became even more prevalent, although large-scale landownership continued to exist alongside it.[6] Want of capital and manpower were probably the two most important factors that inhibited productivity and sometimes even dictated the type of production. For instance, in 1863, despite the four-fold increase in land prepared for cotton seeds, a large part of American and Egyptian seeds available to the cultivators were not being used. The reason for this was that American and Egyptian cotton required more labor than the local variety, and "the native farmers, however desirous to increase cotton cultivation cannot calculate upon the amount of labor required to make it productive and remunerative."[7] Large-scale landowners were successfully planting American cotton seeds for they had the capital to hire extra labor.

Defective tillage, deficient manure, and high transportation costs were other factors that plagued agricultural production and resulted in low productivity during the eighteenth and nineteenth centuries.[8] Agricultural implements remained rudimentary, and cotton gins, in existence since the early nineteenth century, were mostly owned by British or American capital.[9]

---

[1]PRO, SP 105/126, Consul Werry, İzmir, 17 May 1797 to Levant Company, London. Other *ayans* in the region did likewise; see e.g., SP 105/338, Consul Werry, İzmir, 10 July 1810 to Levant Company, London.

[2]AN, AE Biii 242, Commerce du Levant, 16 December 1812.

[3]PRO, SP 105/338, Consul Werry, İzmir, 7 June 1809 to Levant Company, London.

[4]AN, AE Bi 1053, Consul Peyssonnel, İzmir, 8 July 1751 to Minister, Paris; see also, AE Bi 1062, Consul Peyssonnel, İzmir, 22 July 1775 to Minister, Paris.

[5]Veinstein, "'Ayan'..." (1976), p. 136.

[6]PRO, FO 78/1760, Consul Blunt, İzmir, 23 May 1863 to Foreign Office, London; see also, Reşat Kasaba, *Ottoman Empire and the World Economy: The Nineteenth Century* (SUNY Press: Albany, NY, 1988), pp. 61-65.

[7]PRO, FO 78/1760, Consul Blunt, İzmir, 23 May 1863 to Foreign Office, London.

[8]PRO, FO 78/442, Consul Brant, İzmir, 6 December 1841 to Foreign Office, London.

[9]PRO, FO 78/1760, Consul Blunt, İzmir, 23 June 1863 to Foreign Office, London.

Cloth

From the early seventeenth century to the early twentieth century, cloth was the most important export of western Europe to the Levant.[1] İzmir was no exception. The export of raw materials — cotton, cotton yarn, mohair yarn, wool, and silk in the eighteenth century, and wheat, raisins, figs, and other foodstuffs in the nineteenth century — was complemented by the importation of manufactured goods, namely cloth. Of the European cloth exported to İzmir, in terms of popularity and sales, French cloth was the most important in the eighteenth century and British cloth in the nineteenth century.

In the second half of the eighteenth century, over 180 French manufacturers from Languedoc sent cloth to İzmir, ranging from very expensive varieties to competitively priced types of cloth.[2] Strict classification was imposed on this cloth in order to maintain standards and credibility in the Levantine market. A large number of different types of cloth were sold in the market of İzmir, the most popular of which were the *Londrins seconds*. Though not a luxury cloth, it was above average quality and sold well in İzmir. It was not always bartered, but could be sold for cash. In fact, there was a direct correlation between the market for wheat and the sale of *Londrins seconds* in İzmir. For when wheat sold well, the cash available was used by the Ottoman merchants to buy *Londrins seconds*. When wheat sales were on the decline, French merchants avoided sending too large a quantity of *Londrins seconds* for fear that it would be left unsold, and sent instead lesser quality cloth.[3] When the buyer had nothing to exchange, the seller was forced to sell him cloth on credit, which could be extended for as long as two years. The European merchants were not the only ones selling cloth on credit to shopkeepers and dealers in the bazaar. Non-Moslem Ottoman merchants, who were themselves by the early nineteenth century importers of cloth into İzmir, did so as well. Around 1820, such European and non-Moslem merchants formed an association to protect themselves from fraudulent debtors and impose on them stricter terms of payment.[4]

---

[1] *Parliamentary Papers, Accounts & Papers*, Vol. XCV (London, 1914), Report No. 5247, p. 24.

[2] AN, AE Bi 1054-1055, Draps venus à Smyrne et distingués par qualités. Data included in dispatches of Consul Peyssonnel, İzmir, 2 April 1753 to 20 August 1756 to Minister, Paris.

[3] AN, AE Bi 1054, Consul Peyssonnel, İzmir, 7 July 1754 to Minister, Paris.

[4] ACCM, MQ, 5.1, Mémoire des Députés des Européens et des Drapiers Grecs à l'Union des Boutiquiers Grecs et Arméniens et à la Communauté Juive, İzmir, 5 September 1820.

There were three types of *Londrins seconds*, which took their name from the place of production in the South of France — Carcassonne, St. Clermont, and St. Chinian. They first appeared in the Levantine market as an imitation of the British cloth — hence the name *Londrins*. By the 1830, British cloth was ousted from the Levantine market by the French *Londrins*. There were two qualities of *Londrins seconds de Carcassonne*, both of which did well. The St. Clermont and St. Chinian types were also popular, though more for their color than for their quality.

Londrins seconds totally dominated French cloth exports to İzmir. In the late 1750s, they represented 77 percent of all French cloth exports; in the 1760s, they represented 85 percent; in the 1770s, 93.5 percent, and in the 1780s, 95 percent. Between 1783-88, of all *Londrins seconds* exported to the Ottoman Empire, İzmir's market absorbed 39 percent.[1] The reason for the predominance of *Londrins seconds* was that İzmir supplied a large but middle-range market in Anatolia and Persia. Unlike Istanbul, İzmir had no large group of officials or rich dignitaries who would buy very expensive luxury cloth. Expensive cloth was usually consumed within the city of İzmir and in its immediate environs, such as Chios.[2] Second in marketability came the cheaper *Londres larges*, which did particularly well in the Persian market. The Ottoman-Safavid wars greatly affected the sales of this cloth in İzmir. Other kinds of French cloth that came to İzmir were in small quantities.[3]

For most of the second half of the eighteenth century, the French authorities strongly believed in controlling the market and influencing prices. For instance, they only allowed a limited quantity of high quality cloth to be sent to İzmir, in order to prevent the oversupply from being sent to Istanbul where it would compete with the wares of other French merchants. Thus, it was by accident that luxury quality gold and silver thread cloth reached the market of İzmir in any quantity.[4] Another way to regulate the price of cloth was through the system of *répartitions* (quotas). A merchant was only allowed to sell a certain number of bales of cloth within a specified period of time and within a set price range. This way he could not try to undersell his compatriots. In the second half of the eighteenth century, this restriction was practically abandoned, as the French authorities realized that whatever they

---

[1]AN, AE Biii 283, États des Draps expédiés de Marseille pour les échelles du Levant, İzmir, 1756-1788 and AN, AE Bi 1052, Draps français importés à Smyrne, 1750.

[2]AMAE, CCC, Vol. 8, Consul E. David, Mémoire, Chios, 1823.

[3]AN, AE Bi 1054-1055, Draps venus à Smyrne et distingués par qualités. Data included in dispatches of Consul Peyssonnel, İzmir, 2 April 1753 to 20 August 1756 to Minister, Paris.

[4]AN, AE Bi 1053, Consul Peyssonnel, Mémoire, İzmir, 22 November 1751.

gained by keeping the prices from falling too low, they lost by the limited amount of goods they sold.[1] Other nationalities came in to fill the gap in the market left by the French, for there was always competition in İzmir both among the buyers and among the sellers of cloth.

When introducing a new type of cloth, they usually bartered it against mohair yarn, until it became popular. They were not alone, however, in dealing with mohair yarn. French merchants established in Ankara also bought mohair yarn, usually far cash. When considerable amounts of cash were thus deployed, the French in İzmir found themselves unable to barter their cloth.[2] Other incentives were then placed on the price of the cloth to make its sale attractive. In such cases, the price usually included an *agio*, or discount, based on the expected depreciation of the Ottoman currency between the time of the purchase of the cloth in İzmir and the time it took to transport it to its final destination for sale. So that the Ottoman merchant would not carry the loss from the depreciation of the currency, or pass it on the local consumer and risk pricing the cloth out of the market, the European merchant agreed to carry part of the loss himself. This practice became current especially after the 1760s due to growing inflation and depreciation of the Ottoman currency. The exact amount of *agio* was decided periodically by the European merchants and the Ottoman authorities, though not necessarily in direct consultation with each other. If no *agio* was agreed upon in İzmir, the Ottoman merchant went to another city — Istanbul, Salonica, or Bursa — where there was *agio* in force, to trade there in cash.[3] İzmir not only lost out on cloth sales, but ran the risk of having its market drained of capital.

If the market were particularly depressed and the European merchants were finding it difficult to sell their cloth for cash, they were prepared to give credit. Credit could be extended from three times thirty-one days to three times eighteen months. The longer the terms of credit, the lesser was the *agio* included in the overall price. The *agio* was also used as an added incentive in the following way. British merchants declared an *agio* of 2-3 percent on payments of debts, if these payments were made in "good money", that is, in European currencies. Other Europeans had to follow suit, at least as long as the British were giving this incentive, in order not to have their own

[1] *ibid.*
[2] *ibid.*
[3] AN, AE Bi 1058, Éclaircissements sur la suputation qui a été faite du prix des Londrins Seconds de Carcassonne à Smyrne, in dispatch of Consul Peyssonnel, İzmir, 20 November 1767 to Minister, Paris.

payments made in Ottoman para, which, with the rate of depreciation of the Ottoman currency at that time, was rapidly losing its value.[1]

It is difficult to establish the trends in the prices of the cloth imported into İzmir: French statistics tend to group several types of cloth into one, citing a total value only, or else they give the price of a type of cloth on the basis of different measurements.[2] Nevertheless, if we compare the index of the volume with that of the value of cloth imported into İzmir, we find that initially there was a constant fluctuation between the two indices.[3] After 1766, the index in value rose perceptively higher than the index in volume, showing a rise in the price of imported cloth.[4] In the late 1780s, the gap between the two indices started to close as the increase in price slowed down. These trends are also reflected in the share of cloth that the market of İzmir claimed in relation to French cloth exports to the Levant as a whole. In the years 1750-70, İzmir accounted for 22 percent in value and 30.4 percent in volume of all French cloth exported to the Ottoman Empire. In the years 1771-89, this share increased to 35 percent in value and 34 percent in volume.[5]

The volume of cloth exported to İzmir from France during the years 1750-70 averaged 1, 972 ballots or 986 bales per year.[6] In the years 1770-80, annual cloth exports averaged 2, 191 ballots per year, or an increase of 82 percent. The years of peak consumption were 1779-83, with an average of 2,911 ballots per year. In 1750, cloth represented in value 48.4 percent of all the exports of France to İzmir; in 1760, its share was 73 percent; in 1770 it dropped to 33.5 percent; and in 1780 it rose again to 51 percent. In the years immediately preceding the French Revolution, cloth exports fluctuated between 21 percent and 28 percent. In absolute terms İzmir imported 836,410 *guruş* worth of cloth on an annual average between 1750-70. In the years, 1771-89, it absorbed 1,323,355 *guruş* on an annual average, or an increase of

[1]AMAE, CCC, Vol. 36, Consul David, İzmir, 3 January 1821 to Minister, Paris.

[2]This holds both for data in the Archives of the Chamber of Commerce of Marseilles and in the consular correspondance in the Archives of the French Ministry of Foreign Affairs.

[3]E.g., ACCM, I: 19 and AN, AE Bi 1053, 1056.

[4]For İzmir, see ACCM, I: 20; see also AN, AE Bi 1062-1063 and AE Biii 273-274, 276. For Salonica, see Nicos Svoronos, *Le Commerce de Salonique au XVIIIe siècle* (Presses Universitaires de France: Paris, 1956), pp. 329-331.

[5]AN, AE Biii État du nombre des Draps de 16 aunes de long, déstinés pour le commerce du Levant, admis à l'inspection de Marseille, depuis l'année 1749 jusqu'en 1788 avec leur évaluation.

[6]E.g., ACCM, I:19 and AN, AE Bi 1053, 1056; AE Biii 273.

37 percent. In the peak years of French cloth exports, cloth worth 1,706,966 *guruş* was imported annually.[1]

Although trade between İzmir and France increased until the French Revolution — İzmir's highest exports to France for the century, both in volume and value, were recorded in 1787 — the trade in cloth dropped off in the early 1770s and again in the late 1780s. British cloth, more competitively priced than the French and of a far better quality, had already started to compete with French cloth: in the 1770s, 64 percent of British exports were made up of cloth and in the 1780s, 56 percent. From the 1780s onwards, much British cloth was reaching İzmir via Italian ports.[2] Between 1777 and 1782, however, there was a recovery in French exports due to the American War of Independence (1776-83).

As France and later Spain entered the war against Great Britain, the latter ceased sending goods to the eastern Mediterranean in convoys; only private individuals sent goods at their own risk. As a result British trade with İzmir was constricted.[3] During the Napoleonic Wars, British cloth started to reach İzmir through Malta, and by 1812 through British-held Ionian Islands, Corfu in particular. These trading networks were not exclusively in British hands. Greek merchants also went to Malta or Corfu to get British cloth for distribution in the ports of the eastern Mediterranean, including İzmir.[4]

At the height of popularity of French cloth in the market of İzmir, in the 1750s and 1760s, the mere label indicating that it was made in Languedoc was enough for a bale not to be opened.[5] But, even before the political upheaval of the French Revolution and the subsequent years of warfare between Great Britain and France in the Revolutionary and Napoleonic Wars, which swept away most of the infrastructure of French trade in the Levant, French manufactures had already fallen into trouble. Keeping their prices stable or even lowering them in an attempt to be competitive with British cloth, Languedoc manufacturers were forced to reduce the quality of the cloth

[1]E.g., ACCM, I:20 and AN, AE Bi 1062-1063; AE Biii 274, 276.

[2]For British cloth trade figures for the 1770s and 1780s, see AN, AE Bi 1066. For further details on this trade see also, AN, F12/1850A, Consul Fourcade, İzmir, 10 October 1812 to Minister, Paris.

[3]AN, AE Bi 1066; see also, Frangakis-Syrett, *The Commerce...*, pp. 159, 274.

[4]AN, AE Bi 1054, Consul Peyssonnel, İzmir, 9 May 1754 to Minister, Paris.

[5]AN, AE Bi 1069, Consul Amoureux, İzmir, 6 & 13 December 1790 to Minister, Paris; see also, Edhem Eldem, "La circulation de la lettre de change entre la France et Constantinople au XVIIIe siècle", in H. Batu & J.-L. Bacqué-Grammont, eds., *L'Empire Ottoman, la République de Turquie et la France* (Isis: Istanbul-Paris, 1986), pp. 87-98.

produced, thus losing their credibility in the Levantine market. This in turn made French merchants reluctant to deal in cloth, when they could instead export specie to İzmir. In the last quarter of the eighteenth century, the chaotic monetary and financial situation in İzmir and its chronic lack of specie — which went hand in hand with a tremendous growth in its commercial activities, and in turn created opportunities for monetary speculation — prompted French merchants to engage in a systematic trade in specie and bills of exchange. Besides, by then, British, Dutch, German, and Swiss cloth were taking a substantial share in the cloth market of İzmir.

During the Napoleonic Wars, the absence of French cloth from the market of İzmir for two decades allowed competitors to establish themselves.[1] Once this had happened, it was difficult for the French to recapture the market. In the early nineteenth century, the Americans were the only major trading partner of İzmir who were not exporting to it large amounts of cloth, but rather sugar and tobacco.[2] By then, Greek merchants had also acquired a stronghold in the international cloth trade, importing British and German cloth into İzmir.

In 1820, most prosperous French merchants who had remained in İzmir or had reestablished commercial houses there, were trading with Egypt, not Marseilles. Those who were ostensibly exporting cotton and olive oil to the French port and importing cloth were in fact dealing in informal banking activities: lending at high interest rates and moving funds in and out of the market of İzmir according to the rate of exchange or money-changing.[3] Others were engaged in fraudulent practices, sending cloth to İzmir that was badly finished or bales of cloth that were not of the same quality throughout, in an effort to keep afloat. The result was an even bigger influx of British cloth. Part of the monetary surplus that İzmir got from its active balance of trade with a number of countries including France, was being sent to London, via Malta, to buy British cloth.[4] In the early nineteenth century the situation became worse for the French textile industry. Gold and silk stuffs made in Lyons, and popular in İzmir in the second half of the eighteenth century, were being supplanted not only by Venetian products but also by local products.[5]

---

[1]ACCM, MQ, 5.1, Députation des négociants français, İzmir, 22 July 1820.

[2]AMAE, CCC, 43, Exportation et Importation de Smyrne, 1832; see also, New-York Historical Society Archives, Bradish Papers, Bradish, Istanbul, 20 December 1820 to John Quincy Adams Washington, D.C.

[3]AN, AE Biii 415, Maruscheau Élève, "Réfléxions sur la situtaion politique et commerciale de la France dans les États du Grand Seigneur, 13 November 1820.

[4]AN, AE Biii 243, Félix de Beaujour, Inspection générale du Levant, 5 January 1817.

[5]AN, AE Biii 242, Consul Fourcade, Mémoire, İzmir, c. 1812.

In the early seventeenth century, the western Europeans could go to the local producers and purchase local goods, including cotton, directly from them in exchange for cloth and other goods.[1] In the eighteenth century, this was no longer the case. Non-Moslem merchants had become the intermediaries between local producers and the European merchants in all the major Ottoman ports, including İzmir. The former regime was still in force in the Aegean islands for the purchase of wheat and olive oil.[2] In the nineteenth century western European merchants, having acquired the right to deal with local producers directly, used instead non-Moslem merchants as their agents, whom they sent to the interior of western Anatolia.

One reason for the intermediaries acquiring such a position in the eighteenth century, at least vis-à-vis the French, was the chronic lack of specie that the French economy suffered from throughout the eighteenth century. Pressed to buy cotton and other goods to fill a return cargo to the West and not always having the necessary cash to buy them with, the French merchant used an elaborate system of bartering made possible through the intervention of the non-Moslem Ottoman intermediary. It was credit in kind; in other words, instead of money, the intermediary advanced him goods. The advantage to the Ottoman dealer was that in this way he was creating a link that he could control through which trade had to pass. The Frenchman not only bought everything from him, but also sold his goods to Ottoman buyers and Armenian caravan merchants exclusively through him.[3]

One should not assume from the above that the Ottoman intermediaries were in all respects in a very strong position in the eighteenth century. The western Europeans held in their hands most of the external trade of İzmir for most of the eighteenth century. It was only in the final decades that the position of the European merchant began to be significantly eroded. This was due partly to economic and partly to political reasons. The social and political upheaval of the French Revolution and the period of continuous warfare that ensued between Great Britain and France during the Revolutionary and Napoleonic Wars broke the supremacy of France and left a relative gap in the international trade of the Levant, including İzmir, which the non-Moslem merchants filled. These events, accompanied by a sustained growth in the world-economy, forced France and Great Britain to open up their trade

[1]Daniel Goffman, "İzmir as a Commercial Center. The Impact of Western Trade on an Ottoman Port, 1570-16650" (Ph.D. dissertation, University of Chicago, 1985), pp. 230-232; see also, *idem, İzmir and the Levantine World, 1550-1650* (Seattle, 1990), *passim.*

[2]AN, AE Biii 242, Jumelin, Commerce du Levant, 16 December 1812.

[3]AN, AE Bi 1052, Consul Peyssonnel, İzmir, 29 January 1749 to Minister, Paris.

monopolies at a time when free trade was "in the air" but not yet an established state policy. Jewish, Armenian and especially Greek merchants in İzmir took advantage of these conditions to increase their capital accumulation and enlarge their business activities in the international market at the cost of the European merchants in the port-city.[1]

For instance, by the end of the eighteenth century Greek merchants, who always had a share in the cloth trade, succeeded in ousting the Dutch merchants, who imported Dutch and other European-made cloth to İzmir. They did it in two stages. Greek merchants had established commercial houses in Amsterdam since the 1750s taking advantage of the liberal policies of the Dutch. They did well by sending Dutch cloth to their compatriots in İzmir, who then sold it. Greek merchants dominated both the wholesale and the retail market of cloth in the city. In the 1780s, with the international economic conditions favoring them, they created a monopoly of the buyer's market for Dutch cloth in İzmir and imposed their own prices and conditions of purchase. By the end of the Napoleonic Wars, the worst fears of the Dutch were to be realized. The Greek cloth dealers were fast taking over the entire Dutch cloth trade as they had already taken over the Dutch trade in silk stuffs. The Greeks had another advantage: they knew the internal Anatolian market well and could get their cloth distributed there through their agents.[2]

Greeks continued to expand their trading networks inside western Anatolia. Their success in this sector became apparent with the signing of the Treaty of 1838 between Great Britain and the Ottoman Empire, with which the British extended their trade ventures inland into western Anatolia. Here, they found that Greek and other non-Moslem Ottoman merchants were exporting the local produce, having obtained the monopoly of purchasing these goods from local Ottoman administrators.[3] Thus, the British, who remained in their commercial bases in İzmir, used Greeks and other intermediaries as agents, due to their contacts and expertise.[4] Sometimes they nominated a Greek merchant directly from Europe to represent them in İzmir and its hinterland.[5] As the nineteenth century progressed non-Moslem as well as Moslem Ottoman merchants started to take a more active role in the

---

[1] "The Raya Communities of Smyrna in the Eighteenth Century, 1690-1820. Demography and Economic Activities", *Actes du colloque international d'histoire. La ville néohellénique. Héritages ottomans et état grec* (Athens), pp. 38-39.

[2] Nanninga, *Bronnen...*, pp. 950-951.

[3] PRO, FO 195/128, J. A. Werry, İzmir, 10 September 1839 to Vice-Consul Charnaud, İzmir.

[4] PRO, FO 78/442, Valsamachi to Muhassil of Adramit, 1 January 1841, included in letter of Consul Brant, İzmir, 21 January 1841 to Foreign Office, London.

[5] PRO, FO 78/1020, Consul Brant, İzmir, 5 May 1854 to Foreign Office, London.

process of production and consumption. Greek merchants, either working on their own or as agents of the British, speculated through advance purchases of crops much more extensively than earlier.[1]

Trade in cotton and cloth was an important factor in the economic growth of İzmir and also in the rise of the intermediaries who were actively involved. This trade does not, however, appear to have affected the relations of production in agriculture. The increase in the market orientation of İzmir's cotton production did lead to a relative strengthening of the position of the *ayans*. This strength, however, could not shelter them from the recentralization of the Ottoman state early in the nineteenth century.

[1]Nanninga, *Bronnen...*, pp. 480-481; PRO, FO 195/128, Vice-Consul Charnaud, İzmir, 18 May 1839 to British Ambassador, Istanbul.

THE PORT OF PATRAS IN THE SECOND OTTOMAN PERIOD c. 1700-1830

The development of the economy

During the course of the eighteenth century the Morea, as part of the Ottoman Empire, traded with the European market within the system of the Capitulations and largely through the presence of western merchants who were established there for this purpose (fig. 1). The latter imported into the Morea western manufactured and colonial goods and exported from the area Ottoman raw materials and foodstuffs such as cereals, olive oil, silk, wax, valonia and currants.

For the first three quarters of the eighteenth century, most of the external trade of the Morea, including that of Patras, was greatly dominated by the French. A degree of inter-western competition, in the form of British and Dutch merchants trading in the area, did exist however. Such competition facilitated the participation of local merchants in the economic activities of the area. For instance, the Greeks were strong competitors to the French in the export of olive oil, an important produce of the region, whilst the Jews were dominant in the import and distribution of cloth, the biggest western import into the Morea (V. Kremmydas, 1972: 21, 134, 291, 296-7, 299-300, 307; N. Svoronos, 1956:395). Such local participation in the economy was not unique to the Morea but prevalent throughout the Ottoman Empire (N. Svoronos, 1956; E. Eldem, 1988; D. Panzac, 1991; Y. Triantafyllidou-Baladié, 1991; E. Frangakis-Syrett, 1992).

Nevertheless, the very strong position of the French in the external trade of the Morea meant that in peacetime, the local entrepreneurs were mostly relegated to the position of brokers or of intermediaries coming into contact with the local producers on behalf of the western merchants. By contrast, the internal trade of the region was in the hands of local merchants, both Muslim and non-Muslim. Greeks were also active in the coastal carrying trade, whilst the Jewish and Turkish communities were strong rivals to the westerners in monetary speculative activities (Kremmydas, 1972: 21, 121, 293, 295, 307).

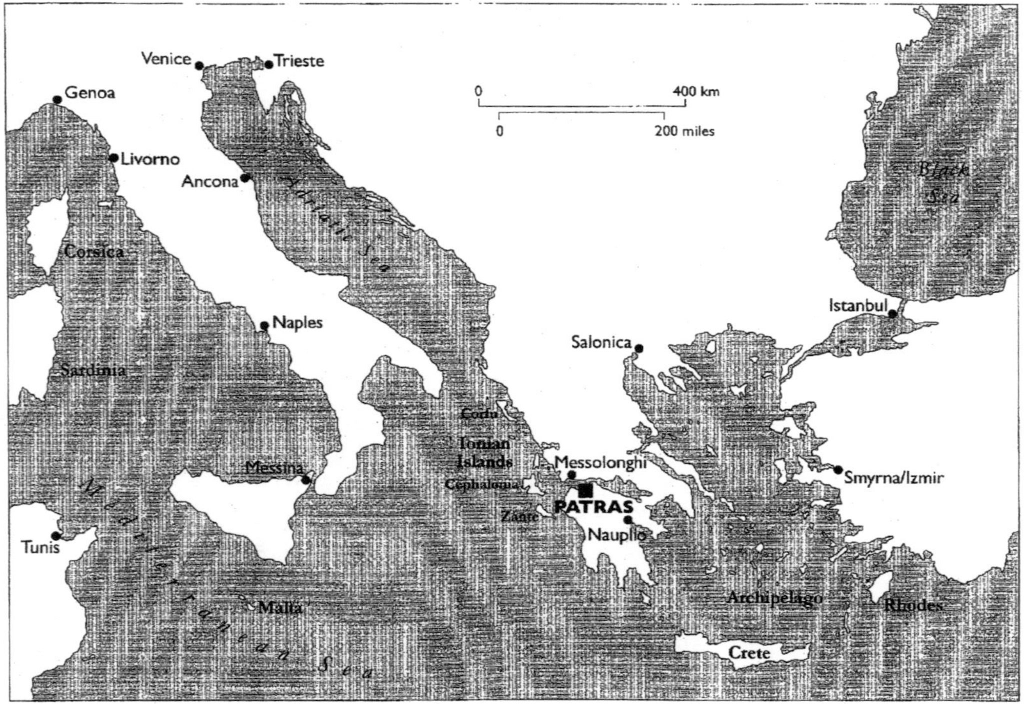

Fig. 1:
Location of Patras, including the principal ports with which it traded.

It was at times of war, however, and particularly during inter-western and Ottoman-western maritime conflicts, that local merchants were able to gain a bigger than otherwise share in the Morea's external trade. It was, in fact, during the Seven Years' War (1756-63) that local entrepreneurs were able to participate — for the first time, in the eighteenth century, to such an extent — in the Ottoman-western trading and shipping networks that linked the Morea with Europe. This was due to a number of reasons: the volume of trade and shipping was increasing as part of European-wide economic developments, whilst the military conflicts going on were disrupting the seas and were breaking up the protectionism that French and British merchants enjoyed in the commerce of the eastern Mediterranean with their respective countries (C. Carrière & M. Courdurié, 1975: 39-80). They were thus unwittingly opening their markets and the seas to other entrepreneurs. For instance, as long as the British and French licensed privateers to attack each other's merchant fleets, making it both onerous (due to high insurance costs) and risky for British or French merchants to hire their own nationals to ship their goods, the neutral Dutch benefited by having their ships handle a considerable part of the British and French carrying trade. It was not only the Dutch who benefited however, for their liberal policies allowed other nationalities, including Moreote Greeks, Jews and Armenians, to carry goods on board Dutch ships and enter the Dutch-Ottoman trade.[1]

Moreover, the Greeks of the Morea, like other Greeks in the eastern Mediterranean, were able to gain by participating in the privateering and even in the piracy that were unleashed during times of conflict in the Mediterranean.[2] Profits thus amassed, contributed to the activities of Greek shipping that also flourished at the time. The Ottoman-Russian War (1768-74) remains a significant starting point for the shipping activities of the Greeks, legal and semi-legal. In co-operation with the Russians they carried out, during the war, widespread privateering and piracy especially after the destruction of the Ottoman fleet by the Russians in July 1770, at the Battle of Çeşme, which strengthened their position in the eastern Mediterranean (C. C. de Peyssonnel, 1785: 78-80). Moreover, at the end of the war, the Greeks were able to buy Russian privateers' ships at good prices.[3]

---

[1] ARA, Consulaatsarchief Smirna, De Scheepvart en de Handel op Smirna, 1762 in J. G. Nanninga, ed., 1952: 715-763.

[2] *Archives Nationales de France*, Paris, AE Bi 859, Consul l'Allement, Messina, 9 Feb. 1782 to Minister, Paris; see also, AE Bi 1087, Consul Fraunery, Trieste, 27 Jan. & 7 Feb. 1789 to Minister, Paris. Hereafter this archive will be cited as ANF.

[3] ANF, AE Bi 861, Consul de Mensil, Mitylene, 25 March 1777 to Minister, Paris.

Great gains were also realized in shipping. By the end of the eighteenth century, multiple maritime conflicts had enabled the Greeks to accumulate enough capital to come into the Mediterranean as international shippers. For instance, in the early 1780s, Moreote ships, but especially ships from Patras, carried out a flourishing trade with Ancôna.[1] In the mid-1780s the Levant accounted for 22 per cent of Messina's imports brought to the Italian port largely by Ottoman Greeks' ships from Malta, Livorno, Genoa, Naples, Messolonghi and, in particular, the Morea. In 1785, the Morea alone, represented 12 per cent of Messina's imports from the Ottoman Empire.[2] Moreote ships carried to Messina mostly silk and wheat for distribution to western Europe, including Marseilles, which was blockaded and could not receive goods by sea from the Levant.[3] They were active, in fact, in a flourishing carrying trade with all the Italian ports throughout the French Revolutionary and Napoleonic Wars, taking advantage of the intermediary role that these ports had acquired in the Ottoman-western trade at the time.[4]

Following their initial capital accumulation through shipping, privateering, and even piracy, Greeks were participating in the Morea's trade with the Italian ports by the end of the eighteenth century. They did so either from their bases in the Morea or by establishing commercial agencies in the Italian ports, whose liberal policies allowed them to do so.[5] Thus, they were well placed to turn favorable international situations to their advantage. For instance, when the Dutch used a land route that passed through Trieste, in order to by-pass the blockading of their ports by the British Navy during the American War of Independence, the Greeks benefited from it:

> Le commerce de Trieste au Levant n'est pratiqué que par les Grecs, facteurs des maisons de leur nation sujettes et établies dans les états du Grand Seigneur.
>
> Il a été jusqu'à présent très limité; leurs fonds sont peu considérables et il est borné à la Morée, à Salonique, à Smyrne et aux Isles de l'Archipel. L'accroissement qu'il a paru prendre pendant les deux ou trois dernières années, est du aux Hollandois qui avaient pris le parti de faire passer par Trieste et transporter par terre les soies et cottons qu'ils tiraient du Levant et

---

[1] ANF, AE Bi 168, État des marchandises arrivées des états du Grand Seigneur à Ancôna, 1780-84.

[2] ANF, AE Bi 859, État des marchandises arrivées des états du Grand Seigneur à Messine, 1785.

[3] ANF, AE Bi 859, L'Allement, Messina, 29 Aug. & 3 Sept. 1785 to Minister, Paris.

[4] ANF, AE Bi 860, État de Navigation, Messina, 1790.

[5] ANF, AE Bi 168, Consul Benincasa, Ancôna, 13 Feb. 1784 to Minister, Paris; see also, AE Bi 859, L'Allement, Messina, 22 May 1784 & 4 Feb. 1786 to Minister, Paris.

qui y acheminaient par la même voie beaucoup d'articles de leurs manufactures et surtout des draps.[1]

*

In the eighteenth century the port of Patras was not yet the important entrepôt that it was to become in the following century. Nevertheless, it was one of the most active ports in the Morea's trade with western Europe. Together with Nauplia, Patras was the most important wheat exporting port of the Morea (Kremmydas, 1972: 20-21). At least some of the wheat exported must have been grown locally, but Patras acted as a bulking or collecting center for much of the region around the Gulf of Corinth, as well as for the more extensive coastal plains to the west, in Elis.

The other major export, of course, was currants. Félix de Beaujour (1800:20) believed that currant cultivation was introduced from Naxos around 1580 and that the first exports arrived in Marseilles and elsewhere in western Europe at the beginning of the seventeenth century (Oxford Dictionary, 1989: 149; M. Epstein, 1908: 109). The British, who were among the principal purchasers of currants from south-western Greece from at least the end of the sixteenth century, turned to Patras for their purchases in the early seventeenth century to by-pass the various impositions that the Venetians placed on currant exports from Zante (A. C. Wood, 1935: 67-68). Even so, currant cultivation seems to have been relatively unimportant in the Patras district at the time of its return to Ottoman rule in 1715. The French, as the principal western traders in the Morea in the eighteenth century, did not share the British interest in currants. Although they were primarily interested in wheat, they also imported an array of goods from Patras.[2]

Other crops were grown in the Patras district in the eighteenth and early nineteenth centuries. These included cotton and tobacco in the plain, according to Leake, who also noted on 30 May, 1805 that land on its edge had been prepared for cultivating *kalamboki* (maize) under irrigation. Whilst maize was probably grown for the subsistence of the cultivators, cotton and tobacco were commercial crops, destined for sale. Silk was also produced in the district probably for export, like the wool, wax, leather and juniper berries also

[1]ANF, Marine B7/446, Bertrand, 19 Oct. 1782 included in memorandum on Commerce des ports de l'Europe..., 1 Feb. 1783.

[2]Archives de la Chambre de Commerce de Marseille, Marseilles, I, 26-28, États éstimatifs des marchandises venant du Levant. Hereafter this archive will be cited as ACCM.

reported by Leake (1830, II: 122, 141-142). Patras continued to export such goods to the end of the Ottoman period and beyond.[1]

Whilst much of the prosperity of Patras in the second Ottoman period can be attributed to the export of commercial crops from the hinterland, principally wheat and currants, the town was also a significant importing center for cloth not only from Marseilles but from elsewhere in Europe, too, brought to Patras by Venetian and Dutch merchants (Kremmydas, 1972: 140, 290). Already by the 1770s, following the demographic growth in Europe which led to an increasing demand for foodstuffs, Patras was emerging as a principal entrepôt exporting wheat not only from the north western Peloponnese but also from the whole of south western Greece. Furthermore, as an increasingly competitive western textile industry turned to the Moreote market to sell its produce, in return for Ottoman goods including currants, and as a growing British commercial activity in the area further stimulated the currant trade, Patras also emerged as the principal exporter of the fruit to Europe, particularly Trieste (H. Giannakopoulou, 1991:418). Currants from other areas, such as Crete, could not compete in the European market with the variety exported from Patras (Y. Triantafyllidou-Baladié, 1988:188). This led to a demographic and economic growth in the Patras district in the last quarter of the eighteenth century, which offset the destructive effects of the Orlov Rebellion (1770) and its aftermath (F. C. Pouqueville, 1813:51).

However, the breakthrough in the economic growth of Patras came at the end of the eighteenth and beginning of the nineteenth centuries, roughly from the French Revolutionary Wars to the end of the Napoleonic Wars, after which the economic conditions for the continued growth of Patras were largely in place.[2] This is borne out by the statistics: between 1794-1814 Patras shipped 30 per cent of all Morea's exports; this doubled in the period 1815-20 (Kremmydas, 1980; 59). There were a number of reasons for this. The continuous problems that their textile industry faced in the last quarter of the eighteenth century weakened the commercial position of the French in the eastern Mediterranean and strengthened that of their competitors, particularly the British, whose cloth was doing better than the French despite the setback which the British suffered during 1778-83 following their decision to withdraw their forces from the Mediterranean temporarily.[3] Furthermore, the political

[1]See, for example, Public Record Office, London, FO 32/81, Consul Crowe, Patras, 2 Feb. 1838 to FO, London; FO 32/100, Crowe, Patras, 30 Sept. 1840 to FO, London. Hereafter this archive will be cited as PRO.

[2]ANF, AE Biii 243, F. de Beaujour, Athens, 6 May 1817.

[3]ACCM, J 1562, Mémoire, Paris, 1790.

and economic upheaval that the French Revolution and its aftermath brought to France led to its temporary commercial demise in the area.

As France had hitherto been the dominant western commercial force in the Morea, the gap that its departure left behind was filled primarily by the British and the Moreote Greeks. The former were enjoying a growing economy and were undergoing the Industrial Revolution, whilst not suffering any of the political turmoil of France, and the latter — with their compatriots established all over the Mediterranean — had been accumulating capital, contacts and expertise and were poised to fill the void created by the French debacle (E. Frangakis-Syrett, 1987:73-86). Moreover, British military and naval successes, including the taking-over of Malta (c. 1800) and the Ionian Islands (c. 1809) in the Mediterranean, gave them bases from which the Greeks of Patras could undertake trade with Britain and the British with Patras, enabling the taking over of a large part of the external trade of Patras by the Greeks. The significance of this was not missed by the French diplomatic service, as was later noted by one of its members :

> S'il est vrai que les Grecs ne se soucient pas de faire le voyage d'Angleterre, il est constant que les Anglais ont eu le souci de leur épargner les trois-quarts du chemin en établissant des entrepôts à Malthe et à Corfu où les sujets Ottomans peuvent venir échanger leurs produits contre ceux de la Grande-Bretagne.[1]

Moreover, the implementation of the Continental System by Napoleon in 1807, which closed the rest of Europe to the British, however inefficiently it might have been implemented, made ports like Patras, in the eastern Mediterranean, look very attractive as potential markets for their goods.

It was not only Britain but also the Italian ports and the Netherlands that increased their trade with Patras in that period. Currants, of course, were a principal export not only for the British market but also for the others making it one of the district's dominant commercial crops.[2] In 1794-95, currants represented 24.2 per cent of total exports from the north-western Peloponnese, whilst in 1798-1801, 27.9 per cent (Kremmydas, 1980:155). As a result of this demand the British Consul in Patras reported in 1815 that: "It is intended by the principal inhabitants to extend the culture of the currant vine in the district of Patras, as its fruit is generally preferred to that of the other districts,

---

[1]ANF, AE Biii 243, Miège, Renseignements sur le commerce du Levant, Livorno, 13 May 1825.

[2]PRO, SP 105/131, Consul Strane, Zante, 12 May 1807 to Levant Company, London.

and of the islands".[1] A start had already been made by 1805 when Leake observed that the prosperity of the town had grown largely because of the cultivation of currants which had become so common that the plain of Patras "consists, for a distance of two or three miles from the town, of continued vineyard of those dwarf grapes" (W. M. Leake, 1830, II: 141). Even after the end of the Napoleonic Wars, currants continued to be important to the district's economy: in 1817-21 they represented 54.6 per cent of total exports of the port of Patras (Kremmydas, 1980:150). However, as already noted it did not export only currants. Increasing quantities of wheat and other goods such as cotton were exported.[2] An increase in the export of wheat was, at least partly, the result of more land being put under cultivation a development which may be explained by the observed growth in the number of settlements in the uplands of the port's hinterland, by 1830. Patras' internal market also grew, as shown by the growth in the port's imports, although some of these imports were distributed to its wider hinterland along the Gulf of Corinth and in western Greece (Kremmydas, 1980: 72-75). The general increase in the trade of Patras as a whole should also explain the town's demographic growth, from 3,832 people in 1700 (table), to an estimated 10,000 to 16,000 people in the period 1805-15 - a rate higher than that in the rest of the Morea (Kremmydas, 1980: 47).

It was in this period that the Italian ports, besides Malta and the Ionian islands, emerged as the principal trading partners of Patras, thus contributing to its commercial growth. There were a number of reasons for this, though the port's location was of fundamental importance (fig. 1). During the French Revolutionary and Napoleonic Wars, the Italian ports attracted a large part of Patras' trade simply because when they were not occupied by the French or blockaded by the British Navy they were neutral. For as the British stationed naval forces off Toulon, the French naval base in the Mediterranean, thus blockading Marseilles, merchants in the French port turned to Livorno or Genoa for their trade, carrying goods to them overland. They were not the only ones. Between 1793 and 1814, the Holy Roman Empire, including Austria, relied on Trieste and other Italian ports for its trade with the eastern Mediterranean, including Patras, especially when the Dutch ports were also blockaded, as was the case between 1795 and 1814 with the exception of the years of the Peace of Amiens (1801-03).[3] Whilst Livorno had traditionally been an entrepôt for British goods in wartime, from 1793 to 1808, Trieste,

[1]PRO. SP 105/135, Consul Cartwright, Patras, 24 Sept. 1815 to Levant Company, London.
[2]ANF, AE Bi 860, État de Navigation, Messina, 4 May 1790.
[3]ANF, AE Biii 243, Miège, Renseignements ... See also, Appendix C.

Ancôna and Venice, protected by the French and unmolested by British warships, were relatively secure, leading to an active trade between the Greeks in Patras and their compatriots and other merchants established in these ports. After 1808, with the arrival of the British Navy in the Adriatic, these ports may not have looked so attractive, although Greek ships, as neutrals, could obtain a license to enter the Adriatic by stopping at Malta.[1] By then, however, the merchants in Patras had turned to Malta and subsequently to the Ionian islands for their trade.[2]

Chronic scarcity as well as growing inflation of the Ottoman currency led to a highly speculative and lucrative trade in money in the eastern Mediterranean which intensified towards the end of the eighteenth century. Patras both received from and sent money to Ottoman, Ionian, Italian and other ports in the Mediterranean in an active trade in money. Although the movement of specie in and out of Patras purely for speculative purposes cannot be discounted, it was also tied to the needs of trade. As entrepôts, the Italian ports both sent and got money from Patras in Greek and other ships for purchases, and subsequent distribution to Europe, of Ottoman foodstuffs and raw materials, or through the sale of European cloth. Specie was sent to Patras from Zante (after 1809) and London (after 1815) to purchase currants for the British market, whilst specie was also sent from Patras to Malta (during and after the Napoleonic Wars) to purchase cloth.[3]

It was particularly in the carrying trade that the Greeks used their neutrality to their best advantage and succeeded in taking over a large part of Patras' freight business. The British Government actively encouraged the Greeks of Patras among others to come to Malta in their own ships to trade giving them licenses to do so.[4] British warships were also assigned by the British Government to escort, among others, convoys of Greek ships in their journey between Patras and Malta (Kremmydas 1980:50). Moreover, British merchants freighted Greek ships, providing them with licenses, in order to carry British-owned cargo.[5]

---

[1]PRO, SP 105/132, Strane, Patras, 19 March 1810 to Levant Company, London.
[2]PRO, SP 105/132, Strane, Patras, 19 Oct. 1809 to Levant Company, London.
[3]ANF, AE Biii 243, F. de Beaujour, Inspection..., 5 June 1817.
[4]PRO, CO 158/16, J. Hunter *et al.*, Malta, 18 April 1810 to E.F. Chapman, London.
[5]PRO, CO 158/16, The Committee of British merchants, Malta, 29 Aug. 1810 to King George III.

After the end of the Napoleonic Wars both the commercial role of the Italian ports in the Mediterranean and the participation of the Greeks in its carrying trade decreased. Patras, by contrast continued to grow, even after 1815, strengthening its commercial ties with Britain in the process. Whilst Patras exported currants, primarily, to other markets besides the British, the latter remained its principal and, by far, its biggest customer whose ability to absorb Corinthian currants kept on increasing, as did Patras' ability to meet this demand during the course of the nineteenth century (P. Pizanias, 1988:58-62; N. Bakounakis, 1988:82-85; V. Lazaris, 1986: 40-43). Patras also continued an active trade with the Ionian Islands, themselves part of the British commercial network.[1] (E. Frangakis-Syrett, 1994: 9-34).

This growth was interrupted by the Greek War of Independence during which Patras suffered considerable devastation (N. Bakounakis, 1988a:20-21, 47-50). Indeed, descriptions of the town in that period make grim reading. In early 1822, the British Consul for the Morea, whilst visiting the town reported "that there does not remain a single house at Patras".[2] Eight months later, he again reported that "Patras had been entirely reduced to ashes",[3] which accounts for the drop in the 1830 population figures (table). Greco-Ottoman hostilities in the area, both in land and at sea, also placed great obstacles to trade during this period (D. Themeli-Katifori, 1973, I: 47-54).[4] Nevertheless, Patras was able to overcome this setback largely due to its commercial links with Britain. Between 1814 and 1835 there was a 76 per cent increase in British purchases of currants exported from Patras, whilst by 1845 there was a further increase of 182 per cent (N. Bakounakis, 1983: 167). Direct links were established between Patras and London, Liverpool, and Hull.[5] This led to tremendous economic growth for the district of Patras as well as to a pattern of monoculture which became as characteristic of the land use in its district as did also the port's orientation towards the international market and its continued role as an entrepôt. (E. Frangakis-Syrett, 1993: 387-410).

---

[1]For example, PRO, SP 105/136, Cartwright, Patras, 20 Jan. 1818 to Levant Company, London; SP 105/139, Consul Green, Patras, 9 Jan. 1821 to Levant Company, London.

[2]PRO, SP 105/140, Green, Zante, 14 Feb. 1822 to Levant Company, London.

[3]PRO, SP 105/140, Green, Patras, 28 Oct. 1822 to Levant Company, London; on devastation caused by the war, see also, PRO, SP 105/139, Green, Patras, 7 April 1821 to Levant Company, London.

[4]For example, PRO, FO 78/136, Pt I, G. Moore, Zante, 9 March 1823 to Levant Company, London.

[5]PRO, SP 105/135, Cartwright, Patras, 29 Feb. 1816 to Levant Company, London; see also, SP 105/137, Green, Patras, 21 Oct. 1819 to Levant Company, London.

The town and its setting

To Dodwell (1819:115) at the beginning of the nineteenth century Patras was

> ... like all other Turkish cities, composed of dirty and narrow streets; the houses are built of earth baked in the sun; some of the best are whitewashed; and those belonging to the Turks are ornamented with red paint. The eaves overhung the streets, and project so much, that opposite houses sometimes almost come into contact, leaving but little space for air or light, and keeping the street in perfect shade; which in hot weather is agreeable, but I conceive far from healthy.

A few years later, Galt (1813:63) characterized it as "... a wretched Turkish town", whilst Bramsen (1820:96) thought that the main street was the only good one in the place. It was overlooked by a much neglected castle where many of the town's Muslims appear to have lived. Muslims (Turks) constituted perhaps a third of the total population of about 10,000 in 1805. There were also a few Jews and Franks (European merchants and Consuls) but the majority of the people were Greek Orthodox Christians. In terms of population at this time, the town may have ranked third or fourth in the size hierarchy of urban centers in the Peloponnese after Mistra (15-18,000), Tripolitsa (15,000) and Nauplia (7-10,000) (Kremmydas, 1972:18; E. Dodwell, 1819:116; W. M. Leake, 1830, II: 144). Population figures for eighteenth-century Patras vary considerably nevertheless. In 1765 Chandler estimated the town's population at 10,000 whilst three decades later two widely differing estimates of 6,000 and 30,000 are given by Olivier and Castellan respectively (Kremmydas, 1972:18).

Ships anchored in the roadstead in front of the town but, though the holding ground was good and some protection was offered on the south by a shallow curve in the coast, there was little shelter from the west and winds, "the latter of which sometimes blows with great impetuosity down the gulph" (sic) (Dodwell, 1819:119) and forced "vessels to fly off ... to some of the Ionian isles for shelter" (S. S. Wilson, 1839: 481). Small craft, however, sheltered behind a mole.

The eighteenth-century town was pleasantly situated "upon an amphitheater at a little distance from the sea" (F. C. Pouqueville, 1813:51), and stood upon "a bluff of marl rock..." between two small alluvial plains (Naval Intelligence Division, 1945, III: 193). The westward plain extends to the headland of Mavrovouni at the entrance to the Gulf of Corinth/Lepanto and merges with a tract of sand dunes, lagoons, and swamps in that vicinity. The area is dominated to the south by the detached ridge of Mt. Skollis (965 m). Some three miles east of the town in the eighteenth century there was an extensive marsh, probably malarial (Dodwell, 1819:116), and perhaps responsible for Patras' reputation as an unhealthy town (T. Watkins, 1792:329; J. Murray, 1840:26), though much of the narrow plain in this direction consists of alluvial fans formed by rivers flowing through rugged hills from the dominant bastion of Mt. Panakhaikon (1926 m). The hill country of folded shales, sandstones and conglomerates broadens out south and west of Mt. Panakhaikon, and is backed by a high escarpment running southwards which effectively forms the boundary to the Patras district (Naval Intelligence Division, 1945, III: 189-193). These hills were covered with woods of oak, fir and Aleppo pine, even in the late nineteenth century, though there were also extensive tracts of cultivation (A. Philippson, 1895).

Rural settlements and population

The increased export of commercial crops through the port of Patras and the demand for foodstuffs from the growing population of the town itself are likely to have affected the hinterland. An expansion in the amount of land devoted to currants has been suggested above though response to rising demand would be delayed for the six years required for the vines to mature and become productive (F. de Beaujour, 1800:220; F. Strong, 1842:176). Increased demand for wheat could be met more quickly, either by selling more "surplus" or by putting more of the annually-sown land under that crop, possibly at the expense of another.

Rising demand for agricultural produce from the hinterland of Patras is also likely to have affected both the rural population and their settlements. Population probably grew overall; villages may have become bigger; some long-abandoned sites may have been reoccupied;[1] some completely new villages may have been established. Whist the data are not available to trace change in land use in any detail, information does exist in two sources dating from either end of the Ottoman period to test the validity of the propositions about the likely effects upon population and settlement.[2]

---

[1]A Venetian source records 12 "*ville distrutte*" in the *Territorio di Patrasso*. See, Querini-Stampalia Library, Venice, Codex XXVII, Cl.III, Breve descrittione del Regno di Morea ; and Museo Civico Correr, Venice, Codex no. 3248-49.

[2]Archivio di Stato, Venice, Grimani dai Servi 54. N. 158, Libro Ristretti della Famiglie e Animi effettive in Cadana Territorii del Regno [di Morea] (for 1700); and Commission Scientifique de Morée, 1835, *Relations du Voyage de la Commission Scientifique de Morée,* Paris and Strasbourg, Vol. 2 (for 1830). Hereafter they will be cited as Grimani, Libro Ristretti ... and *Commission Scientifique* ... respectively.

The earliest source is an age-sex breakdown of the population of named settlements dated to 1700 and known as the Grimani Census.[1] The data appear to have been collected reasonably carefully at a time of security and stability in the region; they are thought to be reliable (V. Panayotopoulos, 1985). The latter source is an enumeration of population, settlement by settlement, carried out at the end of the War of Greek Independence, a period of considerable upheaval and dislocation. It was conducted by men attached to the French *Mission Scientifique de Morée* (1835) working closely with the surveyors of the French Military Mission.[2] The data are incomplete and sometime inconsistent, as might be expected from a source compiled before the Peloponnese had settled back to some semblance of normality.

Names in both sources can be identified on modern topographical maps and the resultant patterns analyzed. This exercise has been carried out for the present, *Eparkhia* of Patra. Although the hinterland of Patras was probably larger in the eighteenth century than the modern *eparkhia*, this administrative district provides a convenient geographical unit for analysis. Its boundaries lie between 16 and 50 kms from the town and its area is some 844 km^2. The principle of distance decay suggests that this territory is close enough to the town and sufficiently small for the proposed effects of development in the town to be relatively great, despite the rugged trackways which, until recently, connected the port with the interior. The modern *eparkhia* also corresponds in a broad sense with the *Territorio di Patrasso* of 1700 and the *Éparchie de Patras* of c. 1830.

The proportion of the total settlements identified (69.0 per cent and 91.3 per cent respectively) and the proportion of the population living in them (84.0 per cent and 92.8 per cent respectively) show that the identification exercise has produced samples of sufficient size for reasonable inferences to be drawn from the data.

One hundred settlements were named in the *Territorio di Patrasso* by the Grimani Census (table; fig. 2). Of these 69 have been identified and all lie within the boundaries of the present *eparkhia*. The total population of the district was 10,521 souls. Since the town of Patras contained 3,832 souls, the rural population consisted of 6,689 people. They lived in settlements with a

[1]Grimani, Libro Ristretti ...

[2]*Commission Scientifique ...*

mean size of 96.9 souls, though the range lay between 5 (Asteri) and 388 (Zumbata). Patras was thus completely dominant as a population center. It contained 36.4 per cent of the district's entire population, and was about 40 times larger than the average village and nearly 10 times the size of the next largest settlement, Zumbata.

Of the identified and therefore located settlements, 13 (18.8 per cent) lay below the 100 m contour and thus, generally speaking, in the lower lying land of the district. Another 32 identified settlements (46.4 per cent) were located between the 100 m contour and the 400 m contour; empirical investigation suggests than the 400 m contour generally coincides with a sharp break of slope which marks the lower edge of the truly mountainous terrain in the *eparkhia*. A further 24 of the identified settlements were found above the 400 m contour, that is, in truly high and generally mountainous terrain.

The mean size of settlement identified below the 10 m contour in 1700 was 73.6 souls. The zone as a whole contained 54.3 percent of the population in all of the identified settlements in the *eparkhia*. Patras itself, however, contained 80.0 per cent of the population of the identified settlements in this zone. In the zone between 100 and 400 m, the mean identified settlement had a population of 65.4 souls, whilst the identified settlements in the zone contained 23.8 per cent of the total population of the identified settlements in the *eparkhia*. The mean size of the identified settlement found above 400 m was 85.6 souls and the zone contained 22.2 per cent of the population in the *eparkhia's* identified settlements.

The *Commission Scientifique* listed 127 places in the *Éparchie de Patras* (table; fig. 37). This suggests an overall increase of 27 on the number of settlements existing in 1700, though we cannot be entirely sure about this because the bases on which localities were selected for inclusion in the two sources are unknown. However, an increase in the number of inhabited places is the likely outcome of economic expansion at a technological level where mechanization of farming was unknown and growth in output therefore largely reflects higher inputs of labor. The total population of the district also appears to have grown to 13,357 individuals.[1] The increase of 2,836 people (27.0 per cent) gives an annualized rate of 0.21 per cent over the period 1700-1830.

[1]This total has been calculated by subtracting the number of families in two settlements which were identified as lying outside the boundaries of the modern *eparkhia* (20) from the total number of families (2.382) given by the *Commission Scientifique* for the *Éparchie de Patras* and multiplying the result by the mean family size accepted by the French at the time (4.75).l

Although this is not an unreasonable rate of population growth by modern standards, it can be accepted as no more than indicative here because of the distortions which the figures may have suffered through the upheavals of the War of Independence and the earlier Orlov Rebellion.

Patras itself (437 families, about 2,076 individuals) is considerably smaller than the earlier estimates would have suggested, and this must be a direct result of death and flight during the war. With 15.4 per cent of the *eparkhia*'s total population, it was less dominant in its district than in 1700 which would hardly have been the case for a port city in "normal" times. The mean size of the rural settlements had also fallen to 88.8 individuals, a decline of about 8 per cent. The range was between about 5 people (one family at Neokhori) and 432 (91 families at Kastritsi). (M. Wagstaff, 2001).

However, amongst the 17 identified rural settlements lying below the 100 m contour the mean size had grown to 106.1 individuals (an increase of 44.2 per cent). Mean size amongst the 48 identified settlements in the 100 to 400 m zone was 74.1 individuals. This represents an increase of 13.3 per cent in the mean size of settlements compared with 1700. The height zone as a whole contained about 3,557 people, that is 27.2 per cent of the total within the boundaries of the modern *eparkhia*. A substantial increase (69.8 per cent) over the situation in 1700 is indicated. Fifty-one of the identified settlements from the *Commission Scientifique*'s list were located above the 400 m contour. The number represents a 112.5 per cent expansion in the zone since 1700. The mean size of the settlements here was 97.2, an increase of 13.5 per cent compared with 1700.

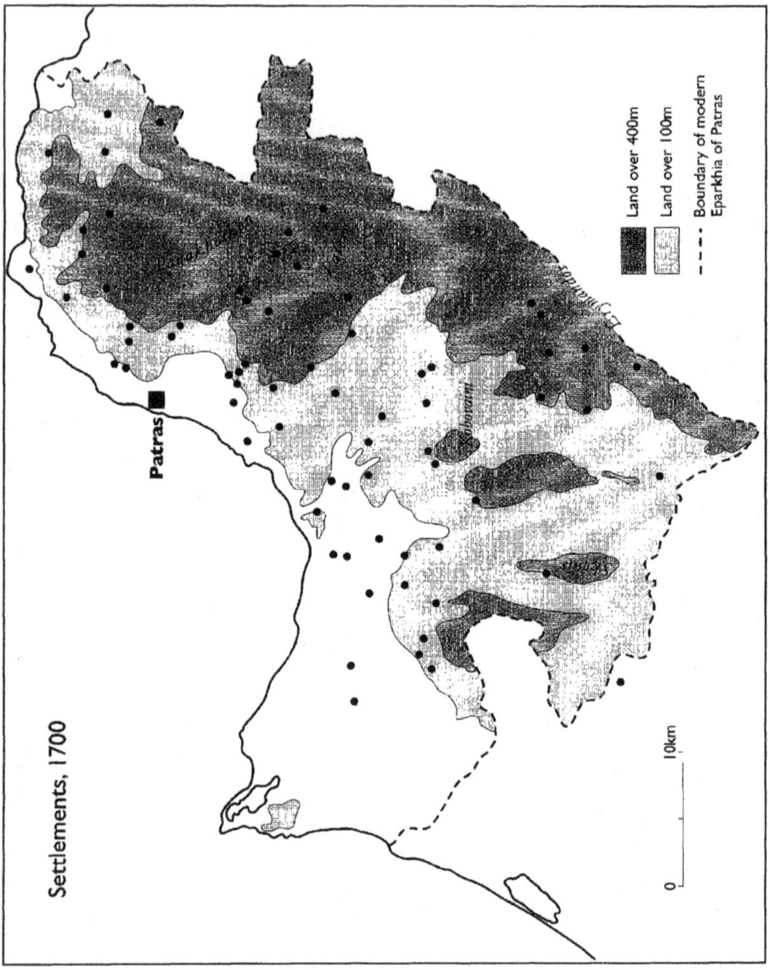

Fig. 2:
Distribution of identified settlements, 1700.

Discussion

It is conceivable that the various indications of growth in the number of settlements and the total population between 1700 and 1830 are artifacts of the comparison of flawed and incompatible data sets. Nonetheless, the changes are often of such considerable magnitude that even a skeptic might concede that they represent something genuine. We believe that they are consistent with the economic expansion in the Patras district discussed in the first part of the paper.

A comparatively large increase in the number of identified settlements in the zone below 100 m (5.0 or 38.5 per cent), accompanied by an increase in the mean size of the rural population, is probably consistent with the more intensive use of land implied by the reported spread of currant cultivation in the plain near Patras itself. The small change in the percentage of the total rural population in identified settlements in this zone (1.4) suggests that the changes are unlikely to have been due to the war.

The increase in the number of identified settlements in other height zones, if it is not an artifact of the data sets and the shortcomings of the identification exercise, is probably too great to be accounted for solely by the establishment of refugees from the war in relatively inaccessible and more secure locations. It is more likely to be a result of long-term expansion in economic activity and a related growth in the population of the district as a whole. The available figures, for all their shortcomings, suggest that population grew at annualized rates of 0.5 per cent in the 100-400 m zone and 1.2 per cent above 400 m. If these growth rates are correct, they are low enough to be compatible with natural increase, perhaps supported by a small amount of immigration in the case of the higher zones. Small rates of growth in population accompanied by an apparent expansion in the number of rural settlements seems consistent with the action of a long-term process. A possible explanation is colonization, either of land completely unused in the past or of fields which have not been used within recent times.

The recognition of *distrutte* settlements by the Venetian authorities and of *hali* (empty) settlements by their Ottoman counterparts is suggestive in this connection. Of the 61 settlements identified and located from the Ottoman *Defter-i Mufassal* of 1715-16 which were reported from the Kaza of Balya Badrc,[1] 11 were described as *hali* (empty) (18.0 per cent). Most of these (63.6 per cent) were concentrated in the 100-400 m height zone. Settlement foundation or reoccupation, accompanied by land colonization, can perhaps be seen as a response to general economic growth, stimulated by the demand mediated through the port of Patras. It affected the more distant, higher and marginal land, as well as the neighboring plains. The colonists themselves may have come from villages within the Patras district itself, but they may also have been drawn from the higher villages in the interior of the Peloponnese where economic opportunities were more limited. Examination of settlement patterns in the Patras *eparkhia* for the period 1700 to 1907

[1]Tapu Arşiv Dairesi Başbakanlık, Ankara, Tapu ve Kadastro Genel Müdürlüğü, No. 24, Mora Liva.

certainly suggests that 1700-1830 was the phase when the number of "new" settlements increased most rapidly (27 more settlement names in 1830 than in 1700), followed by the period 1830-79 (25 more settlements named at the end of the period than at the beginning). If these conclusions linking population and settlement growth with economic expansion are correct, then the generalized economic development recognized for the whole of north-western Peloponnese in the second half of the nineteenth century actually began under Ottoman rule, a hundred or so years earlier.

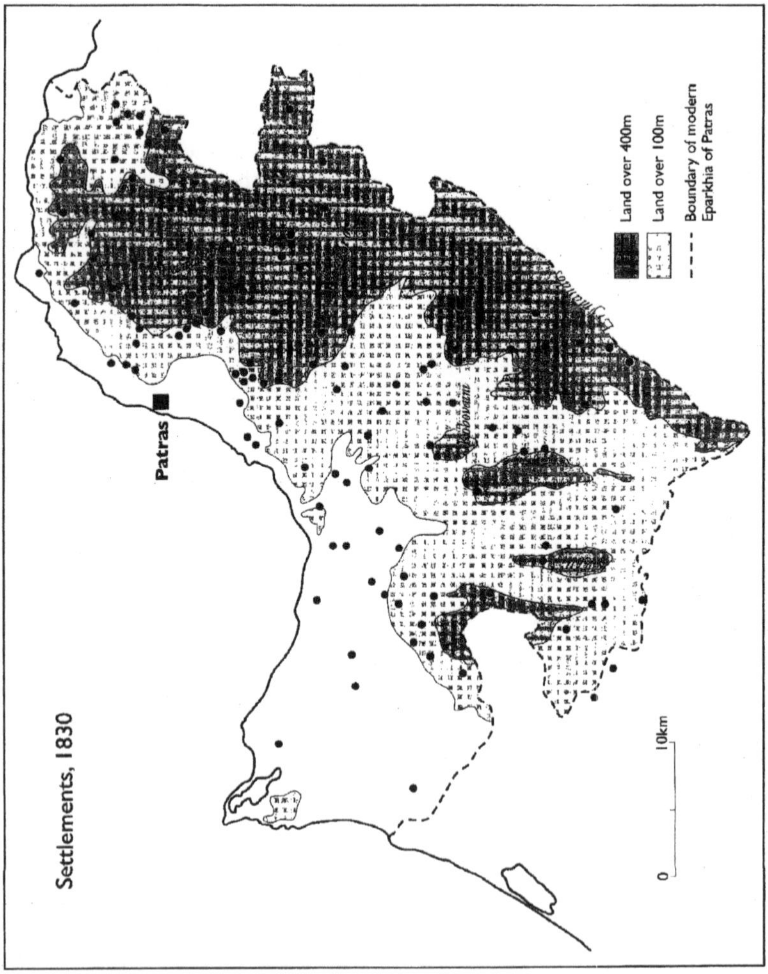

Figure 3:
Distribution of identified settlements, 1830.

Table
Comparative data on settlements and population
1700 and c. 1830

	1700*	1830*
Total number of settlements	100	127
Total number of settlements identified (including Patras)	69	117
Number in height zone <100 m	13	18
100-400 m	32	48
>400 m	24	51
Total populations (souls/individuals)	10,521	13,357
Population of Patras	3,382	2,076
Total population without Patras	6,689	11,281
Total population in identified settlements (including Patras)		
(souls/individuals)	8,842	12,395
percentage of total	84.2	92.8
Population of identified settlements by height zone		
<100 m	4,789	3,879
100-400 m	2,095	3,557
>400 m	1,958	4,959
Mean size of settlements (without Patras)		
(souls/individuals)	96.9	88.8
Mean size of identified settlements by height zone		
<100 m	73.6	106.1
100-400 m	65.4	74.1
>400 m	85.6	97.2

*Grimani. Libro Ristretti...

** *Commission Scientifique* ...

BIBLIOGRAPHY

Bakounakis (N.), 1983, *Recherches sur la ville de Patras. La Renaissance, 1828-1858,* unpublished Diplôme de l'EHESS, Paris.

Bakounakis (N.), 1988, "La vigne et la ville : qui finance la culture?" in G. Dertilis, dir, *Banquiers, usuriers et paysans,* Paris. 322 p.

Bakounakis (N.), 1988a, *Πάτρα, 1828-1860, (Patras, 1828-1860)*, Athens, 285 p.

Beaujour (Félix de), 1800, *Tableau du Commerce de la Grèce, formé d'après une année moyenne, depuis 1787 jusqu'en 1797*, A. A. Renouard, Paris.

Bramsen (J.), 1820, *Travels in Egypt, Syria, Cyprus, the Morea, Greece, Italy etc.*, H. Colburn, London, vol. 2.

Carrière (Charles) et Courdurié (Marcel), 1975, "Grandes heures de Livourne au XVIIIe siècle", *Revue Historique*, Vol. CCLIV, 39-80.

Commission Scientifique de Morée, 1835, *Relations du Voyage de la Commission Scientifique de Morée*, Paris & Strasbourg, vol. 2.

Dodwell (E.), 1819, *Classical and Topographical Tour through Greece during the Years 1801, 1805 and 1806,* London.

Eldem (Edhem), 1988, *Le Commerce français d'Istanbul au XVIIIe siècle*, unpublished Ph D thesis, Université de Provence.

Eldem (Edhem), 1999, *French Trade in Istanbul in the Eighteenth Century,* Brill, Leiden.

Epstein (M.), 1908, *The Early History of the Levant Company,* Routledge, London.

Frangakis-Syrett (Elena), 1987, "Greek Mercantile Activities in the eastern Mediterranean, 1780-1820", *Balkan Studies*, Vol. 28/1, Thessaloniki, 73-86.

Frangakis-Syrett (Elena), 1992, *The Commerce of Smyrna in the Eighteenth Century, 1700-1820*, Centre for Asia Minor Studies, Athens, 375 p.

Frangakis-Syrett (Elena), 1993, "Patras", *Review*, Vol. XVI, 387-410.

Frangakis-Syrett (Elena), 1994, "Monoculture in Nineteenth-Century Greece and the Port-City of Patras", *Journal of the Hellenic Diaspora*, Vol. 20/2, 9-34.

Frangakis-Syrett (Elena), 2000, "Commercial Strategies and Competition in the Levant: the British and the Dutch in Eighteenth-Century İzmir", A. Hamilton, A. de Groot & M. van den Boogert, eds., *Friends and Rivals in the East*, Brill, Leiden, 135-158.

Galt (J.), 1813, *Letters from the Levant*, London.

Giannakopoulou (H.), 1991, "*Μια άλλη όψη του σταφιδικού ζητήματος: η περίπτωσις της Αιτολωακαρνανίας κατά τον* 17° *και* 18° *αιώνα*", ("Another aspect of the problem of currants : the case of Etoloakarnania in the 17th and 18th centuries"), *Proceedings of the First Archaeological & Historical Conference of Etoloakarnania*, 399-418.

Greene (Molly), 2000, *A Shared World,* Princeton University Press, Princeton, NJ.

Kremmydas (Vasilis), 1972, *Το εμπόριο της Πελοποννήσου στο 18° αιώνα, 1715-1792, (The Commerce of the Peloponnese in the 18th century, 1715-1792)*, Athens, 418 p.

Kremmydas (Vasilis), 1980, *Συγκοιρία και εμπόριο στη προεπαναστατική Πελοπόννησο, 1793-1821, (Conjuncture and Commerce in Pre-revolutionary Peloponnese, 1793-1821)*, Athens, 271 p.

Lazaris (V.), 1986, *Πολιτική ιστορία της Πάτρας (A Political History of Patras)*, Athens, vol. 1, 384 p.

Leake (W. M.), 1830, *Travels in the Morea*, John Murray, London.

Murray (John), Publisher, 1840, *A Handbook for Travellers in the Ionian Islands, Greece, Turkey, Asia Minor and Constantinople...*, London, 392 p.

Nanninga (J. G.), ed., 1952, *Bronnen tot de Geschiedenis van den Levantschen Handel. Derde deel: 1727-1765*, M. Nijhoff, 'S-Gravenhage.

Naval Intelligence Division, 1945, *Geographical Handbook Series: Greece*, Hydrographic Department, Admiralty, London.

The Oxford English Dictionary, 1989, 2nd ed., vol. IV.

Panayotopoulos (Vasilis), 1985, *Πληθυσμός και οικισμοί της Πελοποννήσου, 13°-18° αιώνας (Population and Settlements in the Peloponnese, 13th-18th centuries)*, Commercial Bank of Greece, Athens, 414 p.

Panzac (Daniel), dir., 1991, *Les Villes dans l'Empire ottoman: Activités et Sociétés*. CNRS, Paris, vol. 1. 416 p.

Panzac (Daniel), 1996, *Commerce et navigation dans l'empire ottoman au XVIIIe siècle*, Isis, Istanbul.

Peyssonnel (Charles-Claude de), 1785, *Lettre de M. de Peyssonnel ...*, Amsterdam.

Philippson (A.), 1895, "Zur Vegetationskarte des Peloponnes", *Petermanns Geographische Meiteilungen*, N° 41, 273-279.

Pizanias (P.), 1988, *Οικονομική ιστορία της ελληνικής σταφίδας, 1851-1912. (The Economic History of Greek Currants, 1851-1912)*, Commercial Bank of Greece, Athens, 159 p.

Pouqueville (F. C.), 1813, *Travels in the Morea and the Ottoman Empire...*, H. Colburn, London.

Svoronos (N.), 1956, *Le Commerce de Salonique au XVIIIe siècle*, P.U.F., Paris, 423 p.

Strong (F.), 1842, *Greece as a Kingdom. A Statistical Description of that Country from the Arrival of King Otto, in 1833, down to the Present*, Longman, Brown, Green and Longmans, London.

Themeli-Katifori (D.), 1973, *Η δίωξις της πειρατείας και το θαλάσσιον δικαστήριον κατά την πρώτην καποδιστριακήν περίοδον, 1828-1829, (The Suppression of Piracy and the Maritime Court in the first Capodistrian period, 1828-1829)*, University of Athens Press, Athens, vol. 1, 257 p.

Triantafyllidou-Baladié (Yolande), 1988, *Το εμπόριο και η οικονομία της Κρήτης, 1669-1795, (The Commerce and Economy of Crete, 1669-1795)*, Iraklion, Crete, 335 p.

Triantafyllidou-Baladié (Yolande), 1991, "Le marché des produits agricoles de la Canée aux XVIIe et XVIIIe siècles. Le mécanisme des échanges et les pratiques du crédit", Panzac, D., ed., *Les villes dans l'empire ottoman: Activités et Sociétés*, CNRS, Paris, vol. I, 299-320.

Wagstaff (Malcolm), 2001, "Family Size in the Peloponnese (Southern Greece) in 1700", *Journal of Family History*, Vol. 26/3, 337-349.

Watkins (T.), 1792, *Travels through Switzerland, Italy*..., London.

Wilson (S. S.), 1839, *A Narrative of the Greek Mission, or Sixteen Years in Malta and Greece*, London.

Wood (A. C.) 1935, *A History of the Levant Company*, O.U.P. London.

NETWORKS OF FRIENDSHIP, NETWORKS OF KINSHIP: EIGHTEENTH-CENTURY LEVANT MERCHANTS

All too often when one deals with the commercial history of the eastern Mediterranean in the 18th century, and in particular with the external maritime trade of the Ottoman empire with Europe, also called the Levant trade, a number of distinctions are made and dichotomies implied between the two groups active in this trade, namely the European and Ottoman merchants, which upon closer examination do not always bear out. Differences can be found, especially in the earlier part of the 18th century, in a number of areas related to commerce: namely, in the trading practices and overall business strategies of each group, in their legal status and in their capital resources as well as access to capital and markets. Although differences did thus certainly exist between the two groups of merchants, it is perhaps more remarkable, and probably less well understood, that their trading practices also contained common features and that the commercial networks of European and Ottoman merchants often overlapped with each other, whilst the differences dividing them displayed greater fluidity than expected. In the closing decades of the 18th century, as the world economy was both expanding and undergoing major changes, the differences between the two groups started diminishing altogether.

In trying to establish common areas of commercial activity and practice as well as differences between them, the activities of the British and the Greeks, in particular, as representatives of western European and Ottoman merchants respectively, will be examined. However, given the interlocking nature of the commercial networks and practices of both groups, references will also be made to other merchants who were active in the Levant, namely the Dutch, French, Jewish and Armenian merchants. The relative absence of Muslim merchants is primarily due to the fact that this study examines primarily the external maritime trade of the western part of the Ottoman empire with the West whilst the internal, landed or coastal, trade of the empire, where Turkish merchants were particularly active and prominent, is only considered in relation to the external, western-bound maritime trade of the empire.

I. Capital, credit and the Levant trade

For most of the 18th century, and certainly for the first three quarters, there were two areas where the clearest demarcations between Ottoman and western merchants could be made: namely in their capital resources and access to capital as well as in their legal status in Ottoman trade. In general terms, the capital resources at the disposal of the larger commercial houses in London, Marseilles or Amsterdam, which were active in the Levant trade, although in themselves not always astounding in scale, were much larger than the sums most merchants or merchants-cum-bankers in the Ottoman centers could muster. For instance, the Marseilles-based international trading house of Roux Frères, which was active in the French Levant trade for the entire 18th and into the early 19th centuries, had a truly world-wide network of commercial activities. They were able to place their activities in the Ottoman market within a truly international conjuncture of market fluctuations and patterns of demand not only in the commodities markets but in the money markets, too. Moreover, besides trade, Roux Frères were also active in merchant banking, shipping and insurance. In terms of capital resources and scale of activities, the house of Roux Frères may well have represented the upper end of the scale of European firms active in the Levant trade. In fact, it could well have been in a league of its own, judging from archival evidence of its world-wide activities. There were certainly large fortunes to be found amongst the Ottoman elite. However, despite possible exceptions to the contrary,[1] the Ottoman elite was not, as a group, interested in investing heavily in trade,[2] and, for a host of reasons, found other areas of investment, such as tax-farming or lending to the state, more lucrative and desirable.[3]

For the western trading houses, the scale and availability of their capital resources impacted not only the scale of their operations but also the geographical extent of their networks. Respectable London firms in the Levant trade such as Edward and Arthur Radcliffe or Frye & Mitford, had widespread networks of correspondents and associates since the early 18th century. Although their networks may not have been literally global, as in the case of Roux Frères, they did include multiple centers mostly in coastal areas of the Ottoman empire, apart from the Mediterranean, as well as further afield in

[1]We have evidence of Ottoman investors, Muslim and non-Muslim, in shipping. See, Çızakça, Murat, *A Comparative Evolution of Business Partnerships in the Islamic World and Europe with Specific references to the Ottoman Archives* (Brill: Leiden, 1996): pp. 88-122.

[2]Genç, Mehmet, "Osmanlı iktisadi dünya görüşünün ilkeleri", *İ.Ü. Edebiyat Fakültesi Sosyal Dergisi*, III (1999): pp. 237-40.

[3]For investment in tax-farming, see Çızakça, *A Comparative Evolution of Business Partnerships*: pp. 140-5; 153-7.

western Europe. Ottoman merchant houses, too, could have agents in a number of cities in the Ottoman empire and Europe. However, for most of the century, their networks were not of the same extent and scale as those of the Europeans. This changed in the last quarter of the 18th century. Higher levels of capital accumulation, among other factors, allowed Ottoman merchants, too, to establish a truly international network of agencies and partnerships.

Whether they were trading in Europe or with the Levant, European merchants tended, in the 18th century, to combine commerce with other activities such as shipping, merchant banking or insurance.[1] Such a strategy had evolved partly in order to gain greater control over operations and partly in order to spread risks. Employing spare funds in making advances, usually short-term, to fellow merchants was a widespread practice. If the reputation of a commercial house was strong enough and its capital resources of a proportionate scale, then the firm could further employ such funds in acceptances or in discounting of bills, in essence becoming a private banker alongside its trading activities. Owning a ship for long-distance blue water trade was not unusual for a British house trading with the Levant. In an age of irregular shipping schedules, owning the means of transportation gave one an advantage, as well as a considerable capital asset. Given the vagaries of communication over great distances and the delays involved, another feature of long-distance international trade, merchants in Europe could wait sometimes up to two years before they could reap any returns on their capital outlay. The correspondent for the British house, or *factor* as he was called at the time, might have had to wait for a similar length of time in order to realize any returns on the capital of his *principal,* as his employer was called in the 18th century, or on his commission. For instance, when he purchased cotton or silk in the Levant to send to his employer in Europe, the correspondent took his commission also in cotton or silk, rather than in cash, since this was a barter exchange; he then sent home his commission to be sold for his own account. The Levant agent then had to wait between one and a half to two years before any cash came to him from the transaction.[2] In order to counteract delays in investment returns as well as to offset risks, further strategies were adopted. Although such strategies were not exclusive to the Levant trade, they became fundamental to the way it was carried out. One of these strategies was the widespread practice amongst merchants of simultaneously entering into many transactions, which could originate either in the Levant or in Europe, by

[1]Joslin, D. M., "London private bankers, 1720-1785", in Carus-Wilson, E.M. (ed.), *Essays in Economic History*, II (London: St. Martin's, 1966): pp. 341-3.

[2]Davis, Ralph, *Aleppo and Devonshire Square. English Traders in the Levant in the Eighteenth Century* (London: Macmillan, 1967): p. 82.

having part shares in them. Such commercial transactions could involve any market in the Mediterranean and Europe that the trading house, which spearheaded and saw the transaction through, had contacts with. Such a multiplicity of transactions spread out risks as well as created a constant turnover of capital. For at any point in time any one of these transactions could mature allowing the merchant(s) to invest the proceeds in another shared transaction.

Such strategies were also part of the need to stretch one's capital further by adding to it that of one's associates. This would suggest that the capital resources of such firms, while larger than those of most Ottoman merchants, were not enormous. This was even more the case when it came to the capital resources that their correspondents in the Levant were able to have at their disposal. There are a number of reasons for this. For most of the 18th century the doctrine of mercantilism held sway in the thinking of the major European states. Accordingly, British and French government authorities tried to prohibit, or restrict, the outflow of specie from their states by their nationals trading abroad. Although such policies met with only relative success,[1] they did nevertheless have an impact on the amount of capital resources European merchants in the Levant could dispose of. Further, such policies influenced the way trade was conducted by the Europeans in the Ottoman empire as the latter tried to overcome such monetary restrictions.

Besides the doctrine of mercantilism, conditions in the European money markets did not yet lend themselves to an unlimited flow of capital and credit. Even the most advanced European economies of England and the Netherlands were still developing their capital markets. Their banking sectors were in the course of evolving into a separate sector as the bigger private bankers were starting to move away from their other businesses in order to specialize in banking. Although access to capital and credit was still developing in the West, the major European economies were nevertheless further advanced than the state of the credit and capital markets in the Ottoman empire would suggest. However, an area where the Ottomans had made important advances in the mechanics of credit was in their sophisticated system of bills of exchange which was widely used within the empire. However a comparison between the rates of interest in Britain, where the legal

[1]For instance, British merchants were always trying to import foreign currrency into İzmir even at times when, unlike their French and Dutch counterparts, they were not allowed to do so, according to Levant Company regulations. Public Record Office, London, SP 105/118, Levant Company, London, 27 April 1750 to British Consul Crawley, İzmir. Hereafter, these archives will be cited as PRO.

maximum rate of interest was lowered in 1714 to five per cent and the Ottoman empire, where interest rates three times this figure were current amongst merchants in urban centers, is illustrative of the tightness of credit and indicative of a less developed banking sector. Moreover, in the large Ottoman interior, far higher, in essence usurious, levels of interest rates remained current, even beyond the 18th century, further indicating different levels of development between the British and Ottoman money markets. However, not all European capital markets were as developed as the British or the Dutch. For instance, major Italian ports, all of which were active commercial partners of the Ottoman empire, could experience considerable volatility in their money markets. Although these city-ports were important entrepôts for the passage of specie, as well as for goods in European-Ottoman commerce, they could, at certain times of the year, experience scarcity of specie in their money markets[1] at levels that were similar to the scarcity of specie that the Ottoman economy experienced. It should be noted, however, that specie scarcity was more endemic as well as more acute in the Ottoman empire than it was in Europe.[2]

For all of the above reasons, Europeans trading in the Levant did not often dispose of much larger capital resources than Ottoman merchants. This was so even when the capital resources of their employers in Europe were larger. The situation, of course, varied according to the amount of business that the particular *factor* was able to undertake and thus the amount of commission income that he was able to accrue over time, which could render him greater or lesser capital liquidity. It also depended on whether he disposed of any personal fortune upon being established in the Levant. On the whole, however, a periodic lack of funds was common among most British *factors*; it was even more common amongst their French counterparts. Such conditions of trade led the Europeans to adopt practices which were not different from those of the Ottomans: for instance, they borrowed at high interest rates from other European or Ottoman lenders, as well as regularly investing any spare capital they might have had in money lending as well as in merchant-banking, including speculating on the value of various currencies, alongside their

[1]Archives Nationales de France, Paris, AE Bi 600, French Consul Raulin, Genoa, 14 Jan. 1793 to Minister, Paris. Hereafter, these archives will be cited as ANF.

[2]Frangakis-Syrett, Elena, "The Ottoman monetary system in the 18th century: problems and solutions", paper delivered at the *Fifteenth Symposium of the International Committee of Pre-Ottoman and Ottoman Studies,* London School of Economics, London University, 8-12 July, 2002.

commodity trading.[1] Most of these activities were carried out on behalf of and with the knowledge of their employers and, where the funds were theirs, on their own account. The very high premium given to cash in the Ottoman economy made such practices all the more desirable and lucrative for both European and Ottoman merchants to pursue. Should they have the funds available, the latter were just as likely to engage in some kind of merchant banking activity, including money lending or money changing, besides trade. After all, in the absence of a fully developed institutionalized banking sector, being a merchant-cum-private banker was still common practice even in 18th-century Europe.

The cash-flow problems of the Europeans also impacted the dynamics of their relationships with the Ottomans. It strengthened the merchant/broker relationship that emerged between the European in the Levant, as employer, and the Ottoman, as broker. Contrary to official regulations, the Europeans sold their goods to Ottoman merchants for credit of either several months long or until the next caravan came. However, they also themselves often bought goods on credit until their shipment of goods came or until their bill(s) of exchange matured.[2] In so doing they came increasingly to rely on the contacts and ability of a good broker, who would get them the goods when they needed them, or who would have inside knowledge of the trust worthiness and reputation of, for instance, Turkish, Jewish or other local buyers from places miles away to whom they had to trust their goods. A good broker thus became an invaluable asset. It was not only the Europeans who had local merchants, mostly non-Muslims, namely, Armenians, Greeks or Jews, as their brokers. Ottoman houses did likewise.[3] Specializations amongst brokers indicate as much. For instance, sales of imported goods, which were invariably made on credit and rarely for cash, were conducted by the *house* broker, that is the European merchant's broker, who dealt with the *street* or Ottoman buyer's broker.[4] The reverse also held true where Armenian or Turkish silk merchants, for instance, might sell directly, or through their brokers, to the brokers of the Europeans. Ottoman brokers became crucial links through which networks of information, market opportunities and personal contacts flowed. Brokers had

---

[1] Frangakis-Syrett, Elena, "The economic activities of the Ottoman and western communities in 18th-century İzmir", Fleet, Kate (ed.), *The Ottoman Empire in the Eighteenth Century*, *OM*, XVIII [LXXIX]/1 (1999): pp. 22-6.

[2] ANF, AE Bi 1052, French Consul Charles de Peyssonnel, İzmir, 29 Jan. 1749 to Minister, Paris. He is the father of Charles-Claude de Peyssonnel; they both served as Consuls in İzmir.

[3] ANF, AE Biii 242, Commerce du Levant, Ordonnance de 20 sept. 1810.

[4] *Parliamentary Papers, Tariffs* (London, 1843): II, p. 98. The reference holds for the 18th century, too.

also the right to trade on their own account, at times "unofficially" mortgaging their employers' funds to do so.[1]

As expected with 18th-century international commerce, conditions in the market and the laws of supply and demand were fundamental principles governing the Levant trade. However, the daily conduct of trade was also affected by the constraints on the capital resources of the participants leading to, besides credit, a widespread use of barter. This having been said, selling and buying for cash was still preferable to the "tedious road of barter", as echoed in the merchants' correspondence,[2] for it was difficult to calculate one's profits where barter was involved, since it required selling the goods one got in exchange for one's own, before one could make any returns on one's capital outlay. It also increased the risks of not making a profit if the market for a bartered good had, in the interim, changed. Thus if barter could be avoided, even partially, with the substitution of a certain amount of cash, a merchant could get better terms and more advantageous prices. Equally, if there was the need to conclude a sale fast, to load the goods aboard a ship about to depart, or if the market was soft and needed further incentives, the offer of some cash, besides credit and/or barter, was highly desirable. In other words, given the tightness of capital amongst all the participants in the Levant as well as the chronic scarcity of specie in the Ottoman economy, cash carried an especially high premium and affected trade in fundamental ways.

II. Protectionism and the liberal Dutch

Another clear area of demarcation between European and Ottoman merchants, for most of the 18th century, was their legal status and the way it affected them. European protectionism prohibited Ottoman merchants from having direct access to the major markets of Britain and France even when the Capitulations gave British and French merchants, along with other Europeans, access to the Ottoman market, as well as preferential tariff treatment. As a result, Ottoman merchants had to develop different strategies, such as becoming *beratlıs* or brokers, in order to enter those markets. *Berats*[3] gave

---

[1]ANF, AE Bi 1059, French Consul Charles-Claude de Peyssonnel, (son of Charles de Peyssonnel), İzmir, 9 June 1769 to Minister, Paris.

[2]E.g., the correspondence of Colvill Bridger who traded in Aleppo in the middle of the 18th century. I would like to express my thanks to Mr. James Bridger for making this collection available to me.

[3]A *berat* gave an Ottoman the right to trade as a European by making him a national of the European country which had issued it to him, in return for a handsome fee. On *berats*, see Bağış, Ali İhsan, *Osmanlı Ticaretinde Gayri Müslimler* (Ankara: Turhan Kitabevi, 1983): pp. 39-70.

direct access to those markets to a limited number of merchants; being a broker gave indirect access to a larger number of Ottoman merchants who could, at least in theory, trade for themselves through their employers. There were, nevertheless, other opportunities that Ottoman merchants could exploit in order to gain access to the British or French markets. Throughout the 18th century Anglo-French maritime wars, which pitted one power against the other, offered intermittent access to the British and French markets through an Italian port, mostly Livorno, to Ottoman and other merchants.[1]

However, and this is important, even when there were no exceptional circumstances, Ottoman merchants were able to trade with the European market, *at large*, although not with Britain or France directly, through the Italian entrepôts or the Dutch ports and their networks. For example, Jewish merchants could charter a British ship in İzmir to send goods to their associates or commission agents in Amsterdam.[2] In the early 18th century, in particular, the size of the Jewish community of Livorno trading with the Levant must have been considerable, judging from the competition that the British *factory*[3] in İzmir encountered when British merchants, who were not members of the Levant Company, started sending cloth to Jewish merchants established in Livorno. The latter dispatched cloth, usually in European ships, to their associates in İzmir and were able to take business away from the British factory there.[4] Apart from Livorno,[5] Trieste, Ancona, Genoa or Messina routinely served as European bases for Ottoman Levant traders throughout the 18th century. What is less clear from the sources, however, is the exact nature of the business relationship between the Levant-based and the European-based Jewish, Armenian or Greek merchants, and the extent of their networks. That is, did Armenian or Jewish merchants in İzmir, or elsewhere in the empire, have associates or commission agents with whom they traded on a regular basis, and were these agents based in multiple European centers? What is certain is that as a group the Ottomans did not confine themselves to the role of broker in Ottoman-European trade but also participated in the empire's trade with the West. It would ultimately appear that an Ottoman merchant chose to participate, or not, in any given European market(s) based more on whether he had the capital resources to do so, than on whether he had the right legally to do it. Indeed, the entry of the Ottomans in the late 18th and early

1 Carrière, C. and M. Courdurié, "Grandes heures de Livourne au XVIIIe siècle", *Revue Historique*, CCLIV (1975): pp. 40-1.
2 PRO, SP 105/207, *The Mary*, İzmir, 13 March 1721. (The ship was bound for Amsterdam).
3 The term *factory* was used at the time to denote a mercantile community.
4 PRO, SP 105/115, Levant Company, London, 21 June 1699 to Consul Raye, İzmir.
5 E.g., PRO, SP 105/207, *The Mary*, İzmir, 5 Feb. 1721 (The ship had come from Livorno).

19th centuries into *all* the networks of European-Ottoman trade was the double result, on the one hand, of their own growing economic prosperity, which allowed them to establish themselves in multiple European centers and, on the other hand, the increasing volume of world trade which put pressure on the major European markets of Britain and France to ease and finally end their policies of protectionism.[1]

In the course of the 18th century, well before the British or the French had adopted a policy of economic liberalism, the Dutch were already exercising such a policy. In the process an interesting interplay between European and Ottoman merchants emerged,[2] for the Dutch made no legal distinctions between the various participants in their trading networks. It was not only Ottoman merchants who took advantage of this regime. The British also did likewise. *Factors* of British houses established in various ports in the Levant made purchases for their principals as easily for the London market as for the Dutch. At the same time, Dutch firms in Amsterdam traded both through other Dutch houses in the Levant, who acted as their correspondents, and through Ottoman merchants. For instance, de Vogel of Amsterdam employed in the 1760s as his agents in İzmir David van Lennep & Co., Clement van Saan and Fremeaux & Hopker[3] as well as the Ottoman Greek Bartholo Cardamici.[4] In addition, there were British merchants, established in an Ottoman port, who were acting as agents for Dutch companies in the Netherlands to whom they sent Ottoman goods, invariably in Dutch ships. Their correspondents, who traded from other Ottoman ports for them, could be either British or Dutch merchants, or both. We have the example of George Abbott in Istanbul who was acting as *factor* for William Allen in Manchester;[5] both families had a long-standing presence in the empire and in the Dutch Levant trade.[6] In 1781, G. Abbott arranged for his correspondents in Thessaloniki, Messrs Bartholomew Edward Abbott & Co. to send, on behalf

[1]For instance, in 1825, the Levant Company, membership in which conferred on one the right to trade with the Levant, was abolished, PRO, FO 78/136, Memorandum, Levant Company, London, 1825.

[2]Frangakis-Syrett, Elena, "Commercial practices and competition in the Levant: the British and the Dutch in 18th-century İzmir", in Hamilton, A., A. H. de Groot, and M. H. van den Boogert, (eds.), *Friends and Rivals in the East* (Brill: Leiden, 2000): pp. 135-58.

[3]ARA, de Vogel, 21 Dec. 1762 to Jean Boilley in Nanninga, J.G. (ed.), *Bronnen tot de Geschiedenis van den Levantschen Handel. Derde deel: 1727-1766* ('S-Gravenhage: Verkrijgbaar bij Martinus Nijhoff, 1952): pp. 477-8.

[4]ARA, de Vogel, 19 Nov. 1762 to Bartholo Cardamici, İzmir in Nanninga, *Bronnen tot de Geschiedenis Derde deel*: p. 475.

[5]The Abbott family had a long-standing presence in the Ottoman empire, having traded as Abbott & Co. in Ankara in mohair yarn in the 1720s.

[6]The family had traded under the name of Allen & Shaw in İzmir in the 1720s. PRO, SP 105/207, *The Asia*, İzmir, 28 Oct. 1721. Allen's associate in Amsterdam at the time was a Pietro Antonio de Leopaul. SP 105/207, *The Olive Branch*, İzmir, 24 Jan. 1721.

of his principals, cotton to Amsterdam for the order of Messrs Van der Viet & Sons. Abbott's correspondent in İzmir, Joseph Franel, also sent mohair yarn on another Dutch ship bound for Rotterdam to the order of the Amsterdam house.[1] Another arrangement was for the British to establish themselves in the Netherlands and to trade in the Levant through a combination of British and Dutch houses there. In the late 18th century, the well-known house of Messrs David van Lennep & Enslie in İzmir, apart from their other trading activities, acted also as correspondents for Richard Wallis in Istanbul,[2] sending goods to the Netherlands on the order of the principals of Wallis, namely the firm of Hope & Co. of Amsterdam.[3]

In the mid-18th century there were also Ottoman firms, Greek, Jewish and Armenian, established in the Dutch ports.[4] Of the three communities, it was the Ottoman Greeks, who were the most successful in developing their commercial networks in the Dutch Levant trade in the second half of the 18th century.[5] They were all trading with the Levant through a network of associates who were their co-religionists and often from the same family. We have the examples of Armenian houses in Istanbul whose agents in İzmir were sending figs or currants, on behalf of their principals, on Dutch ships, destined for the Amsterdam market.[6] However, there were also Ottoman houses trading with the Dutch port through Dutch agents or associates. Further, some Ottoman merchants evolved, over time, from being agents for Netherlands-based Dutch houses to trading themselves directly with the Netherlands. For instance, the family of Cardamici, who had been agents in İzmir for de Vogel in Amsterdam, in the 1760s, were trading in Istanbul 20 years later as Raphael Cardamici & Sons, with Paolo Cardamici as their correspondent in İzmir. They were sending goods to their Dutch correspondent or agent, in Amsterdam, on Dutch bottoms. Here we see a complete inversion of roles, with the Ottoman being the principal and the European, the agent. Further evidence of the Ottomans entering into partnerships with European firms in the Dutch Levant trade can be found in the late 18th century. By then they were following similar practices and strategies as their European counterparts,

---

[1]PRO, SP 105/187, Chancery, Istanbul, 15 Feb. 1781.

[2]Following the usual pattern, we find that the Wallis family was no newcomer to the Levant trade, having been present since the very early 18th century.

[3]PRO, SO 105/187, Chancery, Istanbul, 30 April 1781.

[4]Frangakis-Syrett, Elena, *The Commerce of Smyrna in the Eighteenth Century, 1700-1820* (Athens: Centre for Asia Minor Studies, 1992): p. 255.

[5]ARA, Fremeaux, van Lennep and Enslie, 29 June 1782 to van Haften, in Nanninga, J. G. (ed.), *Bronnen tot de Geschieddenis van den Levantschen Handel. Vierde deel: 1765-1826* ('S-Gravenhage: Verkrijgbaar bij Martinus Nijhoff, 1966): pp. 339-41; see also, Frangakis-Syrett, *The Commerce of Smyrna:* p. 256.

[6]PRO, SP 105/187, Chancery, Istanbul, 19 and 21 Feb. 1781.

entering into commercial transactions in part on their own account and in part on account of their Dutch or other European partners.[1] The British and the Ottomans were not the only ones participating in the Dutch Levant trade. For instance, French, Danes and Italians, usually established both in the Ottoman empire and in the Netherlands, traded with Amsterdam or Rotterdam.[2] However, the British and Ottoman merchants were probably the two groups who took most advantage of the liberty afforded them to do so.

Although the Levant Company endeavored to keep all non-members, or *non-freemen* as they were called, out of its trading networks,[3] it was nevertheless keen to ensure that as much business as possible came to its members, through commission fees, from any nationality, including the Ottomans, trading in the Levant! It actively encouraged *strangers,* that is non-British nationals as well as *non-freemen*, to consign goods to a British *factor* in any Ottoman port — on a British or non-British ship — on account of any merchant, European or Ottoman. The British factor acted as a commission agent, receiving or sending goods on behalf of these merchants. Commission fees were charged at the usual rate of two per cent.[4] The Levant Company also received a consulage fee at the rate of one per cent.[5] Although members from both groups of European and Ottoman merchants could thus interchange roles within the broad framework of Ottoman-European trade, it should nevertheless be made clear that, throughout the century, *the largest volume* of this trade was carried out by Europeans and not by Greek, Jewish, Armenian or Turkish merchants. This was because until the very late 18th century the Ottomans did not dispose of the capital, organization and networks of interlocking partnerships and agencies outside the Ottoman empire, and perhaps even within the empire, necessary to carry out the empire's maritime trade with the West, on a scale, scope and extent comparable to that of the Europeans. Ottoman merchants did, nevertheless, have in their hands the empire's internal trade, which accounted for the largest part, by far, of Ottoman commerce overall in the 18th century.

---

[1]PRO, SP 105/187, Raphael Cardamici, Istanbul, 1 June 1781.

[2]PRO, SP 105/187, Chancery, Istanbul, 13 March 1781.

[3]PRO, SP 105/129, British Consul Werry, İzmir, 13 July 1804 to Levant Company, London.

[4]This was standard practice at the time. For instance, a commission agent in any Italian port, or *comissionario,* as he was called, also charged the same rate. For Trieste, see Katsiardi-Hering, Olga *Η ελληνική παροικία της Τεργέστης, 1751-1830* [*The Greek Community of Trieste, 1751-1830*] (Athens: University of Athens Press, 1986): II, pp. 431-2. For Livorno, see Vlami, Despina, *Το φιορίνι, το σιτάρι και η οδός του κήπου* [*Florin, Wheat and Garden Street*] (Athens: Themelio, 2000): p. 92.

[5]PRO SP 105/211, The Printed Orders of the Levant Company, London, 9-12 Oct. 1744.

III. The organization of the British Levant trade

If we look at the way the British organized their Levant trade in the 18th century which, in very broad terms, was not too dissimilar to the French or Dutch, we discern three superimposed levels of organizational structure. At the first level, there were the *factors*, or correspondents, acting basically as commission agents for their principals in Britain and elsewhere in Europe. At times, their principals might be other houses in the Levant. The *factors* were the underpinning on which all trading activities rested and constituted the primary networks of the Europeans in the Ottoman empire. The networks were formed through interlocking partnerships between the various *factors* present in different Ottoman ports. Besides being business partners, the *factors* were often related by ties of kinship. They often came from families who had been present in the Ottoman empire for successive generations.

Superimposed on these primary networks, which existed *within* the empire, were the international networks of their principals and those of the associates of their principals. These networks constituted the second level of organization of the Levant trade. They, too, were formed through interlocking partnerships; the latter often took the form of associateships or agencies spread all over the Mediterranean and the Atlantic ports — from Livorno to Portugal and the Netherlands. The geographical extent of these networks depended on the activities of the principal house in Britain. Multiple partnerships were also the norm. One or more of the partners in the London house, that employed the *factor* in the Levant, could also combine with other merchants to create separate, though often overlapping, partnerships. The *factor* could have multiple partnerships, too. Although the *factor*/principal partnership formed the organizational basis for the Levant trade, both *factors* and principals traded with a multiplicity of associates at all times. Indeed, it is quite probable that at any given time most of the *factors* in an Ottoman port had participated in some kind of commercial transaction or other with many of the London houses which traded with the Levant although they were not specifically employed as their *factors*. There were also families who traded under different partnership combinations amongst different family members, as the personalities changed with the passage of time or as different commercial opportunities emerged. All these interlocking partnerships came together to create the commercial networks of the Europeans in the 18th century Levant trade.

Surrounding the networks of the *factors* and their principals, there existed a third level of organizational structure through which the Levant trade was channeled. It consisted of the networks of 'friends' of either the *factors* or of their principals. Networks of 'friendship' that tied families or individuals to each other could be as important as the more formal networks of partnership or kinship. Like ties of kinship, ties of friendship were founded on trust and loyalty. At times they served as the precursors to a more formal partnership. Moreover, partnerships were established for specific purposes and usually for a specific length of time. By contrast, ties of 'friendship' might only result in the periodic participation in a commercial transaction(s). However, being more informal, they were also more flexible. Not being bound by time, ties of friendship could last from one generation to another.

Interlocking partnerships based on ties of kinship and friendship and the networks they created were not unique to the Levant trade. They can be observed in other parts of the world in the 18th century as, for instance, among the families and networks that dominated the long-distance trade of colonial America. Such an example is the Brown family of Rhode Island whose networks of agents stretched to the four corners of the North Atlantic. They were active through their commercial bases from ports in North America and England to West Africa and the West Indies. Like the Roux Frères, who also traded in other parts of the world, besides Europe and the Levant, including the French colonies in the West Indies, the networks of the Browns were truly extensive.[1] Smaller in scope, but not too dissimilar in basic structure and organization, were the networks that Ottoman merchant families created when they increased the scope of their activities in the late 18th and early 19th centuries. Their networks, based primarily on kinship and secondarily on friendship, came to encompass Europe and the Levant.[2]

A *factor* was usually a young man sent to the Ottoman empire at the early stages of his career. However, it was possible for an older, well-established merchant, who had probably stayed on in the Levant from his early factorage years and had subsequently become an independent merchant, to act as a *factor* although probably doing so on an incidental rather than an on-going basis. In general factorage residencies of around eight to ten years were

---

[1]Hedges, James B., *The Browns of Providence Plantations* (Cambridge: Harvard University Press Mass., 1952), *passim.*

[2]Frangakis-Syrett, Elena, "Greek mercantile activities in the eastern Mediterranean, 1780-1820", *Balkan Studies*, XXVIII/1 (1987): pp. 73-86; see also, *Idem*, "Commerce in the eastern Mediterranean from the 18th to the early 20th centuries: the city-port of İzmir and its hinterland", *International Journal of Maritime History*, X/2 (1998): pp. 147-50.

the norm. Such residencies had a twofold purpose: to solve the need to conduct trade from a base in the Ottoman empire and to allow a young man to amass enough experience and capital to become subsequently partner in a London house, which he had served as *factor* and to which he might be related, trading with the Levant. Once in the Levant, the *factor* was instructed to buy and sell by the principal(s) with whom he had the primary relationship and for whose firm he was sent out, in the first place, to trade. Selling and buying for his principal(s), on commission, also formed the basis of his income. His commission depended on the value of goods consigned to him from Europe, which he sold, re-investing the profits in purchases of Ottoman goods, which he sent to his principal(s) back in Europe. Naturally, the amount of business that a *factor* did was based primarily on the amount of sales and purchases he was required to do for them. His income was further supplemented by purchases and sales on behalf of other firms in London. A prudent *factor* always sought business from multiple houses whenever possible.

There were further opportunities for commission work, however, given that a *factor* had himself several different partnerships on the basis of which he traded. That is, an incoming *factor* had a partnership with stipulated responsibilities not only with the house he represented but also with the departing *factor*, whom he was replacing. He may also have had a separate partnership with one of the partners of the firm he worked for. It was also usual for one of the partners of the firm he represented, possibly the most active one, to give him at times consignments of goods on his behalf, besides those on behalf of the entire firm. Further, his principal(s) might have had other partnerships, on behalf of which the factor might be asked to buy or sell goods. In addition, there were the agents of the London house, based in different ports in Europe, for whom the *factor* was asked to buy or sell. And then there were the 'friends' of his principal(s), in London or elsewhere within the network of the firm's business, for whom the *factor* might be asked to carry out commercial transactions in the Levant. All this generated further business and commission income for the *factor*. To ensure that the *factor* always got the best deal possible, miles away from their supervision, he was often given the additional incentive of participating himself in the commercial transaction by having a part share in it. He was after all a *bona fide* member of these networks of partners and friends. Finally, the principal, in London, at times sold goods that his factor had dispatched to him from the Levant, *on behalf of* his employee and for a commission fee. This reversal of the factor/principal relationship, which was quite usual in the Levant trade, brought multiple partnerships, in a way, full circle.

In terms of the amount of business generated through these networks, the *factor*/principal relationship is again indicative. The principal may send a consignment fully on his own account; or on account of himself and of all the partners in the house; or in part on his account and in part on account of other merchant(s) who may be associated with him through another partnership(s). He might equally instruct his *factor* to buy goods on behalf of other merchants who were not in a formal partnership with him but who were his "friends". In such a case, he might participate himself in the affair, in part, or not at all. He might also ask his *factor* to place the costs on his own account, or on the account of the merchant(s) on whose behalf he had instructed the purchases. Once the *factor* had completed the purchase of goods he had received instructions for, he had to be ready to dispatch them for sale to any of his principals' associates, located in different markets in Europe, according to which market offered the best terms.

Since some time usually elapsed from when the initial instructions to buy a specific commodity were first sent, to the time when the purchase had been actually completed, the *factor* in İzmir, Aleppo or Cyprus had to be prepared to buy for any of the Italian, Dutch or British markets. An effective communications network existed between the various associates in the different European ports, with both the principal and the *factor*, for the sharing of information at all times and in a timely manner. Associates in these ports might also be offered part shares in any of the transactions, thus spreading the costs as well as further ensuring the potential for success of the affair in question where they, too, would have a personal stake. While the desire to dispatch goods to the best possible market had to be balanced with the availability of a ship going there, generally-speaking the ability to choose from different markets in Europe, through a network of agents, gave the merchants more options even with the irregular shipping schedules of the 18th century.

IV. Two case studies

A British merchant in Aleppo

Colvill Bridger, who went out to Aleppo in the mid-18th century as *factor* for the house of Radcliffe & Stratton, and the merchants he formed partnerships with are an excellent example of the networks of kinship and 'friendship' in the Levant trade. Adamantios Korais too, who went to

Amsterdam from İzmir in the late 18th century as *factor* for an Ottoman Greek house, and the activities he undertook and partnerships he formed give an equally good example of the networks of kinship and 'friendship' of the Levant trade amongst the Ottomans in the late 18th century.

Bridger spent 11 years in Aleppo (1754-1765).[1] His expertise in international trade came from his previous residence in Lisbon, where he had traded for his own account. At the beginning of his factorage Bridger had four different partnerships — with Radcliffe & Stratton, with Richard Stratton, with William Hammond and with Charles Frye. His principals, Radcliffe & Stratton, were a partnership between the well-known house of Edward & Arthur Radcliffe[2] and the experienced merchant, Richard Stratton.[3] Bridger set up another partnership, as was the custom in the Levant trade at the time, with the departing *factor*, William Hammond, whom he was replacing. This partnership gave Hammond a share in the profits from Bridger's commission for a year. It was a way for the departing *factor* to be further rewarded for his stay in the Levant and for giving over his business contacts and good name to the merchant who was succeeding him. As was also customary, Hammond joined Radcliffe & Stratton, presumably as a senior partner, upon his return to England. This had also been the case with Richard Stratton who had previously served as *factor* in Aleppo for the Radcliffe house before Hammond had, in turn, replaced him.[4]

We can assume that the amount of business in Aleppo in the 1730s and 1740s warranted a factorage house, rather than the presence of a single *factor* for Stratton traded in Aleppo through the factorage partnership of Radcliffe & Stratton. Upon his return to London, Stratton continued his partnership with the Radcliffes and actively traded on his and their behalf. He also established another partnership with Hammond, the incoming *factor*, as the latter would do with Bridger five years later. Upon joining the Radcliffe house, Stratton had brought with him his business connection with Frye & Mitford. During his time in Aleppo, he continued to act as a *factor* for them, as well as for the 'friends' of Frye & Mitford, at times even requesting that he might be their sole *factor* in the Levant and recipient of their consignments.

---

[1]Private Papers, Colvill Bridger, Aleppo, 27 April 1755 to Edward & Arthur Radcliffe, London. Hereafter, this collection will be cited as PP.

[2]On the activities of the Radcliffe house see, Davis, *Aleppo and Devonshire Square, passim.*

[3]Stratton crowned a successful career with the Directorship of the Bank of England. Namier, Sir Lewis and J., Brooke, *History of Parliament*, III (London: HMSO, 1964): p. 685.

[4]Stratton stayed in Aleppo 16 years (1733-1749) which was an unusually long period for a British factor. In his last three years, however, he was no longer a factor for the Radcliffes, trading instead for his own account. Davis, *Aleppo and Devonshire Square*: p. 91.

Bridger, too, acted as *factor* to another member of the house of Frye & Mitford, namely Charles Frye. The latter had been a *factor* in İzmir in the 1740s; by the mid-18th century, he had joined the family firm in London. As for the Radcliffes, they brought to their relationship with Stratton their partnership with the Barkers in London and Istanbul. In this manner, the circle of 'friends' that both the *factor* and his employer could rely upon could expand from within.

One of the most important links in the organization of the Levant trade were the firms that acted as clearing houses for the *factors* throughout the Ottoman empire facilitating the movement of funds between them and their principals in Europe. Established in Istanbul for successive generations, the Barkers were in a good position to specialize in merchant banking and are a good example of such a firm. The funds generated by the imports from the West for the needs of the empire's capital left a surplus for the Europeans of all nationalities trading in Istanbul.[1] This was unlike the situation in the other Ottoman centers, where trade between the empire and Europe left mostly a deficit for the Europeans.[2] As a result, western merchants established in the capital dealt extensively in merchant banking operations for their fellow merchants in other Ottoman centers. Their funds circulated within the empire through the channels of local clearing houses and Ottoman merchant bankers. At all times they combined their merchant banking activities with trading. For instance, in the 1720s, Edward Barker in London was the principal of Chadwick & Uvedale in İzmir.[3] In the 1730s, the factorage of Radcliffe & Stratton in Aleppo and Benjamin Barker, nephew of Edward Barker and factor of the Barker house in Istanbul, were acting as each other's factors. They were participating in silk and cloth consignments at the rate of two-thirds for the Radcliffes and one-third for the Barkers.[4] In the 1750s, Benjamin was joined by another member of the family, George Barker. Trading as Benjamin & George Barker, they carried out merchant banking operations for a number of British merchants established in different Ottoman ports. They also acted as a clearing house for Bridger as well as participated with the latter in commercial transactions that either party might organize. It is unlikely that the Barkers had such a relationship solely with Bridger. For instance, Hammond had also acted as a principal to Benjamin & George Barker sending them cloth and

[1]On the trade of Istanbul in the 18th century, see Eldem, Edhem, *French Trade in Istanbul in the Eighteenth Century* (Brill: Leiden, 1999): *passim.*

[2]Frangakis-Syrett, *The Commerce of Smyrna:* Appendix B, Tables 1 and 2 on Ottoman exports to and imports from Marseilles, 1700-1789 (by Ottoman port), pp. 257-60.

[3]PRO, SP 105/207, *The Asia:* İzmir, 28 Oct. 1721.

[4]Davis, *Aleppo and Devonshire Square*: p. 90.

other consignments and the reverse would also have held. Moreover, even after Hammond had departed from Aleppo, there were consignments where all three, namely, Bridger, Hammond and the Barkers participated.[1] In the 1760s the Barkers, who were by then trading in Istanbul under the name of Humphreys & Barker, were acting as a clearing house to another merchant, Thomas Landsdown, among their other activities. The latter merchant was a factor in Aleppo for the house of Isaac Hughes & Sons of London and a contemporary of Bridger.[2] Moreover, Humphreys & Barker had an agreement with Landsdown for Joseph Chitty, his correspondent in İzmir, to draw on him as long as Landsdown could draw on the firm in Istanbul.[3] Besides Humphreys & Barker, there was also the house of Ashby & Humphrys in Istanbul whose services as a clearing bank Landsdown also used. The principals of Landsdown had further links with İzmir, having the long-established family of Lee, who were trading under the name of Lee & White in İzmir, act as factors for them.[4] It was all part of the long-established and overlapping networks of friendship and kinship.

Going beyond the Ottoman empire, to the various ports in Italy or the Netherlands, Bridger and, before him, Hammond, and Stratton before him, all had a connection with the Amsterdam house of Muilman & Sons. The latter had also had a long-standing connection with the Levant. In the 1720s, they were acting as agents, under the name of Muilman & Meulemaer, for the factorage house in İzmir of Henry, John and Thomas March.[5] In the 1750s, Bridger had a commercial connection with the house of Earle & Hodgson in Livorno,[6] while Landsdown traded with the Italian port through William Bellamy and John Francis Rivaz & Co.[7]

---

[1] PP, Bridger, Aleppo, 27 April 1759 to William Hammond, London; see also, PP, Bridger, Aleppo, 19 May 1759 to Benjamin & George Barker, Istanbul.

[2] PRO, SP 110/37, Thomas Landsdown, Aleppo, 5 Feb. 1762 to Humphreys & Barker, Istanbul; see also, SP 105/37, Landsdown, Aleppo, 29 Jan. 1762 to Isaac Hughes & Sons, London.

[3] PP, Bridger, Aleppo, 30 May 1759 to Joseph Chitty, İzmir; see also, Bridger, Aleppo, 30 May 1759 to Benjamin & George Barker, Istanbul and Bridger, Aleppo, 11 Sept. 1759 to Hammond, London.

[4] PRO, SP 105/37, Landsdown, Aleppo, 19 Jan. 1762 to Lee & White, İzmir. In the 1750s, there was the partnership of D'Aeth & Lee in İzmir and the partnership of D'Aeth & Barker active in Istanbul and in the 1740s in Venice, too. PRO, SP 105/118, Levant Company, London, 27 April 1750 to Treasurer, İzmir.

[5] PRO, SP 105/207, *The (Dutch) Wendale*, bound for Amsterdam, İzmir, c. 1723.

[6] PP, Bridger, Aleppo, 26 April 1759 to Earle & Hogdson, Livorno.

[7] PRO, SP 105/36, Landsdown, Aleppo, 15 Oct. 1759 to John Francis Rivaz & Co., Livorno; see also, SP 110/37, Landsdown, Aleppo, 26 Oct. 1761 to William Bellamy, Livorno.

A Greek merchant in Amsterdam

Once the Ottoman merchants started creating their own international trading networks through multiple partnerships, in the last quarter of the 18th century, they greatly resembled their European counterparts. The distinguishing characteristics that had earlier differentiated the two groups were thus, in large part, eliminated. Partners came together to take out shares in commercial transactions dividing the profits, or losses as the case might be, amongst them when the affair was concluded. As was also the norm in accounting practices at the time, they kept detailed records of all transactions and balanced out each other's accounts at regular intervals, or at the conclusion of an affair. Judging from the fast growth of the Ottoman Greeks' networks and the success of their partnerships, theirs was a winning combination. Yet they also appeared to have had a higher rate of bankruptcy than the Europeans. The latter tended to be more conservative as well as more averse to risk-taking; their firms were longer-lasting than those of the Greeks.[1] In many other respects, however, the Greeks did not differ much in their methods from those employed by the British or other European firms to carry out business in the Levant especially as far as the individual merchant was concerned.

Kinship played a very important role in keeping the partners' networks together as their members were either related or married to each other or both. Ties of kinship were also valuable in giving cohesion to a partnership of firms, separated from each other by great distances, trading in new places and markets, where business contacts were crucial and access to capital was not easy. Whilst ties of kinship were stronger amongst the Greeks than amongst the western Europeans, and remained so for a long period of time,[2] the principle was basically the same in both cases. Besides kinship, like their European counterparts, the Greeks, too, had their networks of 'friends'. A great majority of Ottoman Greeks, who led in the establishment of international trading networks, came from the island of Chios and migrated to İzmir, since the western Anatolian city was the premier port in Ottoman-European trade and its importance far outweighed that of any other port in the empire, including Istanbul. As the Ottoman Greeks became increasingly prosperous and active in İzmir's trade with Europe, so the Chiots emerged as the economic leaders of this community.[3] By the end of the 18th century,

[1]ANF, AE Biii 242, French Consul Fourcade, Mémoire, İzmir, c. 1812.

[2]Kinship remained important until the early 20th century.

[3]On the rise of the Chiot merchant community in this period, see Frangakis-Syrett, Elena, *Οι Χιώτες έμποροι στις διεθνείς συναλλαγές, 1750-1850 [Chiot Merchants in International Trade, 1750-1850]* (Athens: Agricultural Bank of Greece, 1992), *passim*.

some of the most important commercial houses in the city were owned by Chiots;[1] they were also prominent in some of the city's most important trades, such as the cloth trade.[2]

Adamantios Korais was a merchant in Amsterdam trading with the Levant from 1773 to 1778.[3] He came from a well-to-do family of Levant merchants who had migrated from Chios to İzmir. His father, Ioannis Korais, had traded with Amsterdam and Livorno and was a partner in the apparently important Catholic Chiot house of Dimitri Bachatori in İzmir, for whom Korais also did some commission business while in Amsterdam. Korais' father-in-law, Adamantios Rysios, had also participated in the Dutch Levant trade.[4] Korais had initially gone to Amsterdam to represent the house of Stathi Thomas. However, like Bridger, Korais had more than one set of principals. The other house he was agent for, was the firm of Ioannis Avgerinos. In the 1770s, this firm, which was Chiot in origin, had its head office in İzmir and a network of partners in the empire and abroad — namely, the firm of Loukas Calvocoressis in Istanbul, the firm of Dimitrios Kourmoulis in Venice and the agency of Adamantios Korais in Amsterdam. In addition, the firm of Avgerinos had an associate in Trieste and more partners in İzmir.[5] A multi-layered relationship existed amongst the partners of Avgerinos located in the different cities who appeared to be independent firms whilst at the same time following directions from the head office.

The firm of Stathi Thomas, the primary principal of Korais, also traded through multiple partnerships. The Thomas-Korais partnership was supplemented by another between Thomas and the house of Petrocochino & Pateraki in Istanbul. The Petrocochino family was a particularly extensive one, its members trading at the time under different commercial combinations

---

[1]ANF, F/12, 1850A, État général des maisons du commerce ottoman établies à Smyrne, 1820.

[2]ARA, Fremeaux, van Lennep and Enslie, 29 June 1782 to van Haften in Nanninga, *Bronnen tot de Geschiedenis... Vierde deel*: pp. 339-41; see also, PRO, FO 78/136, British Consul Werry, İzmir, 13 April 1822 to Levant Company, London.

[3]Although he started as a merchant, Korais spent most of his life in academic and literary pursuits in France. As a result of his writing and publishing activities, he came to acquire a special place in the cultural history of Greece as an intellectual father of the nation.

[4]Slot, B.J., "Commercial activities of Korais in Amsterdam", *O Eranistis*, XVI (1980): pp. 69-70, 76. On the trading activities of Korais see also, Petrou, Stamatis, *Γράμματα απο το Αμστερντάμ* [*Letters from Amsterdam*] (Athens: Hermes, 1976).

[5]Slot, "Commercial activities of Korais": pp. 59-60, 69.

in Istanbul, İzmir,[1] Salonica, Odessa, Amsterdam,[2] Livorno,[3] Trieste[4] and elsewhere in the empire and abroad. As for Stathi Thomas, he was an experienced merchant who must have brought a string of 'friends' and contacts to the partnership. He had been a former partner of one of the most important Ottoman Greek merchant-cum-banking houses in Amsterdam, which had traded as Thomas & d'Isay (Isaiou in Greek). Following the end of his partnership with Korais, in 1778, Thomas formed a new four-year partnership with the Petrocochino and Ralli families and traded under the new name of Thomas, Ralli & Petrocochino.[5] Like the Petrocochino, the Ralli, too, would establish in the late 18th century one of the most extensive Chiot networks in the Levant trade where family members played a key role. Trading under the name of Ralli Brothers, their network became truly global in the early 19th century, more widespread than even that of the Browns: it encompassed India, Persia, America, the Far East and Africa.[6]

As for the d'Isay family, Thomas' former partners in Amsterdam they, too, had started off in İzmir. In the late 18th and early 19th centuries, they were trading through two different firms, Manoli d'Isay & Son and Cristodoulo Manoli d'Isay. They were considered to be amongst the most important Ottoman houses in the city at the time.[7] Following the end of the partnership with Thomas, d'Isay had continued to prosper in Amsterdam acting as a correspondent for a number of houses in İzmir, including G. Mavrogordatos, G. Anastas & Co. as well as one of the employers of Korais, the firm of Avgerinos. The latter, as was the custom amongst the westerners too, was trading with Amsterdam through more than one agent. Like the Barkers in Istanbul, d'Isay also served as a clearing house for many Greek merchants in Amsterdam, including Korais. Following the end of his

[1]ANF, AE BIII 242, Fourcade, İzmir, c. 1812; see also, ANF, F/12, 1850A, État général des maisons du commerce ottoman établies à Smyrne, 1820.

[2]Frangakis-Syrett, *The Commerce of Smyrna*: p. 256; see also, *Idem*, *Οι Χιώτες έμποροι*. pp. 42-4.

[3]Vlami, *Το φιορίνι, το σιτάρι*. pp. 147, 149.

[4]Katsiardi-Hering, *Η ελληνική παροικία της Τεργέστης*. II, pp. 579-92.

[5]Slot, "Commercial activities of Korais": pp. 71-2.

[6]Frangakis-Syrett, *Οι Χιώτες έμποροι* pp. 38-9, 58-9. For examples of Greek commercial networks that were established in the course of the 19th century, see Herlihy, Particia, *Odessa. A History, 1794-1914* (Cambridge, Mass.: Harvard University Press, 1986); *idem*, "Greek merchants in Odessa in the 19th century", *Harvard Ukranian Studies*, III-IV (1979-80): pp. 399-420; Pepelasis-Minoglou, Ioanna, "The Greek merchant house of the Russian Black Sea: a 19th-century example of a traders' coalition", *International Journal of Maritime History*, X/1 (1998): pp. 61-104.

[7]*He was considered by his contemporaries to be one of the wealthiest men amongst the Greeks* in the Dutch city at the time, whilst the d'Isay family firms in İzmir were considered to be amongst the richest in the city. ANF, F/12, 1850A, État général des maisons du commerce ottoman établies à Smyrne, 1820; see also, Slot, "Commercial activities of Korais": p. 71.

partnership with Thomas, and independently of the latter, Korais acted as agent of Pateraki in Istanbul, a former partner of Thomas and member of the earlier Thomas-Korais circle of associates. In his final years in Amsterdam, one more 'friend', Ambrosio Ralli of İzmir, joined the circle of merchants Korais did commission work for.

As agent for either firms, like Bridger, Korais bought and sold goods on commission for his principals. Buying in Amsterdam he had to be prepared to send the goods to İzmir, Istanbul or Venice, or in other markets where his principals had partners, according to the conditions in any of these markets. As was the case with Bridger too, whilst Korais was arranging the purchase and shipping of Dutch cloth to the Levant or to the Mediterranean at large, the various partners of his principals were offered the possibility of participating in the transaction. Both Korais and Bridger made extensive use of the internal Ottoman and inter-European as well as Ottoman-European networks of bills of exchange to have funds remitted to them for purchases or to debit one of the partners in the empire or in Europe or to remit profits to the empire or elsewhere in Europe. Bridger and Korais at times purchased on credit and both men used any surplus cash in short-term money lending operations; indeed, the principals of Korais in the Levant seemed to do so even more ardently than he did himself. Both men gave detailed and frequent accounts of their business activities to their principals, including accounting for all funds used by them, and sought instructions from them. It is to be expected that these two merchants, one from Aleppo and the other from Amsterdam, participating in the same Levant trade at different periods in the 18th century, during which time trading practices, whilst evolving, had not yet changed radically, should display such striking similarities in the way they traded.

* * *

In this study we have sought to demonstrate the differences and the similarities in the commercial strategies and practices of the Ottoman and European merchants in the trade between Europe and the Ottoman empire in the course of the 18th century. We have aimed to show the reasons why such differences or similarities existed and how these differences diminished in the latter part of the century as the volume of international trade increased and the world economy changed. Monetary conditions, such as access to credit, the state of the capital markets and the level of capital accumulation, both in Europe and the Ottoman empire, emerged as perhaps the most pivotal reason accounting for the participation, or not, of Ottoman merchants in the international networks of the Levant trade, alongside the Europeans. The legal status of either group of merchants, in view of the prevailing system of Capitulations in Ottoman-European trade, and government policy on the part of the European states, such as the implementation of the doctrines of mercantilism and protectionism by Britain and France, or indeed the absence of a belief in such doctrines on the part of the Netherlands, were certainly instrumental in enabling or in hindering Ottoman merchants from taking part in all sectors of Ottoman-European trade alongside their European counterparts. However, what ultimately defined whether or not the Ottomans participated in all the networks of the Levant trade, and the degree, extent and timing of such participation, depended on the prevailing monetary conditions and the way such conditions were modified as the economy underwent major changes in the last quarter of the 18th century.

Through an analysis of the organization of the British Levant trade, it also becomes apparent how crucial to the functioning of the Levant trade were the networks that these merchants created, built on kinship and 'friendship', as defined in this study. Further complemented by interlocking partnerships, these networks formed the organizational structure of the Levant trade. In the center of this organizational structure there was the *factor*/principal relationship, with its multiple partnerships, constituting the very underpinning of the Levant trade. This relationship was further complemented by the equally important employer/broker relationship in the Ottoman empire, between the European merchant as employer and the Ottoman merchant as broker-*cum*-independent merchant. Both relationships could not have flourished nor could they have operated as effectively without the networks of kinship and 'friendship' surrounding them. There are many reasons for this. Such networks enabled effective strategies, such as shared participation in commercial affairs, to operate effectively. Further, the networks ensured adequate supervision amongst trading partners located miles away from each other and made full use of the communications and transportation facilities that were available at the time. Finally the networks allowed the Levant traders to command multiple markets at the same time, which stretched from one end of the Mediterranean to the other and reached as far as the Atlantic ports, at a time when their capital resources and corporate structures were not what multi-national companies could command a century later.

Kinship, friendship and interlocking partnerships were key to the success of these networks and of the trade that was channeled through them. The ability to create similar networks of overlapping partnerships amongst kin and friends that Ottoman merchants, and in particular the Greeks, did when they started trading in earnest outside the Ottoman empire alongside their European counterparts, is a fundamental reason for the striking similarities by then between the two groups of merchants European and Ottoman as well as for the success that crowned the endeavors of these merchants. Networks of kinship and 'friendship' ultimately became a defining characteristic as much for the Europeans as for the Ottomans in the 18th-century Levant trade.

7. View of Manisa.
(From Cornelis de Bruin, *Voyage de Corneille le Bruyn au Levant ...*)

8. View of the Citadel and of the Caravan Bridge of İzmir. (Author's collection)

THE ECONOMIC ACTIVITIES OF OTTOMAN AND WESTERN COMMUNITIES IN EIGHTEENTH-CENTURY İZMİR

During the course of the 18th century the integration of the Ottoman empire, in particular its coastal areas, into the international market, advanced considerably setting the scene for its near-complete integration in the 19th century. As this integration was affected mainly through trade with the West, İzmir, a coastal port in the western part of the empire, emerged as the major port in this trade relationship with the West and became the principal vehicle for the empire's integration. It was a process that took most of the century to evolve.

Whilst in the first half of the 18th century İzmir averaged only a 19 percent share of the goods exported from all major Ottoman ports to France, the empire's principal western trading partner, and was surpassed by Alexandria and even more so by the islands of the Aegean Archipelago, from the late 1740s on its prominent position vis-à-vis the other Ottoman ports' trade with France, became increasingly apparent, and after 1751 İzmir's position in Ottoman-French trade was unrivaled. Beginning in the 1760s, İzmir's exports to France grew faster than the trade of the Ottoman empire as a whole: as a result, İzmir also captured an ever-increasing share of the empire's total trade. From 1745 to 1789, an average of 34 percent of the annual exports of the Ottoman empire passed through İzmir. Salonica and Kavala, which had emerged by the 1770s as the principal ports after İzmir, were still considerably behind. In the 1780s the export trade of the above ports, combined with that of Alexandria and İskenderun, represented only 65 percent of İzmir's exports.[1] İzmir also dominated the empire's importation of French goods. From 1749 to 1789, an annual average of 30 per cent (four percentage points less than the exports) of all French imports to the empire entered through İzmir. Its greatest rival was Istanbul but İzmir actually surpassed it.[2] It was, in fact, İzmir's ability to export to the West raw materials necessary for the former's growing

---

[1]For a fuller exposé of the trade of İzmir in the 18th century and its place within the trade of the Ottoman empire see Frangakis-Syrett, Elena, *The Commerce of Smyrna in the Eighteenth Century, 1700-1820*, Athens, 1992, pp. 119-130.

[2]*ibid.*, p. 119; see also Frangakis, Elena "The Ottoman City Port of İzmir in the Eighteenth and early Nineteenth Centuries, 1695-1820", in: *Revue de l'Occident Musulman et de la Méditerranée*, XXXIX/1 (1985), pp. 149-152.

textile sectors, (such as silk, particularly in the earlier part of the century, cotton, cotton yarn, mohair yarn, various types of wool), and foodstuffs, (such as wheat and olive oil), and to import western manufactured cloth, dyestuffs (also related to manufacture) and colonial goods of mass consumption (such as sugar and coffee), that laid the basis for the commercial growth of İzmir.

The marrying of good-quality cotton from the environs of İzmir to the needs of an expanding textile industry in Languedoc and the whole Provence region solidified the trading partnership between İzmir and Marseilles and accounts to a large extent for the considerable commercial success of the former. Whilst in the opening years of the century, 1700-1702, İzmir's share of the total value of the empire's cotton exports to Marseilles was around 10 percent, in 1750-1754 it was 44 percent surpassing the 70 percent mark in 1785-1789, peak years in French trade, resulting in an ever-increasing commercial growth for İzmir.[1]

Whilst French trade in the Levant peaked in the last quarter of the 18th century, most of which was handled by İzmir, the city's trade continued to grow at the turn of the century as it turned to other European trading partners, namely the Italian ports and subsequently Britain, benefiting from the expansionary phase of the world economy and other favorable conditions. The result was a spectacular commercial growth for İzmir in the late 18th and early 19th centuries which was, in many respects, the culmination of 18th century economic developments.

The competition that the European merchants faced when buying cotton from local purchasers, who intended it for consumption in the local manufacturing centers in Ankara or elsewhere in Anatolia, which catered to a domestic market, showed that there was also a lively internal trade.[2] However, İzmir's exports surpassed its imports for most of the century and its external trade, it would appear, constituted the biggest sector in the city's economy, although it also commanded and was supported by an extensive internal trading network. In the absence of adequate data it is difficult to determine how much of the internal trade was linked to the international market and the external trade and how much of it was part of the internal economy. Perhaps the most telling example of local economic growth was the spectacular increase in the economic activities, such as trade, shipping and, to a lesser

---

[1] Frangakis-Syrett, E., *The Commerce of Smyrna,* p. 233.

[2] Archives Nationales de France, Paris, AE Bi 1053, Consul Peyssonnel, Mémoire, İzmir, 22 November 1751. Hereafter this archive will be cited as ANF.

extent, maritime insurance and local production of cloth of the local Ottoman communities, particularly in the latter part of the 18th century, which represented considerable capital accumulation. There was also an increase in İzmir's market, particularly in the city and its immediate environs, including islands in the Aegean Archipelago such as Chios.[1] However, a large part of İzmir's imports was not consumed on the spot but distributed to its very extensive hinterland that included large areas of Anatolia and reached as far as Iran. At the same time, it collected and exported to the West an increasing amount of the agricultural production of large areas of Anatolia and of the islands in the Aegean Archipelago.

An active European commercial presence dominated İzmir's external trade, the biggest sector in the city's economy, for most of the century. The principal European mercantile communities were the French, British and Dutch, who had established themselves in the city from the early 17th century, and who enjoyed certain non-reciprocal trading advantages vis-à-vis the local merchants due to the prevalent system of the Capitulations.[2] Yet their trading activities were closely inter-linked with the local merchants in a number of ways. For instance, these Europeans set themselves up in the city and traded mainly through local merchants who acted as their brokers. They were themselves probably also active in the bazaar of the city, if not directly, by buying and selling from a stall, at least indirectly by negotiating deals regarding stocks which they might have had for sale in their warehouses or concerning goods that they wanted to purchase.

They certainly did not have a standing network or establishment of their own in the interior of western Anatolia. Given the level of capital resources that these merchants disposed of in the 18th century, they did not have the funds to venture inland on a scale that would have made them competitive *vis-à-vis* the local merchants. If they went themselves to the interior, which they might occasionally have done, they did so accompanied by their broker and, in this case, also their dragoman. The problem of the language and the lack of security in the interior were definite reasons also to deter them from making it a regular practice. Besides, for goods brought to İzmir from further afield, such as Persian or Bursa silk, Ankara mohair yarn or certain types of wool, it made sense for the European merchants to deal with

[1] *Ibid.*

[2] ANF, F/12, 549, Réforme du tarif des douannes en Turquie, Conseil Général du Commerce, 16 December 1804; see also Public Record Office, London, SP 105/129, British Factory, İzmir, 31 January 1804 to Levant Company, London. Hereafter this archive will be cited as PRO. See also Goffman, Daniel, *İzmir and the Levantine World, 1550-1650*, Seattle, 1990, *passim*.

these goods once they reached the city's bazaars. Moreover, Persian silk was transported exclusively by Armenian caravan merchants whilst Bursa silk or Ankara mohair yarn were, to a large extent, the monopolies of Jewish and Armenian and, to a lesser extent, Turkish merchants who brought the goods themselves to İzmir selling them to other local merchants. The latter, serving as intermediaries, would sell them to the European merchants through the latter's brokers.[1] In fact, the extensive trading networks of İzmir inside the Ottoman empire, which meant that goods came from afar or were carried far, made use of intermediaries necessary. Intermediaries, like the brokers, were usually non-Muslim local merchants, Armenians, Greeks or Jews. In some cases both the functions of the intermediary and the broker might be carried out by the same person. Indeed, even when European merchants bought olive oil directly from the producers, which was the case in the Aegean islands, paying cash for it usually through İzmir — which acted as a clearing house — western manufactured cloth, that was imported into İzmir by western merchants, was carried to the same Aegean islands by local merchants. No direct barter exchange of olive oil for cloth between the western merchants and the local producers seemed to have taken place.

The Turks were not only merchants but also land proprietors and, in some cases, large-scale producers as well as local administrators and customs officials. The Turks played their most important role in the commercial activities of İzmir as large landowners and producers of cotton and wheat, while, as *ayans*, as most large-scale landowners usually were, they had other responsibilities apart from trading. As merchants, their role in the economic life of İzmir had some of the characteristics of that of non-Muslim merchants. Some Turkish merchants traded with the Europeans in mohair yarn, cotton, cotton yarn and leather on credit through non-Muslim intermediaries.[2] Most of them, however, were active in the inter-Ottoman trade linking İzmir with the rest of the Ottoman empire and did not act as intermediaries or brokers for the Europeans. As such they did not come into contact with the Europeans much and, hence, there are not many references to their commercial activities in the western sources which leads to an underestimation of their economic activities. Nevertheless they were active both in the internal caravan trade routes and in the coastal trade of the empire.[3] As landowners and merchants

---

[1] Matterson, Clarence, English Trade in the Levant, 1693-1753, unpublished Harvard University Ph.D. dissertation, 1936, p. 142.

[2] ANF, AE Bi 1055, Consul Gilly, İzmir, 28 June 1755 to Minister, Paris.

[3] ANF, AE Biii 242, Consul Fourcade, Mémoire, İzmir, c. 1812. See also PRO, SP 105/188, Ambassador Sir Robert Ainslie, Istanbul, 1782, 1783, 1786.

they, of course, both lent to and borrowed money from non-Muslims and Europeans.

If the trading activities of the European merchants seemed to have been closely linked with the local merchants, particularly non-Muslims, the Europeans nevertheless enjoyed many special advantages. For instance, it was the more advanced western economies that set the tone for the trade exchanges between the West and the Ottoman empire, for it was the needs of the growing textile industries in Western Europe which brought about the demand for the raw materials that became İzmir's principal exports. Nowhere was this more obvious than in the demand in Europe for Ottoman cotton that resulted in a surge of cotton exports from İzmir which accounts, to a large extent, for the commercial growth of the city. It is rather early to speak of a significant export orientation of the local economy, since it is difficult to quantify the amount exported *vis-à-vis* the amount produced in İzmir's environs, especially since many of its principal exports were produced in areas beyond its immediate hinterland. Yet by the end of the 18th century, at least part of its economy was becoming export oriented, propelled principally by the needs of the western economies, whose representatives the western merchants were.[1] Moreover, for the greater part of the century western merchants, based in the Levantine port, were the ones who mostly imported goods to İzmir from the West or exported İzmir's goods to the international market. It was not till 1798 that the first Ottoman ships, freighted by local merchants in İzmir, officially reached the port of London, with local merchants' goods on board.[2] Similarly, it was not till the last two decades of the century that the French, intermittently, allowed the local merchants to import goods from İzmir directly to Marseilles without paying the foreigners' 20 per cent import duty. This duty was finally abolished only in the early 19th century. Western merchants enjoyed further advantages. They virtually monopolized the insurance sector, mainly maritime insurance. In addition, most of the carrying trade between İzmir and western Europe, and even İzmir and other Ottoman ports in the eastern Mediterranean, apart from the lighterage sector, was in the hands of western shippers for most of the century, except during times of European maritime conflict.[3]

---

[1] *Ibid.*; see also, Cunningham, A.B. (Ed.), "The Journal of Christophe Aubin: A Report on the Levant Trade in 1812", in: *Archivum Ottomanicum*, VIII (1983), p. 43.

[2] PRO, SP 105/122, Levant Company, London, 30 January 1798 to Consul Werry, İzmir.

[3] *E.g.*, ANF, AE Bi 271, États des batiments, 1756,1763; see also Échinard, Pierre, *Grecs et Philhellènes à Marseille (de la Révolution Française à l'Indépendance de la Grèce)*, Marseilles, 1973, pp. 65, 82-85; Raymond, André, *Artisans et commerçants au Caire du XVIIIe siècle*, Damas, 1974, II, p. 168, and Efthymiou-Hadzilakou, Maria, *Rhodes et sa région élargie au XVIIIe siècle: les activités portuaires*, Athens, 1988, pp. 282-286.

The advanced western economies, dictating the nature of the trade exchange, stood to influence the local economy as a whole. Yet, on the level of the individual merchant or the daily practice of trade, the westerner, although enjoying many advantages, was not all powerful, as the following example well illustrates. The Ottoman economy suffered from a chronic lack of specie coupled with a devaluationary trend in its currency which became progressively more acute in the second half of the century and which resulted in a lucrative trade in money. Apart from benefiting from this lucrative trade — in which the local merchants were also active although only in the closing decades of the century — the westerners also enjoyed the advantage of seeing their currencies circulate side-by-side with the local currency and even being preferred to the Ottoman.[1] At the same time, however, the western economies, particularly the French, suffered too from a periodic lack of specie.[2]

In other words, the French merchant was often in need of cash, a situation exacerbated by the slow rhythm of the Levant trade where it could take up to two years for a merchant to realize any returns on his capital outlay. Pressed to buy Ottoman goods, to take advantage of a shipping opportunity or a propitious market, but not having the cash to buy them with, or a shipment of cloth to barter them with, the French merchant while waiting for his shipment of cloth, or a bill of exchange or cash, turned to the local merchant who advanced him the desired Ottoman goods. It was a kind of credit, only instead of advancing him money, the local merchant was advancing him goods.[3] Since the French merchant was not only bartering or buying for cash but was frequently making purchases on credit, he tended to stay with the local merchant, who could accommodate him at all times, rather than going directly to the Ottoman purchasers or sellers. In this way the local merchant was securing an important place for himself in the organization of trade in İzmir. There was another way in which the local merchant profited from the above transaction. This was by carefully manipulating the profit margins in cash, barter and credit sales. By reselling the Frenchman's cloth at a *lower* price, but for cash, when cash was available in the market of İzmir, the local merchant was able to use this cash to buy cotton, cotton yarn, wool, etc. at a lower price than that which he had sold the goods to the Frenchman for, as the latter was either bartering or purchasing on credit. The French

---

[1]Carrière, Charles, "Réfléxions sur le problème des monnaies et des métaux précieux en Méditerranée orientale au XVIIIe siècle", in: *Commerce de Gros, Commerce de Détail dans les Pays Méditerranéens, XVIe-XIXe Siècles*, Nice, 1976, p. 1-20.

[2]*E.g.*, ANF, AE Bi 600, Consul Raulin, Genoa, 14 January 1793 to Minister, Paris.

[3]ANF, AE Bi 1052, Consul Peyssonnel, İzmir, 29 January 1749 to Minister, Paris.

merchant usually reserved his cash for olive oil or wax purchases, two goods which were always sold for cash in İzmir.[1]

Since cash was *also* scarce in the Ottoman empire, European merchants were forced very frequently to *sell on credit* with a 12 or a 24 month repayment period being the usual practice. Although, after a residence of some time the European merchant would know the credit worthiness of the various local merchants, at least initially, it was advantageous for him to have a trustworthy local merchant as a broker or as an intermediary in such dealings. It would also appear that the local merchants' expert knowledge of the Ottoman market and their many contacts in the region gave them a versatility that the European merchants could not always match. For instance, in the early 19th century, when they acquired greater direct access to the international market, they were able, given a propitious opening in the market, to exploit the credit system and knowledge of the market quite well. Having bought goods, such as cloth, on credit from the European merchants, they then sold them for cash. With this money they bought, for instance, a supply of wheat which they then sold for cash, and with the proceeds bought yet more wheat, which they again sold for cash. Thus, they were able to reap profits from two sales of wheat before they had to repay their European creditors.[2]

There were other factors which resulted in the business activities of the western communities becoming closely inter-linked with those of the Ottomans. The scarcity of specie both in İzmir and, at times, in the markets in Europe, referred to above, caused both European and Ottoman merchants to lend money extensively at high interest rates when they had capital available and, when they were short of capital, to borrow, at times quite heavily. There was the risk, however, that if a merchant defaulted on his loans, his creditors might be unable to pay their debts which could start a chain reaction of bankruptcies.[3] Even more than the westerners, it was the local merchants, as money-lenders, independent merchants or brokers, who borrowed most heavily and speculated the most. A down-turn in the market or an extraneous event, such as a major epidemic which could bring trade to a standstill, could result in widespread insolvency amongst them, which could totally disrupt the city's money market and overall economy, especially if there had been an excessive number of promissory notes in circulation and interest and exchange rates were

[1]*Ibid.*
[2]ANF, AE Biii 242, Miège, Renseignements sur le commerce du Levant, Livorno, 13 May 1825.
[3]ANF, AE Bi 1063, Consul Peyssonnel, İzmir, 9 June 1777 to Minister, Paris.

very high. As brokers, their insolvency could also affect their European principals' fortunes. For it was usual practice for the brokers sometimes to use not only their own capital but also that of their principals in their own ventures, losing not only their but also their principals' money if the venture floundered. In such a case the European merchant apparently preferred to keep the broker in his employ and try to recover his capital from the broker's salary rather than take him to court and risk never recovering his money.[1] Although a really fraudulent broker could be boycotted by the entire European community, the relations between broker and principal were usually amicable.[2]

The dynamics between the western and local mercantile communities were constantly changing. One important factor, for example, which made the western mercantile communities potentially vulnerable *vis-à-vis* the local merchants was intense inter-western competition, as well as competition within a community: thus, one French merchant might undersell another Frenchman in order to attract business in a soft indigo or cloth market. Although western merchants, by acting as a united body, did periodically attempt to refuse demands of local merchants, such as an increase in the rates of commission, such unity did not usually last long. Of course, the local merchants or brokers, too, competed against each other but competition seemed to be more intense amongst the Europeans. Such competition could also result in the underestimation of the prices of imports in the İzmir market and the overestimation of the exports' prices at levels higher than that which they fetched abroad.[3] Moreover, at periods of acute monetary shortage, in particular, competing European merchants were willing to extend credit, anywhere from 93 days to 54 months, as a way of attracting a sale.[4] Furthermore, if a major European community decided to give an incentive to its local creditors to pay their debts, say in European currency, by giving them a discount of two to three per cent, the other communities had to follow suit if they did not want their payments made in increasingly weaker Ottoman currency.[5]

---

[1]ANF, AE Bi 1059, Consul Peyssonnel, İzmir, 9 June 1769 to Minister, Paris. These were, apparently, current practices in the Levant. See also, Frangakis-Syrett, Elena, "Trade Practices in Aleppo in the Middle of the 18th Century: the Case of a British Merchant", in: *Revue du Monde Musulman et de la Méditerranée*, LXII/4 (1991), p. 124.

[2]ANF, AE Bi 1052, Consul Peyssonnel, İzmir, 5 March 1749 to Minister, Paris.

[3]ANF, AE Bi 1045, Consul Peleran, İzmir, 28 February 1732 to Minister, Paris.

[4]This was a practice current in the Levant; see also, Frangakis-Syrett, E., "Trade Practices in Aleppo", pp. 127-129.

[5]Archives du Ministère des Affaires Étrangères, Paris, CCC, Vol. 36, Consul David, İzmir, 3 January 1821 to Minister, Paris. Hereafter this archive will be cited as AMAE.

The French state authorities and the British Levant Company tried to lessen this competition by decrees that aimed at regulating not only the westerners' trading practices but also supply and demand in the market of İzmir. During the first half of the 18th century, in particular, the Governors of the Levant Company in Britain tried to regulate the number of ships that were allowed to reach the Levantine port annually,[1] whilst the French authorities attempted to set limits on the amount of goods their merchants could sell within a certain period of time and fix the minimum sale price.[2] Such measures failed to control the market, which remained highly competitive, and only rendered uncompetitive the community on which they were imposed. For many reasons, such restrictive measures were abandoned in the second half of the 18th century although both authorities continued to uphold the monopolistic privileges granted to their merchants through the Capitulations.

Wars gave the local merchants their best chance of upsetting this monopolistic system and gaining greater direct access to the international market. Maritime conflicts that involved Britain and France, the major economic powers in the area, caused the domination of these warring powers over İzmir's trading networks with the West to weaken while the relentless privateering that they unleashed upon each other harmed their merchant marine and maritime trade even more. As it became dangerous and onerous, due to high insurance costs, to carry goods in British or French ships, and sometimes impossible to reach a blockaded port, such as Marseilles during the Seven Years' War (1756-1763), neutral countries' carriers, such as the Dutch, emerged to fill the gap. At the same time, at least part of İzmir's trade with the West was redirected to other outlets, such as the Italian port of Livorno.[3] This was particularly significant for the Ottoman merchants since the *porto franco* status of Livorno and the liberal economic policies of the Dutch state meant that Ottoman merchants were allowed to participate in İzmir's external trade that went through those channels. Of course, there had always been contraband trade between London, Livorno and İzmir during peacetime, despite the efforts of the British Levant Company to curb it, in which both Ottoman and British merchants participated illegally. However, the rise to prominence of Livorno during wartime as an entrepôt in the Ottoman-European trade gave new opportunities to Ottoman merchants established there to participate in

---

[1]*E.g.*, PRO, SP 105/116, Levant Company, London, 13 August 1719 to Consul Cooke, İzmir; SP 105/117, Levant Company, London, 1 September 1730 to Consul Boddington, İzmir; *ibid.*, Levant Company, London, 13 March 1739 to Treasurer Tooke, İzmir.

[2]*E.g.*, ANF, AE Bi 1045, Consul Peleran, İzmir, 6 September, 7 October and 7 November 1732 to Minister, Paris; AE Bi 1053, Consul Peyssonnel, İzmir, 22 September 1751 to Minister, Paris.

[3]Carrière, Charles and Courdurié, Marcel, "Grandes heures de Livourne au XVIIIe siècle", in: *Revue Historique*, CCLIV (1975), pp. 40-41.

İzmir's trade with the West. Similarly, the Seven Years' War greatly boosted the participation of Jewish, Greek and Armenian merchants in the trade of İzmir with western Europe alongside western merchants and using Dutch carriers.[1] It was during this period that Ottoman-Greek commercial houses, in particular, established themselves in the Dutch ports to trade with İzmir, no longer as intermediaries but as independent merchants, and continued to do so long after peace had been re-established.[2]

As privateers, Ottoman entrepreneurs also turned wars to their advantage by operating under letters of marque from powers on both sides of a conflict. It was not only European wars that resulted in advantageous situations for the Ottomans. Wars where the Ottoman empire was involved could also present economic opportunities, such as that of privateering in the eastern Mediterranean during the Russo-Ottoman War (1768-1774) and thus accumulate capital. It also afforded them the opportunity to purchase ships at low prices from Russian privateers, at the end of the war, which made this war and its aftermath a formative period for the Greeks' subsequent prominence in the carrying trade in the area.[3]

It was in the last quarter of the 18th and in the early 19th centuries, however, that propitious economic and political conditions came together eventually to end the exclusivity of the British and French merchants in their countries' trade with İzmir. The Ottomans, who continued in their role as intermediaries and brokers to the westerners, now also took an active role in the port's external trade with the West as the frequent and large-scale wars, which diminished the western warring powers' commercial competitiveness, were combined with an expansionary phase in the world economy. This led to an increase in the volume of international trade and called for an end to the hitherto monopolistic trading privileges of the French and British merchants. Moreover, the intensity of the political and military upheaval brought about by the French Revolution and the French Revolutionary (1792-1801) and Napoleonic (1803-1815) Wars that followed it, caused the major economic

---

[1] Algemeen Rijksarchief Consulaatsarchief Smirna, 2dd, de Scheepvaart en de Handel op Smirna, 1762, in: *Bronnen tot de Geschiedenis van den Levantschen Handel. Derde deel: 1727-1765*, Nanninga, J. G. (ed.), Gravenhage, 1952, pp. 715-763.

[2] ANF, F/12, 1850A, État général des maisons de commerce …, İzmir 1820; see also Slot, B.J., "Commercial Activities of Korais in Amsterdam", in: *O Eranistis*, XVI (1980), pp. 69, 71, and Zolotas, I., *Ιστορία Χιου* [*History of Chios*], Athens, 1926, III, pt. I, p. 301, 312, 366-367 and Frangakis-Syrett, Elena, *Οι Χιώτες έμποροι στις διεθνείς συναλλαγές 1750-1850* [*Chiot Merchants in International Trade, 1750-1850*], Athens, 1995, *passim*.

[3] ANF, AE Bi 861, Consul du Mensil, Mitylène, 25 March 1777 to Minister, Paris. For more information on Greek shipping activities in the late 18th and early 19th centuries see also Frangakis-Syrett, Elena, "Greek Mercantile Activities in the Eastern Mediterrranean, 1780-1820", in: *Balkan Studies*, XXVIII/1 (1987), pp. 73-86.

power in the eastern Mediterranean, France, to lose its dominance and greatly decrease its commercial activities in the area.[1]

The intermittent blockading of Marseilles by the British meant that after 1792 and until 1815 the French port was not able, as hitherto, to dominate İzmir's trade with the West; Genoa, Livorno, Ancona and Trieste temporarily took over that role, benefiting, in particular, İzmir's non-Muslim merchants (Greeks and Jews especially) who had established branches in these ports and who took control of a considerable amount of İzmir's trade with the West.[2] It was not only Marseilles that was affected, however. In 1781-1782, the last years of the American War of Independence, the Dutch were forced, as their ports were blockaded by the British Navy, to turn to a land route for their cloth exports to the Levant, taking them through Europe to Trieste and then on to İzmir by sea, thus abandoning part of their lucrative carrying trade and making Trieste a nucleus for at least some of their trade. They did the same for their Ottoman imports from İzmir. The fact that İzmir's Dutch trade did not decrease to any noticeable extent in those years shows the efficacy of the alternative trading networks that Ottoman merchants had by then set up. Ottoman merchants, particularly Greeks, established in the Italian port once again, greatly benefited from the increasing flow of trade that was directed there.[3] Whereas in the past British merchants preferred to send their cloth to İzmir directly, rather than through entrepôts in the Mediterranean, Britain's military involvements and the existence of the Continental System forced them to accept the sale of their cloth, already a very popular product in the İzmir market, conducted in trading outposts in the Mediterranean, such as Malta or Corfu, rather than London. Once again, Ottoman merchants established there were able to take a growing share of this prospering business and thus take advantage of the special conditions for international trade that war had created.[4]

---

[1]Archives de la Chambre de Commerce de Marseille, Marseilles, MQ, 5.1., Mémoire presenté à M. le Consul Général de France à Smyrne par les députés du commerce français, İzmir, 22 July 1820. Hereafter this archive will be cited as ACCM.

[2]Frangakis-Syrett, *The Commerce of Smyrna*, pp. 172-174; see also Frangakis, Elena, "İzmir — an International Port in the Eastern Mediterranean, 1695-1820", in: *Actes du IIe Colloque International d'Histoire*, Athens, 1985, I, pp. 118-119.

[3]ANF, Marine B/7, 446, Bertrand, 19 Oct. 1782; see also Katsiardi-Hering, Olga, *Η ελληνική παροικία της Τεργέστης 1751-1830* [*The Greek Community of Trieste (1751-1830)*], Athens, 1986, II, pp. 547-558; for more information on Greek commercial networks, see also Kremmydas, V., *Έμποροι και εμπορικά δίκτυα στα χρόνια του Εικοσιένα (1820-1835)* [*Merchants and Trading Networks during the Greek War of Independance (1820-1835)*], Athens, 1996, pp. 56-66, 176-184 and Pepelasis-Minoglou, I., "The Greek Merchant House of the Russian Black Sea: A Nineteenth-Century Example of a Traders' Coalition", in: *International Journal of Maritime History*, X/1 (1998), pp. 65-72.

[4]ANF, AE Biii 242, Jumelin, Commerce du Levant en général, c. Sept. 1812; see also PRO, SP *105/133*, The Treasurer, İzmir, 25 Aug. 1812 to Levant Company, London, and Frangakis-Syrett, Elena, "The Greek Mercantile Community of İzmir in the first half of the Nineteenth Century", in: *Les Villes dans l'Empire Ottoman: Activités et Sociétés*, Daniel Panzac (ed.), Paris, 1991, I, p. 395.

It was not only in commerce but also in the carrying trade that the Ottomans met with considerable success, in the last three decades of the 18th century, as a large part of İzmir's carrying trade in the eastern Mediterranean passed into their hands at the expense mainly of the French.[1] For the first three quarters of the 18th century, the French had the largest share of İzmir's freight: French ships not only carried goods of French merchants between İzmir and Marseilles, sometimes via an Italian port, but also carried goods of Ottoman merchants, Muslim and non-Muslim, between İzmir and other Ottoman ports in the eastern Mediterranean. Local capital accumulation from trade, piracy and privateering, which were all activities that intensified during the course of the second half of the 18th century, allowed the emergence of local entrepreneurs, particularly Greeks, in the coastal trade of İzmir. Having successfully invested in short-distance shipping, they moved into the long-distance carrying trade: by the turn of the century they were carrying goods between İzmir and the Italian ports as well as Marseilles, or between the Italian ports themselves. Chiots, based primarily in İzmir, provided the capital to finance such shipping expeditions and purchased the cargo, whilst Hydriots, Spetsiots, and Psariots furnished the ships and crew.[2] The abnormal conditions of the French Revolutionary and Napoleonic Wars greatly strengthened Ottoman shipping activities and their ships increased in number, although, compared to western ships, they remained small in tonnage.

Apart from the above sectors, the Ottoman communities were active in monetary speculative activities in which western merchants, French as well as British and Dutch, were also particularly active in the second half of the 18th century. The reasons for such activities have largely to do with the problems of the Ottoman economy: its chronic lack of specie and the devaluationary trend of its already weak currency, *vis-à-vis* the European currencies, as already referred to, which resulted in greater inflation rather than in greater capital liquidity. These problems were accentuated by the wars which, depleting the Ottoman treasury, increased the Porte's need for specie, forcing it to turn to another source of precious metals for its mint: imported foreign currency. Such economic conditions adversely affected the activities of all merchants, both western and Ottoman, but they also presented them with opportunities for profit. Such an opportunity was trade in money.

---

[1] Frangakis-Syrett, "Greek Mercantile Activities", pp. 73-86; see also ANF, AE Bi 168, Consul Benincasa, Ancona 13 February 1784 to Minister, Paris and AE Bi 859, Consul L'Allement, Messina, 14 January and 4 February 1786 to Minister, Paris.

[2] AMAE, CCC, Vol. 8, Consul David, Mémoire, Chios, 1823; for more details on Ottoman Greeks' participation in the local carrying trade see, Triantafyllidou-Baladié, Y., "Transports maritimes et concurrence en Méditerranée orientale au XVIIIe siècle: l'exemple de la Crète", in: *Actes du IIe Colloque International d'Histoire*, Athens, 1985, I, pp. 23-24.

Since the 17th century there had always been a lucrative trade in money with specie imported into İzmir from the West.[1] In the 18th century, this was a trade which the westerners were particularly active in, the French and Dutch more so than the British since, for the greater part of that century, the latter could only operate in this trade clandestinely.[2] Silver Spanish piastres and especially Austrian thalers, were imported into İzmir from Marseilles and elsewhere in the West as a commodity to be traded in. The Italian ports, serving as entrepôts for other European markets, exported specie to İzmir in return for Ottoman goods.[3] Although specie could go from İzmir back to Europe, the flow of silver was usually in the reverse direction, particularly in the last two decades of the century.[4] Yet it did not remain in İzmir either: some of it was sent to the Far East and India for the purchase of goods such as Indian cloth; specie was also sent, through Malta, to London for the purchase of British cloth; a large part of it, fluctuating in amount according to the needs of the treasury, was sent to the Ottoman capital for minting into Ottoman currency and part of it was sent to the West in the form of repatriated profits of western merchants.[5]

Specie was also imported into İzmir for another reason and that was speculation.[6] As French cloth faced the relentless competition of the British textile industry, French merchants turned to specie as an alternative export to İzmir. They imported specie to İzmir in return either for cotton or some other Ottoman good, although the transaction was not a direct exchange; in the latter part of the century, specie was imported increasingly in return for bills

---

[1]ANF, AE Biii 235, Commerce du Levant, Mémoire sur les sequins, 1686.

[2]PRO, SP 105/118, Levant Company, London, 27 April 1750 to Consul Crawley, İzmir; see also Davis, Ralph, *Aleppo and Devonshire Square. English Traders in the Levant in the Eighteenth Century*, London, 1967, p. 242.

[3]ANF, AE Bi 168, Consul Benincasa, Ancona, 24 Feb. 1785 to Minister, Paris; see also Svoronos, Nicolas, *Le Commerce de Salonique au XVIIIe siècle*, Paris, 1956, pp. 337-339.

[4]For more details, see Frangakis, Elena, "The Balance of Trade and Balance of Payments between İzmir and France, 1700-1789", in: *Communications grecques presentées au Ve Congrès international des Études du Sud-Est Européen*, Athens, 1985, pp. 134-137 and table 1. See also Carrière, Charles and Courdurié, Marcel, "Un sophisme économique. Marseille s'enrichit en achetant plus qu'elle ne vend. Réfléxions sur les mécanismes commerciaux levantins au XVIIIe siècle", in: *Histoire, Économie et Société*, (1984), p. 38.

[5]ANF, AE Bi 1057, Consul Peyssonnel, Précis du mémoire... en faveur de l'agio sur les éspèces, İzmir, 29 April 1769.

[6]For relevant secondary literature on this complex subject, see *e.g.* Rebuffat, F. and Courdurié, M., *Marseille et le négoce monétaire international, 1785-1790,* Marseilles, 1966; see also Carrière, C., Courdurié, M., Gusatz, M. and Squarzoni, R., *Banque et capitalisme commercial (La lettre de change au XVIIIe siècle),* Marseilles, 1976, and Eldem, Edhem, Le commerce *français* d'Istanbul au XVIIIe *siècle*, unpublished University of Provence Ph.D. thesis, 1988, especially chapter 2 and *idem*, "La circulation de la lettre de change entre la France et Constantinople au XVIIIe siècle", in: *L'Empire Ottoman, la Republique de Turquie et la France*, Batu, H. and Bacqué-Grammont, J.-L. (eds.), Istanbul-Paris, 1986, pp. 87-97.

of exchange.[1] These practices are best illustrated by the activities of the İzmir correspondents of the house of Roux Frères, the latter based in Marseilles and operating world-wide, who imported specie into İzmir sent to them by other agents of the house of Roux and which they sold, making their profits from the rate of exchange. These profits they sent back to Roux in the form of bills of exchange, which they purchased in İzmir in the most advantageous currency, and drawn upon any economic center in Europe that would give them the highest return, the funds finally making their way back to Roux in Marseilles.[2] Although handsome profits could thus be made, these were also highly speculative activities for, at any point, there could be a flood of specie in the market of İzmir lowering their exchange rate *vis-à-vis* the Ottoman currency. There could also be a dearth of suitable bills of exchange to remit the profits to Europe with, causing the bills to become expensive and thus cutting away at the profits from the first part of the operation.[3] It was as difficult to predict the best time for one's shipment of specie to arrive in İzmir as it was to wait for a long time for the bills to become abundant, for thus capital remained idle when it could have been used for money-lending, if not for commerce.[4]

Arbitrage was also practiced whereby bills of exchange were bought and sold for speculative purposes. Speculators manipulated successfully the fluctuations in the prices of these bills which reflected the relative dearth or abundance of such bills in the market of İzmir. As Amsterdam was a major financial market — indeed a large number of bills from İzmir were drawn upon Amsterdam — the Dutch were also very active in these speculative activities which, by the end of the century, were even surpassing their commercial activities.[5] It was not only the westerners who practiced arbitrage. A very large number of bills of exchange, which the Europeans purchased in İzmir, were underwritten by Ottoman, mostly non-Muslim merchants, whose credit worthiness the European merchants constantly monitored.[6] Moreover, these bills were often drawn upon the associates of the İzmir merchants who were themselves established in various places in Europe — Amsterdam, Vienna, Livorno, Trieste, Ancona. All these activities allowed the local

---

[1] *E.g.*, ACCM, LIX/735, R. Franchetti, İzmir, 13 August 1788 to Roux frères, Marseilles; LIX/750, Denis Rolland et Cie, İzmir, 19 March 1790 to Roux frères, Marseilles.

[2] *E.g.*, ACCM, LIX/750, Denis Rolland et Cie, İzmir, 13 December 1788 and 5 January 1789 to Roux frères, Marseilles.

[3] *E.g.*, ACCM, LIX/735, R. Franchetti, İzmir, 20 October 1790 to Roux frères, Marseilles.

[4] *E.g.*, ACCM, LIX/735, R. Franchetti, İzmir, 10 March 1790 to Roux frères, Marseilles.

[5] ANF, F/12, 549-550, Mémoire sur le commerce du Levant, 1777.

[6] *E.g.*, ACCM, LIX/750, Denis Rolland et Cie, İzmir, 18 December 1788, 24 March and 13 July 1789 to Roux frères, Marseilles.

communities an important share in the speculative monetary practices as well as bringing to them a considerable level of capital accumulation.[1] All communities, both western and local, also dealt, to varying degrees, in money-lending.

In conclusion, the 18th century was, in many respects, a formative period for İzmir. The integration of İzmir's hinterland into the international market progressed significantly during the course of the century, resulting in the emergence of İzmir, in the second half of the 18th century, as the principal port of Ottoman trade with the West, as well as in the take-off in İzmir's economy in the last quarter of the 18th and in the early 19th centuries. Although it took the whole of the 19th and early 20th centuries for İzmir and its western Anatolian-cum-Aegean islands hinterland to be fully integrated into the world economy, the process, which proved irreversible, had begun in the previous century and the export-orientation pattern for a large part of its agricultural produce had already been established.

The obvious beneficiaries of such an integration were, since they were also the principal agents, the western mercantile communities in İzmir as well as the western economies, whose needs were met by the western merchants, and the local mercantile sector as a whole. İzmir's commercial growth reflected an increase in the westerners' commercial activities too — including activities complementary to trade, such as, shipping and insurance — with the western economies gaining not only from the repatriation of profits but also from the nature of the goods exchanged which aided particularly the growing textile industries of the West. When the French and British merchants' monopolistic rights in İzmir's trade with the West came to an end, under a conjuncture of international economic and political developments in the final decades of the 18th and early 19th centuries, re-enforced by the special wartime conditions in the Mediterranean at the time, their commercial dominance was for the first time seriously challenged, and even temporarily overtaken, by the local communities. However, as the opening-up of the western economies, particularly the British and the French, was itself the result of the needs of those economies for more raw materials and markets for their goods, and was initiated by them, this development also stood to benefit the western economies. Therefore, western merchants also stood to benefit in the long term, as shown by the expansion of their commercial and other economic activities in the 19th century, although, by then, they had, once more, to

[1]*E.g.*, ACCM, LIX/750, Denis Rolland et Cie, İzmir, 10 August and 27 November 1790 to Roux frères, Marseilles.

contend, at times, with strong local competition which differed, due to different economic conditions, from that in the previous century and touched upon every aspect of İzmir's trade and economy.

Local merchants also benefited from the commercial growth of İzmir in the 18th century, even when the westerners dominated İzmir's external trade, for a number of reasons; partly, because the westerners were either unwilling or unable, due to the level of capitalist development of their economies, to commit large capital resources or enlarge significantly their scale of operations, thus allowing the local merchants to maintain their dominance in the trading networks of the Ottoman interior and thus to compete with them; partly, because the wars gave the locals the opportunity to overcome the trading monopolies of the westerners and, finally, partly because the locals were able to participate in lucrative sectors of international trade and thus in the process of integration of İzmir's economy into the international market. Jewish merchants, for instance, became brokers of the western merchants, thus reaping a profit from the westerners' transactions, whilst they were, at the same time, active in the trade of İzmir with its hinterland, that is, the trading networks that brought the goods from the interior to İzmir for purchase by the Europeans. Further, the ability of the Armenians, and even more of the Greeks, to gain control of the cloth trade — cloth being the most sought-after European import into İzmir, the 'centerpiece', one could say, in the trade exchange — was important in a number of ways: its increasing importation led to increasing profits and contributed to the local merchants' capital accumulation whilst their knowledge of the Ottoman market, as far as this commodity was concerned, must have facilitated their successful establishment in the western European ports, at the turn of the century, from where they sent cloth to İzmir in return for Ottoman raw materials.

At the same time, the fact that a Ralli, a member of the successful Greek entrepreneurial family, was the *sarraf* of the powerful Karaosmanoğlu at the end of the 18th century shows that the local merchants were also active in traditional areas of the Ottoman economy, such as merchant banking, moneylending and other monetary activities, re-enforcing their capital accumulation. Their successful participation in the carrying trade in the Mediterranean showed that they were also able to diversify their economic activities in order to take advantage of new economic opportunities as these arose. Their success, here, was partly due to the fact that shipping was still interconnected with their basic activity — trade; partly due to the fact that their international networks of commercial establishments and kinship worked to their advantage and were even re-enforced through shipping and, partly due to the fact that they were more willing than the westerners to risk the war-ridden Mediterranean waters, in the late 18th and early 19th centuries, even while manipulating the system by getting licenses to navigate from both the French and the British.

Thus, by the end of the 18th century, Ottoman merchants were able to participate in all sectors of İzmir's economy, including external trade, formerly almost totally a European preserve. Despite this however, they also displayed extreme fragility in their businesses with a high rate of bankruptcy which occurred after a few years of over-hectic, over-speculative economic activity. Yet, overall, Ottoman merchants emerged as credible competitors to the Europeans, not necessarily able to shut the westerners out from trading or carrying out any other economic activity in İzmir, but rather, able to act as serious rivals. As for the western Europeans, although they had, by the end to the 18th century, lost their exclusive rights in the external trade of İzmir they were by no means displaced. They continued to be a very strong commercial force in the area branching into other sectors of the region's economy in the course of the 19th and early 20th centuries as their capital resources were strengthened and their commitment and need to invest such resources in the region's economy increased.

COMMERCIAL PRACTICES AND COMPETITION IN THE LEVANT: THE BRITISH AND THE DUTCH IN EIGHTEENTH-CENTURY İZMİR

In the eighteenth century, Dutch and British merchants, together with the French, constituted the major European mercantile communities in İzmir. They played a crucial role in the way trade was carried out between İzmir and the West as well as in the evolution of the trade relationship of the entire region with the West. The British and the Dutch had each a different impact on the area which, in many respects, reflected the different ideologies and economic policies of their respective countries and the different needs of their national economies. Perhaps the two most important and distinct ways that the Dutch affected the region's economy were, firstly, the leading role that they played in the integration of İzmir into European financial circuits, and, secondly, the way they allowed local, that is Ottoman, entrepreneurs to enter their commercial and financial networks. In the process they influenced the level of capital accumulation realized by the local merchant communities. The British affected Ottoman-European trade in a distinctive manner, particularly in the early nineteenth century, by leading in the penetration of western commercial capital into the hinterland of İzmir. For they thus laid the foundations for the changes that would take place in Ottoman-western commercial relations of the nineteenth century when western capital would play a larger role than formerly in the region's commercial sector.

Since the nature of the commercial relations with the Ottoman empire of both groups was broadly similar — they both exported manufactured and colonial goods to İzmir and imported from there raw materials for their textile sectors in addition to agricultural goods — they influenced İzmir's commercial sector in similar ways. This was a fundamental reason why the Dutch and the British were rivals in the trade of İzmir — a rivalry which affected the tactics and practices of both merchant groups as each strove to realize maximum profits. Moreover, their contemporaneous commercial presence also ensured a highly competitive business climate, one in which the French, who were the strongest mercantile group in İzmir at the time in terms of resources and commercial activity, could, at best, dominate, but never control, the commercial sector of the city-port. Indeed, İzmir's economic milieu remained fiercely competitive and open to all groups, Ottoman and European, throughout the eighteenth century, leading to different tactics for each group. In order to counter rivalry from the Ottoman merchants, for example, inter-European cooperation could be sanctioned by diplomatic representatives on the spot. Such cooperation could take the form of a common front by the British and the Dutch, and sometimes by the French too, with the aim of forcing the terms of a commercial transaction on a particular group, or groups, of local merchants. However, such cooperation was often a temporary measure, brought on by special circumstances and likely to be short-lived, for it attempted to reverse the trend of İzmir's competitive commercial world. Longer-standing and potentially more effective was cooperation, often incurred in wartime, on the level of individual entrepreneurs, be they Dutch, British or Ottoman.

Once established in İzmir, as European merchants, both the Dutch and the British had a similar status *vis-à-vis* the local authorities. The way the two communities were administered in İzmir, as well as elsewhere in the Levant, also had similarities, just as there were points of resemblance in the way they related to the Ottoman merchants, for the dynamics at work between the local and the major European merchant communities were broadly similar. However, the political and diplomatic influence that each country could bring to bear on the Porte could, at times, make a difference. The two commercial communities also found themselves hampered, or aided, as the case might be, by the regulations of their states or by the foreign policies of their governments.

Both the British and the Dutch carried out their trade in İzmir, as they did elsewhere in the empire, in small mercantile communities under the protection of their countries' respective consular and other diplomatic representatives. There were many points of community in the way these representatives acted and interacted with their nationals in the Levant. Operating on the basis of the privileges granted to their governments through the Capitulations, they attempted to protect, regulate, and, in the process, exercise a certain control over the trading activities of their nationals. This control was much greater in the British than in the Dutch case, although it started to wane amongst the British too in the latter part of the eighteenth century as the European economy entered an expansionist phase. Nevertheless, each country had quite different corporate structures through which to administer and, perhaps, to regulate the trading activities of its nationals in the Levant.

The British traded under the auspices of the Levant Company, a monopoly operating under a royal charter granted for the first time in 1581 by Elizabeth I.[1] The charter initially gave the company exclusive rights to the Levant trade for a period of seven years. After the company had demonstrated trade and shipping activity on a large and profitable enough scale, the charter was renewed in 1593 for a period of twelve years, and in 1605 the company was given a perpetual charter.[2] The Levant Company was headed in London by a governor, a deputy governor and assistants. The leadership was made up of important City of London figures, some of the governors of the company even having held the office of Lord Mayor of London.[3] Merchants trading in the Levant could also hold important offices during their careers, such as the directorship of the Bank of England.[4]

Unlike the Netherlands, where trade to the Levant was open to all, merchants in Britain had to become members of the company, or *freemen* as they were called, in order to trade in the Levant. The requirements for becoming a member were residence within a twenty-five mile radius of the City of London and the privilege to exercise the profession of 'mere' merchant as opposed to retailer in the City of London.[5] Upon admission the *freeman*, if over 26 years of age, paid £50 and, if under 26, £25; all sons and apprentices of *freemen* were admitted upon paying only 20 shillings. Later, in the mid-eighteenth century, the amount for admission was reduced to £20.[6] *Freemen* could also act as agents for non-members of the company, including non-British merchants. For the Levant company, despite its monopolistic attitude towards trade with the Ottoman Empire, was keen to ensure that as much trade or shipping as possible pass through the hands of British *freemen* and thus actively encouraged non-*freemen* and *strangers*, as non-British (including Ottoman) merchants were called, to deal with British *freemen* in the Ottoman

[1] David MacPherson, *Annals of Commerce, Manufactures, Fisheries and Navigation* (4 vols, London, 1805), ii, pp. 168-171-201-202, 242.

[2] M. Epstein, *The Early History of the Levant Company* (London, 1908), pp. 17, 19.

[3] Epstein, *The Early History*, pp. 67-72.

[4] For example, Richard Stratton of Radcliffe & Stratton, partner in the important London firm of Edward & Arthur Radcliffe, culminated a successful commercial career in the Levant trade — he also served as a factor in Aleppo earlier on — by becoming director of the Bank of England in 1750-1758. Sir Lewis Namier & J. Brooke, *History of Parliament* (London, 1964), iii, p. 685. For information on the trading activities of Richard Stratton, see Elena Frangakis-Syrett, "Trade Practices in Aleppo in the Middle of the Eighteenth Century. The Case of a British Merchant", *Revue du Monde Musulman et de la Méditerrannée*, 62/4 (1991), pp. 123-132, and on the trading activities of the Radcliffe firm, see Ralph Davis, *Aleppo and Devonshire Square* (London, 1967), *passim*.

[5] Public Record Office, FO 78/136, Levant Company Memorandum, 1825. Hereafter this archive will be cited as PRO.

[6] *Acts of Parliament*, 26 March 1753. An Historical View of the Conduct and Proceedings of the Turkey Company; see also, A Bill for Enlarging and Regulating Trade into the Levant Seas.

ports, the latter acting as agents. There were two main reasons for the adoption of such a policy: to promote the business of their members and to create another source of revenue for the company. Thus both European (for instance Dutch) and Ottoman merchants could consign goods to a British *freeman,* or *factor,* in İzmir. The goods could be consigned on a British or non-British ship coming from Amsterdam or any other port, on account of a non-*freeman* or an Ottoman merchant, the British *factor* acting as agent or broker. As such he received the goods in İzmir or dispatched them from the port, at all times ensuring their ultimate destination and generating the payment of a consulage fee to the Levant Company.[1]

Besides the above source of revenue, the Levant Company also charged its own members consulage fees and levies over and above any charges from Ottoman and British customs. These *ad valorem* duties, calculated on the value of the goods and not on the value of the ship carrying them, varied according to the needs of the company. The levy was to be paid within sixty days of the ship's arrival at the port of İzmir, the consulage within thirty days.[2] If these duties were not paid at the prescribed times, the company charged 1% interest per month till the account was settled. Revenue was also raised by the company by offering British legal protection to non-British European merchant communities in return for a fee. It was raised, too, by the British consul, as was the case with the other consuls in İzmir including the Dutch, through the granting of *berats* by which official legal protection was afforded, in return for a fee, to Ottoman merchants in İzmir for the purposes of trading on the international market on the same legal premise as the European merchants.[3] And, finally, merchants guilty of violating the company's regulations by trading in illicit goods were subject to an elaborate system of fines, which could be as high as 20% of the value of the goods in question. Prohibiting trade in money was one such regulation. Merchants caught importing specie to İzmir paid a 20% fine collected in the imported specie.[4] For a number of reasons — such as the lucrative nature of trade in money — this prohibition no longer held by the end of the century.[5] Income raised from all the above sources was used to meet the expenses of maintaining the company's establishments, including the consulate in İzmir, of paying its officials, and of offering presents, and, where necessary, of paying for *avanias,* or extraordinary payments, to the Ottoman authorities. An important

[1]PRO, SP 105/211, Printed Orders of the Levant Company, 19 October 1744.
[2]PRO, SP 105/337, Factory meeting, İzmir, 11 April 1758.
[3]De Groot, *The Ottoman Empire and the Dutch Republic,* p. 39.
[4]PRO, SP 105/118, Levant Company, London, 27 April 1750 to Consul Crawley, İzmir.
[5]PRO, SP 105/337, Consul Hayes, İzmir, 15 May 1789.

area of activity and decision-making for the company was its shipping policy through which it aimed at controlling the Levant trade. The company was forced intermittently in the first half of the eighteenth century to give up this right,[1] and did so once and for all in the second half of the century.[2] Whilst its right was in force the Levant Company dispatched goods at prescribed times in ships of its own, called *general* ships, and the *freemen* had to send their goods in these ships too. The approval of the governing body of the company was needed to send another ship at an intermediate date.

In the case of the Dutch, trade was open to all. Dutch shipowners could carry goods on behalf of any nation, whilst Dutch merchants could consign goods to any merchant they wanted in İzmir, be he European or Ottoman.[3] Besides the Dutch, British and other European merchants established in İzmir could also trade with Holland. They did so either on their own account or acting as correspondents for Dutch merchants in Holland. Moreover, Dutch firms in İzmir could act as correspondents for British firms established elsewhere in the Ottoman empire, and trade with Holland on their behalf in addition to pursuing their own independent trading activities with the Dutch ports.[4]

The Dutch merchants also had a somewhat different organizational structure from the British for controlling their trade in the Levant. This was based on Colleges of Directors, as they were called, which were in fact more akin to Chambers of Commerce than anything else. Amsterdam was the first to establish a College of Directors of Levant Trade and Navigation in the Mediterranean in 1625. Similar colleges were soon set up in Leiden Hoorn, Enkhuizen and Medemblik, and, in 1670, in Rotterdam.[5] The colleges acted in some ways similarly to the Chamber of Commerce of Marseilles, although they enjoyed greater independence in commercial matters *vis-à-vis* their state governments than did the French Chamber of Commerce.[6] Nor were the colleges restrictive as far as trade in the Levant was concerned since trade was open to all. They were supposed, rather, to ensure that no abuses take place in

---

[1]PRO, SP 105/116, Levant Company, London, 13 August 1719 to Consul Cooke, İzmir; SP 105/117, Levant Company, London, 1 September 1730 to Consul Boddington, İzmir.

[2]*Acts of Parliament*, 26 March 1753. An Historical View; see also, PRO, SP 105/211, Printed Orders of the Levant Company, 1744.

[3]Masson, *Histoire du commerce français ... au XVIIIe siècle*, p. 375; see also, PRO, SP 105/207; Charles R. Boxer, *The Dutch Seaborne Empire: 1600-1800* (New York, 1965), pp. 90-95 and Jonathan I. Israel, *The Dutch Republic* (Oxford, 1995), p. 1001.

[4]PRO, SP 105/187, British Chancery, Istanbul, 15 & 21 February 1781 and 26 March 1781.

[5]David W. Davies, *A Primer of Dutch Seventeenth-Century Overseas Trade* (The Hague, 1961), pp. 43-44.

[6]Masson, *Histoire du commerce français ... au XVIIe siècle*, pp. 123-124.

any area of the Dutch Levant trade. Evidence on the ground, however, suggests that Dutch consuls in İzmir did try at times, in the eighteenth century, to direct the trading activities of their nationals, alongside their British and French colleagues.

At the end of the eighteenth century, the college in Amsterdam — together with Rotterdam it was one of the two most important Dutch ports in the Levant trade — was made up of eight directors, a secretary and an inspector of ships.[1] These colleges undertook such duties as supervising the consuls stationed in the Ottoman ports, inspecting goods destined for the Levant trade, and requesting and organizing convoys to the Levant. An area where the colleges did exercise a certain control was shipping: Dutch ships usually left for the Levant in convoys and had to be of a certain size. On the whole, they were bigger than the British in tonnage and larger still when compared to the ships the French employed in their Levant trade. Funds for the maintenance of the ambassador and other consular authorities, as well as for customary gifts and extraordinary payments to Ottoman officials, were raised by the imposition of a 2% tax on all imports and exports payable at the home port and by levying a fee on all ships going to or coming from the Levant in the Dutch ports.[2]

Irrespective of the way each country organized its Levant trade the merchants of both communities, whilst in an Ottoman port, were under the administration and legal control of their consul and his fellow officers, although here again there were certain differences: for instance, although the British consul was under the British ambassador, he himself was appointed by, and represented, the Levant Company. The Dutch consul answered both to the Dutch ambassador and to the Directors of Levant Trade in Amsterdam. As a result, any legal action concerning the Dutch merchants went through four different judicial channels.[3] For example, legal actions brought by the merchants were decided by a majority vote of the consul and the assessors in İzmir, the latter being state officials who helped him administer the Dutch community together with the treasurer and the secretary. Their decision was then reviewed by the Dutch ambassador in Istanbul, the Directors of Levant Trade in Amsterdam, and the directors general of the state. An important function of these officials, for both communities, was regulating the relations

---

[1]Masson, *Histoire du commerce français ... au XVIIIe siècle*, p. 374.
[2]*Ibid.*, pp. 374-375; Davies, *Primer*, p. 44.
[3]Archives Nationales de France, AE Biii 243, Réglements concernant le commerce de la nation hollandaise, 1815. Hereafter this archive will be cited as ANF.

of their nationals with the Ottoman authorities, especially local customs officials, and sorting out problems their nationals might have with each other as well as with other European or local merchants.

Although such administrative structures created the necessary stability and protection to trade in the Levant for the Dutch and the British, already from the early eighteenth century onwards the restrictive policies undertaken, at times, by the respective consular authorities could conflict with the way the Levant trade was carried out. The intense competition amongst all groups trading in İzmir and the demand for Ottoman goods in the western markets, in addition to the ability of İzmir to absorb, and distribute to its large hinterland, prime western imports, led to a highly volatile market in the eighteenth century, which was difficult to predict but also equally difficult to control. Perhaps the most important way in which British and Dutch consular authorities — the British rather more than the Dutch, and the French more than the British — attempted to control the trade of their nationals, was by controlling the market. They aimed to achieve this either by controlling prices or by controlling supply and demand. They found such aims increasingly difficult to attain as the century went on. Indeed, already from the early eighteenth century on, it was not only the market conditions in İzmir that the British or the Dutch authorities had to take into account, but also conditions in other major markets in the Ottoman empire with which İzmir was connected, such as Istanbul or Thessaloniki. For the commercial networks, both Ottoman and European, which increasingly connected the major markets in the maritime regions of the empire with Europe as well as with each other, were at the same time advantageous to the Europeans and a source of intense competition.

In the 1730s, for instance, as the French were strengthening their position in Ottoman-European trade,[1] the British and the Dutch started feeling the competition, since they were all dealing in basically the same commodities. The import trade in cloth thus became a test case when the Dutch authorities in İzmir, like their British counterparts, attempted to fix minimum prices for Dutch-imported cloth. In doing so they had to take into account not only the prices that various qualities of their cloth, as well as corresponding qualities of British and French cloth, commanded in European commercial circles in Istanbul and Thessaloniki, besides İzmir, but also the prices that Ottoman Jewish, Armenian and Greek merchants and cloth retailers

[1]Charles Carrière, *Négociants marseillais au XVIIIe siècle* (2 vols, Marseilles, 1973), i, pp. 396-427; see also Frangakis-Syrett, *The Commerce of Smyrna*, pp. 119-138.

charged in Istanbul for the European cloth they brought from İzmir. Underselling a competitor, a practice which could become fiercer in a soft market, especially at a time of a general commercial crisis as was the case in the 1730s, was a risky proposition. For it could also result in widespread bankruptcy. The price war in İzmir in the early 1730s took place in the midst of a French economic crisis in Marseilles and Paris that spread all over Europe, triggering defaults in London, Amsterdam, Cadiz and Seville,[1] as well as in İzmir and other centers in the Ottoman empire.[2]

There were many major problems in trying to regulate the pricing of goods in the Levant trade apart from the existence of empire-based commercial networks. One such problem was the result of specie substitution practices that had evolved in the Ottoman markets where barter and credit were used extensively in addition to, or indeed instead of, money, whether in specie or in bills of exchange, in order to effect a sale. Such practices had a direct impact on the prices of goods traded, making the fixing of a minimum price for western goods an impossibility. For prices depended on the quality and demand not only of the goods being sold but also of the Ottoman goods being bartered against them. A European who wanted to undersell his competitors had only to offer more cloth for the goods he was buying from the Ottomans in order to do so. Whilst some Ottoman goods, such as cotton or cotton yarn, commanded a steady price, mohair yarn and other products varied so greatly in quality that they could not bear a fixed price. Moreover, according to the state of the market, manufactured goods were at times *only in part* bartered against local goods, with the remaining balance being paid in cash, thus complicating the whole procedure still further.[3]

Since barter was tedious and speculative, depending, as it did, on the sale of the articles exchanged, another way of overcoming specie shortage was by extending credit to a potential buyer. A credit period varied in length from two weeks to two years, with the likelihood of being somewhere in-between. As might be expected, the length of the credit period affected the price of goods, reflecting both the degree of risk involved and the interest that the seller was foregoing by not realizing his cash for a given period of time. However, Dutch or British merchants, and especially captains, often found it advantageous to drop their prices and sell quickly rather than wait for long

---

[1]Carrière, *Négociants marseillais*, i, pp. 441-442; see also, Robert Paris, *Histoire du commerce de Marseille de 1660-1789. Le Levant* (Paris, 1957), p. 447.

[2]ANF, AE Bi 1045, Consul Peleran, İzmir, 28 February & 7 October 1732 to Minister, Paris.

[3]A.B. Cunningham ed., "The Journal of Christophe Aubin: A Report of the Levant Trade in 1812", *Archivum Ottomanicum*, 8 (1983), p. 38.

periods of time to be reimbursed. The European merchants in particular needed to have a certain amount of cash in hand from time to time in order to pay for the preparation and transport of their purchases to the west.[1] However, even they could not always avoid selling on credit. Indeed, credit was at times considered the only way to do business.

Another factor that seriously frustrated the efforts of both communities' consular authorities to control the pricing of goods, and hence the market, consisted of the problems associated with the Ottoman currency, namely its weakness and its scarcity. Its weakness and volatility in relation to the European currencies, particularly in the second half of the eighteenth and in the early nineteenth centuries, became especially important to trade in view of the way such volatility affected the rates of exchange of the Ottoman currency and hence the value of the goods exchanged. The scarcity of the Ottoman currency, on the other hand, caused (at least in part, for there were also other reasons) an extensive circulation of multiple western currencies in the market of İzmir and in other major Ottoman economic centers. Such a currency situation led to endless possibilities of profit in İzmir's particularly lively and speculative currency market. At the same time, it rendered more complex commercial transactions that dealt in commodities from different countries in different currencies, for there also existed the option of speculating in such currencies as opposed to using them only in commercial transactions. Moreover, given the fact that such monetary conditions were characteristic of the market of İzmir, they were also reflected in the pricing system of the goods exchanged. That is, the pricing of a commodity was also affected by the value of the Ottoman currency, itself sometimes the result of intense currency speculation. This rendered the pricing of these goods even more complex. It also made it more difficult for European authorities, such as the Levant Company which was trying to influence the price of British cloth, to take into account calculations that were based on the specific conjuncture of a currency market many miles away.

Another way to control prices was by controlling supply. This was a policy preferred primarily by the French and one which the British and Dutch, often jointly, were able to undermine. For when the French merchants in İzmir were given a quota by their consul of so many cloths of various qualities to sell in a set period of time, at a fixed minimum price, in order to

[1]Private Papers, Colvill Bridger, Aleppo, 30 May 1755 to Edward & Arthur Radcliffe, London. Hereafter this collection will be cited as PP.PP, Bridger, Aleppo, 30 May 1755, to Richard Stratton, London.

force the local market to accept a certain price level, they failed to have the desired result. For the British and the Dutch stepped in instead, filling the gap left by the French in the demand for western cloth at prices that the İzmir market commanded.[1] As a result, even the French abandoned this policy in the second half of the eighteenth century when the market forces were getting even stronger and the organization of trade more complex. However, in the early part of the eighteenth century, the British also tried to control supply, albeit rather more indirectly, by controlling shipping to İzmir — that is by deciding the time(s) when company ships were to be sent to İzmir — through the regulations of the Levant Company.[2] This policy, too, had to be abandoned by the second half of the eighteenth century due to pressure from British manufacturers and other economic interests at home, as well as to the changing needs and conditions of the Levant trade in the latter part of the century.[3]

The market of İzmir had certain advantages that were not found everywhere else in the Levant and which played an important role in the dominant position the city-port came to enjoy in Ottoman-western trade. Such advantages were the existence of a large hinterland to which İzmir was well connected, and the most extensive commercial networks, at sea and on land, both to the west and within the empire at large, encompassing many areas of the Ottoman interior, reaching as far as Persia, and giving İzmir a pivotal position within the empire's commercial routes. Such networks also meant the near guarantee, for a ship from the west or a caravan from the east, that the goods thus brought to İzmir would find buyers, and that the caravan dealers or the European captains would find goods to take on their return journey to eastern Anatolia and Persia in the east or to Europe in the west. This was an important asset in the eighteenth century that differentiated this market from all others in the Levant. The need either to return half full or to go to several markets before enough freight had been obtained for the return journey to Europe, as was the case with the Syrian or Greek ports, greatly diminished the appeal of these markets.[4] However, the multiplicity of buyers and sellers in the İzmir market also meant that competition could at times be so acute as to increase the prices of the goods traded. As a result, Ottoman goods could become almost too expensive for the markets in Europe and profit margins for the Europeans were often slim.

---

[1] ANF, AE Bi 1045, Consul Peleran, İzmir, 28 March 1735 to Minister, Paris; see also, AE Bi 1053, Consul Peleran, İzmir, 22 September 1751 to Minister, Paris.

[2] E.g., PRO, SP 105/117, Levant Company, London, 13 March 1739 to Treasurer Tooke, İzmir.

[3] *Acts of Parliament*, 26 March 1753. An Historical View ...

[4] Frangakis-Syrett, *The Commerce of Smyrna*, pp. 119-123 and Appendix B, pp. 257-260; see also, Paris, *Histoire du Commerce*, pp. 437-443.

What made competition even more acute was the fact that British merchants — and we can assume that similar demands were placed on the Dutch too — usually had certain price limits within which to buy or sell and which were set by their employers or associates in the west. Unlike the western governments, the latter were not trying to exercise control over the market but rather over their agents, who were using their capital miles away. They were also trying to ensure that goods could be procured at a price that would allow for profits to be made in the western markets. Whilst the prices of goods bought or sold became the object of endless negotiations between the Europeans and the Ottomans, it was often in the terms of sale or purchase that bigger or smaller profit margins could be realized. These terms might establish whether any amount of cash were to be included in the payment and the specific currencies being used, or whether it was to be done entirely on credit, and in that latter case the length of credit applied; or even whether any barter was to take place and in that case the quality of the goods bartered. Finally, an important component in the profitability of any transaction was the speed with which goods were likely to reach their destinations and thus the possibility of capturing a good market. Indeed, the appearance of a ship bound for Europe often speeded up the conclusion of a deal as far as the European was concerned, and could affect prices too. Similarly, the appearance of a caravan could force the hand of a reluctant local seller, for he stood to lose a sale that he might have secured if more goods suddenly came to the city's bazaar.

The existence of two groups of entrepreneurs, the Ottomans and the Europeans, each with their own special assets and advantages, locked in tight commercial rivalry, was a characteristic of İzmir. Each group, European or Ottoman — the former including the Dutch and the British — entered the commercial world of Izmir with their own strengths and weaknesses. For their part, the British and the Dutch, as was also the case with the other major trading power, the French, had a privileged and legally advantageous position *vis-à-vis* the Ottoman merchants in İzmir owing to the Capitulations. They had far better contacts and knowledge of the European markets and manufacturers. They also tended, on the whole, to dispose of greater capital resources than the locals. The result was that, for a good part of the eighteenth century, the Europeans — at times including the British and the Dutch — dominated certain sectors of the external trade of İzmir with the west. For example, they dominated the purchase of Ottoman goods once they had been brought from the interior to the port, and they dominated their export to the major markets in Europe, such as Britain or France. They also prevailed in the importation of western goods to İzmir. The British and the Dutch, together with the French, and, to a lesser degree, with other Europeans, were also predominant in deep water shipping and maritime insurance. Together with the French, the British participated in Ottoman coastal shipping, even if the French were much more active in this sector than the British.

However, all of these assets did not make *individual* European merchants all-powerful in their everyday dealings with the Ottoman merchants. For their part, the latter had an unequaled knowledge of the local markets in the interior, contacts with, as well as access to, both producers of Ottoman exports and consumers of western imports in the city and its hinterland. As brokers to the British or the Dutch, the local merchants were often more than just their employees. They frequently participated in ventures of their own thanks to their knowledge of, and entries to, the internal networks — even if they might, at times, 'borrow' their employers' capital to do so.[1] All this allowed the local merchants to dominate the internal domestic landed and maritime trade networks of İzmir. For if the Europeans were the ones who got the goods on board western-bound ships, it was the locals, who brought these goods to them from the interior. Whilst the British and the French, unlike the Dutch, aimed at maintaining for most of the century a near-exclusivity of their home markets — largely barring the local merchants from direct access to them — the Ottoman merchants had a near-monopoly of the internal markets and economy in the city's hinterland and throughout İzmir's internal and vast commercial networks. Although the Europeans, including the Dutch and the British, could, and did, venture inland, they only did so on a limited scale and somewhat sporadically before the early nineteenth century. The bitter competition the Europeans faced when they started going into the Ottoman interior for purposes of trade in a concerted manner — both before and, for a while, even after the 1838 trade convention that laid the legal foundations for such an entry —shows just how well guarded that interior economy was by the local entrepreneurs.

In the eighteenth century, therefore, the Ottoman interior and its commercial networks remained largely closed to the Dutch and the British. Ottoman merchants, Muslim and non-Muslim, were not the only ones, however, who disposed of commercial networks within the Ottoman empire. The British, in particular, had their own networks of merchants who were stationed in some of the major city-ports or other urban centers in the empire.

[1]E.g., ANF, AE Bi 1052, Consul Charles de Peyssonnel, İzmir, 5 March 1749 to Minister, Paris; PRO, SP 105/116, Levant Company, London, 2 July 1717 to Consul Cooke, İzmir.

They were usually employees, or *factors*, of a commercial firm; their employers were called principals and were usually stationed in London. The *factors* could also work for more than one merchant house and the latter could be outside Britain too — for example in the Mediterranean. The Dutch do not seem to have disposed of quite so extensive a network of agents as the British. Moreover, there was an important difference: unlike the British, Dutch commercial houses in the Netherlands were willing, at all times, to have Ottoman merchants act as their agents or corespondents in İzmir. This may have had both positive and negative results. Such practices may have given the Dutch merchants a better, albeit indirect, access to the interior than their British rivals,[1] but may also have facilitated the entry of local merchants from İzmir into the Dutch markets later in the century.

As far as the British merchants were concerned, it should be noted that they were all stationed in Ottoman centers such as İzmir which were well connected with the western markets since all their activities revolved around the trade of the empire with Europe. Besides, they did not usually have any extensive contacts with the commercial networks in the hinterland of those centers, for such networks were invariably in the hands of local Ottoman merchants.[2] This is not to say that the British did not derive advantages from the existence of their commercial networks. Since a number of merchants in different cities in the empire were all working for the same firm in London, they could exchange contacts and information concerning the best market for cotton or silk, or send funds to each other to make a purchase. In view of the scarcity of specie in the Levant under which all merchants, European and Ottoman, labored, availability of funds was an important asset. For this reason, a significant link in these networks for British factors was the existence of a house that could be stationed in Istanbul and which acted largely as a merchant-*cum*-banker, even if there were still no clear divisions between the activities of a merchant and those of a merchant banker and the same person was often both.[3] A frequent method of transferring funds within the empire, practiced by all Europeans, not only the British, was the use of the internal Ottoman circuits of bills of exchange — an area where Ottoman and European networks overlapped and complemented each other.

---

[1]De Vogel, 19 November 1762 to Bartholo Cardamici, İzmir, in Nanninga, *Bronnen*, iii, p. 475.

[2]For more details on the commercial networks of the Europeans and the way these functioned, see Elena Frangakis-Syrett, "Commerce in the Eastern Mediterranean from the Eighteenth to the Early Twentieth Centuries: The City-Port of İzmir and its Hinterland", *International Journal of Maritime History*, 10/2 (1998), pp. 126-36, 141-5.

[3]See e.g., Frangakis-Syrett, "Trade practices in Aleppo", pp. 124-125, 127.

The result was a relationship of competition and cooperation, of constantly varying dynamics, played out on all levels of trade and at every opportunity, and which influenced commercial strategies as well as practices between the Europeans — be they British or Dutch — on the one hand and with the Ottomans on the other. For example, a strategy local merchants might resort to in order to force the hand of the British, particularly in the silk trade, was to stand together and refuse to sell below a minimum price. This could even mean that the local merchants would buy from one another in order to keep prices up. In such cases, the British could retort equally vigorously by selling whatever silk they had already purchased in the bazaar, instead of shipping it abroad, claiming that they could thus make better profits than on the western markets. The means by which the British called the Ottomans' bluff seemed to work, at least temporarily, in a business world where impressions could, at times, be as effective as reality.[1] However, it could also backfire as a tactic, or be shortsighted. For it seems that the British sometimes bought silk — even going directly to local dealers in the environs to do so — not with the intention of sending it to England, but rather in order to sell it on the local market. However, the more hands the commodity went through the more expensive it became for those merchants who were the ultimate exporters. The Levant Company consequently tried to prohibit such a practice.[2] Although the tactic of going into the immediate hinterland of İzmir in order to make more advantageous purchases was not extensive in the eighteenth century, it was certainly also practiced by the Dutch, whose agents went inland in order to buy cotton in advance, i.e. before the harvest was in.[3] Whilst this could give the Dutch a competitive edge over their rivals, it was also considered a speculative practice, for the merchant could end up offering a higher price than what the cotton ultimately fetched. He could also do very well out of it, however.

At times, and if the right conditions for such tactics existed, cooperation between entrepreneurs could take the form of quite formidable combinations, or syndicates, in order to overcome competition from rival

[1]PP, C. Bridger, Aleppo, 27 July & 19 May 1759 to William Hammond, London; see also, PP, Bridger, 15 August 1759 to Benjamin & George Barker, Istanbul.
[2]PRO, SP 105/211, Printed Orders of the Levant Company, 1744.
[3]De Vogel, 19 November 1762 to Bartholo Cardamici, İzmir, in Nanninga, *Bronnen*, iii, p. 475.

merchants.[1] Such was the case with Ottoman Greek merchants originating from the island of Chios, who dealt initially in the retail, and subsequently in the wholesale, sectors of Dutch-imported cloth in İzmir.[2] In the period from the late eighteenth to the early nineteenth centuries their combination, or syndicate, dealt a near-mortal blow to the Dutch importers of cloth in the city and all but ousted them from the sector.[3] This was made possible by a number of advantages that the Chiots, in this case, were able to exploit to the utmost. For instance, they enjoyed strong family and local ties and were able to use such bonds of kinship to build up confidential networks, contacts, information, expertise and credit, thereby augmenting their capital resources. As a result they were able to increase their businesses from selling in the city and its immediate hinterland to selling further afield in Anatolia in the course of the late eighteenth century. Realizing, for a number of reasons, a good level of capital accumulation and benefiting from their other assets, they proceeded to a qualitative growth of their business. From sellers of Dutch-imported cloth they became importers of such cloth from Dutch merchants and manufacturers in the Netherlands and elsewhere in Central Europe.

An important reason for the rapid growth that the İzmir Chiots experienced in their business was the particular conjuncture of events in the European political and military scene that worked in their favor. In the early 1780s, for example, Dutch trade to İzmir suffered greatly from the blockades of Dutch ports by the British navy. The Dutch consequently had to redirect at least some of their trade to the Adriatic and the port of Trieste, whilst using overland routes for the rest of the way. Most of the trade of Trieste with İzmir, however, was carried out at the time by Ottoman merchants, many of them Greek houses related to the Chiot cloth merchants in the Levantine port.[4] Moreover, growth in the western economies, including the Dutch, in some

[1] Fremeaux, Van Lennep and Enslie, 29 June 1782 to Van Haaften in Nanninga, *Bronnen*, iv, pp. 339-341; see also Directors, 24 July 1760 to States General in Nanninga, *Bronnen*, iii, pp. 400-401.

[2] The tactics used by the Chiot combination or syndicate in the late eighteenth century in order to achieve their aims are worth noting. Closing ranks, all thirty houses that made up the combination elected four deputies who were the only ones authorized to buy cloth from the Dutch. Buying in bulk, and being an important buyer, the syndicate could secure lower prices for their purchases which they passed on to their members by selling the cloth to them at a slightly higher price but a price that still allowed the members to sell at a profit on the İzmir market. At the same time the syndicate realized a profit from the sales to its own members which it also passed on to them; in turn, the members made a contribution to the syndicate. No one seems to have defected from the syndicate which, in view of other factors, too, went from strength to strength in the next three decades, or so.

[3] *Rapport fait à M. le chargé d'affaires* Testa sur les drapiers, Hochepied, İzmir, 19 February 1818, in Naninga, *Bronnen*, iv, pp. 950-951.

[4] ANF, Marine B/7, 446, Bertrand, 19 October 1782, in Commerce des ports de l'Europe, 1 February 1783.

respects served the interests of the Chiots better than the interests of the Dutch merchants in İzmir. Dutch manufacturers, for instance, actually benefited from such competition. As for the Dutch merchants in İzmir, they continued to import cloth to the city-port and even to sell it to Chiot wholesale merchants in the early nineteenth century, although most likely on a smaller scale than before.[1] Nor were the Dutch the only ones to suffer competition from the concerted actions of the Chiots. The latter tried to dictate terms to the French merchants too. Whilst there are some similarities with the Dutch-Chiot rivalry, this particular competition was less auspicious for the Chiots for a number of reasons, including the vitality of the French economy and the stronger commercial presence of the French as compared to the Dutch in İzmir.[2] As for the Chiots, they lost their initial solidarity as they were ultimately divided along social and economic lines. By the early nineteenth century the more prosperous merchants had become cloth importers and had joined an Ottoman-European association of cloth importers in the city whose aim was to regulate the extension of credit and enforce payments from the union of Ottoman (Greek, Armenian, and Jewish) cloth retailers in the bazaar. The less prosperous Chiots were in the cloth retail trade and are likely to have joined the union.[3]

Certainly, not all local rivalries were as formidable, or represented the tide of economic changes as aptly, as the competition between the Chiots and the Dutch. Nevertheless, the above example should not be seen as an isolated case either, but rather as a consequence of the liberal policies of the Dutch who had allowed Ottoman merchants to participate in their commercial networks, and, by the second half of the eighteenth century, to establish themselves in Dutch ports. It was a policy of which the British in İzmir were fully aware and which they decried. In the early nineteenth century, faced by the forces of economic change that favored an end to protectionism and determined to maintain some exclusivity for its members, the Levant

[1]The debts that Dutch merchants accumulated — as did the British and French merchants — from credit offered to Chiot cloth buyers and on which the Chiots reneged when they were forced to abandon their businesses and flee the city at the outbreak of the Greek War of Independence, in 1821, are evidence of the continuing participation of the Dutch in this sector. PRO, FO 78/136, Consul Werry, İzmir, 13 April 1822 to Levant Company, London; see also FO 78/136, British Ambassador, Istanbul, 17 July 1822 to Levant Company, London and FO 78/136, British Ambassador, Istanbul, 10 January 1823 to Levant Company, London.

[2]Ministère des Affaires Étrangères, Centre des Archives Diplomatique de Nantes, FC/CAE, Vol. 30, Consul Méchain, İzmir, 25 February 1818 to French Ambassador, Istanbul. Hereafter this archive will cited as MAE, CADN.

[3]Archives de la Chambre de Commerce de Marseille, MQ 5.1, Agreement presented by a deputation of European and Greek cloth importers to the Union of Greek and Armenian shopkeepers and to the Jewish community, İzmir, 5 September 1820. Hereafter this archive will be cited as ACCM.

Company opted for a compromise. It allowed Ottoman Greeks to trade with London through its members in the hope of preventing them from trading independently with other merchants in the British port and deterring them from establishing themselves in Britain as they had done in Holland, lest they '[thus] in time monopolize all the trade to the utter exclusion of both factors and members at home.'[1] British perceptions of the threat posed by the activities of the Greeks notwithstanding, it is worth noting here that, in the late eighteenth and early nineteenth centuries, the Dutch suffered even greater and more detrimental rivalry from the British as the latter seized an increasingly larger share of İzmir's European trade. Indeed, in the process the British actually ousted an erstwhile rival of both, the French. The French mistakenly also blamed the Ottoman Greeks, rather than the British, for their misfortune, which was, of course, due to a number of other factors besides Greek or even British competition.

At times competition could also come from one's own compatriots. For instance, in the early eighteenth century, the British, as *freemen* of the Levant Company, faced competition from other British merchants who were not members of the company and who were thus trading illicitly with İzmir from their bases in Livorno, a free port which allowed the establishment of all merchant groups. These 'Italian' merchants, as the Levant Company called them, exported British, and even French, cloth, to İzmir and from there imported Ottoman silk and mohair yarn for the British market.[2] Such activities certainly damaged the interests of the British merchants in İzmir. For they also strengthened the position of the Ottomans who were established in the Italian port and traded with İzmir. At the same time the Levant Company had what one might call a pragmatic attitude towards Livorno, for it did allow its members to receive goods from Ottoman merchants established there so as not to surrender potential business and consulage fees to its rivals. However, neither these 'Italian' merchants nor the Ottomans trading from Livorno were allowed to make any serious inroads into British trade with İzmir or, as far as the Ottomans were concerned, to acquire any foothold in the British commercial networks, as was the case with the Dutch. Indeed — and this is where a major difference with the Dutch lies — it was only in the very early nineteenth century that the British allowed the Ottomans to start entering their economy and networks as independent merchants,[3] and they even dissolved the

[1]PRO, SP 105/129, Consul Werry, İzmir, 13 August 1804 to Levant Company, London.

[2]Clarence, Matterson, "English Trade in the Levant, 1693-1753", (unpublished Harvard University Ph.D. dissertation, 1936), pp. 196, 295.

[3]PRO, SP/105 129, British merchants, İzmir, 31 January 1804 to Levant Company, London; see also SP 105/126, Consul Werry, İzmir, 17 July 1797 to Levant Company, London.

Levant Company in the process. This, however, was a time when the British economy stood to gain from such liberal policies and was poised to go even further, that is, to call for free trade. In the interim period, namely in the late eighteenth and early nineteenth centuries, the British attempted to cooperate with Ottoman merchants in areas where such cooperation would be most advantageous to them.[1] For instance, when British merchants started using the Ionian Islands and Malta as entrepôts for their trade with İzmir, they cooperated with Greek merchants who were already established there.[2] This was a policy that served well British (and not only Greek) interests, especially during the Napoleonic wars when the Continental System was in force.[3]

Wars, particularly naval conflicts, could be disruptive of all merchant activities, and both the British and the Dutch were vulnerable to their potentially negative effects. In the Seven Years' War, for example, the Levant Company had to relax its protectionist stance and allow the port of Livorno to become an entrepôt for British trade with İzmir even if such a measure risked strengthening the position of Ottoman merchants who were already established in the Italian port. And war could be still more detrimental to British commercial interests in the Levantine port. Such was the case with the naval operations in Europe during the American War of Independence which forced the British to write off the Mediterranean strategically. As a consequence British trade with İzmir fell dramatically and in two separate instances — in 1779 and 1782 — was temporarily wiped out.[4] It is thus ironic that, whilst the Dutch ports were blockaded by the British navy and the Dutch could not send goods to İzmir by sea, British goods were not always reaching that market either.[5] It is equally interesting, and illustrative of the efficacy of the Trieste-based Ottoman Greek networks, that Dutch trade with İzmir, as opposed to the Dutch merchants themselves, did not suffer, any more than did the Dutch and other European manufacturers who continued sending cloth to İzmir. In fact the contrary occurred: taking advantage of British difficulties, the share of Dutch trade in the overall trade of İzmir with Europe actually increased in this period.[6]

---

[1] Elena Frangakis-Syrett, "The Greek Mercantile Community of İzmir in the First Half of the Nineteenth Century", D. Panzac, ed., *Les villes dans l'Empire ottoman: Activités et Sociétés* (Paris, 1991), i, pp. 391-416.

[2] PRO, SP 105/132, Consul Werry, İzmir, 9 July, 27 September 1809 and 4 October 1810 to Levant Company, London.

[3] ANF, AE Biii 242, Consul Fourcade, Mémoire, İzmir, c. 1812.

[4] ANF, AE Bi 1066, for the years 1776-1782.

[5] For the relevant trade figures, see Frangakis-Syrett, *The Commerce of Smyrna*, Appendix C, pp. 274-275.

[6] *Ibid.*, p. 275.

Partly as a result of successful assaults on Dutch commercial interests as shown above, and partly as a result of the prominence of the Dutch financial circuits in the European-Ottoman monetary circuits, in the latter part of the eighteenth century the Dutch merchants in İzmir turned even more than other Europeans to monetary activities as an alternative area of profit and as a way of offsetting potential losses from commodity trading. There are a number of reasons for this, and which are not unique to the Dutch but could also be applied to others, particularly the French. In the eighteenth and early nineteenth centuries the pressure to alleviate specie scarcity which was so prevalent in the Ottoman monetary system had led to a number of monetary activities, some of which could be quite speculative and were practiced by both Ottoman and European merchants. Such activities were particularly prevalent in an active commercial market like that of İzmir. Moreover, they became alternative activities to commodity trading since they could be potentially more lucrative than trading in goods. Even the British, although to a lesser extent than the Dutch, turned to these activities in the late eighteenth century.[1] They reinforced the complementarity of Ottoman and European entrepreneurs active in the Ottoman empire at the time as merchants-*cum*-bankers. Indeed, when we examine the business strategies of the British and the Dutch in eighteenth-century İzmir it is in some respects almost impossible to differentiate between strictly commercial and strictly monetary practices, the last including a certain amount of informal banking operations. Given the monetary constraints that all merchants labored under in the Levant — the Ottomans to a greater extent than the Europeans — both the Dutch and the British in İzmir saw monetary practices as an alternative to purely commercial operations. The two communities lent to, and borrowed from, each other and everyone else in İzmir,[2] even contravening the regulations of their own states against such practices whenever necessary. Both the British and the Dutch also carried out trade in money. That is to say, they imported western currencies to İzmir not only in order to trade with them but also in order to sell them as a commodity on the local market. It was a lucrative trade.[3] The Dutch acted officially. The British participated unofficially early on in the century, risking a penalty, and then did so officially later on. For a number of reasons, at the height of the trade in money in the empire in the late eighteenth century, İzmir became the port of entry for it *par excellence*, attracting even more foreign specie than Istanbul.

---

[1]PRO, SP 105/337, Consul Hayes, İzmir, 15 May 1789.

[2]E.g., ANF, AE Bi 1055, Consul Gilly, İzmir, 28 June 1755 to Minister, Paris.

[3]For more details see Elena Frangakis, "The Balance of the Trade and Balance of Payments between İzmir and France", *Communications grecques presentées au Ve congrès international des études du sud-est européen* (Athens, 1985), pp. 127-138.

Whilst monetary activities were thus undertaken by the merchants alongside their commercial dealings throughout the period under study, speculative monetary activities such as arbitrage in specie or in bills of exchange, or speculating on the difference in value between specie and bills of exchange, became more widespread in İzmir in the second half of the eighteenth and in the early nineteenth centuries.[1] This was because of the dual problems of the Ottoman economy and its monetary system, namely specie scarcity and the weakness of the Ottoman currency in the foreign exchanges, which became particularly acute at that point.

For a number of reasons, including the size of the Ottoman empire and the need to send tax revenue at periodic intervals to the capital from the provinces, bills of exchange had been widely used amongst the Ottoman administrative and commercial elite ever since the seventeenth century. As the trade of the empire with Europe grew in the eighteenth century, to the internal Ottoman networks of bills of exchange were added external western networks linking, for commercial and other purposes, such Ottoman markets as Istanbul and İzmir with the European financial circuits. İzmir served as an important link in these financial networks because of its extensive commercial networks with many markets both within the empire and within Europe. Moreover, in view of the fact that bills of exchange in different currencies circulated widely between İzmir and various European economic centers at all times, opportunities existed for an array of speculative activities.

One such speculative monetary activity practiced by the merchants in İzmir was a form of arbitrage whereby bills of exchange in different currencies were bought and sold in the local market for speculative purposes. Profits were made by successfully manipulating the fluctuations in the prices of such bills. These fluctuations, however, were based on a number of factors, including the relative dearth or abundance of the bills in the market of İzmir, and profits were not always guaranteed. As Amsterdam was a major financial market — indeed, a large number of bills of exchange from İzmir were drawn on Amsterdam, for commercial or speculative purposes — the Dutch were very active in these circuits. In the closing decades of the century, such activities at times even surpassed their commercial dealings.[2] As was the case

[1]For more details on monetary speculative activities in İzmir, see, Frangakis-Syrett, *The Commerce of Smyrna*, pp. 139-154; see also, Edhem Eldem, "La circulation de la lettre de change entre la France et Constantinople au XVIIIe siècle", Hamit Batu & Jean-Paul Bacqué-Grammont, eds., *L'Empire Ottoman, la Republique de Turquie et la France* (Istanbul/ Paris, 1986), pp. 87-96.
[2]ANF, F/12, 549-550, Mémoire sur le commerce du Levant, 1777.

with their commercial networks, the Dutch were not the only ones who were active in their monetary circuits; Ottoman merchants were equally so. A large number of bills of exchange drawn on Europe and purchased by Europeans other than the Dutch in İzmir were underwritten by Ottoman entrepreneurs whose associates were established in centers such as Vienna, Livorno, Trieste and Ancona, as well as in Amsterdam.[1]

Whilst the Dutch were still economically active in İzmir in the early nineteenth century, their activities had been diminished, albeit for different reasons than their French counterparts who were also not doing as well as formerly. By contrast, the British were enlarging their commercial activities and were adopting new strategies such as entering the Ottoman interior, İzmir's hinterland, more systematically and aggressively than ever before. They were certainly not the only ones sending agents to the interior in the first quarter of the nineteenth century; the French, and to a lesser extent the Dutch, were also doing so.[2] Nevertheless the British did so on a large scale, and, in the process, laid the foundations of an extensive commercial presence in the interior that would bear fruit in the following decades.[3] These activities on their part were commensurate with the growing needs of their economy which had just undergone the Industrial Revolution and whose demand for raw materials and new markets was increasing. The commercial success of the British was also being reinforced by the competitiveness of their textile sector and by the greater capital resources at the disposal of their merchants.

In the course of the eighteenth century the economic needs and policies of Britain and the Netherlands shaped to a considerable extent the trading activities, practices, and strategies of their nationals in İzmir, and account for many of the differences that existed between the two merchant groups. Inter-European conflicts affected their commercial fortunes and their activities. At the same time, the practices, and strategies of the British and the Dutch were also influenced by the local conditions: by the Ottoman economy as much as by the conditions in the market of İzmir. İzmir, dominating the empire's trade with Europe and commanding the most extensive commercial networks both

---

[1]E.g., ACCM, LIX/750, Denis Rolland & Cie, İzmir, 18 December 1788, 24 March and 13 July 1789 to Roux Frères, Marseilles.
[2]MAE, CADN, FC/CAE, Vol. 30, Consul Méchain, İzmir, 16 March 1818 to French Ambassador, Istanbul; see also, FC/CAE, Vol. 38, Dupré, İzmir, 3 November, and 16 December 1829 and 19 January 1830 to French Ambassador, Istanbul.
[3]PRO, FO 195/128, Vice-Consul Charnaud, İzmir, 18 May 1839 to British Ambassador, Istanbul; see also, FO 195/128, J.A. Werry, İzmir, 19 September 1839 to Vice-Consul Charnaud, İzmir and FO 195/128, Taya Pasha, Kütahya, 28 October 1839 to Consul Brant, İzmir.

within the empire and with Europe, offered the British and the Dutch many advantages and opportunities in trade and in monetary activities which are reflected in the array of dealings in which the two groups participated. The commercial world of İzmir was also defined by intense competition. Indeed, competition affected all aspects of Dutch and British activity as well as the relations between the two mercantile communities. On the level of the individual merchant and of day-to-day commercial dealings, the two nations also displayed remarkable similarities as they both traded in similar commodities, often with similar means, and frequently faced similar economic or monetary conditions. Thus whilst the market of İzmir largely defined the potential of their fortunes, the policies of their respective states and their national economies went a long way towards defining their fates.

TRADE PRACTICES IN ALEPPO IN THE MIDDLE OF THE EIGHTEENTH CENTURY
The case of a British merchant*

Bridger's business partnerships

Colvill Bridger, the son of Henry Bridger — a merchant in London — was a factor in Aleppo from 1754 to 1765. This was a difficult period, overall, for British trade (B. Masters, 1988: 30-33). When Colvill Bridger arrived in Aleppo the British factory consisted of six other factors, namely, Smith, Edwards, Vernon, Lansdown, Hays, and Free. He initially went out to Aleppo as a factor for the Radcliffe house which was a partnership between Edward and Arthur Radcliffe and Richard Stratton**; the latter took care of most of the Levantine trading on behalf of the Radcliffes, who were also the senior partners.***

It was Richard Stratton who initially made him the offer to go to Aleppo and take over from William Hammond as a factor in the house of Radcliffe & Stratton. At that time, Bridger was himself established in a mercantile house in Lisbon, "whereof he was the head"[1]. As was the custom at the time, Bridger was to share his profits for one year with the departing factor, Hammond. After that, Bridger was to have the benefit of all the business of the Radcliffe & Stratton house to himself for three years. At the end of the three years, the Radcliffes' nephew was to come out to Aleppo and share all the benefits of the factorage with Bridger. Furthermore, Bridger was to make a separate agreement with Hammond to enter into a partnership for four to five years which was finally reduced to three years to coincide with the nephew's arrival in Aleppo. It was to be extended for another year only if the nephew did not come. However, the nephew came early, that is, only after a year and nine months that Bridger had been in Aleppo. Moreover, the Radcliffes wanted their nephew to have a share in the profits of the Bridger-Hammond partnership also.

---

* This is an exploratory article based on the private papers of Colvill Bridger which were made available to me by Mr. James Bridger to whom I would like to express my thanks.

** Richard Stratton was a successful merchant who also became Director of the Bank of England, 1750-1758. (Sir L. Namier & J. Brooke, 1964, vol. III: 493).

*** For more details on the activities and business milieu of Bridger, see Frangakis-Syrett (1998: 126-36, 141-45) and (2002: 183-200).

1 Colvill Bridger, Aleppo, 27 April 1755 to Edward & Arthur Radcliffe, London.

From the arrival of Bridger in Aleppo to the commencement of the partnership with the Radcliffes, Bridger entered into an agreement with Stratton to give the latter a quarter of all profits he made in that interim period.[1] Bridger had also opened a sterling account with Richard Stratton before he left England, who received and paid money for him from time to time, but this was most likely a favor that Stratton did for him.

Although William Hammond was also associated with the house and Bridger considered him as one of his main principals, he also had a separate and partly secret trading partnership with him, initially contracted for three years, to start the second year Bridger was in Aleppo. Bridger paid him £150 annually, plus commission, for Hammond to act as Bridger's factor and buy cloth and other goods on his behalf as well as sell Bridger's Ottoman exports to London. This reversal of the factor/principal relationship was apparently quite common, though in the case of Bridger it had to be kept secret from the Radcliffes or had secret clauses. It was a lively partnership. For instance, Hammond would send cloth to the house of Benjamin & George Barker of Istanbul three quarters for his own account and a quarter for Bridger, leaving it up to Bridger to make up his mind whether it was profitable, each time, to have such a consignment sold on his behalf or not. Similarly, Bridger would ask Hammond for consignments of cloth, indigo or cochineal only if the prices in London would allow him to make a profit.[2] Bridger could be an exacting businessman to deal with. For instance, when Hammond sent some cloth to the Barker house and offered a quarter of the sale to be done on Bridger's account, the latter instructed the Barkers to include him in the sale only if the price were remunerative enough; if the money were to come in within a reasonable amount of time; and only if the Barkers thought that indigo or cochineal would not render him a better account in the Istanbul market or come sooner than cloth.[3]

The Barkers had been partners of the Radcliffes in the 1730s and 1740s and by the 1750s were their bankers and active correspondents. Bridger also used the Barkers as a clearing house as well as had trading connections with them. By 1759, as trade was not doing very well, Bridger offered £100 per annum for the continuance of the partnership, instead of £150, on the basis that he had not been getting the big consignments he thought he would have and the more frequent but smaller consignments were not bringing enough business.

[1]Bridger, Aleppo, 18 Nov. 1759 to Henry Stratton, London.
[2]Bridger, Aleppo, 27 April 1759 to William Hammond, London.
[3]Bridger, Aleppo, 19 May 1759 to Benjamin & George Barker, Istanbul.

Another principal was Charles Fry for whom Bridger traded in the Levant on commission. There were other merchants, for whom Bridger did business on commission, though to a lesser extent, at least whilst the Radcliffes were his main principals — such as John Harding, Kingscote & Walker, Thomas Ph. Vernon, Geoffrey Whatley.[1] Bridger had also trading connections with Muilman & Sons of Amsterdam. In 1755, Bridger took over another factorage when John Free died in Aleppo (R. Davis, 1967: 91).

According to Davis a factor needed 2,200 to 2,400 piastres per annum, half of which was spent on living expenses and the rest for business expenses such as payment of the *scrivan's*, or clerk's, salary. Bridger calculated that he needed 3,000 piastres to live on, so he was probably being overgenerous with his living expenses to his principals or Davis had looked at rather frugal factors. (Davis: 87). Whatever the case might have been, Bridger seemed to have had other expenses such as the purchasing of a *berat* for his scrivan from the British Ambassador in Istanbul. And if the factor were unlucky with his *scrivan*, then his expenses were considerably higher. This appears to have been the case with Bridger whose *scrivan* died in 1759 relatively early to be able to repay Bridger for some of the expense that the British merchant incurred in getting him a *berat* and whose estate was too poor (perhaps because of the Perso-Ottoman Wars which had affected the silk trade considerably) to give Bridger any compensation.[2] The clerk's estate was unfortunately too small to do more than supply the family he had left behind. Like the French merchants' Jewish brokers in İzmir, Bridger's *scrivan* also used the money of his employer to speculate with and left various monthly accounts of the British merchant unpaid, which Bridger had to settle.

Bridger had in his employ also a number of Syrian warehousemen. They had the freedom to trade with the West. There is no mention, in Bridger's correspondence, that he paid their *berat*. He did pay them a wage, however, whilst their brokerage was paid by the silk merchants. Syrian warehousemen whose activities were almost indistinguishable from those of the British factors, in particular, made ample use of the banking facilities of the Radcliffe house, by regularly drawing on the Barkers in Istanbul or asking the latter to pay third parties on their behalf. Sometimes the sums involved were quite considerable. For instance, in 1759 the Barkers were asked to pay 15,000 piastres, "in good money", in exchange for some diamonds they had

[1]Bridger, Aleppo, 12 Oct. 1759 to Hammond, London.

[2]Bridger, Aleppo, 20 April 1759 to James Porter, Esq., British Ambassador, Istanbul; see also, Bridger, Aleppo, 19 May 1759 to B. & G. Barker, Istanbul.

gotten from Syrian warehousemen.[1] The sum well exceeded what Bridger expected to make in commission in a period of two years from his main principals.

Bridger also traded with Jewish merchants bartering cloth for silk. Prompted by his principals to always drive a hard bargain with them, buying their silk at the lowest possible price, he conceded, at times, that he almost drove them away and cautioned his principals that, in the long term, such tactics may not be beneficial to them. He strongly endorsed doing business with them.[2]

The Seven Years' War and trade

What affected all aspects of trade was the Seven Years' War (1756-1763). On the whole war dampened trade, decreased the volume of goods exchanged, and rendered transportation, with increased insurance and other costs, onerous and risky. It also contributed to the recurring monetary shortage in the market of Aleppo. War also made it difficult for Bridger to predict the arrival of his orders. Ships were not only delayed but tended to arrive at an inopportune time, that is, together with other ships due to convoying, thus causing gluts in the market and upsetting the factors' best-laid plans.[3] Cloth orders contracted once the war started. Bridger's former own orders to a single principal for 231 bales of cloth were replaced by smaller orders, and by his desire not to keep cloth surpluses in his warehouse even though he received consignments less frequently. His order to each of his principals in 1759 were more in the region of 100 bales.[4]

The war also greatly strengthened the ties between Aleppo and Livorno as most British goods were sent there from London and then on to the Levant under heavy escort. The same route was used for goods sent to London, using convoys all the way. Neutral ships were also preferred. In 1759, for instance, Bridger asked the Radcliffes to send their goods either on a Dutch, Ragusan or Danish ship for it was rumored, that Swedish and "Imperial" ships (of the Holy Roman Empire) were going to be attacked by privateers sent by the King of Prussia. Further precautions were taken to ensure the safe arrival of

[1]Bridger, Aleppo, 16 May 1759 to B. & G. Barker, Istanbul.
[2]Bridger, Aleppo, 27 April & 19 May 1759 to Hammond, London.
[3]Bridger, Aleppo, 16 Feb. 1759 to Hammond, London.
[4]Bridger, Aleppo, 30 May 1755 to E. & A. Radcliffe, London and Bridger, Aleppo, 8 June 1759 to Hammond, London.

the goods such as consigning and loading the goods in the name of a foreigner, usually a Dutch merchant, and endorsing them to Bridger with bills of lading being sent overland directly to him.[1]

The war could also produce advantageous situations, such as high demand for British cloth whenever French cloth could not reach Aleppo.[2] In fact prospects of peace in early 1759 made Bridger worry that he might not be able to sell all of his cloth. From the lack of success that the Levant Company had in forbidding its members and officers from trading in French cloth however, one can assume that British cloth also had difficulties getting through.[3] An area where the British had a clear advantage over the French, at least until 1759, was in the trade of indigo and cochineal. The difficulties the French were experiencing, and the fact that before the war they had been importing three times more indigo than the British, meant that the French left an important gap in the market which the British could profit by filling. In fact as early as 1755 the mere rumor of war increased demand for these "money goods".[4] There was a double advantage in trading in these goods — besides commission, they could be sold for cash and the factors in Aleppo saw them as a way of having cash remitted to them. Moreover, these goods could be purchased by Bridger either in London or in Livorno through Earle & Hodgson, his correspondents in the Italian port.[5]

Land and sea transportation

Besides war there were other hazards to trade such as the risks involved in transportation, which were accentuated in Aleppo because of its being land-locked and thus relying on a caravan for the transportation of goods from the port of shipment to its marketplace and vice versa. Besides the actual time lost in arranging camel transportation from İskenderun (Alexandretta) to Aleppo, and the additional costs involved, there were unpredictable hazards such as some of the goods being left behind whilst unloading them from the ship and loading them on to camels, or the outright "losses" that sometimes occurred

[1] Bridger, Aleppo, 26 April 1759 to Messrs. Earle & Hogdson, Livorno; see also, Bridger, Aleppo, 30 May 1759 to E. & A. Radcliffe, London.

[2] Bridger, Aleppo, 15 Aug. 1759 to B. & G. Barker, Istanbul; see also, Bridger, Aleppo, 11 Sept. 1759 to Hammond, London.

[3] Bridger, Aleppo, 16 Feb. & 27 April 1759 to Hammond, London.

[4] Bridger, Aleppo, 24 April 1755 to Charles Frye, London.

[5] E.g., Bridger, Aleppo, 21 April 1759 to Robert Pasley, Lisbon; Bridger, 26 April 1759 to Earle & Hodgson, Livorno and Bridger, Aleppo, 19 May 1759 to Hammond, London.

affecting part of the consignments.[1] Sometimes goods were damaged from careless handling during the caravan journey such as depositing a bale of cloth on a wet surface overnight whilst the caravan rested.[2] Unwarrantable delays sometimes developed due to a shortage of camels which could only be overcome by incurring the extraordinary expense of hiring mules. Although the caravan journey between Aleppo and İskenderun was only a few days long it could take more than a month for goods to be transported during hot weather for camels were then not easily available.[3] Yet Aleppo's strategic position being near so many caravan routes leading to Iraq, Persia and eastern Anatolia probably more than compensated its lack of access to the sea (F. Tabak, 1988: 191).

Because the timing of the arrival of the goods in the London or Aleppo markets was very important, Bridger spent a lot of his time organizing the shipping of his goods. His aim, as that of any other factor, was to get his goods out to London as soon as possible. However, if he did not have enough cargo to fill the ship he had chartered, he had to get additional cargo from the other factors, and, if need be, wait for them till they were ready to send their goods out.[4] When loading goods to a ship he had not chartered, he used his connections, for instance, ensuring that he was recommended to the captain "by the captain's friends" so that his goods would be loaded first.[5] When a ship arrived in İskenderun and there were not enough goods for her to load, Bridger might organize a coasting trade giving recommendation letters to the captain, or arranging for him to pick-up goods from a port in the vicinity, to make his coasting trade more worthwhile.[6]

Money lending and credit

Money was scarce in Aleppo, as it was in every other Ottoman economic center except for Istanbul. Bridger himself lent money to local people and others in Aleppo in the customary practice of every European

[1]Bridger, Aleppo, 22 & 26 March 1755 to Messrs. Longy & Edey, İskenderun; see also, Bridger, Aleppo, 3 July 1755 to Francis Browne, İskenderun and, Bridger, Aleppo, 9 Feb. 1759 to Baltazar Longy, İskenderun.

[2]Bridger, Aleppo, 19 June 1755 to Richard Stratton, London.

[3]*Ibid.*, see also, Bridger, Aleppo, 18 March 1759 to B. & G. Barker, Istanbul.

[4]Bridger, Aleppo, 10 March 1755 to R. Stratton, London and Bridger, Aleppo, 30 May 1755 to E. & A. Radcliffe, London.

[5]Bridger, Aleppo, 16 Feb. 1759 to B. Longy, İskenderun.

[6]Other factors also did so. E.g., Public Record Office, London, SP 110/36, Thomas Lansdown, Aleppo, 17 Jan. 1760 to Captain C. Wilson, İskenderun. Thereafter, this archive will be cited as PRO.

merchant, thus capitalizing on the chronic monetary scarcity of the Ottoman economy but also taking risks, which in 1759 made him into "a very great loser." For credit became so bad once the war started that everybody who had made loans "have been endeavoring to get them in." Bridger incurred a considerable loss of over £1,000 due to the bankruptcy of a certain Bowmesteer to whom he had lent money. In fact, the Radcliffes prevailed on Bridger's father to make up the loss to his son, as a first installment of which the father paid £245 worth of cochineal to the Radcliffes which they sent to Bridger. It was this loss, combined with his clerk's death and the slackness of trade due to wars, famine and natural calamities, that made Bridger resolve to stay in Aleppo longer to recoup his losses (A. Marcus, 1989: 123-124). In fact he calculated that the Bowmesteer debt alone was to take him one or two years to recover from.[1]

Notwithstanding the fact that Bridger took every opportunity to employ his capital on usurious loans, he also frequently ran out of money especially at times of acute monetary shortage in Aleppo. Unlike the other Europeans, the British merchants were not allowed by the Levant Company to export money to the Levant which further aggravated the situation. At such a time Bridger borrowed even from members of his own family. His brother, Richard, upon inheriting the estate of their uncle (whose wrath he did not incur as did Bridger by going to Aleppo), decided to lend Colvill £1,500 at 5 percent interest rate for the first eight months increasing it thereafter to $7^{1/2}$ percent. A vexed Bridger asked his father:

> "Why should he insist on a higher interest from me than what he can have of others unless he looks upon the risque to be greater, if so I beg you would acquaint him that my note in this country will pass amongst all kind of people, as currently as those of the Bank of England will do with you, and perhaps more so."[2]

Predictably, he decided to pay off the loan as soon as his silk was sold unless his brother lowered the interest rate to 4 percent which was what one could get from credit-worthy borrowers in England.

At other times, however, he faced difficulties in getting money for his bills of exchange drawn on Istanbul. It was not only Bridger who suffered hardship. At such instances, other British merchants offered discount of 3

[1] Bridger, Aleppo, 21 April 1759 to Pasley, Lisbon; see also, Bridger, Aleppo, 30 May 1759 to E. & A. Radcliffe, London.

[2] Bridger Aleppo, 21 Dec. 1759 to Harry Bridger, Sussex.

percent on their bills in order to have them accepted, whilst local merchants were discounting theirs by 5 percent.[1] Other circumstances that could lead to Bridger running out of cash was a depletion of his cloth supplies in his warehouse, which was possible during the Seven Years' War when long or unpredictable delays occurred in shipping. This forced him to use his "money goods" in barter agreements presumably against purchases of silk, foregoing thus the cash that he would have otherwise gotten. It was not uncommon for Bridger to become so short of cash that he could not pay the various expenses he incurred from transporting, cleaning and preparing goods for export.[2] Sometimes the only solution was to borrow money. In July 1755, after calculating that he will not be able to "turn into cash" his barter sales for fifteen months or so, he decided to borrow at 12 percent interest to meet his expenses.[3]

Istanbul, the banking capital of the Empire, was almost exclusively the place where Bridger had his bills of exchange, drawn on him, paid out on his behalf; he also had bills he drew on others cashed for him and credited to his account by the house of B. & G. Barker. The Barkers were also the principal means for Bridger's London associates to send him money. For his part Bridger usually drew money from the Barkers to buy goods for his principals which he could not barter for.[4]

One of the important ways in which monetary shortage was alleviated by the merchants in Aleppo was by carrying out their most important trading activities, to a large extent, through barter. The most important barter transaction, and around which most trade was centered, was the exchange of cloth for silk. After more than a month of being at the point of almost closing the sale, which probably came after weeks of haggling and weighing the price levels and the mood of the silk sellers, Bridger would finally conclude his barter deal. He was then able, for example, to report to Frye that he had sold his principal's cloth and tin against silk, and to Harding that he had sold the latter's cloth, tin and pepper against silk.[5] However, competition from French cloth coupled with the specific quality of British cloth that was

---

[1]Bridger, Aleppo, 15 Aug. 1759 to B. & G. Barker, Istanbul.

[2]Bridger, Aleppo, 30 May 1755 to E. & A. Radcliffe, London and Bridger, Aleppo, 30 May 1755 to R. Stratton, London.

[3]Bridger, Aleppo, July 1755 to John Harding, London.

[4]Bridger, Aleppo, 30 May 1759 to B. & G. Barker, Istanbul; see also, Bridger, Aleppo, 30 May 1759 to Joseph Chitty, İzmir and Bridger, 11 Sept. 1759 to Hammond, London.

[5]Bridger, Aleppo, 30 May 1755 to Frye, London; see also, Bridger, Aleppo, 30 May 1755 to John Harding, London.

sometimes available, which might not be of the best, made barter difficult. In such cases, cloth had to be bartered for less sought after goods than silk.[1]

The Levant Company's official policy was against giving credit because of the risks involved. Nevertheless, we know from the British Consul in Aleppo, Wilkinson, how British merchants used every possible way to get around the regulation, such as selling cloth for a bag of money which the merchant never opened but handed back being given a note for it. The money was to be paid when the next caravan arrived.[2] Although no one doubts that merchants all over the Levant did not follow the company's regulations on "trusting"[3] any more than they did other "restrictive" regulations, such as not importing specie, nevertheless it is interesting to note how very widespread credit was. How, for instance, the Radcliffes, a large and one would guess rather conservative house, would instruct Bridger "to sell for time" — that is, to sell for money giving credit for a number of months and usually up to a year. At the same time, Bridger took upon himself to guarantee the credit-worthiness of the merchants he concluded such deals with.[4] Despite the agreed-upon twelve to fifteen months credit period with 4 percent discount it was possible for the local merchants to pay their debt off with silk before their time was up with the arrival of the next caravan or the new *recolta*.[5] In fact, Davis mentions the opposite as happening, too: that is, British merchants bought silk on credit with the understanding that they would exchange it for cloth when their next ship arrived (Davis: 185-186). This practice was current in İzmir, too, particularly among the French merchants.[6]

The most common combination, in order to conclude a sale, was a mixture of barter and cash or, to be more precise, of barter and credit. In early 1759, whilst British cloth was not doing well in Aleppo, Bridger bought silk at 18 piastres per *rotillo* (a higher price that what he had bought it for in 1755) with two-thirds of the price being paid in cash, at twelve months credit, and one-third of the price being bartered against cloth. Another way to realize a barter deal, whenever British cloth was not particularly popular, was to mix cloth with "money goods", thus making the deal more attractive to the silk merchant. Whenever Bridger held in his warehouse types of cloth which were

[1]Bridger, Allepo, 16 Feb. 1759 to Hammond, London.

[2]PRO, SP 105/116, Levant Company, London, 22 June 1715 to Consul Wilkinson, Aleppo.

[3]E.g., PRO, SP 105/116, Levant Company, London, 2 July 1717 to Consul Cooke, İzmir.

[4]Bridger, Aleppo, 11 Sept. 1759 to Hammond, London; see also, Bridger, Aleppo, 10 March 1755 to Harding, London and Bridger, Aleppo, 24 April 1755 to Frye, London.

[5]By *recolta* here it is meant the annual collection of the silk cocoons (Davis: 76).

[6]Archives Nationales de France, Paris, AE Bi 1052, Consul Peyssonnel, İzmir, 29 Jan. 1749 to Minister, Paris.

particularly popular then a sale for cash or credit could be realized where part of the money could be given after three or six months, and the rest after twelve months, or other variations thereof.[1] In fact, sometimes there was strong demand for cloth in Aleppo with the greatest impediment to its sale being "the badness of credit".[2] What could also delay a sale were the price limits that the factor had from his principal. If these were particularly stringent, the factor would probably sell his other principals' consignments first and leave last those goods, for which he had to drive a harder bargain, or simply wait for market opportunities to improve. It was a particular triumph for Bridger when he could sell well under his principals' limits.[3]

Cloth

The merchant's ability to sell cloth in the market of Aleppo also depended to a very large degree on what type of cloth and of what quality, color and pattern he could dispose of and whether that particular type was popular at the time. In fact sometimes quality could be sacrificed and a bale or piece of cloth be sold if the colors and list were right; that is, if they were vivid, discernible colors and the list were fine.[4] Therefore, a lot of care was taken to state exactly what type of cloth was needed when ordering shipments from London and emphasis was placed on having the order executed correctly. If the colors ordered were too fancy or the pattern too complex, samples were sent to ensure compliance. To make sure that the cloth that Bridger got, given the competition he was facing would sell, he even sent to London, along with the order, assortments as given to him by the local merchant and would-be purchaser. And if the buyer were a particularly important merchant and "friend to the house", then he was not to be "disobliged".[5]

Whereas color and the general appearance of the cloth determined the ease with which it was sold, its quality affected the price. Levantine customers were, on the whole, exacting customers. Poor quality not only as far as the texture of the fabric was concerned but also the way it was cut and whether it fulfilled the required measurements or not, greatly affected the price. Moreover

---

[1]Bridger, Aleppo, 16 Feb. 1759 to Hammond, London ; see also, Bridger, Aleppo, 15 Aug. 1759 to B. & G. Barker, Istanbul.

[2]Bridger, Aleppo, 12 July 1759 to Hammond, London.

[3]Bridger, Aleppo, 30 May 1755 to E. & A. Radcliffe, London.

[4]The strip that bordered the cloth was called list and was usually made of a different material than the rest of the fabric. Bridger, Aleppo, 30 May 1755 to George Whatley, London ; see also, Bridger, Aleppo, 19 Feb., 10 March & 19 June 1755 to R. Stratton, London.

[5]Bridger, Aleppo, 8 July 1755 to E. & A. Radcliffe, London.

a cloth consignment had to be as good as the quality of the sample cloth that had been shown ahead to the purchaser for else the factor himself who might have priced it higher, initially, would lower the price and complain to his principal. Often cloth was also priced according to the reputation a London merchant house had acquired over the years. The same held in İzmir for French cloth manufacturers. The Radcliffes had the reputation of sending the best cloth that reached the market of Aleppo, so that cloth shipments of other London merchants were often compared against the Radcliffes' cloth for quality.[1]

Price mechanisms

Many events affected the price of goods, causing them to fluctuate. News of a new silk *recolta* about to reach the market usually lowered the price of silk as well as forced wavering sales through. Conversely the arrival of a ship, or accidental arrival of more than one ship, could force silk prices up for factors were then more likely to want to catch the opportunity to send silk to London and hence more eager to purchase. According to how much cloth a ship brought from Europe, cloth prices could also fall. The news of the arrival of a caravan affected prices of all the goods the caravan had to buy or sell. The Perso-Ottoman Wars, in their turn, affected not only silk prices and supplies but also cloth prices, for the non-arrival of Persian caravans also brought a drop in demand for cloth.[2]

During the Seven Years' War, the news of the arrival of a ship in Livorno from England, could affect prices in a Levantine market for it signaled the near certain arrival of goods, as ships from the Italian port to the Levant were rarely captured. Conversely, the news or rumors that a French ship loaded with indigo had been captured by the British could lead to the increase in the price of indigo.[3]

There was no end to the tricks factors resorted to in order to turn a situation to their advantage as, for instance, ordering a ship "to hide" in Cyprus instead of waiting in İskenderun so as to give the impression to the

[1]Bridger, Aleppo, 30 May 1755 to R. Stratton, London; see also, Bridger, Aleppo, 31 Jan. 1755 to Harding, London.
[2]Bridger, Aleppo, 5 April 1755 to Stratton, London; see also, Bridger, Aleppo, 16 Feb. 1759 to Hammond, London.
[3]Bridger, Aleppo, 27 July 1759 to Hammond, London; see also, Bridger, Aleppo, 30 June 1759 to B. & G. Barker, Istanbul.

local merchants that the factors were in no hurry to buy.[1] At another instance, when the prices at which local merchants were buying silk from the place of production were too high despite the fact that the *recolta* was good and hence abundant, which would have driven the price of silk in the market of Aleppo even higher, Bridger took several bales of silk, that he had prepared to send to England, and sold them instead in the bazaar declaring that whilst he could get such high prices in Aleppo, he would not send any silk to England. Apparently, Bridger's plan succeeded for he drove prices drown in two markets of the environs.[2]

Sometimes deliberate or incidental circumstances could affect prices such as the *paşa* of Tripoli fixing a minimum price for silk, or the "planters" at Antioch buying off one another in order to keep up the nominal price of silk. Particularly large purchases by a European community, an Ottoman dignitary or local artisans also drove prices up. Another source of competition was the East India Company whose cloth shipments reached Basra by sea and were distributed to Baghdad, Mosoul, Diarbekir and Damascus which, if in large enough quantities, could affect cloth prices in Aleppo.[3] Finally, it sufficed for one merchant only to start buying to affect prices, so volatile and competitive could be the market.[4]

Bridger's profits

Factors' profits were usually 8 percent with 3 percent made on sales of cloth, and other goods coming from Europe, and 5 percent on silk and other Ottoman purchases averaging on the whole 7,000 piastres per annum (Davis: 91-92). It would appear that Bridger was getting rather less, for in the first half of the Seven Years' War he was making an income of 10,000 piastres on a single large biannual consignment. Such consignments usually did not exceed 100,000 piastres. One such consignment represented around 200 bales of cloth and some other merchandise. Allowing for an exaggerated account of his own expenses (he calculated them at 3,000 piastres per annum) he still had to share these profits with the Radcliffes' nephew. This situation could not have gone on for very long and Bridger must have wished either for bigger consignments,

[1]Bridger, Aleppo, 22 April 1755 to Harding, London.
[2]Bridger, Aleppo, 27 July & 11 Sept. 1759 to Hammond, London; see also, Bridger, Aleppo, 15 Aug. 1759 to B. & G. Barker, Istanbul.
[3]Bridger, Aleppo, 12 July & 19 May 1759 to Hammond, London; see also, Bridger, Aleppo, 18 March 1759 to B. & G. Barker, Istanbul.
[4]Bridger, Aleppo, 22 April 1755 to E. & A. Radcliffe, London.

and hence more profits, or for a break-up of the partnership and the departure of his partner from Aleppo. It is not likely that he would have voiced his such concerns, but would have tried instead through other means to raise his income, had not Richard Stratton's death in 1759 made it even more unlikely for the Radcliffes to increase their consignments to Aleppo for he was the firm's driving force. It was then that their nephew's departure and break-up of the partnership started to appear increasingly attractive to Bridger. Especially as he hoped to maintain his trading partnership with William Hammond, who was considered one of the most important British merchants trading with Aleppo at the time as well as with his other principals such as John Harding, Charles Frye and others not only in London but elsewhere in Europe and the Levant.

Thus, contrary to Davis, who gives the impression that Bridger did not want his partnership to break up he, in fact, did (Davis: 92). He saw factorage without a partner in Aleppo for two to three years more as the only way for him to make good some of the losses he had incurred by 1759, given the strong possibility that trade would pick up at the end of the war which he thought was imminent. His only concern, when the Radcliffes did eventually break up the partnership in November 1759, was that it would take effect:

> "As soon as we [Bridger and Radcliffe] have made returns for the Effects in our hands belonging to our different Principals ... [ensuring] that what goods may arrive or commissions given from hence forward to be for my sole Account or Benefit ...".[1]

From the family papers it would appear that Bridger, who stayed much longer than he had initially anticipated, traded successfully and was able to retire thereafter in England to a very comfortable life in the country where he built an elegant family mansion.

Conclusion

Colvill Bridger was an extremely dedicated businessman who lived and breathed trade, drove hard bargains with everybody, despite the courteous way with which he did it, and pursued relentlessly every possible avenue of profit. His detailed correspondence to his various principals, associates, partners, correspondents and others with whom he had a business interest gives us an insight into the most minute workings of a British merchant's trading,

[1]Bridger, Aleppo, 21 Nov. 1759 to E. & A. Radcliffe, London; see also, Bridger, Aleppo, 21 Dec. 1759 to Harry Bridger, Sussex.

merchant banking and other monetary activities in Aleppo in the middle of the eighteenth century and his network of activities and contacts. Moreover, Bridger's case was not unique but fairly representative of a European merchant's economic activities in the Levant at the time.

Merchants' private papers are also important because they are relatively scarce, as a source, compared to the voluminous correspondence on the subject by the various European consuls and other administrators. They are also important because they give a first-hand account as opposed to the administrators' often second-hand or overall accounts for the latter were, usually, more interested in the general picture than in the individual case and may have had political or legal considerations not shared by the merchants.

BIBLIOGRAPHY

Boogert, van den (M.), 2000, "European Patronage in the Ottoman Empire: Anglo-Dutch Conflicts of Interest in Aleppo (1703-1755)", Hamilton, A., de Groot, A. & van den Boogert, M., eds., *Friends and Rivals in the East,* Brill, Leiden.

Boogert, van den (M.), 2001, "Ottoman Dragomans and European Consuls: The Protection System in Eighteenth-Century Aleppo", unpublished Ph.D. dissertation, Leiden University.

Davis (R.), 1967, *Aleppo and Devonshire Square,* Macmillan, London.

Frangakis-Syrett (E.), 1998, "Commerce in the Eastern Mediterranean from the Eighteenth to the Early Twentieth Centuries: The City-Port of İzmir and its Hinterland", *International Journal of Maritime History* (X)/2: 125-154.

Frangakis-Syrett (E.), 2002, "'Networks of Friendship, Networks of Kinship: Eighteenth-Century Levant Merchants", *Eurasian Studies* (I)/2: 183-205.

Marcus (A.), 1989, *The Middle East on the Eve of Modernity,* Columbia University Press, New York.

Masters (B.), 1988, *The Origins of Western Economic Dominance in the Middle East,* New York University Press, New York.

Masters (B.) 1999, "Aleppo: The Ottoman Empire's caravan city", Eldem, E., Goffman, D. & Masters, B., *The Ottoman City between East and West,* Cambridge University Press, Cambridge.

Namier (Sir L.) & Brooke (J.), 1964, *History of Parliament,* vol. III, HMSO, London.

Tabak (F.), 1988, "Local Merchants in Peripheral Areas of the Empire: The Fertile Crescent during the Long Nineteenth Century", *Review* (XI)/2:179-214.

THE ARMENIAN, GREEK AND JEWISH COMMUNITIES OF SMYRNA IN THE 18th CENTURY (1690-1820)
Demography and economic activities*

Smyrna was one of the most important cities in terms of population and economic activity in the Ottoman Empire in the eighteenth century. It numbered 100,000 people. Its growth reflected the emergence of large urban centers that occurred in the Empire at the time.[1] Its population would have grown even more had it not been for a series of environmental hazards that plagued the city at recurring intervals throughout the 18th century.[2]

In common with other large Ottoman cities, Smyrna was visited almost annually by the plague. It came by sea through the ports of Istanbul and Alexandria or by land through the caravan route from the East.[3] Epidemics caused by malignant fevers, due to poor sanitary conditions, were a frequent aftermath to plague and caused even greater devastations to the population than the plague at certain years. To these calamities were added earthquakes due to the bedding of volcanic rock of the city and fires which occurred often due to the system of wooden houses which was adopted because of the earthquakes.[4] Fires were often the result of an earthquake.[5] The most devastating earthquakes occurred in the second half of the 17th century and in the first half of the 18th century. Plague attacks were heavier in the second half of the 18th century and in the early 19th century.

---

*A number of editorial changes have been made by the author from the original publication in 1985. In the title of the article the term [*raya*], used to denote non-Muslim subjects of the Ottoman Empire, has been changed to [Armenian, Greek, and Jewish], deemed to be more appropriate.

[1] L. Erder, The Making of Industrial Bursa: Economic Activity and Population in a Turkish City, 1835-1975, PhD, Princeton University, 1976, p. 41.

[2] See PhD thesis of present author, The Commerce of İzmir in the Eighteenth Century, 1695-1820, London University, 1985, pp. 52-83; see also, *idem, The Commerce of Smyrna in the Eighteenth Century 1700-1820,* Athens, 1992, pp. 43-65.

[3] Ferrières-Sauveboeuf, Comte de, *Mémoires historiques et géographiques des voyages du Comte de Ferrières-Sauveboeuf faits en Turquie, Perse et en Arabie depuis 1782 jusqu'en 1789,* Paris, 1790, p. 136.

[4] P. Lucas, *Voyages du Sieur Lucas fait par ordre de Louis XIV dans la Turquie en Europe, l'Asie Mineure, la Syrie et l'Égypte*, Paris, 1742, p. 210.

[5] Public Record Office, SP/105/126, Consul Werry, Smyrna, 31 Jan 1797 to Levant Co, London. Hereafter these archives will be cited as PRO.

It has been calculated that between 1739 and 1741-2, the city lost twenty per cent of its population due to a combination of calamities: recurring and prolonged outbreaks of plague which took place throughout these years, an earthquake in 1739 and a fire in 1742.[1] Between 1758 and 1763, heavy attacks of plague together with an earthquake in 1763 in the Frankish quarter (that is, the European merchants' quarter) depopulated the city by twenty-five per cent.[2] Attacks of plague in 1735, 1765, 1769, 1771, 1784 and 1788 are calculated to have caused an overall loss to the city's population of five to fifteen per cent.[3]

The following table on the population of Smyrna, which dates from the middle of the 17th until the early 19th century, has been compiled from accounts of travelers. Unfortunately, these do not cover periods when most calamities occurred. It should also be stressed that these figures are not very reliable and should be treated with caution. Unfortunately, no other sources exist. Settlements such as Buca, Bornova and Sevdiköy, around Smyrna, which grew to sizeable market centers by the end of the 19th century, were in the 18th century only small villages.

Another demographic feature of 18th-century Smyrna was the numerical superiority of the Turks over the Greeks. This may in part have been reversed in the 19th century. An increase in the Greek population began in the final decades of the 18th and continued into the 19th century, as immigrants from Morea to a large extent, but from elsewhere too, came to settle in the fertile plains around the city.

All major non-Muslim[4] communities of the Empire were represented in Smyrna besides a sizeable European community. In fact Smyrna was the most cosmopolitan city in the Levant in the 18th century, known for its 'Frankishness' at a period when Europeans were not very prominent in the Empire. In the 19th century, the city was to be known as *gavur* İzmir, infidel Smyrna, due to the economic prominence of the Christians.

---

[1]M. A. Katsaitis, *Δύο ταξείδια στη Σμύρνη, 1740 καὶ 1742*, (*Two Voyages to Smyrna, 1740 and 1742*), ed F. Falbos, Athens, 1972, p. 173.

[2]PRO/SP/105/119, Levant Co, London, 16 Dec 1763 to Consul A. Hayes, Smyrna.

[3]D. Panzac, «La peste à Smyrne au XVIIIe siècle», *Annales*, 28, 1973, pp. 1071-1093; p. 1085.

[4]The term [*raya*], used in the original publication of the article, in 1985, to denote non-Muslim subjects of the Ottoman Empire, has been changed to [non-Muslim Ottoman/local] in the text.

THE POPULATION OF SMYRNA (1653-1837[1a-y])

Date	Total	Turks	Greeks	Armenians	Jewish	Europeans
1653	90,000[a]	60,000	15,000	7,000	7/8,000	–
1657	90,000[b]	60,000	15,000	8,000	6/7,000	–
1675	55,000[c]	30,000	10,000	–	–	–
1676	45,000[d]	–	–	–	–	–
1678	80,000[e]	–	–	–	–	–
1693	50,000[f]	–	–	–	–	–
1699	24,000[g]	14,000	8,000	400	1,500	200
1701	27,000[h]	15,000	10,000	200	1,800	200
1714	100,000[i]	60,000	20,000	8,000	–	–
1723	300,000[j]	–	–	–	–	–
1725	62,500[k]	50,000	8,000	–	4,500	–
1731	76,000[l]	50,000	8,000	–	4,500	–
1733	28,000[m]	15,000	10,000	600	2,000	–
1739	100,000[n]	80,000	10,000	2,000	6,000	–
1768	120,000[o]	–	–	–	–	–
1776	102,000[p]	65,000	21,000	6,000	10,000	200
1778	150,000[q]	97,000	30,000	8,000	12,000	2,000
1784	120,000[r]	–	–	–	–	–
1786	150,000[s]	–	–	–	–	–
1794	100,000[t]	–	–	–	–	–
1800	100,000[u]	–	–	–	–	–

[1]a) L. d'Arvieux, Ch. de, *Mémoires du Chevalier d'Arvieux, 1653-1657*, Paris, 1735, p. 43.
b) J. B. Tavernier, *Les six voyages de J.-B. Tavernier en Turquie, Perse et aux Indes*, Paris, 1712, 6 vols; vol. 1, p. 104.
c) J. Spon, *Voyage d'Italie, de Dalmatie, de Grèce et du Levant fait aux années 1675 et 1676*, Amsterdam, 1679, 2 vols; vol. 1, p. 230.
d) G. Wheeler, *Voyages de Dalmatie, de Grèce et du Levant*, Amsterdam, 1723, 2 vols; vol. 1, p. 227.
e) C. Le Bruyn, *Les voyages du Corneille le Bruyn au Levant*, Le Haye, 1732, p. 83.
f) G. Careri in T. Baykara, *İzmir şehri ve tarihi*, İzmir, 1974, p. 56.
g) Motraye in *İzmir Şehri* …, p. 56.
h) P. de Tournefort, *Rélation d'un voyage du Levant*, Paris, 1717, 2 vols; vol. 2, p. 495.
i) P. Lucas, *Voyage du Sieur Paul Lucas fait dans la Turquie* …, Rouen, 1742, p. 212.
j) Ch. St Maure in *İzmir Şehri* …, p. 56.
k) Miranda in *İzmir Şehri* …, p. 56.
l) M. Tollot, *Nouveau voyage fait au Levant aux années 1731 et 1732*, Paris, 1742, p. 267.
m) C. Thompson, *The Travels of the late Charles Thompson*, Reading, 1744, 3 vols; vol. 3, p. 289.
n) R. Pococke, *Voyages de Richard Pococke*, Paris 1772, p. 17.
o) J. H. Baron de Riedesel, *Voyages en Sicile, dans la grande Grèce et le Levant*, Paris, 1802, p. 233.
p) M.G.F.A. Choiseul-Gouffier, Comte de, *Voyage pittoresque dans l'Empire ottoman*, Paris, 1842, p. 346.
q) D. Sestini, *Lettres à ses amis en Toscane pendant le cours de ses voyages en Italie, Sicile et Turquie*, Paris, 1789, p. 3.
r) M. d'Ohsson, in *İzmir Şehri* …, p. 56.
s) L. F. Ferrières-Sauveboeuf, Comte de, *Mémoires … des voyages … faits en Turquie…*, 2 vols.; Paris, 1790, vol. 2, p. 233.
t) J. Dallaway, in *İzmir Şehri* …, p. 57.
u) G. Olivier, in *İzmir Şehri* …, p. 57.
v) M. J. Tancoigne, *Voyages à Smirne en 1811-14*, Paris, 1817, p. 26.
w) C. Iconomos (tr B. Slaars), *Études sur Smyrne*, İzmir, 1868, p. 138.
x) C. Texier in *Études* …, p. 139.
y) *Journal de Smyrne*, in *Études…*, p. 139.

Date	Total	Turks	Greeks	Armenians	Jewish	Europeans
1812	106,000[v]	60,000	25,000	10,000	5,000	6,000
1817	150,000[w]	—	60,000	—	—	—
1836	150,000[x]	75,000	40,000	10,000	15,000	10,000
1837	130,000[y]	45,000	55,000	5,000	13,000	12,000

The major European nations in Smyrna in the 18th century were the French, British and Dutch. A number of other European nations were also present in smaller numbers — Italians, Danes, Swedes, etc. who were active mainly in the carrying trade. What brought the Europeans to Smyrna were the opportunities offered to trade. Conveniently situated for the Aegean Archipelago, Smyrna was the outlet for a vast hinterland that stretched beyond Eastern Anatolia into Iran. In the 18th century, it had developed into the principal entrepot linking commercially the Ottoman Empire with the West.[1] By the early 19th century, Smyrna had the biggest network of trade inside the Ottoman Empire, too.

The city was divided into separate quarters where each community lived. The Europeans lived in the Frank Street which was 15 feet wide and extended nearly half the length of the city. It was situated next to the market place and hans, in the economic center of the city.[2] The Greek and Armenian quarters were next to the European one, near the center of the city. The Turkish quarter was on the upper part of the city, around the citadel, away from the bazaars. The Jewish quarter was situated next to the Turkish one. The Jewish cemetery, just outside the city, was considered an important landmark at the time and testified to the standing of the Jewish community.

Each community had its own religious establishments due to a policy of toleration on the part of the State. The Turks had 19 mosques. The Greeks had 2 large churches. The revenue of its Bishop was among the largest of the Orthodox clergy in the Empire.[3] The Armenians had one church and the Jews

---

[1]See article of present author, «The Ottoman city-port of İzmir in the 18th century, 1695-1820», *Revue de l'Occident Musulman et de la Méditerranée*, Vol. 39/1 (1985), pp. 149-162. See also, Frangakis-Syrett, "18. Yüzyıldan 20. Yüzyılın Başlarına Kadar İzmir Ekonomisine Bir Bakış", *21. Yüzyıl Eşiğinde İzmir Uluslararası Sempozyum*, İzmir, 2001, pp. 71-81. On the social aspects of the non-Muslim communities of the city-port in the eighteenth century, see e.g., Onnik Jamgocyan, "Une famille de financiers arméniens au XVIIIe siècle: les Serpos", Daniel Panzac, ed., *Les villes dans l'Empire ottoman: Activités et sociétés*, Paris, 1991, Vol. I, pp. 365-390; Marie-Carmen Smyrnelis, "Une société hors de soi. Identités et relations sociales à Smyrne aux XVIIIe et XIXe siècles" (unpublished thèse de doctorat, École des Hautes Études et Sciences Sociales, Paris, 2000); Roxane Argyropoulos, "La communauté grecque de Smyrne au temps des lumières", *Études balkaniques*, 2002, pp. 110-15.

[2]E. Flandin, *L'Orient*, Paris, 1852, p. 45.

[3]F. Hasselquist, *Voyages and Travels in the Levant*, London, 1766, p. 21.

8 synagogues. Two of the synagogues were burnt down in the fire of 1742, which had started in the Jewish quarter, and again in 1772.[1] The Europeans had three convents. Although the Europeans had an active social life in Smyrna, there was not a lot of interaction between them and the local communities.[2] The Ottoman Greeks were those with the greatest amount of interaction, on the social level, with the western Europeans. The case of a European marrying a Greek woman was rather rare and actively discouraged by the nation states in Europe. Nevertheless, there was a great deal of interaction on the economic level between Muslims and non-Muslims, Ottomans and Europeans.

According to one source, Jews first came to Smyrna from Spain and Portugal in the early 17th century. More Jews came later from Ankara, Crete, Corfu and Yanina. According to another source, Portuguese Jews came to Smyrna much later, at about the middle of the 17th century.

> «Les juifs Portugais et Italiens ne sont pas établis au Levant que depuis 40 ans. Ils ne sont sous la protection des Consuls de France à Smyrne que depuis 10 à 12 ans, que le Sieur Fabre, Consul, leur accorda sa protection moyennant une partition de 100 à 150 piastres par famille».[3]

They kept their Portuguese identity and status till the early 18th century, after which date they appear as Ottoman subjects. According to European sources, the Jewish community was active economically throughout the 18th century, at times constituting a threat to European commercial interests.

It is thought that the Armenians first came to Smyrna from Djulfa, Tiflis, Tocat, Ankara, Erivan, Kayseri and Erzerum in the early 17th century. According to a 19th century Armenian source, claims were made for an Armenian presence in Smyrna from as early as 1380. These claims are based on the existence of tombstones in St Stephen's church, the principal Armenian church in the city, dating from the late 14th century. They were settled in the *Apano-mahalla*; they left after 1500 for their subsequent quarters, next to the Greeks.[4] An important Armenian community existed in

---

[1] M.-A. Katsaitis, *Δύο ταξείδια*..., p. 173.

[2] There were always exceptions to the rule as was the case with the French Consuls Peyssonnel, father and son, and their interactions with the Turkish landowning family of Karaosmanoğlu.

[3] Archives Nationales de France, AE Biii 235, Commerce du Levant: Mémoire sur les Juifs, 1693. Hereafter this archive will be cited as ANF, see also, *The Jewish Encyclopaedia*, 1905, p. 414.

[4] Y. K'osean, *Hayk'i Zmi'wrnia ew i Srjakays*, (*The Armenians in Smyrna and its environs*), Vienna, 1899, pp. 85-98.

Manisa, a town near Smyrna that had economic ties with the city, from 1636, as found from tomb inscriptions in its church.[1]

*

As trade was the most important sector in the city's economy, all three communities were involved in trade, although each was in a different sphere. Armenians held in their hands the city's trade with the East. They had the near-monopoly in the provisioning of the city's market with goods from Iran, particularly silk, and had a considerable share in the trade with Erzerum, Tokat, Sivas, Diyarbakir, Kayseri, Antalya and Ankara. They were also the main carriers of goods between Smyrna and the East and in control of the caravan trade. Jews were involved in the trade of Smyrna with Bursa whilst the Turks were the main rivals of the Armenians in the city's inland trade with the rest of the Ottoman Empire and owned the largest number of camels in this trade. The Turks were also prominent in the Ankara mohair yarn and Bursa silk trades.

For a long time the Armenians supplied the East with European cloth brought thither from Smyrna. To the Western Anatolian city they brought precious raw materials such as silk and goat wool. By the early 19th century, however, the British were supplying the Iranian market with cloth from Basra thus diminishing the number of caravans coming to Smyrna.[2] Armenians were also the agents and secretaries of Turkish landowners, both in the city and in the countryside, around the city, as was the case with wheat-producer and large landowner Araboğlu.[3] They were their bankers and *hommes d'affaires*. Other Armenians were shopkeepers in silk stuffs and cloth but their number was small. Greeks controlled the upper end of the market in this sector.

The Jews were the brokers and money-lenders *par excellence* of Smyrna. Almost all trade passed through their hands. They were the ones who came in contact with the European merchants. «Les Juifs sont les agents et les ouvriers de tout le commerce de Smyrne. Il n'est pas un négociant turc, grec ou européen qui n'ait un Juif à son service ou exclusivement attaché à sa *maison*».[4] They also held in their hands the retail trade of imported coffee,

---

[1] *ibid*, pp. 131-140.
[2] ANF, AE Biii 242, Mémoire sur le commerce de Smyrne, Fourcade, Smyrna, 1820.
[3] ANF, AE Bi 1054, Araboğlu, Ismail Ağa, Governor of Bergama to Consul Peyssonnel, Smyrna, 9 May 1754.
[4] ANF, AE Biii 242, Mémoire ..., 1820.

indigo and pepper. They collected silk from Bursa, cotton from Manisa, chevron wool, wax and galls which they cleaned and prepared for export.[1]

Men rich enough to tax-farm the customs in Smyrna were from the Jewish and Turkish communities. The most powerful customs official in the 18th century was a Jew called Isaac Ağa. He farmed simultaneously the customs of Smyrna and Istanbul.[2] Among the brokers, the Sidi family were among the most active at the end of the 18th century with Daniel, Abraham and Leon Sidi being the most prominent. The last was broker to the powerful Dutch commercial house of Richard van Lennep. There was also Jacob Sidi who was a hare skin merchant.[3] As monetary problems continued to plague the Ottoman economy (shortage of specie, recurrent depreciation) and whilst banking was still informal, usury was rife in answering the needs of trade for money. It was practiced by all three communities, although the Jews were mostly involved in the negotiations of loans.

The Greeks were responsible in collecting taxes from the other communities for the State. They were also responsible for health in the city-port and they were the ones to issue the ships with clean or foul bills of health according to whether they considered the city to be free of plague or not.[4] They were also in control of the wholesale and retail trade of cloth of all qualities. Cloth was the most important import into Smyrna from Western Europe. They distributed it to the city and its environs including the island of Chios. By the end of the 19th century, the Greek community, and in particular the Chiots, many of whom had moved to Smyrna by that time, was distributing cloth to cities all over Anatolia. It was not until the middle of the 19th century, that European merchants were able to penetrate fully into Anatolia economically, or send their own agents there. Even then it was usually Greeks who went inland acting as representatives for European firms.[5]

---

[1]ANF, AE Bi 1053, Mémoire, Peyssonnel, Smyrna, 22 Nov 1751.

[2]ANF, AE Bi 1057, Consul de Jonville, Smyrna, 26 May 1763 to Minister, Paris.

[3]A. Galanté, *Histoire des Juifs d'Anatolie: les Juifs de Smyrne*, Istanbul, 1937-9, vol. 1, p. 143.

[4]PRO/SP/105/126, Consul Werry, Smyrna, 17 June 1800 to Levant Co, London.

[5]O. Kurmuş, "The Role of British Capital in the Economic Development of Western Anatolia, 1850-1913", PhD, London University, 1974, p. 87; see also, Reşat Kasaba, *The Ottoman Empire and the World Economy*, Albany, NY, 1988; *idem*, "Economic Foundations of a Civil Society: Greeks in the Trade of Western Anatolia, 1840-1914", D. Gondicas & C. Issawi, eds., *Ottoman Greeks in the Age of Nationalism*, Princeton, NJ, 1999, pp. 77-87. Elena Frangakis-Syrett, "The Implementation of the 1838 Anglo-Turkish Convention on İzmir's Trade: European and Minority Merchants", *New Perspectives on Turkey*, 7, 1992, pp. 91-112; *idem*, "The Economic Activities of the Greek Community of İzmir in the Second Half of the Nineteenth and Early Twentieth Centuries", D. Gondicas & C. Issawi, eds., *Ottoman Greeks in the Age of Nationalism*, Princeton, NJ, 1999, pp. 17-44; Gerasimos Augustinos, *The Greeks of Asia Minor*, Kent, Ohio, 1992; Sia Anagnostopoulou, *Μικρά Ασία, 19ος αιώνας-1919 (Asia Minor, 19th Century-1919)*, Athens, 1998.

«Les Grecs et particulièrement les Sciottes, sont les maîtres absolus des ventes en détail des draps, des toileries, des soieries et des dorures. Ils font la loi aux européens, sont étroitement liés entre eux et payent comme ils l'entendent».[1] Despite the Greeks from Morea, Yanina, the Aegean islands and even Ambelakia, who came to Smyrna at the end of the 18th century, it was the Chiot community, which became the most prosperous. They played an important role in the expansion overseas of the trade activities of the Greeks in Smyrna at the turn of the century.

Despite their multiple economic activities, the local communities did not dominate one of the most important economic sectors of the city — external maritime trade. This was for most of the 18th century in the hands of the Europeans. The latter, settled in the principal ports of the Ottoman Empire (Smyrna being the most important amongst them), carried out trade with Western Europe. Local merchants could not do the same as the laws of some of these European countries excluded them.[2] In addition, their status quo in the Empire placed them at a disadvantage *vis-à-vis* the Europeans, who enjoyed preferential treatment based on the Capitulations.

It was not always so. Before the 18th century Jewish, Greek and Armenian merchants from Smyrna took an active part in the international trade. Often they had a sister company based in a Western port. Thus in 1553, the Armenians established themselves in Livorno, where they traded in Indian prints, Iranian silk and cotton from Manisa.[3] In 1563, they went to Amsterdam although periods of peak trade activity there, were 1661-1665 and 1701-1705. In 1612, they established themselves in Marseilles where they acquired the monopoly of the Iranian silk trade to the French port.[4] By the end of the century, however, they were to lose these rights to the French merchants. A 20% import duty levied on all foreigners exporting to Marseilles excluded them, in effect, from this trade. Nevertheless in the 18th century they traded in Iranian silk from Amsterdam and from a number of Italian ports. In the middle of the 17th century, their trade activities linked Smyrna with the North Sea.[5]

---

[1]ANF, AE Biii 242, Mémoire, 1820; see also, ANF, AE Bi 1053, Mémoire, 22 Nov 1751.

[2]PRO/SP/105/121, Levant Co, London, 26 May 1797 to Consul Werry, Smyrna.

[3]Chalhan de Cirbied (tr F. Macler), «Notes de Ch. de Cirbied sur les Arméniens d'Amsterdam et de Livourne», *Annahir*, 1, 1904, pp. 8-16.

[4]C.-D. Tekeian, «Marseille, la Provence et les Arméniens», *Mémoires de l'Institut Historique de Provence*, 1929, XI, pp. 5-63.

[5]K. Kévonian, «Marchands Arméniens au XVIIIe siècle», *Cahiers du monde russe et soviétique*, April-June 1975, pp. 199-244.

At the end of the 17th century, the greatest rivals to British and French trade in Smyrna were the Jews: «... their trade consists of goods which in quality and quantity are similar to our own — cloth from Holland and England, silk stuffs from Italy, paper etc.».[1] In fact, the Jewish merchants maintained from their base in Livorno a share in the international trade of Smyrna throughout the 18th century, although a rather small one. Greek merchants were also active in the international trade through Amsterdam and the Italian ports in the latter half of the 18th century.

By the beginning of the 18th century, the needs of the West for the raw materials of the Ottoman Empire became greater as its manufacturing industries got under way. European merchants were settled in the Ottoman ports to export these raw materials to Europe — for their own account — and import into the Empire European manufactured cloth and colonial products — mass consumer goods such as coffee and sugar and dyestuffs for the dyeing of cotton yarn which was one of the main exports of Smyrna. In this trade network, the non-Muslim Ottoman merchants became the intermediaries between the foreign merchants and the Ottoman producers. Although the European merchants would have preferred to do away with the intermediaries, the nature of trade in Smyrna was such that made them indispensable. «... in Smyrna one can only do business through the intervention of the local people, who distribute goods to greater distances and receive goods from afar which they give us in exchange for our own».[2] Smyrna's extensive hinterland and vast network of trade assured the Europeans of a return cargo in a relatively short period of time. Merchants in Marseilles sent their goods to Smyrna when they wanted a return cargo quickly. Their agents were thus pressed to buy Ottoman raw materials but did not always have the necessary cash to buy them with. For most of the 18th century, there was shortage of money both in France and the Ottoman Empire. Unlike Istanbul, where rich Ottomans lent the Europeans money, and the reverse, in Smyrna Jews, Armenians and Greeks lent them goods. This transaction took place in the following manner. A French merchant would sell some of his cloth for cash and use this money to buy olive oil and wax, which were the only two goods sold for cash in Smyrna. With the rest of the money he paid off bills of exchange that he might have drawn upon him. He then worked out a bartering plan according to which the local intermediary supplied him with cotton wool, mohair yarn, cotton yarn etc. He supplied him with Ottoman goods, usually in advance, for the Frenchman might not have the cloth in his hands yet. It was credit in

[1] ANF, AE Biii 235, Commerce de Levant, 1693.
[2] ANF, AE Biii 242, Commerce de Levant en général, Jumelin, 16 Dec 1812.

kind — only instead of advancing him money he was advancing him goods. The advantage to the local merchant was that in this way he was creating a link through which trade had to pass. The Europeans not only bought everything from them but sold their goods to Ottoman buyers and Armenian caravan dealers through non-Muslim merchants almost exclusively. There were other ways in which the intermediary could profit from this operation. Selling the cloth that the French merchant sold him at a lower price, he used the cash to buy raw materials at a lower price from what he sold them to the European merchant in exchange for cloth. For, when buying for cash one could get a better price than in a barter exchange.[1] The same happened the other way round, too. European merchants sold cloth to local merchants giving them six months to two years credit. They, in turn, sold it to other Ottoman merchants, who took it into Anatolia to exchange it for silk or another raw material. The money was eventually paid.

Although on the level of the individual merchant the Europeans were not always rich, on the national level they disposed of large capital resources. It was on this level that they warded off, successfully during the middle decades of the 18th century, the local merchants. It was particularly so with the British and Dutch mercantile communities. During that time the European merchants became the link in the market of Smyrna (and by consequence of a large part of the Anatolian market) with the international western market.

Competition amongst the European merchants themselves, gave the local merchants an opportunity to come into the international market. British trade in Smyrna was dominated by a small number of merchants with considerable capital resources. These merchants tried to control the market in order to keep prices at levels that suited them. This was not always to the interests of smaller merchants who co-operated with the Ottomans and aimed at underselling the Levant Company merchants.

> «We are informed that some members of this Company have made private contacts with Armenians and other strangers, not free (i.e., not members) of this Company for the delivering of cloth at certain prices in Turkey which is highly prejudicial to our trade».[2]

Reaction from the mercantile establishment was prompt. They wrote to the British Consul in Smyrna: «We hope with your just endeavors to prevent or at least to restrain as much as possible the clandestine importation at your

---

[1]ANF, AE Bi 1052, Consul Peyssonnel, Smyrna, 29 Jan 1749 to Minister, Paris.
[2]PRO/SP/105/115, Levant Co, London, 21 June 1699 to Consul Raye, Smyrna.

place by Jews and all others not entitled to trade within our privileges».[1] The only time when the Ottomans could trade in the international market were periods of warfare between the major nations, France and Britain, as it happened in the Seven Years War (1756-1763). At all times, a certain number of local merchants could trade under the protection of a European nation. This protection was given to the Ottoman merchant at a fee — the *beratlı* system. In the 18th century, however, this was not very widespread. Nevertheless, most of the time, Ottoman merchants, including Turkish, could trade with the liberal Dutch or Italian ports, as the trade between Smyrna and Genoa or Livorno, in the 1720s, indicates.

*

At the end of the 18th and beginning of the 19th centuries, there was spectacular growth in world trade. Expansion of the industrial sector in W. Europe created greater needs for raw materials and markets for the finished products. World trade could no longer function on the basis of monopolies and restrictions of the type propagated by the Levant Company. Free trade was what the world economy needed. In Smyrna, the main beneficiaries of these developments were primarily the non-Muslim communities and the Greeks in particular. They experienced spectacular economic growth and an expansion of their activities that went far beyond the walls of the city.

One by one the major European nations abandoned their monopolistic laws and allowed Ottoman merchants into their trade: France and then Britain. Between 1781 and 1815, the Chamber of Commerce of Marseilles, bowing to pressure from French manufacturers for abundant supplies of raw materials, four times repealed the law that discriminated against foreign merchants by imposing an import duty of 20% on all goods entering Marseilles under their names.[2] Every time French merchants, whose interests in the Levant were thus affected, managed to have the decision revoked. After 1815, however, the decision stood. Free trade had won the day. As a result, a number of Greek merchants, most of them from Smyrna, established themselves in the French port. In fact, the first Greek merchants went to Marseilles in the 1780's. For the majority of them Smyrna was the center for their trade activities and the principal merchandise they traded in was cotton. They did not stop at that. They soon expanded in the wheat trade supplying W. Europe at times of

[1] PRO/SP/105/116, Levant Co, London, 2 July 1717 to Consul Cooke, Smyrna.
[2] ANF, AE Biii 242, Sur l'article 30 ... , Commerce du Levant, 28 Sept 1814.

harvest failure. They established family branches in Odessa and Taganrog in the Black Sea, and in Istanbul, in order to undertake this trade.

In addition, they imported wool, mohair yarn, hare skins from Smyrna and olive oil from the Aegean Archipelago. They exported cloth, cochineal, silk stuffs, coffee and cocoa to a number of ports in the Ottoman Empire such as Salonica, the ports of the Peloponnese, Alexandria. From Marseilles, they traded with the Italian ports of Genoa, Livorno, Trieste, Ancôna and Venice and with the Spanish ports of Lisbon and Barcelona. From Lisbon they sent to Smyrna Spanish piastres. One of the first Greek merchants to acquire a truly international network of trade was Barthelemi Badetti — a Catholic from Chios. He was active in trade for two decades since his arrival in the French port in 1798.[1] Another illustrious merchant was Peter Homeridis Schilizzi, descendant from one of the most important families of Chios. In 1804 he arrived in Marseilles and a year later established the commercial house of «Peter Schillizi & Co». With the end of the Napoleonic Wars, a new wave of Chiot merchants arrived in Marseilles. Among the most important ones were Pandia & Augustus Ralli, Yannis & Eustratios Petrocochinos, Michael & Yannis Vuros, Nicolas & Pantelis Argentis, Paraschewas Sechiaris. The first two established the house of «Ralli-Argenti» which was the French branch of an international business which had its base in Smyrna under the name of «Sechiari and Argenti» and another branch in Istanbul under the name of «Petrocochino and Argenti».[2]

Apart from French trade, Ottoman merchants were able to turn to British trade which was until then a prerogative of British nationals and members of the Levant Company only — apart for some *beratlıs*. «Their protection at the Porte has sufficient influence to represent with success the advantages that would arise to the revenue in procuring a free footing as they trade in Holland, and I am well assured from good authority they are encouraged to hope, it will be obtained for them. The Turkish Ambassador is instructed to ask for the same privileges for Ottoman subjects [to trade] to England, that the British have in Turkey».[3] The same happened with the

[1] P. Échinard, *Grecs et Philhellènes à Marseille*, Marseilles, 1973, pp. 62-9.

[2] *ibid.*, pp. 60, 89; see also, Elena Frangakis-Syrett, *Χίωτες έμποροι στις διεθνείς συναλλαγές, 1750-1850* (*Chiot Merchants in International Trade, 1750-1850*), Athens, 1995, pp. 45-50; *idem*, "The Greek Mercantile Community of İzmir in the First Half of the Nineteenth Century", Daniel Panzac, ed., *Les villes dans l'Empire ottoman: Activités et sociétés*, Paris, 1991, Vol. I, pp. 391-98; Vasilis Kremmydas, *Εμποροι και εμπορικά δίκτυα στα χρόνια του εικοσιένα* (*Merchants and Trading Networks in the 1820s*) Athens, 1996, *passim*. Despina Vlami, *Το φιορίνι, το σιτάρι και η οδός του κήπου (Florin, Wheat and Garden Street)* Athens, 2000, *passim*.

[3] PRO/SP/105/126, Consul Werry, Smyrna, 17 June 1797 to Levant Co, London.

Dutch. In fact, the Dutch State was the first to follow a liberal policy and allow non-Muslim merchants to settle in Amsterdam. By the middle of the 18th century, there was a sizeable Greek community established there which traded with Smyrna. The well-known Greek intellectual, Adamantios Korais, was sent to Amsterdam in the 1770s, as a representative of his family firm in Smyrna.

Apart from economic developments, the French Revolution and the Napoleonic Wars were a series of political and military events that played a crucial role in the growth of the economic activities of the local communities. They broke the economic dominance of France in the Eastern Mediterranean, including Smyrna, which had lasted for most of the 18th century. The French cloth industry was already suffering in the decade before the French Revolution. The political events of the Revolution caused an unparalleled upheaval in the country not least of all in its economy. French traders abroad were unsettled. Much of the direct trade between Marseilles and the Levant was disrupted. The Italian ports were able to take a good part of it as the spectacular growth in the trade between Smyrna and the Italian ports, and in particular Trieste and Ancôna, in this period, illustrate.[1] Greek, Armenian and Jewish merchants who had established themselves in the ports of Livorno, Genoa, Ancôna and Trieste were in a position to take charge of much of the re-directed trade. As the port of Marseilles was no longer able to furnish French merchants with sufficient quantities of raw materials, they turned to the Italian ports for their supplies and thus to the Ottoman, mostly non-Muslim, merchants established there.[2]

Another area where the Napoleonic Wars were crucial for its development was local participation in the carrying trade. Throughout the 18th century, the French to a large extent, (and other European nations such as the Danes, the Dutch, the British or the Swedes, and the Ragusans to a lesser extent), dominated the carrying trade in the Eastern Mediterranean. They also dominated the carrying trade between the Ottoman Empire and Western Europe. During the Napoleonic Wars, open warfare between France and the other European nations led them to carry out privateering against each other. Initially the Greeks carried out privateering on behalf of Britain against France and the reverse. Soon they came out as pirates against all nations and on behalf of their own communities. At the same time the dominance of the

[1] In 1801, 61% of Smyrna's imports came from Trieste and Ancôna and 70% of its exports went to these ports. Trade between Smyrna and the two ports previously was around 15-20%.
[2] ANF, AE Biii 243, Renseignements sur le commerce du Levant, Livorno, 13 May 1825.

Europeans in the carrying trade weakened as it became too risky and uneconomical to cross the seas. These developments stimulated a process that was already under way and which became apparent in the first two decades of the 19th century — that of the Greeks, not only of Smyrna but of the Aegean islands, too, taking a share in the carrying trade. They did not limit their activities to the coastal trade of Western Anatolia or to the trade of Smyrna with the other Ottoman ports, but sent their ships further afield to Italy, Holland, France and even Britain. The first Ottoman Greek ships to leave Smyrna for London were in 1798.[1]

After the French Revolution when French traders came back to do commerce in Smyrna, they found that it was more profitable to co-operate with the Ottoman merchants than compete against them. Some had lost part of their capital, others their commercial house. Still others found that they could trade with the Levant through an Ottoman merchant direct and without undergoing the expense involved in establishing themselves there. The Greeks were again those who co-operated most with the French. There are a number of reasons for this. The Greeks spoke the language; knew the French market well and had numerous contacts from their activities there. Thus a bill of lading was signed by a captain in Smyrna who undertook to deliver within a certain period of time goods to Marseilles. Upon the dispatch of the bill of lading to the French port, the merchant drew, on the consignee, a bill of exchange representing 9/16 of the value of the goods. The merchant in using this capital bought goods which he then dispatched to his corespondent in Marseilles. The latter was reimbursed for his money when the goods were sold. Proceeds from the sale were sent to the Ottoman merchant in either specie or in a bill of exchange. In this way, the merchant in Marseilles financed the merchant in Smyrna. At the end of the venture both sides had made a profit. The goods, which were consigned to the French merchant, served as a guarantee for the loan. In addition, the French merchant received an interest rate of 15-20% on his money.[2] Frenchmen invested their capital with local merchants in another way. They sold them goods on credit which the locals sold in Smyrna for cash. With the proceeds they bought wheat. Their profits consisted in their ability to buy and sell wheat twice before they had to repay their French creditors. For the French merchant it was more profitable to trade in this way than to keep an establishment in Smyrna.[3]

[1]PRO/SP/105/121, Consul Werry, Smyrna, 20 June 1797 to Levant Co, London.
[2]ANF, AE Biii 242, Commerce du Levant, 28 Sept 1814.
[3]ANF, F/12, 1850 A, État général des maisons de commerce, 1820.

During the final decades of the 18th century, Greek and Jewish merchants founded commercial houses with correspondents in Livorno, Trieste, Ancôna, Genoa, Austria and Spain. Jewish and Greek trading houses were among the richest in Livorno. The Armenians together with the Turks continued in their control of the trade within the interior of the Ottoman Empire. Saumon Nubar, J. Sciachum and C. Chumarian were among the most important ones.[1] In the early 19th century Armenian merchants were establishing themselves in London to trade with the Ottoman Empire.

The biggest Greek commercial houses, in the late 18th century, in Smyrna, were those of Dimitri Rodocanachi & Co, Ralli Suhari & Argenti, Ralli Petrocochino & Argenti, Parodi & Mavrokordato and Frangiadi & Rodocanachi. The richest house in the early 19th century was considered to be Fratelli Vlasto. Another prosperous house was that of Dimitri and Alesandro Sevastopoulo as were also those of Manoli d'Isay & Son and Cristodoulo Manoli d'Isay. The last family had been active in Amsterdam since the 1760's. Amongst those who were also doing well in Smyrna were Demetrio Cartaro, Antoni Negroponti Schillizi and Luca Negroponti & Son. Figli de Giorgio Dromocaiti & Etio Christoforo were directing a rapidly expanding business, as were Fratelli Badetti & Co, with Barthelemy Badetti being established in Marseilles. The other two Catholic houses in Smyrna were those of Angello, Alliotto & Co and the Egyptian house of Nicolo Mussabini.[2]

The Greeks in Smyrna amassed great fortunes. Many of them however, did not keep them for long. It was rare for a commercial house to maintain the same level of business for more than two decades. The merchant accumulated too many debts and eventually found himself unable to pay bills of exchange drawn upon him. In the early 19th century, according to the French Consul, there was a very large number of Greek houses in Smyrna who disposed of some capital. Of these only two had been in existence for more than two decades — Mavrogordato & Co and Antonio Bachatori. In the early 19th century, only the former was still active and prosperous.

Whilst the Greeks and Jews were particularly active in the mercantile and informal banking sectors, the Armenians were present in the manufacturing sector. The biggest factory that Smyrna possessed was established in the 1770's by an Armenian company under Government protection and in imitation of a similar project in Istanbul. It employed up to

---

[1] *ibid.*

[2] ANF, AE Biii 242, Mémoire, 1820.

500 workers and printed cloth and muslins for export to Switzerland, Germany and England. It also catered for an important internal market that went beyond the hinterland of Smyrna and comprised of a large part of Anatolia.[1] It should be stated that the manufacturing sector was small compared to the city's mercantile sector. For the economy of Smyrna, part of the Ottoman economy, was largely pre-capitalist where the most developed sector was merchant capital. Finally, the non-Muslim communities were absent from large scale landownership and production for the market which was a prerogative enjoyed by Turks mostly.

The growth of Smyrna as a principal port of the Ottoman Empire benefited the local communities on the whole. Certainly, commercial dominance by the West did limit their trading activities. Towards the end of the century however, world economic development and political events allowed them to come back to the world economy with renewed vigor and success. This was particularly so in the case of the Greek community. It should be stated that the European economies were not losing in this way either. For the Ottoman merchants were still importing European cloth and colonial goods to Smyrna and exporting raw materials to Europe. That is, local mercantile capital was allowed to grow and take a share in the increased trading and banking activities that the industrial growth of the Western economies generated.

[1] On Ottoman manufacture and red dyeing, see Olga Katsiardi-Hering, *Τεχνίτες και Τεχνικές βαφής νημάτων* *(Artisans and techniques of dyeing yarn)*, Athens, 2003, *passim.*

GREEK MERCANTILE ACTIVITIES IN THE EASTERN MEDITERRANEAN, 1780-1820

This study focuses on the mercantile activities of Greeks whose bases were mainly Smyrna, but also other ports in the eastern Mediterranean, with western Europe and vice-versa. Many of these Greek merchants formed part of an extended family company, which had branches all over the eastern and western Mediterranean, and who cooperated with each other. This extended family company expanded continuously from one port to another in the Mediterranean, usually maintaining a head office in the eastern Mediterranean. The period under study, 1780-1820, is the most crucial period in the economic development of the Greeks in the eastern Mediterranean in the eighteenth and early nineteenth centuries. Considerable rates of capital accumulation and economic growth occurred in this period which enabled them to set up these multiple trading bases.

The reasons for this growth were both economic and political. The last decades of the eighteenth and the beginning of the nineteenth centuries, coincided with an expansionary phase of the world economy, and the beginnings of the Industrial Revolution in Britain, which led to a remarkable increase in the productivity of the British textile industry. The needs of western Europe, and particularly of Britain, for raw materials and markets for their finished products also increased. The eastern Mediterranean was one such market. Smyrna, the biggest international port in the eastern Mediterranean at the time,[1] experienced spectacular economic growth in its trade with western Europe.[2] The French Revolution of 1789, and the French Revolutionary and Napoleonic Wars that followed, in the years 1792 to 1815, brought French commercial domination in the eastern Mediterranean, since the beginning of the century, temporarily to an end. The military confrontation between the two major European powers, Britain and France, forced on France and Britain the opening-up of their trade monopolies to facilitate their trade at a time

---

[1]*Archives de la Chambre de Commerce de Marseille, Marseilles,* Série I, 19-20, États des marchandises envoyées en Levant et Barbarie (1749-1789); and Série I, 26-28, États des marchandises venant du Levant et de Barbarie (1700-1789). Hereafter this archive will be cited as ACCM.

[2]Frangakis, Helen, *The Commerce of İzmir in the Eighteenth Century, 1695-1820* (Ph.D. thesis, University of London, 1985), pp. 173-176.

when free trade was "in the air" but not yet an established state policy. Between 1792 and 1815 France, seeing its merchant marine beleaguered by the continuous attacks of British privateers and warships, turned to neutrals in order to facilitate its trade. It repealed its law that excluded foreigners from trading in Marseilles three times until the law stood in favor of the foreigners.[1] When the law was not in force French goods, sent to Smyrna from Marseilles and consigned to Greek merchants, could be confiscated by the French consul in the Levantine port.[2] Increasingly though the French authorities became more accommodating as French merchants found it either too difficult or too expensive to trade on their own with the Levant.[3] In some cases cooperation on an individual basis between a French merchant and a Greek shipper, or merchant, had started even before the French Revolution, for the French were already experiencing difficulties in their Levant trade.[4]

The Continental System, 1806 to 1814, placed obstacles in the trade of Britain with France's satellites, allies, and associated powers, which included most of Europe. Britain, with a rapidly expanding economy, sought the eastern Mediterranean market in a larger scale than ever before. It also relaxed the monopoly laws governing British trade with the Levant. The peace that Britain signed with the Ottoman Empire in 1797 was followed, a year later, by the first Ottoman Greek ships to leave for London.[5]

Although by the end of the Napoleonic Wars the more dynamic economy of Britain had replaced French commercial domination by British in the Levant there existed a gap of forty years or so, 1780-1820, during which the Greek merchants, along with the other Ottoman non-Muslim merchants, Armenian and Jewish, took over a large part of the trade of the eastern Mediterranean ports with the West, hitherto carried out largely by European merchants. The Europeans, armed with the Capitulations (trade agreements contracted between the Ottoman Empire and a number of western European countries and which favored the latter) had hitherto enjoyed certain legal advantages over their Ottoman counterparts. Added to this, were the monopolistic principles of their national economies and their superior organization, in terms of transportation and insurance, which combined to

[1] *Archives Nationales de France*, Paris, Série AE Biii 242, Sur l'article 30 de l'ordonnance du 20 Sept. 1810. Commerce de Levant, 28 Sept. 1814. Hereafter this archive will be cited as ANF.

[2] *ANF*, AE Bi 1065, Consul Amoureux, Smyrna, 23 Dec. 1791 to Minister Paris.

[3] *ANF*, Série F12/1850 A, État général des maisons de commerce, Smyrna, 1820.

[4] *ANF*, AE Bi 168, Consul Benincasa, Ancôna, 6 Nov. 1786 to Minister, Paris.

[5] *Public Record Office*, London, Series SP 105/121, Consul Werry, Smyrna, 30 June 1797 to Levant Company, London. Hereafter this archive will be cited as *PRO*.

further exclude their Ottoman counterparts for most of the eighteenth century, from a large part of the eastern Mediterranean trade with the West. Whatever exclusivity the Europeans enjoyed came to an end in the first quarter of the nineteenth century.[1] The non-Muslim community that benefited most from these changes, even more than the Jewish or the Armenian, was the Greek mercantile community. This can be seen from their remarkable expansion in ports all over the Mediterranean, and beyond, in a short period of time, and their dominant position in the carrying trade, particularly within the eastern Mediterranean.

The reasons for this are multiple and some of them originate in the decades preceding 1780. Indeed even before 1780, the Greeks were able to take advantage of every weak link in the monopoly network that France and Britain had sought to establish. The free port of Livorno was a haven for semi-clandestine trade between western Europeans who wanted to avoid the cumbersome monopolistic laws of their own countries and chose to associate with Ottoman merchants and the latter, who operated freely from Livorno.[2] From the 1760s and 1770s Greek commercial houses, originating mostly from Smyrna, but also from Istanbul, such as Petrocochino, Prassacachi Brothers, Skaramangas were established in Livorno.[3] The Greeks were at no time the only Ottoman community trading in the Italian ports and Jewish merchants figured prominently, during most of the eighteenth century, particularly in Livorno.[4] Yet in the last quarter of the century, it would appear, the Greeks did start overtaking the other communities in the trade of the Italian ports with the eastern Mediterranean. They also challenged the position of the western Europeans, who were established in these ports and were trading with the Levant. Apart from Livorno, the Greeks were particularly prominent in Messina, Ancôna, and Trieste.[5] The following observation was made by the French consul in Trieste in 1782:

> The trade of Trieste with the Levant is practiced mainly by the Greeks whose principals are in the Ottoman Empire. Until recently their trade was

[1]Frangakis, Elena, "The Raya Communities of Smyrna in the Eighteenth Century, 1690 1820: Demography and Economic Activities", *Actes du Colloque International d'Histoire. La ville néohellénique. Héritages ottomans et état grec*, Vol. 1 (Athens, 1985), pp. 27-42.

[2]PRO, SP 105/115, Levant Company, London, 21 June 1699 to Consul Raye, Smyrna.

[3]Zolotas, I., *Ιστορία της Χίου* (*History of Chios*) (Athens, 1926), vol. III, Pt. 1, pp. 301, 312, 366-367.

[4]ANF, AE Biii 243, Miège, Renseignements sur le commerce du Levant, Livorno, 13 May, 1825. Hereafter cited as Renseignements.

[5]Katsiardi-Hering, Olga, *Η Ελληνική Παροικία της Τεργέστης, 1751-1830* (*The Greek Community of Trieste, 1751-1830.* (Athens, 1986), 2 vols, *passim.* For Livorno see, Vlami Despina, *Το φιορίνι, το σιτάρι και η οδός του κήπου (Florin, wheat and Garden Street)* (Athens, 2000), pp. 79-112.

> limited; their capital outlays were not very considerable and their activities were limited to Morea, Salonica and Smyrna; the increase that has taken place in the last two or three years is due to the Dutch who have been bringing to Trieste silk and cotton from the Levant and then taking it by land to Holland, Imperial Germany, and Switzerland. They use the same route for their exports of cloth and bulky goods to the Levant.[1]

In 1785, 22 percent of Messina's imports came from the Levant and 6 percent of its total exports went to the Levant with Smyrna accounting for a third. In that year, 9 percent of Smyrna's imports came from Genoa, Livorno, and Messina and an equal amount of its exports went to those ports.[2] Silk cloth exports to the Levant which were, to a large extent, handled by Greeks, constituted an important sector of Messina's Levantine trade. Apart from silk cloth the Greeks also dealt in olive oil, which they purchased from the islands of the Aegean Archipelago and transported it to Messina, usually in their own vessels. From Messina the oil was transported, in Genoese vessels, to Genoa and Livorno where it was treated. The final destination was the soap manufacturers in Marseilles where the cargo was smuggled in without paying the 20 percent duty levied on all foreign trade. Oil transported to Marseilles in this way was cheaper than if it were bought in the Aegean islands, by French merchants, and transported to Smyrna and then on to Marseilles in French ships.[3] In addition to these goods the Greeks carried from Messina, as well as from other Italian ports, specie to the eastern Mediterranean.[4]

After 1793 Marseilles was no longer able to dominate the trade of the eastern Mediterranean with western Europe, as it had done formerly, supplying not only the French with Ottoman goods, but also Imperial Germany, Switzerland, and Belgium. Genoa, Livorno, and Trieste took over this role. Furthermore, in the years 1793 to 1814, as Marseilles could not send French goods to the Levant by sea either, it had to use overland routes to Livorno, Genoa, Trieste, and Ancôna. These ports thus became the markets for French goods to the eastern Mediterranean supplying western Europe with Ottoman goods, too.[5] As the Adriatic coast was relatively calm and free of British attacks and privateering until 1809, the ports of Trieste and Ancôna, in particular, benefited from Marseilles' loss of trade. Until 1789 Marseilles accounted for over half of the trade of Smyrna with western Europe, which

---

[1] *ANF*, Série Marine B/7, 446, Bertrand, 19 Oct. 1782 in Commerce des ports de l'Europe, 1 Feb. 1783. The Dutch were using a land route because the British were blockading their ports in the last years of the American War of Independence, 1781-1782.

[2] *ANF*, AE Bi 859, Consul l'Allement, Messina, 14 Jan. 1786 to Minister, Paris.

[3] *ANF*, AE Bi 859, Consul l'Allement, Messina, 3 Sept. 1785 to Minister, Paris.

[4] *ANF*, AE Bi 859, Consul l'Allement, Messina, 4 Feb. 1786 to Minister, Paris.

[5] *ANF*, AE Biii 243, Renseignements.

itself accounted for over half of the Ottoman Empire's trade with the West. In 1801 to 1803, during the Peace of Amiens, 51.2 percent of Smyrna's exports to the West went to Trieste and Ancôna and 44 percent of its European imports came from these two ports.[1] As trade was directed to these ports the Greeks, who were well established there, were in a good position to take hold of a large part of this trade. The better established the Greeks were in the Italian ports, the more successful they were likely to be in penetrating major economies as those of France. Such were the fears expressed by the French consul in Smyrna, M. Fourcade, in 1820. He was right:

> ... The Greeks who have for the last fifty years been cherishing the hope for a happier future without success, have ended by forming numerous establishments in Italy, which despite our exclusion of them, will form a barrier which we can overcome only by attracting them into our economy....[2]

Holland was equally important to Greek economic development. Unlike Britain and France, Holland had a liberal policy that allowed foreign merchants to establish commercial houses in its ports. Mavrogordatos, who had one of the most solvent commercial houses in Smyrna,[3] was amongst the first, together with d'Issay to set up business in Amsterdam in the 1760s. In 1762, during the last year of the Seven Years' War, over two dozen Greek companies or individual merchants sent goods to Smyrna from Rotterdam and Amsterdam, on Dutch ships.[4] Although most of these houses were exporting Dutch and other European-made cloth to Smyrna and elsewhere in the eastern Mediterranean and importing into Holland Ottoman raw materials, a good number of these houses speculated in money, too. From the late 1760s, as the monetary problems of the Ottoman economy grew, so did its chronic shortage of specie intensify. One of the most effective ways to alleviate the Ottoman market of specie shortage was to import bullion, in specie or in bills of exchange. Until the 1780s trade in money was mostly in the hands of western European merchants. It was not so for the bills of exchange whose circulation within and without the Empire was much more difficult to monitor. Ottoman merchants, therefore, actively participated in this sector.

---

[1] *ARA*, Totaal Bedrag van de Invoer en Uitvoer te Smirna in de jaren, 1801-1803, in J. G. Nanninga, ed., *Bronnen tot de Geschiedenis van den Levantschen Handel. Vierde deel, 1765 1826* ('S-Gravenhage, 1966), pp. 1542-1571.

[2] *ANF*, AE Biii 242, Consul Fourcade, Mémoire, Smyrna, 1820. Hereafter cited as Mémoire.

[3] *ibid.*; see also, *ANF*, F/12 1850 A, État général des maisons du commerce ottoman établies à Smyrne, 1820.

[4] *ARA*, Consulaatarschief Smirna, 2dd, de Invoer en de Uitvoer met Nederlandschen Scheppen te Smirna, 22 Feb.-22 Aug. 1762, in Nanninga, *Bronnen... derde deel, 1727-1765* ('S-Gravenhage, 1952), pp. 715-763. In this bitter Anglo-French conflict Holland was neutral. It saw, therefore, its Levantine trade increase and was thus better able to allow Ottoman merchants in it.

Bills of exchange were used in the following way: when the market of Smyrna experienced acute shortage in a certain foreign currency (foreign currencies circulated together with, and sometimes instead of, the local currency) bills of exchange in that currency were sent to the port. It was a lucrative enterprise for these bills were in high demand and could be cashed at a high rate of exchange *vis-à-vis* the Ottoman currency. A high proportion of bills of exchange written in Smyrna or Istanbul were eventually drawn upon in the international financial centers of Amsterdam, Livorno, Venice, and Genoa.[1] Greeks, established in Holland, did not only enter the commercial sector of the Dutch economy but also its international financial and speculative networks. It greatly aided their rate of capital accumulation for profits from speculation were almost double those from trade at the time.[2] Apart from trade, the house of Mavrogordatos was also active in monetary speculation.[3] In the early 1800s, there were many Greek merchants in Dutch cities who could claim residence of several decades in the country and exercise political rights in the municipalities although they maintained close economic contacts with the eastern Mediterranean.[4]

In 1787, over fifty Greek companies or individual merchants sent goods to Smyrna from the Dutch ports. Although in 1762 the number of Greek merchants sending goods to Smyrna from Holland did not outnumber their Jewish and Armenian counterparts, who were also active in the Dutch trade, in 1787 they clearly did outnumber them.[5] A reason for Greek predominance in the Dutch trade was probably the fact that the Greeks had control of the cloth trade in the market of Smyrna, and in most of western Anatolia, and the Aegean islands, both wholesale and retail. This gave them a leverage with the Dutch exporters of European cloth into Smyrna. Cloth was the single most important commodity exported by the Dutch in the Levant. In fact between 1784 and 1818, they practically took over Dutch exports of cloth to Smyrna and to the rest of Anatolia.[6] Other factors also contributed to the predominance

---

[1]Eldem, Edhem, "La circulation de la lettre de change entre la France et Constantinople au XVIIIe siècle", *L'Empire Ottoman, la République de Turquie et la France*, eds., H. Batu and J. L. Bacqué-Grammont (Istanbul-Paris, 1985), p. 91.

[2]*ACCM*, I, 26-28.

[3]Eldem, "La circulation", p. 97.

[4]Algemeen Rijkarschief, 'S-Gravenhage, Arschief van de Nederlandsche legatie te Constantinopel, no. 132, July 1803 in Argenti, Philip, *Diplomatic Archive of Chios, 1577-1841* (Cambridge, 1954), Vol. I, pp. 36-45.

[5]*ARA*, Consulaatarschief Smirna, dd[3], De Invoer en de Uitvoer met Nederlandschen Scheppen te Smirna, 22 Aug. 1786-22 Feb. 1787, in Nanninga, *Bronnen ... vierde deel, 1765-1826*, pp. 1428-1466.

[6]*ARA*, 349, Fremeaux, van Lennep and Enslie to van Haaften, 29 June 1782; and ARA, 120, Rapport fait à M. le chargé d'affaires Testa sur les drapiers par J. de Hoschepied, Smyrna, 19 Feb. 1818 in *ibid.*, pp. 339-341 and 950-951.

of the Greeks in the eastern Mediterranean trade in general besides the liberal policies of the Dutch and of the Italian ports: their ability to enter sectors other than trade in goods or monetary speculation, such as the carrying trade, and their ability to expand simultaneously into a very large number of ports in the Mediterranean and in western Europe.

The following example is representative of how it happened. After a family council in 1804, it was decided that Peter Schillizi Homerides should leave from Smyrna for Marseilles, taking a ship-load of goods for sale and letters of introduction to merchants and friends of the family. Having sold these goods, he returned to Smyrna for a brief period of time before going back to Marseilles to found, in 1805, the house of Peter Schillizi Homerides. After five years of successful business Homerides dissolved the company. By then the British, who were blockading the French coast, had for the most part stopped the trade of Marseilles with the Levant. After a brief sojourn in Paris, in October 1814, Homerides reached Costanza, through Salonica, taking advantage of the land route, with a considerable amount of goods. Soon after that, as the seas were open once more after the end of Anglo-French hostilities, he returned to Marseilles where he reopened his company.[1] Besides the Schillizi, the Ralli family (both were Chiot families whose businesses originated mostly in Smyrna although they were active also in Istanbul) is another good illustration of the complexity of the Greeks' mercantile activities and the speed with which they expanded their business. In 1815, Pandia and Augustus Ralli together with John and Eustratio Petrocochino, set up the company of "Ralli, Argenti" in Marseilles, as the French branch of the house of "Sechiari & Argenti" based in Smyrna, with a second branch in Istanbul under the name of "Petrocochino & Argenti".[2] In 1818, two other Ralli Brothers, John and Stratis, left Livorno to set up a corresponding branch in London. They traded in silk and cotton from Persia and Anatolia, through Smyrna and Istanbul and exported to the eastern Mediterranean British cloth and French silk stuffs. Five years later, they set up the company of "Ralli & Petrocochino" in London and imported there wheat from the Black Sea.[3]

---

[1]Homeridis Schillizi, Peter, *Βιογραφία Αυτοσχέδιος (An autobiography)* (Athens, 1871), Vol. 2, p. 6.

[2]Échinard Pierre, *Grecs et Philhellènes à Marseille de la révolution française à l'indépendance grecque* (Marseilles, 1973), pp. 62-79. See also, Smyrnelis, Marie-Carmen, "Colonies européennes et communautés ethnico-confessionnelles à Smyrne; co-existence et réseaux de sociabilité (fin du XVIIIe - milieu du XIXe siècle)", Georgeon, F. & Dumont, P., eds., *Vivre dans l'empire ottoman. Sociabilités et relations intercommunautaires* (Paris, 1996), pp. 173-194.

[3]Syriotis, Mikes A., "*Ο οίκος των Αδελφών Ράλλη*", (Ralli Bros."), *Chiaka Khronika* (1911), Vol. 1, pp. 101-110; Karidis, Vyron, "Greek Shipping in the Black Sea, 1815-1856: The Evidence from South Russian Ports" (unpublished paper given at the 1987 *International Symposium of the Modern Greek Studies Association*, Providence, Rhode Island). See also, Frangakis-Syrett, Elena, *Οι Χιωτες Εμποροι στις διεθνείς συναλλαγές, 1750-1850 (Chiot Merchants in International Trade, 1750-1850)* (Athens, 1995), pp. 41-60.

The Greeks also displayed extreme agility in taking advantage of new trading opportunities and in shifting their commercial ventures to new trade routes, as the old sea routes during wartime became full of privateers and usually led to ports that were blockaded. In 1785, the port of Odessa was declared a free port. By 1820 an important Greek mercantile community was already established there. The house of Rodocanachi was amongst the most important houses in Odessa with branches in Smyrna, Istanbul, Marseilles, the Italian and Dutch ports, and after 1820, in London, too.[1] It dealt in Russian wheat, British cloth, French silk stuffs, cotton, wool, olive oil, and other Ottoman foodstuffs and raw materials, and specie. With the beginning of the French Revolutionary Wars sea routes leading to French and French-controlled ports became almost impassable. A number of land routes thus came into use. One route started at Constanza (the point of departure of Schillizi Homeridis in 1814) and went along the Danube to Vienna; another route was a tortuous land passage from Salonica through Yugoslavia to southern Switzerland and then on to Marseilles, or on to northern Switzerland and then on to western Europe.[2] The Greeks used these routes extensively. In the land route to Marseilles they carried cotton and colonial coffee to the French port in return for Orleans-made fezzes and French cloth from Languedoc and Lyons. It was a very profitable trade.[3]

The Greeks also carried out a considerable trade, from their bases in Smyrna and Istanbul, with Austria.[4] In 1789, Greek houses established in Vienna traded in cotton which they got from Smyrna, and at times, from Volos, too. They used their contacts in the port of Trieste in order to acquire specie to send to Smyrna or Volos to purchase cotton with . To transport the specie to the Levantine port they used western European ships. The French consul in Smyrna saw this as an additional source of consulage, and placed an extra levy on all specie carried in French ships on behalf of foreigners. The

---

[1]Herlihy, Patricia, "Greek Merchants in Odessa in the Nineteenth Century", *Harvard Ukrainian Studies* (1979-1980), Vols III/IV, pp. 399-420; see also, Records of Baptisms from the chapel of "Our Saviour", Finsbury Park; Saint Sophia Parish Records Archive, Bayswater, London, 1830s; G. M. Rodocanachi, Merchant, 9 North Buildings, Finsbury Circus and Rodocanachi, Son & Co., Merchants, 26 Finsbury Circus, see *Robson's Commercial Directory of London ...for 1841* (London, 1841), p. 815. See also, Papelasis-Minoglou, Ioanna, "The Greek Merchant House of the Russian Black Sea: A Nineteenth-Century Example of a Traders' Coalition", *International Journal of Maritime History* (1998), Vol. X/1, pp. 61-104. Kardasis, Vasilis, *Ελληνες ομογενείς στη νότιο Ρωσσία, 1775-1861 (Greeks in Southern Russia, 1775-1861)* (Athens, 1998), *passim*.

[2]A. B. Cunningham, ed., "The Journal of Christophe Aubin : A report on the Levant Trade in 1812", *Archivum Ottomanicum* (1983), Vol. 8, pp. 24-25. See also, Harlaftis, Gelina, *A History of Greek-Owned Shipping* (London, 1998), pp. 39-60.

[3]*Archives du Ministère des Affaires Étrangères*, Paris, Série CCC, Vol. 8, Consul David, Mémoire sur Scio, Chios, 1823-1825. Hereafter this archive will be cited as AMAE.

[4]*ANF*, AE Biii 242, Mémoire.

French consul in Trieste, however, proposed the abolition in Smyrna of this levy. The French, he argued, no longer had the monopoly of the carrying trade in the Mediterranean and Greek merchants could very easily charter another nation's ships. In fact, the British first lowered and then abolished altogether levy on specie carried in their ships on behalf of foreign merchants.[1] Buying with cash in the eastern Mediterranean at the time gave the purchaser a distinct advantage and a discount on the price. In 1811-1812, British cloth, coffee, sugar, spices, and dyes rose suddenly in price in the market of Smyrna due to the war and to large purchases made for Russia and Austria in cash and on credit, where these goods were much in demand.[2]

In the 1780s and 1790s, the Greeks used their status as beratlees (holders of Ottoman Imperial licenses that gave them special privileges allowing them to operate under the protection of a European Power) to their advantage at a time when the berats gave a valuable opening to international trade and particularly to British trade, which was the last to abandon protectionism.[3] Yet, by the early 1800s a lot of British trade with the eastern Mediterranean was carried out away from the confines of the Levant Company. British merchants were bringing British cloth to Malta or Corfu (after both islands came under British control) contracting Greek merchants, who were already established there, to send the cloth out to their partners, or associates, in the eastern Mediterranean, and predominantly in Smyrna.[4] They had already started to trade with Britain from the early 1800s, as the most dynamic economy of western Europe was in the process of abandoning monopoly regulations. In 1804, the Smyrna Factory of the Levant Company, which had hitherto held the exclusive right, officially at least, to British trade with the port, complained vigorously of the infiltration of Greek merchants into its business to the head of the Levant Company in London through their consul in Smyrna, F. Werry:

> ... from a thorough conviction that the limited trade allowed to beratlees only, will not prevent other Greeks from carrying on a simulated trade to England, on which supposition the merchant and the factory will be equally sufferers. It is needless to repeat what many gentlemen in Your Worshipful Company are so well informed of the decay of the opulent Dutch establishments here occasioned solely by the Greeks being permitted to trade to Holland, and the French who had granted a free trade to Marseilles....[5]

---

[1] *ANF*, AE Bi 1087, Consul Fraunnery, Trieste, 27 Jan. and 24 March 1789 to Minister, Paris.

[2] *ANF*, F12/1850 A, Fourcade, Smyrna, 14 April 1812 to Minister, Paris.

[3] *PRO*, SP 105/129, Consul Werry, Smyrna, 13 Aug. 1804 to Levant Company, London.

[4] PRO, SP 105/132, Consul Werry, Smyrna, 9 July 1809 to Levant Company. London; see J. Blow Williams, *British Commercial Policy and Trade Expansion, 1750-1850* (Oxford, 1972), pp. 364-365.

[5] PRO, SP 105/129, Consul Werry, Smyrna, 31 Jan. 1804 to Levant Company, London.

In London, Greek merchants came and settled from 1820 onwards. The first Greeks recorded as merchants, who had settled in London, were Eustratio Ralli & Co., and Ralli & Petrocochino, in 1820, operating from Billiter Square and Bond Street respectively.[1] These merchants traded mainly in Russian wheat. Their associates, established in Istanbul, also played a key role in this network of trade. In 1825 the Levant Company was abolished altogether leading to a free trade between Britain and the eastern Mediterranean.

The ability of the Ottoman Greeks also to break the predominance of western European nations, and principally of the French, in the carrying trade, not only within the eastern Mediterranean, but also between the eastern Mediterranean and western Europe, and at times within western European ports, was paramount in their process of capital accumulation. Undertaken mostly during wartime such carrying trade, though risky, was particularly lucrative. Neither the Armenian nor the Jewish mercantile communities ventured much in this sector, which may partly account for the greater economic growth of the Greeks.

Besides the western Anatolian coastline, where Turkish shippers were also present, the Greeks were particularly active in the carrying trade of the Italian ports with the Levant. In the 1760s, the French were the only nation involved in the carrying trade of Ancôna with the Ottoman Empire, although they had already suffered a serious setback during the Seven Years' War (1756-1763).[2] After the end of the Russo-Ottoman War (1768-1774), the Greeks were able to buy a large number of ships at low prices from Russian privateers.[3] With the outbreak of the American War of Independence, the French and the British carrying trade between Ancôna and the Levant fell into the hands of the Greeks. So that, whereas in 1777 there were only three or four Greek ships, by 1785, there were twenty to twenty-five Greek ships active in this route, which represented almost a third of the ships employed in this carrying trade.[4] However, Greek ships were small, on the average under 100 tons, whereas French ships were over 200 tons, with the result that the bulk of trade between Ancôna and the Levant was still carried by French

---

[1] *Robson's Improved London Directory... for 1820* (London, 1820), p. 471.

[2] *ANF*, AE Bi 271, États des batiments, 1756-1753. See also, Panzac, Daniel, *Commerce et navigation dans l'empire ottoman au XVIIIe siècle* (Istanbul, 1996), *passim*.

[3] *ANF*, AE Bi 861, Consul du Mensil, Mitylene, 25 March 1777 to Minister, Paris.

[4] *ANF*, AE Bi 859, Consul l'Allement, États des batiments, Messina, 27 Aug., 22 Oct., 10 Dec. 1785; 11 Feb., 8 April, 27 May, 17 June, 16 Sept., 21 Oct., 18 Nov. 1786; 6 Feb., 22 May, 18 Sept., 2 Oct. 1790; see also, Vlassopoulos, N. S., *Η ναυτιλία των Ιονίων Νήσων, 1700-1864 (The Merchant Marine of the Ionian Islands, 1700-1864)* (Athens, 1995), vol. I, pp. 108-147; vol. II, pp. 13-36.

ships.[1] At about the same time, Greek ships started to become prominent in the carrying trade of Genoa and Messina with the Levant.[2] In 1782, during the last year of the American War for Independence, trade between Messina and Marseilles was so severely disrupted as to make it unprofitable for the French to carry any goods in this route. The result was that Greek ships, as neutrals, took over part of this trade carrying foodstuffs and other raw materials from southern Italy to Marseilles and Lyons.[3] In 1784, Greeks in Messina were planning to hire French ships with capacities of 150 to 200 tons to expand their carrying trade since the Ottoman foodstuffs that Greek ships brought to Messina even after passing through the hands of several Italian and French merchants undersold similar goods sent through official channels to Marseilles. At the same time, the Court of Naples, which the port of Messina belonged to, was promising Greek merchants to lift some restrictions, which limited their trading activities.[4] The profits that they were able to amass were very considerable. Despite the fact that none of these ships were ever of a size similar to French carriers, their proprietors were able, within a short time, to move from the carrying trade to establishing businesses in the Italian port.[5] Greek ships were equally active in the carrying trade of Ancôna with the Levant.[6]

Expanding further at the beginning of the French Revolution, Greek shippers based in Venice carried Ottoman goods to Messina and sold them to French and Italian merchants there for distribution to Livorno, Malta, and Marseilles.[7] They took back to Smyrna, and other eastern Mediterranean ports, silk cloth and specie and from the 1790s onwards, from Malta in particular, they took to the Levant, British cloth.

During the Napoleonic Wars (1803-1815) Ottoman Greeks, many of them Chiots, from their bases in the eastern Mediterranean, and mainly in Smyrna, took advantage of their position as neutrals in the Anglo-French conflict and, with the right types of licenses issued by the British, navigated the Mediterranean. They formed partnerships with Psariots, Hydriots, and Spetsiots, the Chiots providing the capital to buy cargo and any other necessary expenses for the voyage, and the others furnishing the ships and the

[1] *ANF*, AE Bi 859, Consul l'Allement, Messina, 14 Jan. 1786 to Minister, Paris.
[2] *ANF*, AE Bi 168, Consul Benincasa, Ancôna, 13 Feb. 1784 to Minister, Paris.
[3] *ANF* AE Bi 859, Consul l'Allement, Messina, 22 May 1784 to Minister, Paris.
[4] *ANF*, AE Bi 168, Consul Benincasa, Ancôna, 19 Aug. 1785 and 30 July 1782 to Minister, Paris.
[5] *ANF*, AE Bi 859, Consul l'Allement, Messina, 9 Feb. 1782 to Minister, Paris.
[6] *ANF*, AE Bi 859, Consul l'Allement, Messina, 20 March 1784 to Minister, Paris.
[7] *ANF*, AE Bi 859, Consul l'Allement, Messina, 14 Jan. 1788 to Minister, Paris.

crew. They carried wheat and olive oil from western Anatolia, including Smyrna, the Aegean Archipelago islands, Istanbul, Salonica, and even Egypt as well as colonial goods to French and Italian ports. They were armed with two types of licenses from the British. One license covered them for carrying British and colonial goods, to be shown to the French, thus making it into a legitimate cargo, and the other license covered them for carrying French goods to be shown when intercepted by the British. When these voyages met with success the profits derived were very high, as both freight rates and the prices of the goods sold in the French or Italian ports were high. Yet there were times when these expeditions met with failure and then losses were equally substantial.[1]

If the carrying trade were the fastest growing economic activity of the Greeks, the initial capital for it was usually raised through privateering, and even piracy, that took place during the long series of wars that brought great upheaval to the Mediterranean from the first Russo-Ottoman War (1768-1774) to the end of the Napoleonic Wars in 1815. Both piracy and privateering were well organized.[2] Greek merchants lent their money "à l'hypothèque", to be repaid with interest, to finance a privateer's expedition.[3] The Second Russo-Ottoman War (1787-1792) led to a great flurry of Greek privateering in the Aegean Archipelago. Russian and Greek privateers, working together in the same ship, did not hesitate to attack even Greek ships, which had Ottoman flags, leaving their owners to seek compensation from the Russian Consul.[4] The Russian authorities condoned such actions. The Russian Consul at Trieste refused to seize privateers' prizes or to take inventory of the goods seized by a privateer from a captured Ottoman Greek ship.[5] Greek privateers continued their activities unabated during the French Revolutionary and Napoleonic Wars. So much so that no ship with anything valuable on board ventured unescorted in the Aegean Archipelago during that time.[6] It was not only the Aegean Archipelago that suffered from privateering, but also the routes between the Italian ports and the Levant and between the Italian ports and

---

[1]*AMAE*, CCC, Vol. 8, Consul David, Mémoire sur Scio, Chios, 1823.

[2]*ACCM*, MQ, 5-1, Consul David, Smyrna, 6 April 1825 to Minister, Paris. During the War of Greek Independence piracy and privateering became quite rife.

[3]*ANF*, AE Bi 1087, Consul Fraunnery, Trieste, 27 Jan. 1789 to Minister, Paris.

[4]*ANF*, AE Bi 1087, Consul Fraunnery, Trieste, 30 Jan. 1789 to Minister, Paris.

[5]*ANF*, AE Bi 1087, Consul Fraunnery, Trieste, 7 Feb. 1789 to Minister, Paris.

[6]*PRO*, SP 105/128, Consul Werry, Smyrna, 1 Feb. 1802 to Levant Company, London: see also, SP 105/132, Consul Werry, Smyrna, 20 Nov. 1809 and 10 March 1810 to Levant Company, London and SP 105/133, Consul Werry, Smyrna, 12 July 1812 to Levant Company, London.

France. Finally, Greek merchants were active in marketing the captured goods in the eastern Mediterranean, including such large ports as Smyrna.[1]

In addition to privateers, North African pirates were particularly active in the whole of the Mediterranean throughout this period attacking all ships.[2] The Greeks were able to overcome them by obtaining, from the British, Mediterranean passes that exempted them from seizure, if intercepted by these pirates. The British obtained such passes by paying subsidies to North African states. These pirates were not stopped till after the end of the Napoleonic Wars.

In conclusion the Greeks, based principally in Smyrna but elsewhere in the eastern Mediterranean, too, taking advantage of the freer economies of the Italian ports and of the liberal policies of the Dutch in order to enter international trade, and of the monetary difficulties of the Ottoman economy in order to speculate, amassed considerable capital accumulation and expertise. Moreover, taking full advantage of the favorable international economic conjuncture, and of the military confrontations, that locked the major European Powers in combat with each other and weakened their economic hold in the area, the Greeks advanced their activities. In so doing, they displayed extreme agility and alertness in finding new venues to trade, in expanding to new sectors, such as the carrying trade, or privateering, however risky these might be, and to different ports, usually maintaining a family link with the eastern Mediterranean. All this led them, by the early nineteenth century, to considerable commercial success.

---

[1]Themeli-Katifori, Despina, *Η Δίωξις της Πειρατείας* (Ph. D. thesis, University of Athens, 1973), vol. I, pp. 40-62. See also Hatzioannou, Maria-Christina, "*Οι εμποροκαπετάνιοι μετὰ την Επανασταση*" ("Captains-cum-Merchants after the Revolution"), in *Η Επανάσταση του 1821 (The Revolution of 1821)* (Athens, 1994), pp. 157-172.

[2]*ANF*, AE Bi 859, Consul l'Allement, Messina, 17 May 1783 to Minister, Paris; see also, PRO, SP 105/135, Consul Werry, Smyrna, 17 Aug. 1816 to Levant Company, London.

LES RÉSEAUX COMMERCIAUX ET L'INTÉGRATION AU MARCHÉ MONDIAL DE LA MÉDITERRANÉE ORIENTALE, UN APERÇU HISTORIQUE

Pendant la dernière partie de la période ottomane, c'est-à-dire, de la 2ème moitié du XVIIIe siècle au début du XXe siècle, la région de la Méditerranée orientale fut insérée, surtout à travers le commerce extérieur et ses liens avec le marché international, dans le processus de mondialisation. Car bien que le commerce international ne fût pas le seul facteur dans ce processus, il fut le plus important. L'insertion dans le marché international de la Méditerranée orientale, résultat important de ce processus, a surtout contribué à l'expansion du marché externe ainsi qu'à l'accroissement et à la plus grande unification du marché extérieur ottoman. En outre, ce processus influença, à la fois, plusieurs secteurs de l'économie régionale comme l'organisation du secteur commercial, la production agricole ou le développement du secteur bancaire. Cependant, il faut aussi constater que la mondialisation de la région avança au détriment, peut-on dire, de la régionalisation. Car quoiqu'ils fussent formés des noyaux économiques régionaux, les liens de tels noyaux furent parfois plus étroits avec le marché international qu'avec d'autres marchés plus proches, soit ailleurs dans la Méditerranée orientale, soit dans la Mer noire. Par exemple, en prenant le noyau d'İzmir, comprenant la ville, les îles égéennes ainsi que la côte occidentale et une partie de l'Anatolie centrale, on constate que les liens économiques de ce noyau avec Marseille ou Londres furent beaucoup plus avancés et complexes que ceux avec Syros, en Grèce ou Alep en Syrie. En plus, les liens de la ville avec d'autres marchés régionaux, en dehors de son noyau, furent souvent plus influencés par les besoins du marché international que par les besoins économiques autonomes de la région, bien que ce phénomène tendit à diminuer vers la fin de la période ottomane. En outre, les liens avec le marché extérieur furent parfois développés au détriment des liens autonomes à l'intérieur du marché anatolien.[1] Par exemple, jusqu'à la fin de la période ottomane, İzmir continua à dominer les échanges commerciaux de la côte anatolienne occidentale et des îles égéennes avec l'économie mondiale.

---

[1]Par exemple, les liens économiques de Kütahya avec İzmir — guidés plutôt par les besoins du marché extérieur — furent développés au détriment des liens antérieurs du centre anatolien avec Bursa. Public Record Office, Londres, FO 78/570, Consul D. Sandison, Bursa, 28 fév. 1844 à Foreign Office, Londres. Par la suite l'abréviation de PRO sera utilisée pour les fonds britanniques ainsi que l'abréviation de FO pour le Ministère des Affaires Étrangères de Grande-Bretagne.

Car malgré l'existence de liens directs de ces lieux avec le marché international, ces derniers ne furent jamais assez forts pour éliminer complètement le rôle d'intermédiaire d'İzmir.[1] Sous de telles conditions, et à cause d'autres raisons aussi, pendant toute la période ottomane, l'unification totale du marché intérieur n'a pas été réalisée malgré le niveau avancé du développement du marché.

Or, nous nous proposons d'analyser le processus de mondialisation par l'exemple du nucleus économique d'İzmir et de son *hinterland*, au sens américain du terme, et à travers l'organisation du commerce et des réseaux commerciaux qui furent constitués principalement pour servir le marché extérieur. Cependant il faut noter que le commerce intérieur se servait aussi de ces réseaux. Nous analyserons aussi les activités et les stratégies des agents économiques — les marchands ottomans ainsi qu'occidentaux — dans ces réseaux et les chaînes qui y sont créées pour la circulation des marchandises, des capitaux et de l'information.

Dans un aperçu historique, on commencera par la seconde moitié du XVIIIe siècle, période-clé pour la phase initiale d'intégration, non seulement de l'Anatolie occidentale, y compris İzmir, mais de la région de la Méditerranée orientale, en général, au marché mondial. Cependant İzmir, et son hinterland, constituent un bon exemple pour illustrer le processus de mondialisation puisqu'ils jouèrent un rôle spécial dans l'intégration de l'Empire au marché international. Car İzmir ne fut pas seulement un centre commercial important dans la région, mais elle fut, en effet, le centre le plus important pour l'Empire dans ce processus.[2] Les fonctions politiques, administratives ainsi que financières d'Istanbul, sa rivale naturelle, empêchèrent le capital de jouer un rôle primordial dans ce processus, pour la Méditerranée orientale. Par contre, en développant des réseaux commerciaux plus étendus et plus complexes, non seulement concernant le commerce extérieur de l'Empire ottoman mais aussi en ce qui concerne le commerce intérieur, İzmir devint une sorte de plaque tournante pour la circulation des marchandises au-dedans ainsi

---

[1] *Parliamentary Papers, Accounts & Papers*, Londres, 1900, CVII, Rapport commercial pour les années 1897-1899, p. 48; voir aussi, *ibid.*, Londres, 1902, CX, Rapport commercial pour l'année 1901, p. 14.

[2] Pour le développement d'İzmir , le plus grand port de l'Empire pendant le XVIIIe et le début du XIXe siècles, voir Elena Frangakis-Syrett, *The Commerce of Smyrna in the Eighteenth Century, 1700-1820*, Athènes, 1992.

qu'au dehors de l'Empire.[1] Ce processus avança d'une façon perceptible à partir de la seconde moitié du XVIIIe siècle pour arriver à un apogée au début du XIXe siècle. A la fin des guerres napoléoniennes, İzmir avait acquis une position de domination extraordinaire dans le commerce maritime ainsi que terrestre, extérieur ainsi qu'intérieur, de la Méditerranée orientale ; ce qui fut noté par un observateur perspicace, Félix de Beaujour: «Smyrne n'est pas seulement l'échelle qui fait le plus grand commerce avec l'Europe, c'est celle encore qui fait le plus grand commerce avec la Turquie. La Thrace lui envoie ses laines par Enos, la Macédoine ses tabacs par Cavalla et Salonique, la Grèce et l'Archipel leurs huiles et leurs vins, Brousse ses soies, Ankara ses fils de chèvre, Kütahya, Konya et Adalya leurs laines de chevron, leurs galles et leurs graines jaunes et toute l'Asie Mineure ses cotons. Alep est la seule place turque qui distribue les même marchandises que Smyrne et que les vend en concurrence avec elle aux caravanes de Diyarbakır, de Mossul et de Bagdad".[2]

Du point de vue de densité et de la complexité des réseaux commerciaux et du volume des transactions réalisées, il y a eu peu d'échelles qui purent lui faire concurrence: İskenderun et Alep, ou Alexandrie au XVIIIe siècle et au XIXe siècle, Istanbul et, plus tard, Salonique.[3] En effet, ce fut seulement pendant les dernières décennies du XIXe siècle qu'İzmir commença à céder, relativement, son rôle primordial à l'intégration de l'Empire dans l'économie internationale. La fin de la prédominance commerciale, presque exclusive, d'İzmir dans la Méditerranée orientale fut le résultat de plusieurs facteurs: l'un des plus importants fut le rôle croissant du capital financier, ottoman et surtout occidental, dans le secteur bancaire ainsi qu'industriel de l'économie ottomane. Istanbul fut l'hôtesse par excellence de ce capital comme ce fut auparavant le cas d'İzmir pour le capital commercial, occidental ainsi qu'ottoman. Cependant le commerce continua à être un des secteurs principaux de l'économie ottomane, ce qui permit à İzmir de continuer son rôle important dans cette économie ainsi que dans le processus de mondialisation de la Méditerranée orientale.

---

[1]Archives Nationales de France, Paris, AE Bi 1053. Consul Charles de Peyssonnel, İzmir, 22 Nov. 1751. Par la suite, l'abréviation de ANF sera utilisée pour ce fonds d'archives françaises. Voir aussi, Archives de la Chambre de Commerce de Marseille, I, 26 28. États estimatifs des marchandises venant du Levant et de Barbarie (1700-1789): I, 19-20. États des marchandises envoyées au Levant et en Barbarie (1749-1789). Par la suite, l'abréviation de ACCM sera utilisée pour ce fonds d'archives françaises.

[2]ANF, AE Biii 243, Félix de Beaujour, Inspection générale du Levant, İzmir, 5 juillet 1817. En ce qui concerne les activités commerciales d'Alep au XVIIIe siècle, voir Bruce Masters, *The Origins of Western Dominance in the Middle East*, New York, 1988, pp. 60-68, 146-164.

[3]Pour le XVIIIe siècle, voir Frangakis-Syrett, *The Commerce* ... pp. 257-260; pour le XIXe siècle voir Charles Issawi, *The Economic History of Turkey, 1800-1914*, Chicago, 1980, pp. 82-83, 103-104, 110-112.

ÉVOLUTION HISTORIQUE D'INTÉGRATION

Or, nous nous proposons d'illustrer l'évolution historique du processus d'intégration de la Méditerranée orientale dans le marché international en prenant l'exemple du commerce du coton. Le coton joua un rôle d'importance primordiale pendant la phase initiale de ce processus, notamment durant la seconde moitié du XVIIIe siècle. Pendant cette période il y a eu une croissance économique considérable dans les pays d'Europe occidentale, ce qui se manifesta par l'expansion de leurs industries textiles et par leurs importations de matières premières pour cette industrie. Alors le coton anatolien est devenu la matière première ottomane la plus recherchée par les marchés européens.[1] En effet, vers la fin du XVIIIe siècle, plus le processus d'intégration avança, plus cela fut principalement à cause du coton et du coton en laine qui dominèrent les contacts commerciaux de la Méditerranée orientale avec les marchés européens.[2] Bien que le coton fût exporté de toute la Méditerranée orientale ce fut İzmir qui, pour plusieures raisons, notamment grâce à ses réseaux commerciaux déjà en place, put avancer le plus l'intégration de la région, en exportant le plus grand volume de coton et ainsi en tirant les plus grands avantages de cette conjoncture du marché international.[3]

Au début du XIXe siècle, il y a eu une baisse considérable des exportations du coton ottoman sur les marchés européens, résultat de la concurrence américaine et de l'invention du *coton gin*.[4] Témoin du progrès d'intégration et du degré du développement économique déjà achevés par la région, fut le fait qu'İzmir et son *hinterland* purent s'adapter à cette nouvelle conjoncture. Tous les réseaux du commerce du coton — cultivateurs, banquiers privés, intermédiaires, exportateurs — furent remplacés par ceux du commerce des raisins, des figues, des noix de galles et des garances qui

---

[1]Elena Frangakis-Syrett, "The Trade of Cotton and Cloth in İzmir: from the Second Half of the Eighteenth Century to the Early Nineteenth Century", dans Çağlar Keyder & Faruk Tabak, éds., *Landholding and Commercial Agriculture in the Middle East,* Albany, NY, 1991, pp. 97-104.

[2]Frangakis-Syrett, *The Commerce...,* pp. 231-241; voir aussi, Charles Carrière & Michel Morineau, "Draps du Languedoc et commerce du Levant au XVIIIe siècle", *Revue d'Histoire Économique et Sociale*, t. 46, 1968, pp. 108-121.

[3]Elena Frangakis-Syrett, "The Ottoman Port of İzmir in the Eighteenth and Early Nineteenth Centuries, 1695-1820", *Revue de l'Occident Musulman et de la Méditerranée,* No. 39/1, 1985, pp. 160-162; voir aussi, N. Svoronos, *Le Commerce de Salonique au XVIIIe siècle*, Paris, 1956, pp. 252-253.

[4]En 1820, étant donné que la France avait déjà commencé à importer du coton américain, le coton anatolien représenta seulement 12%, en valeur, des exportations totales d'İzmir à Marseille. Archives du Ministère des Affaires Étrangères, Paris, CCC, t. 35, jan.-juin 1820 et *ibid.*, t. 36, juillet-déc. 1820. Par la suite, l'abréviation AMAE sera utilisée pour ce fonds d'archives françaises. Il en fut de même pour les autres marchés européens où la demande pour le coton anatolien baissa aussi. AMAE, t. 43, 1832; voir aussi, Orhan Kurmuş, "The cotton famine and its effects on the Ottoman Empire", dans Huri Islamoğlu-İnan, éd., *The Ottoman Empire and the World-Economy,* Cambridge, 1987, pp. 160-161.

devinrent, pendant la première moitié du XIXe siècle, les exportations principales de la région.[1] La capacité de l'économie régionale de réagir au marché international se manifesta encore une fois pendant la Guerre civile américaine (1861-1865), quand la croissance de la demande du coton anatolien sur le marché mondial mena, encore une fois, à l'augmentation de la production du coton dans la région.[2] A la fin de la guerre, pendant que la région essayait de s'adapter à la nouvelle conjoncture où le coton anatolien ne fut pas, encore une fois, autant recherché qu'auparavant, il y eut une crise économique régionale. Bien qu'elle fût le résultat de plusieurs facteurs, certes la surproduction du coton contribua à cette crise.[3] Cependant l'évidence du succès de cette adaptation fut le niveau de développement économique atteint par İzmir et son *hinterland* au cours du dernier quart du XIXe et au début du XXe siècles.[4] Au cours des années 1900, pendant qu'İzmir continuait à exporter une certaine quantité de coton, tous les changements de prix de cette denrée sur le marché mondial furent enregistrés tout de suite sur le marché d'İzmir. Cela manifestait le degré de mondialisation de la région, dont les chaînes directes de communication et les échanges faisaient partie, qui se réalisa vers la fin de la période ottomane.[5]

LES RÉSEAUX COMMERCIAUX

Pour mieux comprendre le processus d'intégration, il faut bien analyser les réseaux commerciaux qui, on le constate, font partie du processus en même temps qu'ils en sont le résultat. Étant donné que l'expansion du marché ottoman, extérieur ainsi qu'intérieur, fit partie du processus d'intégration, il faut signaler la contribution importante de ces réseaux à cette expansion. Commençant par la phase initiale d'intégration, il faut aussi constater le rôle très important du capital occidental dans ces réseaux. Cela fut le résultat, en partie, de la position privilégiée des marchands européens qui, pendant la seconde moitié du XVIIIe siècle, établis dans des villes comme İzmir, Istanbul

[1]ANF, AE Biii 415, Importation et Exportation de Smyrne, 1858; voir aussi Lewis Farley, *The resources of Turkey considered with a special reference to the profitable investment of capital in the Ottoman Empire,* Londres, 1862, pp. 94-95; Reşat Kasaba, *The Ottoman Empire and the World Economy,* Albany, NY, 1988, pp. 122-123.

[2]Donald Quataert, "The Commercialization of Agriculture in Ottoman Turkey", *International Journal of Turkish Studies*, t. I, 1980, pp. 38-55; voir aussi, Kurmuş, "The Cotton famine...", pp. 164-165.

[3]PRO, FO 78/1888, Consul Cumberbatch, İzmir, 27 mars 1865 à Earl Russell, FO, Londres; FO 78/1992, Consul Cumberbatch, İzmir, 4 juin et 16 juillet 1867 à Lord Stanley, FO, Londres.

[4]Elena Frangakis-Syrett, "L'économie de l'Anatolie occidentale, 1908-1914" dans M. Bazin, S. Kançal, R. Pérez et J. Thobie, éds. *La Turquie entre trois mondes*, Istanbul, 1998, pp. 239-248.

[5]AMAE, NS, t. 380, Rapports commerciaux d'İzmir pour les années 1900.

ou Alep, purent effectuer la plus grande partie du commerce de l'Empire avec les marchés occidentaux.[1] Les Européens, et en particulier les Anglais et les Français, purent garder leur position privilégiée jusqu'à l'établissement du régime de laissez-faire, au début du XIXe siècle, qui libéralisa les échanges commerciaux entre l'Empire et tous les pays d'Europe, y compris la France et la Grande-Bretagne. A part le commerce avec l'Europe, les Occidentaux jouèrent aussi un rôle très important dans le transport maritime, non seulement entre l'Empire ottoman et l'Europe, mais aussi dans le cabotage, grand et petit, qui relia les divers ports de l'Empire. Le cabotage, appelé aussi caravane maritime à cette époque-là, fut un moyen très efficace de lier les marchés de différentes régions de l'Empire et les Européens y jouèrent un rôle très important en transportant les denrées des marchands ottomans sur leurs propres bateaux.[2] Certes ils ne furent pas les seuls à naviguer alors en Méditerranée orientale : les Ottomans pratiquèrent aussi le cabotage.[3] Cependant les Européens, et les Français en particulier, pour plusieures raisons, dominèrent le cabotage ottoman au XVIIIe siècle. D'Istanbul à Alexandrie et jusqu'à la côte syro-palestinienne ou d'İzmir jusqu'aux ports de l'Afrique du Nord, les circuits du transport maritime, que les Occidentaux ont ainsi créés, contribuèrent à la cohésion et l'accroissement du marché intérieur ottoman.[4] En outre, l'accroissement du cabotage, qui se réalisa pendant la

---

[1]Voir, par exemple, Elena Frangakis-Syrett, "Trade between the Ottoman Empire and western Europe: the case of İzmir in the eighteenth century", *New Perspectives on Turkey,* t. 2/1, 1988, pp. 4-10; *idem, The Commerce...*, pp. 75-103; Svoronos, *Le commerce...*, pp. 141-168; Edhem Eldem, "Le commerce français d'Istanbul au XVIIIe siècle", doctorat de l'Université de Provence, 1988, ch. 2; R. Davis, *Aleppo and Devonshire Square. English Traders in the Levant in the Eighteenth Century,* 1967, *passim.*

[2]En ce qui concerne le commerce intérieur maritime ottoman, ou cabotage, voir, par exemple, Daniel Panzac, "Négociants ottomans et capitaines français: la caravane maritime en Crète au XVIIIe siècle" dans H. Batu & J.-L. Bacqué-Grammont, éds., *L'Empire ottoman, la République de Turquie et la France,* Istanbul-Paris, 1986, pp. 99-118; André Raymond, *Artisans et Commerçants du Caire au XVIIIe siècle*, Damas, 1974, t. II, pp. 184-192; Yolande Triantafyllidou-Baladié, "Transports maritimes et concurrence en Méditerranée orientale au XVIIIe siècle: L'exemple de la Crète", *Actes du IIe colloque international d'histoire,* Athènes, 1985, t. I, pp. 19-37; Maria Efthymiou-Hadzilacou, *Rhodes et sa région élargie au XVIIIe siècle: les activités portuaires,* Athènes, 1988, pp. 193-228; Elena Frangakis-Syrett, "The Coastal Trade of the Ottoman Empire, mid-eighteenth to the early nineteenth centuries" dans J. Armstrong & A. Kunz, éds., *Coastal Shipping and the European Economy, 1750-1980*, Mainz-am-Rhein, 2002, pp. 131-149.

[3]En ce qui concerne les activités des armateurs ottomans, y compris des armateurs turcs, voir par exemple, PRO, SP 105/188, Sir Robert Ainslie, ambassadeur britannique à Istanbul, 1 & 16 mai 1782; 3 fév. & 2 déc. 1783; 27 jan. 1786.

[4]Pour plus de détails sur ces circuits maritimes, voir par exemple, Daniel Panzac, "Affréteurs ottomans et capitaines français à Alexandrie: la caravane maritime en Méditerranée au milieu du XVIIIe siècle", *Revue de l'Occident Musulman et de la Méditerranée*, No. 34, 1982, pp. 23-39; *idem,* "Le commerce du Tripoli de Barbarie dans la seconde moitié du XVIIIe siècle", *Revue d'histoire maghrebine,* t. 69-70, 1993, pp. 141-167; Amnon Cohen, "Ottoman Rule and the Re-Emergence of the Coast of Palestine, 17th-18th Centuries", *Revue de l'Occident Musulman et de la Méditerranée,* No. 39/1, 1985, pp. 163-175; Rhoads Murphey, "Provisioning Istanbul: the State and Subsistence in the Early Modern Middle East", *Food and Foodways*, t. 2, 1988, p. 253.

seconde moitié du XVIIIe siècle, fut aussi témoin de la croissance économique, qui se manifesta dans l'Empire ottoman comme dans d'autres régions de la Méditerranée pendant cette période-là et qui contribua au processus de mondialisation de la région. Alors, l'importance des Européens se trouve dans toute la gamme des activités qu'ils entreprirent, en faisant le commerce, la banque ou le transport maritime et les réseaux qu'ils créèrent ainsi.

Or, prenons le cas typique d'un négociant Anglais établi à İzmir.[1] Dès le début, ce qui est frappant c'est que ce négociant ne fut pas le correspondant d'une maison de commerce à Londres seulement, mais en effet, de plusieures maisons. Ces dernières purent être établies soit à Londres soit ailleurs en Grande-Bretagne, ou bien hors du pays dans des endroits bien reliés au marché britannique comme Lisbonne, Livourne ou Malte. En même temps, la maison de Londres eut, elle aussi, plusieurs correspondants, et pas seulement le négociant d'İzmir, qui étaient établis dans les différentes échelles de l'Empire. En plus, il ne fut pas la seule maison à en faire autant. Par exemple, vers la fin du XVIIIe et au début du XIXe siècles, la maison internationale de commerce et de banque de Roux Frères, établie à Marseille, eut un vaste et complexe réseau d'agents, qui fut vraiment global, y compris de plusieurs agents aux grandes échelles de la Méditerranée orientale.[2]

Ainsi chaque maison en Europe eut tout un réseau de correspondants qui leur était propre, établis dans les grandes échelles de l'Empire ainsi qu'ailleurs dans la Méditerranée, pour faire circuler l'information nécessaire concernant les prix ou la disponibilité du marché ottoman, pour la vente des denrées européennes ou coloniales, ainsi que pour l'achat de matières premières et d'autres produits de l'Empire destinés aux marchés européens. Ainsi, si le marchand Anglais d'İzmir n'arrivait pas à effectuer ses achats de soie pour sa maison-mère, à cause des prix défavorables à Londres par rapport aux prix courants d'İzmir, ou pour d'autres raisons, il pouvait contacter un autre correspondant de sa maison-mère. Par exemple, il pouvait contacter celui d'Alep pour qu'il achetât la soie, si bien sûr la conjoncture du marché à Alep était plus favorable que celle d'İzmir. En plus, par un système efficace de communication, le négociant d'Alep pouvait aussi s'informer s'il y avait un navire disponible dans une échelle proche, par exemple à İskenderun ou à

[1]Pour l'exemple d'un tel négociant, d'après des papers privés, voir Elena Frangakis-Syrett, "Trade Practices in Aleppo in the Middle of the Eighteenth Century. The case of a British Merchant", *Revue du Monde Musulman et de la Méditerranée,* No. 62/4, 1991, pp. 123-132.

[2]Par exemple, ACCM, LIX/735, R. Franchetti, İzmir, 13 août 1788 à Roux Frères, Marseille, LIX/750, Denis Rolland et Cie, İzmir, 19 mars 1790 à Roux Frères, Marseille.

Chypre, pour envoyer à Londres les achats effectués pour le compte du négociant d'İzmir.[1]

Pour que le négociant d'Alep pût effectuer les achats, le correspondant d'İzmir devait aussi lui envoyer les fonds nécessaires. Cela se réalisait par l'intermédiaire d'un négociant-banquier à Istanbul, qui était lui aussi membre du circuit des correspondants de la maison à Londres. A son tour, ce dernier eut à sa disposition tout un réseau monétaire informel appartenant à des hommes d'affaires établis dans des grandes échelles de la région, y compris Alep et İzmir, pour la circulation des fonds dans l'Empire ainsi qu'entre l'Empire et l'Occident.[2] Une telle circulation des fonds était effectuée, plus souvent par la voie de lettre de change ou de notes de crédit; cependant d'autres moyens, des espèces ou des diamants, pouvaient aussi être utilisés. Les réseaux financiers pour la circulation des lettres de change, ainsi que pour d'autres instruments de paiement, comprirent des Occidentaux ainsi que des Ottomans — parmi ces derniers se trouvèrent des entrepreneurs, des banquiers privés, des fonctionnaires et d'autres membres de l'élite ottomane. Les circuits des lettres de change reliant la Méditerranée orientale — particulièrement Istanbul et İzmir — avec de multiples centres financiers européens, bien que souvent ignorés dans l'historiographie,[3] contribuèrent fortement à l'intégration de l'Empire au monde financier européen de l'époque. Car ces circuits financiers, dont le fonctionnement fut plutôt influencé par les forces du marché, contribuèrent aussi à l'approvisionnement du marché avec des fonds et ainsi à l'allégement partiel du manque de numéraire de l'économie régionale. La rareté du numéraire fut un phénomène assez répandu dans l'économie ottomane pendant toute notre période et son allégement, même partiel, fut très important. Ainsi ces réseaux financiers jouèrent un rôle décisif dans le processus de mondialisation de la région.

---

[1]PRO, SP 110/36, Th. Lansdown, Alep, 22 déc. 1759 à M. Lee White, İzmir.

[2]Elena Frangakis-Syrett, "Local and Western Traders in the Ottoman Middle East: İzmir and Aleppo in the Eighteenth Century", communication présentée à la conférence internationale de Middle East Studies Association à Phoenix, Arizona, 19-22 novembre 1994.

[3]Exception à la règle sont les travaux des C. Carrière, F. Rebuffat et M. Courdurié. Par exemple, F. Rebuffat & M. Courdurié, *Marseille et le négoce monétaire international*, Marseille, 1966; C. Carrière, "Réflexions sur le problème des monnaies et des métaux précieux en Méditerranée orientale au XVIIIe siècle", *Commerce de gros, commerce de détail dans les pays méditerranéens*, Nice, 1976, pp. 1-20. Voir aussi, Edhem Eldem, "La circulation de la lettre de change entre la France et Constantinople au XVIIIe siècle" dans H. Batu & J.-L. Bacqué-Grammont, éds., *L'empire ottoman, la République de Turquie et la France*, Istanbul-Paris, 1986, pp. 87-97; Elena Frangakis-Syrett, "The Balance of Trade and Balance of Payments Between İzmir and France, 1700-1789", *Communications présentées au Ve Congrès International des Études du sud-est Européen*, Athènes, 1985, pp. 127-138 et *idem*, "The Ottoman Monetary System in the Long Eighteenth Century", communication présentée au colloque international de l'Institut Français d'Études Anatoliennes à Istanbul, 28-30 novembre 1997.

Par ces réseaux — commerciaux ainsi que financiers — tout un système d'échanges continuels, emmêlés, superposés s'est créé, dont le fonctionnement présupposait et renforçait une circulation efficace et croissante d'informations qui, à son tour, jouait un rôle important vers l'expansion du marché extérieur ainsi qu'intérieur de la région — résultat ainsi que symptôme de l'intégration de la région dans le marché international.

Bien que l'association avec les maisons de commerce en France, en Hollande ou en Angleterre, ne fût pas forcément la même pour chaque négociant du Levant, il y avait des ressemblances. Car ces négociants agirent plus ou moins comme des agents ou des correspondants de maisons à l'Occident. Le partage des profits varia selon les termes du contrat entre le correspondant et sa maison-mère. De plus, les négociants au Levant purent faire des affaires pour leur propre compte. Le contrôle de l'agent par sa maison-mère fut assuré de plusieures façons. Citons-en quelques-unes: les relations personnelles, un consensus commun partagé par tous les membres du réseau, sur la mentalité et les risques acceptables dans les activités commerciales ou usuraires qui furent pratiquées au Levant, ainsi que par toute une stratégie de surveillance assidue. Cette dernière consista en une surveillance continuelle et détaillée des comptes du négociant du Levant pour chaque affaire conclue, ou en plaçant des limites strictes au niveau des prix des marchandises traitées dans chaque affaire, pour pouvoir ainsi mieux contrôler les marges du profit.[1] Bien sûr, il y eut aussi la surveillance exercée par les autorités nationales sur chaque communauté européenne de négociants, qui varia selon la politique suivie par chaque État.[2]

Or, en ce qui concerne les marchands ottomans — l'autre groupe des acteurs économiques importants dans la région — on constate qu'ils ne laissèrent pas le champ libre aux Occidentaux. De plus en plus, au cours de la seconde moitié du XVIIIe siècle et à travers les économies les plus libérales de l'Occident, comme celle de Hollande ou l'Italie, les Ottomans purent participer au commerce international de la région, en utilisant plusieures stratégies. Par exemple, ils se spécialisèrent dans le commerce de certaines denrées comme les draps manufacturés en Europe: tout d'abord, ils s'occupèrent de leur distribution sur le marché ottoman;[3] plus tard, ils élargirent leurs opérations

---

[1]PRO, SP 110/37, Th. Lansdown, Alep, 5 nov. 1761 à S. Touchet, Londres.

[2]PRO, SP 105/211, Règlements de la *Levant Company*, Londres, 1744; ANF, Marine B/7, 435, İzmir, 1740; voir aussi, Frangakis-Syrett, *The Commerce...*, pp. 76-103.

[3]Algemeen Rijksarschief, 349, Frémeaux, van Lennep & Enslie, 29 juin 1782 à van Haften dans J. G. Nanninga, éd., *Bronnen tot de Geschiedenis van den Levantschen Handel*, 'S-Gravenhage, 1966, pp. 339-341. Par la suite l'abréviation ARA sera utilisée pour ce fonds hollandais.

pour inclure l'importation de ces draps de l'Occident, particulièrement de Hollande.[1] Les marchands ottomans se spécialisèrent aussi dans certains marchés comme ceux de Livourne ou d'Ancône, en Italie, qui furent des entrepôts importants pour le commerce du Levant avec l'Europe.[2] Vers la fin du XVIIIe siècle, ils y créèrent leurs propres agences de commerce pour étendre leurs opérations commerciales avec la Méditerranée orientale. Néanmoins, pendant toute notre période, leur plus grand atout fut la domination des réseaux commerciaux intérieurs de l'empire ottoman.[3]

LE LIBÉRALISME DES ÉCHANGES

A la fin du XVIIIe et au début du XIXe siècles, il y eut des développements importants concernant tant les réseaux que le processus d'intégration de la région. Le changement le plus important fut tout d'abord l'ouverture des marchés protectionnistes européens, comme ceux de France et de Grande-Bretagne, aux réseaux commerciaux ottomans.[4] Or, suivant la Révolution industrielle, des négociants ottomans purent s'établir en Occident, y compris en France et en Grande-Bretagne, pour y faire le commerce avec le Levant. Ils réussirent dans ce but en installant, à la fois, différents membres de leurs familles dans différents centres économiques d'Europe, ce qui leur donna accès, en même temps, à plusieurs réseaux commerciaux et financiers occidentaux. En peu de temps, ils se sont ainsi étendus dans toute la Méditerranée, orientale et occidentale, ainsi que dans la Mer Noire, où ils établirent, soit des agences, soit des maisons indépendantes de commerce.[5] Les chefs, et parfois le personnel aussi, de ces maisons de commerce et agences furent liés entre eux par des liens forts de parentèle, non seulement d'amitié, étant tous originaires de mêmes endroits de la Méditerranée orientale.[6] Ils

---

[1]ARA, 120, Chargé d'Affaires Testa à Hoschepied, 19 fév. 1818 dans Nanninga, *Bronnen*, pp. 950-951.

[2]PRO, SP 105/132, Consul Werry, İzmir, 27 sept. 1809 et 4 oct. 1810 à Levant Company, Londres; voir aussi, ANF, AE Biii 243, Renseignements sur le commerce du Levant, Livourne, 1825.

[3]Par exemple, ANF, Bi 1052, Consul Charles de Peyssonnel, İzmir, 29 jan. 1749; PRO, FO 195/1161, Hadkinson, Merrylees & Company, İzmir, 11 juillet et 26 sept. 1878 au Consul Reade, İzmir.

[4]ANF, AE Biii 242, Commerce du Levant, 1814.

[5]S.E. Fairlie, "The Anglo-Russian Trade, 1815-1861", (doctorat de l'Université de Londres, 1955), pp. 261-291.

[6]Un bon exemple de ce phénomène furent liens de parentèle parmi les entrepreneurs de l'île egéenne de Chios. Pour plus de détails sur cela, voir Elena Frangakis-Syrett, *Οι Χιώτες έμποροι στίς διεθνείς συναλλαγές, 1751-1830* Les négociants de Chios dans le commerce international, *1751-1830*, Athènes, 1992, *passim*, Olga Katsiardi-Hering, *Η παροικία της Τεργέστης, 1751-1830 (La communauté grecque de Trieste, 1751-1830)*, Athènes, 1986, t. II, pp. 579-596. Voir aussi, Marie-Carmen Smyrnelis, "Une société hors de soi. Identités et relations sociales à Smyrne aux XVIIIe et XIXe siècles" (thèse de doctorat, École des Hautes Études en Sciences Sociales, Paris, 2000).

purent ainsi développer leurs propres réseaux qui furent superposés et emmêlés aux réseaux occidentaux, tant en Europe que dans l'Empire ottoman. Leur connaissance détaillée du marché intérieur ottoman et leurs réseaux d'agents à l'intérieur de l'Empire furent importants pour le succès de leurs opérations. Ce succès, à son tour, contribua à l'insertion de l'Empire ottoman dans le marché mondial.

Un autre développement, aussi important pour le processus d'intégration de la région, fut l'installation à l'intérieur du pays d'Occidentaux qui jusqu'au début du XIXe siècle s'établirent, dans la majorité des cas, seulement dans les grandes villes-ports de l'Empire. Or, ils purent créer leurs propres réseaux à l'intérieur de l'Empire. D'ailleurs, dans la majorité des cas, ils ne furent plus des agents de firmes occidentales, mais des chefs de maisons de commerce indépendantes, fondées au Levant ou en l'Occident, qui participèrent ainsi au commerce international de la région.[1] Certes, dans toutes leurs activités commerciales, ils rencontrèrent la concurrence des marchands locaux. Selon leurs moyens, les Occidentaux eurent tout un réseau d'agents et de sous-agents. Ces derniers furent le plus souvent des locaux; cependant ils purent être aussi des Occidentaux.[2] Leurs opérations *à l'intérieur du pays* y comprirent des contacts directs avec les cultivateurs ainsi qu'avec des réseaux commerciaux locaux pour la vente des marchandises importées ou l'achat des marchandises ottomanes ainsi que pour leur expédition vers le marché mondial.[3]

La pénétration économique à l'intérieur du pays, par le capital commercial occidental, joua un rôle important pour l'intégration de la région dans le marché international.[4] Cette pénétration fut le résultat de la croissance économique des pays de l'Occident, qui se manifeste à la suite de la Révolution industrielle et qui fut renforcée, du point de vue contractuel, par le traité

---

[1]PRO, FO 195/389, Consul Holmwood, İzmir, 24 nov. 1890 à Sir A. W. White, ambassadeur britannique, Istanbul. Pour plus de détails sur les activités économiques des occidentaux voir aussi, Elena Frangakis-Syrett, "Western and Local Entrepreneurs in İzmir in the Nineteenth and Early Twentieth Centuries" dans Tuncer Baykara, éd., *Son Yüzyıllarda İzmir ve Batı Anadolu*, İzmir, 1994, pp. 77-92.

[2]PRO, FO 195/1620, Vice-Consul Biliotti, Rhodes, 9 oct. 1888 à Sir W. A. White, ambassadeur britannique, Istanbul; *Parliamentary Papers, Accounts & Papers*, Londres, 1902, CX, Rapport commercial pour l'année 1901, p. 4.

[3]PRO, FO 195/1161, Hadkinson, Merrylees & Company, İzmir, 11 juillet et 26 sept. 1878 au Consul Reade, İzmir.

[4]Salgur Kançal, "La conquête du marché ottoman par le capitalisme industriel concurrentiel (1831-1881)", dans J.-L. Bacqué-Grammont & P. Dumont, éds., *Économies et Sociétés dans l'Empire ottoman (fin du XVIIIe siècle-début du XXe siècle)*, Paris, 1983, pp. 360-366.

commercial de 1838.[1] Car en formant leurs réseaux à l'intérieur du pays, les Occidentaux jouirent de plusieurs avantages: par exemple, leurs moyens en capital furent beaucoup plus grands que ceux dont ils disposaient un siècle auparavant; leurs capitaux furent aussi plus grands que ceux dont leurs rivaux, les marchands locaux, en général, purent disposer.[2] En plus, les Occidentaux ont bénéficié de la capacité toujours croissante du marché occidental, à absorber des denrées ottomanes, ce qui favorisa l'expansion de leurs affaires. Ayant ainsi une domination sur les exportations de la région, ils jouirent de tous les avantages des liens réguliers entre la région et le marché mondial, qui furent réalisés par le progrès technologique dans le secteur de la navigation maritime ainsi que dans le secteur du transport ferroviaire.[3] Cependant les Occidentaux eurent aussi à faire face au capital local qui participa d'une manière très compétitive dans tout le secteur commercial ainsi que dans le secteur bancaire informel. Le résultat fut une rivalité aiguë, entre le capital occidental et local, qui caractérisa les secteurs commercial ainsi que bancaire de la région.[4] Cette rivalité contribua, à son tour, aux profits des locaux et ainsi au processus d'accumulation du capital dans l'économie ottomane et éventuellement à la mondialisation de la région.[5]

Témoin du progrès de l'intégration ainsi réalisée fut l'apparition, vers la fin de notre période, des réseaux de spécialisation, évidents plutôt parmi les Occidentaux, entre le secteur bancaire et celui de commerce. A partir de la seconde moitié du XIXe siècle, il n'existe plus le cas du négociant-banquier occidental s'occupant d'affaires financières, au niveau du petit banquier privé, en même temps qu'il exerçait le métier de négociant, comme au siècle

---

[1]Pour plus de détails sur le traité de 1838 et les résaux commerciaux des Occidentaux, voir Elena Frangakis-Syrett, "Implementation of the 1838 Anglo-Turkish Convention on İzmir's Trade: European and Minority Merchants", *New Perspectives on Turkey*, t. 7, 1992, pp. 91-112; voir aussi, Reşat Kasaba, "Open Door Treaties: China and the Ottoman Empire Compared" dans *ibid.*, pp. 78-86.

[2]Un exemple de l'ampleur des capitaux à la disposition des sociétés occidentaux — qui opérèrent dans la région — fut la firme écossaise MacAndrews Forbes & Company, dont les ressources monétaires n'ont pas cependant découragé toute compétition de la part des sociétés locales. MacAndrews Forbes & Company furent de grands exportateurs des réglisses de toute la région. PRO, FO 195/1161, Consul Reade, İzmir, 11 oct. 1878 au gouverneur général, vilayet d'Aydın.

[3]Frangakis-Syrett, "British Economic Activities...", pp. 206-208; 219-223; voir aussi, Charles Issawi, *The Economic History...*, pp. 148-150; 161-163; 170-171; 183-186 et Donald Quataert, "Limited Revolution: The Impact of the Anatolian Railway on Turkish Transportation and the Provisioning of Istanbul, 1890-1908", *Business History Review*, t. LI/2, 1977, pp. 143-145.

[4]Elena Frangakis-Syrett, "Concurrence commerciale et financière entre les pays occidentaux à İzmir (XIXe-début XXe siècles)" dans J. Thobie, R. Pérez & S. Kançal, éds., *Enjeux et Rapports de Force en Turquie et en Méditerranée orientale*, Istanbul, 1996, pp. 117-127.

[5]Salgur Kançal, "Fin de l'empire ottoman: Insertion dans la division internationale du travail (1880-1913). Le Commerce International de 1871 à 1913", *V. Milletlerarası Türkiye Sosyal ve İktisat Tarihi Kongresi Tebliğler*, Ankara, 1990, pp. 395-407. *Idem*, "La conquête du marché ottoman...", pp. 355-409.

précédent. En plus, vers la fin du XIXe siècle, s'il occupait du commerce, l'entrepreneur occidental était, souvent, soit exportateur soit importateur. Cependant, de telles distinctions n'étaient pas aussi marquées parmi les entrepreneurs ottomans où une coexistence entre les réseaux commerciaux et financiers continuait à opérer jusqu'à la fin de la période ottomane. En effet, même au début du XXe siècle, le portrait d'une société ottomane à İzmir était, en général, celui des négociants-banquiers: c'est-à-dire, des importateurs ainsi que des exportateurs qui exerçaient en même temps le métier de banquier privé.[1]

LE CAPITAL FINANCIER OCCIDENTAL

Pendant les deux dernières décennies du XIXe siècle et jusqu'à la Première Guerre Mondiale, pour plusieures raisons y compris les niveaux du développement économique mondial et ottoman, le processus de mondialisation de la Méditerranée orientale réalisa un progrès remarquable. Ce progrès ne se manifesta pas seulement dans le secteur commercial mais, ce qui concerne l'infrastructure — transport et équipements publics — il y eut une avance assez spectaculaire qui fut évidente surtout dans les centres urbains de la Méditerranée orientale.[2] L'intégration de la région au marché mondial des capitaux — dont le résultat fut l'engagement économique croissant du capital financier occidental et l'apparition d'un réseau bancaire occidental dans la région — contribua d'une manière très significative à ce progrès.[3] Le premier champ économique où le capital financier a fait son apparition fut le secteur bancaire, avec l'établissement d'agences de banques européennes ou de filiales dans les centres urbains ottomans, créant ainsi un réseau bancaire dans l'Empire.[4] Cela influença le développement économique de la Méditerranée orientale, y compris son secteur commercial, où il y a eu une modernisation, en ce qui concerne l'organisation du secteur. Il y eut aussi une augmentation et une amélioration du crédit, par la diminution des taux d'intérêt dans les centres urbains de la région et une simplification des paiements internationaux, ce qui

---

[1]Par exemple, Franco, Israël, Tarica, Alalouf & Cie, S. A., İzmir, c. 1908. Papiers privés à la possession du M. A.C. Franco, New York que je voudrais ici remercier.

[2]AMAE, CCC, t. 54, Consul Pellissier, İzmir, 28 avril 1882 à M. de Freycinet, Ministère des Affaires Étrangères, Paris; voir aussi, PRO, FO 195/2090, Consul Cumberbatch, İzmir, 18 juin 1900 à Sir N. O'Connor, ambassadeur britannique, Istanbul et *Parliemantary Papers, Accounts & Papers*, Londres, 1912-13, C, Rapport commercial pour l'année 1911, pp. 14-15.

[3]Christopher Clay, "The Origins of Modern Banking in the Levant: the Branch Network of the Imperial Ottoman Bank, 1890-1914", *International Journal of Middle Eastern Studies*, t. 26, 1994, pp. 589-614.

[4]Jacques Thobie, "European Banks in the Middle East" dans R. Cameron & V.I. Bovykin, éds., *International Banking, 1870-1914*, New York, 1991, pp. 406-440.

influença d'une façon positive le commerce extérieur de l'Empire.[1] En outre, la mise en place de projets d'infrastructure d'une technologie très avancée et d'une capitalisation assez considérable fut l'autre secteur économique où le capital financier joua un rôle primordial. La réalisation de tels projets, comme les transports ferroviaires et urbains pour la circulation des personnes et des marchandises, l'approvisionnement des consommateurs urbains en gaz et autres sources d'énergie, les besoins d'une industrie légère régionale, récemment développée, contribuèrent sensiblement au développement économique de la région. Cela, à son tour, eut un résultat très positif sur le processus de mondialisation de la région. Bien que le capital occidental dominât ces secteurs, le capital local ne fut pas complètement absent. Cependant la présence du capital ottoman fut limitée à des projets d'infrastructure plutôt modestes.[2]

Le capital financier occidental contribua également à l'intégration de la région aussi à travers la stratégie monétaire de la Banque Impériale Ottomane et notamment sa décision de maintenir le bimétallisme, or et argent, du système monétaire ottoman et de favoriser l'or, au détriment de l'argent.[3] D'ailleurs, le pouvoir qu'a la Banque Impériale Ottomane d'influencer le cours du change entre l'or et l'argent dans l'Empire, et de rendre stable ainsi la parité de la livre turque-or vis-à-vis de la livre sterling et, par conséquence de rendre stable les cours de change à l'étranger pour la livre turque-or, facilita considérablement le commerce extérieur de la Méditerranée orientale et ainsi contribua à l'intégration de certains secteurs de l'économie régionale à l'économie mondiale.[4] Pour ce qui concerne les monnaies d'argent, qui circulèrent plutôt à l'intérieur de la région, et bien que la Banque pût influencer leurs marchés, l'insuffisance du numéraire, parmi d'autres raisons, entraîna des variations de cours d'une transaction monétaire à l'autre et d'une région à l'autre de la Méditerranée orientale, ce qui fut significatif de l'absence d'une unification totale du marché intérieur ottoman que la Banque, seule, n'a pas pu accomplir.[5]

---

[1]Elena Frangakis-Syrett, "The role of European banks in the Ottoman Empire in the second half of the nineteenth and in the early twentieth centuries", dans A. Teichova, G. Kurgan-van Hentenryk & D. Ziegler, éds., *Banking, Trade and Industry in Europe*, Cambridge, 1997, pp. 263-276.

[2]PRO, FO 195/1899, Consul Fr. Holmwood, İzmir, 5 nov. 1895 à M. H. Hubert, Chargé d'*Affaires britannique*, Istanbul.

[3]A. Biliotti, *La Banque Impériale Ottomane*, Paris, 1909, pp. 166-177, 180-182; voir aussi Salgur Kançal, "La dualisation de l'espace monétaire ottoman de 1800 à 1913" dans H. W. Lowry & R. S. Hattox, éds., *Third Congress on the Social and Economic History of Turkey*, Istanbul, 1990; pp. 127-137.

[4]Jacques Thobie, "Les choix financiers de *l'Ottomane* en Méditerranée orientale de 1856 à 1939" dans *Banque et Investissements en Méditerranée*, Marseille, 1985, pp. 57-61.

[5]Kançal, "La dualisation…", pp. 131-136; voir aussi, Biliotti, *La Banque*…, pp. 137-138.

Ce dernier facteur influença la fluidité des rapports des circuits monétaires internes de l'Empire qui, à leur tour, influencèrent l'intégration de la région en plaçant certaines limites à ce processus.

LE SECTEUR AGRICOLE

Un secteur économique où le processus d'intégration n'a pas avancé, pour plusieures raisons, autant que d'autres secteurs de l'économie ottomane, fut le secteur agricole. Certes, au moins une bonne partie de la production agricole de la Méditerranée orientale fut liée directement au commerce international; en effet, plus proche des routes ferroviaires et maritimes se trouvèrent les régions agricoles, plus forts et efficaces furent les liens avec le marché extérieur.[1] Il y eut aussi une accumulation relative du capital à travers le commerce international pendant toute notre période, qui fut plus évidente parmi les grands et moyens propriétaires que parmi les petits cultivateurs. Cependant les grands propriétaires agricoles du XVIIIe siècle, dont la production fut exportée avec profit,[2] ne furent pas aussi dominants au XIXe siècle. Une fois que la corvée fût éliminée, le secteur agricole fut dominé, aux XIXe et début XXe siècles, par de moyens ou de petits cultivateurs dont les ressources monétaires étaient limitées.[3] En effet, le manque de capitaux fut caractéristique du secteur rural pendant toute notre période.[4] D'ailleurs, ce qui fut important, les avances technologiques au niveau de productivité agricole furent modestes et par conséquence la productivité resta plus ou moins la même pendant notre période.[5] Finalement, la disponibilité du crédit, l'engagement du capital occidental ainsi qu'ottoman et le niveau d'investissement ne furent pas très avancés dans le secteur rural par comparaison avec les autres secteurs de l'économie régionale. Il en fut de même aussi pour le degré d'intégration du secteur où le processus fut plus limité.

---

[1]PRO, FO 195/1011, Vice-Consul Gérant britannique, Rhodes, 9 fév. 1874 et FO 195/2112, Consul Cumberbatch, İzmir, 15 mars 1901 à Sir N. O'Conor, ambassadeur britannique, Istanbul. Voir aussi, F. Rougon, *Smyrne: situation commerciale et économique*, Paris, 1892, pp. 148 152; Çağlar Keyder, *The Definition of a Peripheral Economy: Turkey, 1923-1929*, Cambridge, 1981, pp. 28-32; Roger Owen, *The Middle East in the World Economy, 1800-1914*, Londres, 1981, pp. 113-114.

[2]Frangakis-Syrett, *The Commerce...*, pp. 39-40, 116-118; voir aussi, *idem*, "The Trade of Cotton...", pp. 101-104.

[3]PRO, FO 78/868, Consul Brant, İzmir, 13 mars 1851.

[4]PRO, FO 78/441, Consul D. Sandison, Bursa, 28 jan. 1841, voir aussi, *Parliamentary Papers, Accounts & Papers* Londres, 1910, CIII, Rapport commercial pour l'année 1909, p. 18.

[5]PRO, FO 78/1760, Consul Blunt, İzmir, 23 mai et 23 juin 1863.

La mondialisation de la Méditerranée orientale fut un processus dont la phase initiale se développa dans la deuxième moitié du XVIIIe siècle et qui acquit son niveau le plus avancé à la vieille de la Première Guerre Mondiale. Au début de la période, du XVIIIe à la première moitié du XIXe siècles, les réseaux commerciaux des locaux ainsi que des Occidentaux jouèrent un rôle primordial dans ce processus. Plus tard, vers le dernier quart du XIXe et au début du XXe siècles, les réseaux du capital financier s'ajoutèrent aux réseaux du commerce et contribuèrent de façon significative aussi à l'intégration de l'Empire au marché mondial.

18. YÜZYILDAN 20. YÜZYILIN BAŞLARINA KADAR İZMİR EKONOMİSİNE BİR BAKIŞ

Antikten itibaren İzmir Yakın Doğu'da önemli bir limandı. Ancak onsekizinci yüzyılda Doğu Akdeniz'le kalmayıp, Osmanlı İmparatorluğu'nun tümünün batıda Avrupa ile, doğuda büyük ölçüde İran ve Uzak Doğu ile ticaretindeki en önemli ve biricik liman haline geldi. Dahası, İzmir'in onsekizinci yüzyılın ortalarında görünür hale gelen ticare yükselişi İmparatorluğun, yayılmacı döneminde olan, — onsekizinci yüzyılın son bölümünde ve ondokuzuncu yüzyılın başlarında Akdeniz bölgesini de içine alan-Avrupa ekonomisinin bir parçası durumundaki Batı ile ticaretinin artışıyla çakıştı. Başka bir deyişle, İzmir sadece İmparatorluğun dış deniz ticaretinin aslan payını almakla kalmadı, sürekli büyüyen, ticari yükselişini göz kamaştırıcı hale getiren bir pay aldı. Süreç içinde, İzmir ticarette her açıdan; ticareti yapılan malların hacminde ve değerinde, limandan çıkan, hem Osmanlı tüccarlarına hem de Batılı tüccarlara hizmet veren ticaret ağlarının yoğunluğunda ve bu ağlar üzerinden gerçekleştirilen iş muamelelerinin hacminde fark edilebilir bir ticari hakimiyet kazandı.

İzmir Osmanlı kıyı taşımacılığında da hakimiyet gösterdi. Üç kıtaya-Avrupa, Asya ve Afrika — ve Akdeniz, Karadeniz ve Kızıl Deniz'i çevreleyen alanlara kadar yayılan Osmanlı İmparatorluğu o tarihte dev bir imparatorluktu. Kızıl Deniz ile Karadeniz denizcilik bölgelerinin arasında konumlanmış olan Akdeniz, bu denizleri ve dolayısıyla bütün Osmanlı denizcilik dünyasını birbirine bağladı. Akdeniz içinde en işlek deniz-hattı İstanbul-İzmir-İskenderiye hattıydı. Bu hat içinde en önemli bağlantı İzmir'di. Bir bütün olarak Osmanlı denizcilik dünyasındaki güzergahlardan %30'undan çoğu ya İzmir'den başlıyor ya İzmir'de son buluyordu; ya da şehir limanını bir uğrak limanı olarak seçmişti. Bunun nedeni İzmir'in — İstanbul'dan Kuzey Afrika'ya — çeşitli Osmanlı denizcilik bölgelerini birbiriyle bütünleştirmekle kalmayıp, İmparatorluğun iç bölgelerinin büyük bölümünü denizcilik bölgeleriyle bütünleştiriyor olmasıydı. İzmir'in geniş ardbölgesi, Batı Anadolu ve Orta Anadolu'dan, Suriye'de Halep'ten; Doğu Anadolu'ya ve daha doğuda İran'a, Irak'ta Musul'a kadar genişleyip, batıda Ege bölgesi ve Yunan ana karasını içinde aldı. İzmir sadece Osmanlı mallarını toplayıp Batıya göndermekle kalmadı, aynı zamanda Batı mallarını ithal edip, Osmanlı iç pazarının büyük bir bölümüne dağıttı. Sonuç olarak, hem Osmanlı dünyası içindeki hem de

Avrupa'yla olan en yaygın ticaret ve deniz taşımacılığı bağlantılarına kavuştu, onsekizinci yüzyıldaki muhtemel rakipleri ancak Istanbul ve İskenderiye'ydi.

Ticaret ve deniz taşımacılığıyla, İmparatorluğu Avrupa'daki belli başlı pazarlardan bazılarına bağlayan finansal ağlarda lider rolü oynamasının yanında, İzmir bölge için önemli bir bankacılık merkeziydi de. Ancak bu alanda İstanbul önemli bir rakipti. Aslında bir iki şehir onsekizinci yüzyılda İmparatorluğun uluslararası pazara ve özellikle de Avrupa mali çevrelerine entegrasyonunu kolaylaştırmada ticaret kadar önem taşıyan bir dizi karmaşık mali faaliyet geliştirdiler. Dahası, İzmir ekonomisinin ikili ticari ve mali doğası şehrin Batı Anadolu ve Ege bölgesinin ekonomik gelişmesinde asli bir rol oynamasını sağladı.

İzmir limanının dikkat çekici ve süreklilik arz eden ticari yükselişinde birçok faktör rol oynamıştı. Bazı faktörler zamanı için önemli de olsa, bu büyümenin temellerini ortaya koymak açısından dönemseldi. Örneğin, onaltıncı yüzyılın sonlarında ve onyedinci yüzyılın başlarında Bağdat üstünde patlak veren Osmanlı-İran savaşları, İran ipek kervanı tüccarlarının o dönemde tesis edilmekte olan Avrupa-Osmanlı ticaretinde temel çıkış noktası olarak Halep'ten vazgeçip İzmir'e yönelmelerine neden oldu. Bu sürecin bir parçası olarak, onyedinci yüzyılın başlarında Fransız, İngiliz ve Hollanda konsoloslukları limanda tüccar topluluklarının yerleşmesine önayak oldular. Diğer faktörler daha da önemliydi: İzmir'in yakın ardbölgesinden Yakın Doğu ve Avrupa arasında doğan ticaret açısında önemli bir başka mataya, pamuğa kolayca ulaşılabilmesi böyle bir faktördü. Çünkü pamuk ithalattı önce İzmir'e Osmanlı-Avrupa ticaretinde değerli bir yer kazandırıp, sonra da bu yeri sağlamlaştırdı. Emparyal siyaset, ticareti şehir limanına, Anadolu kıyısndaki ya da Ege adalarındaki diğer limanlarından uzağa yönlendirdiği için İzmirin konumunu daha da güçlendirdi. İstanbul'a, yani emperyal iktidar merkezine yakınlığı İzmir'in ardbölgesindeki kervan yollarının güvenli olmasını sağlayarak, şehrin büyümesinde rol oynayan bir başka faktördü. İzmir kendisine sağlanan güvenli ardbölgesinin avantajlarını Anadolu'nun içlerinde ticaret ağları tesis etmekte kullandı, bu, İmparatorluktaki en yaygın ticaret ağlarına sahip olma yolundaki ilk adımdı. Güvenli ulaşım ve etkin yerel ticaret ağları İzmir pazarını o dönemde Osmanlı-Avrupa ticaretinde önemli bir yeri olan üçüncü metayla, tiftikle destekledi.[1] Ankara tiftiği ticareti ticareti büyük ölçüde, malı diğer yerel tüccarlara satmak için İzmir'e getiren Türk ve Ermeni tüccarların tekelindeydi. Aracı olarak hizmet eden yerel tüccarlar,

[1]Archives Nationales de France, Paris, AE Bi 1053. Konsolos Charles de Peyssonnel, Mémoire, İzmir, 22 Kasım 1751. Bundan sonra bu arşiv ANF olarak anılacaktır.

simsarları üzerinden bunları Avrupalı tüccarlara satarlardı. Sonuç olarak, onsekizinci yüzyılın başlarında bir batılı için tiftiği Anadolu limanındaki yerel tüccardan almak, üretildiği Ankara'dan almaktan daha ucuzdu, ki bu da İzmir'in ticaret ağlarının maliyet etkinliğini gösteriyordu.[1]

Ancak onsekizinci yüzyılda ve ondukuzuncu yüzyılın başlarında İzmir'e ciddi ticari büyümesini ve Yakın Doğu ticaretindeki su götürmez hakimiyetini kazandırmasının yanında, bu büyüme sürecini İzmir'in tarihindeki önceki dönemlere ait ticari etkinlikten farklı kılan, özellikle öncellikle onsekizinci yüzyılın ikinci yarısında ve ondokuzuncu yüzyılın başlarında Osmanlı-Avrupa ticaretinde yaşanan gelişmelerdi. İzmir'in ekonomik açıdan büyümesi, bu dönemde Osmanlı İmparatorluğu'nun Batıyla ve özellikle de o dönemde Yakın Doğu'nun en önemli ticari gücü haline gelen Fransa'yla ticaretindeki büyümeyi takip etti. Ondokuzuncu yüzyılın başlarında Fransa'nın yerini İngiltere aldı. İngiltere ondokuzuncu yüzyıl boyunca İmparatorluğun temel ticari partneri olarak kalacaktı. Bu gelişmeler İzmir'in tarihine ondukuzuncu yüzyılın başlarında temel ticari partner olarak Fransa'nın yerini İngiltere'nin alması biçiminde yansıdı.[2] 1870'lerde İngiltere İzmir'in ithalatının yarısını karşıladı;[3] İngiltere'nin İzmir'in Batı ile olan ticaretindeki hakimiyeti yirminci yüzyılın başlarına kadar sürdü.

Onsekizinci yüzyılın ikinci yarısında bakıldığında, ekonomik büyümeyle ve birtakım Fransız devlet politikalarıyla güçlenmiş olan Franco-Osmanlı ticaret ilişkilerinin sağlamlaşmasının İzmir'in büyümesi ve Osmanlı-Fransız ticaretine egemen olmasıyla paralel gitmesi pek de supriz sayılmaz. Ticaret istatistiklerinden yararlanılarak İzmir'in 1740'larda hakimiyetini tesis etmesinin ve 1754'te en önemli Osmanlı limanı olarak ortaya çıkmasının izi sürülebilir. Bu yıla gelmeden önce Smyrna'nın Fransa ile ticareti İskenderiye, Suriye limanları ya da Ege adalarınca geride bırakılmıştı. Ancak 1754'ten sonra diğer Osmanlı limanlarına göre yıllık olarak Batı'ya en çok malı açık farkla İzmir ihraç etti. İmparatorluğun dağılmasına kadar temel ihraç limanı olarak kaldı.[4] Bu gelişmelerde bir çok faktör rol oynadı. Ege adalarından göreli olarak sınırlı miktarda tahıl ve zeytinyağı ithal edilebilirken, — bunlar kendi başlarına önemli metalar olsa da ne hacim olarak ne de kapsam olarak,

[1] ANF, AE Bi 1054, Bilan des ecritures de Villamus & Cie. İzmir, 1753.

[2] 1775-1820 arasında İzmir'in Batı Avrupa'dan ithalatı ve Batı Avrupa'ya ihracatının toplam değerlerine ilişkin tablo için bakınız, Elena Fangakis-Syrett, *The Commerce of Smyrna in the Eighteenth Century 1700-1820* (Athens, 1992), s. 274-279.

[3] *Parliamentary Papers, Accounts & Papers,* Annual Commercial Reports Series, 1865-1912.

[4] Elena Frangakis-Syrett, "The Port of Smyrna in the Nineteenth Century" (der.) B. Kiraly ve diğerleri, *War and Society in East Central Europe,* vol. XXIII (Thessaloniki, 1988), s. 261-272 içinde.

büyüyen Fransız pazarında ve diğer batılı pazarlarda Osmanlı mallarına artan ihtiyacı karşılayamazdı —; İskenderiye ve Suriye limanlarının ardbölgelerinin o zamanlarda güvenli olmaması ticaret ağlarını zedeledi ve tüccarların Avrupa'ya gemileri tam yükle geri gönderebilmeleri büyük ölçüde engelledi. Geri dönüş yolculuğu için gerekli malların İzmir'de bulunabileceğinin hemen hemen garantili olması Avrupa'dan tüccarları ve kaptanları limana çekti. Bu, sonuç olarak kervanları da içerilerden İzmir'e çekti. Bütün bunlar mali işlemlerle desteklenen, sürekli, işleyen bir ticari döngü üretti.

İzmir'in Fransa'dan yapılan toplam Osmanlı ithalatındaki payı yüzyılın başlarındaki yaklaşık %20'den sonlarında ikiye katlanıp, %40'a ulaştı. İzmir'in yüzyılın sonlarındaki en yakın rakibi olan Selanik Osmanlı ithalatında sadece %14'lük bir paya sahipti. Ancak, artan sadece İzmir'in Osmanlı-Avrupa ticaretindeki payı değildi, enflasyon oranı göz önünde alındığında bile İzmir'in ticareti mutlak değerlerle arttı: Yüzyılın ikinci yarısındaki ortalama yıllık ihracat, ilk yarısındakinden değer olarak dört kez daha büyüktü.[1] İhracat, onssekizinci yüzyıl sonlarında zaten yüksek olan değerlerini ondokuzuncu yüzyılın başlarında ikiye katladı.[2] Smyrna'nın yaşadığı dizginlenemez ticari büyüme, — Osmanlı-Fransız ticaretindeki temel limanı olan — Marsilya'ya yapılan tüm Osmanlı ihracatı endeksiyle İzmir'in bu Fransız limanına yaptığı ihracatı karşılaştırdığımızda görünür hale gelir. 1700 yılını baz olarak alınca, (örneğin, 1700=100), her iki endeks de onsekizinci yüzyılın ilk yarısında birbirini izleyen periyodik dalgalanmalarla aynı genel artış eğilimini gösterdi; hatta, İzmir bazı yıllarda Osmanlı İmparatorluğunun yaşadığından daha büyük düşüşler kaydetti. Ancak Smyrna'nın ihracat endeksinin İmparatorluğunkinin altına hiç düşmediği 1746'dan itibaren durum değişti; üstelik İmparatorluk ihracatının genelde düştüğü yıllarda Smyrna'nın endeksi büyüme gösterdi. Hem İmparatorluk hem de İzmir için zirve yıla, endekslerin 428 ve 806'ya çıktığı 1788'de ulaşıldı.

İzmir aynı zamanda İmparatorluğun Avrupa ile olan ithalatına da hakim oldu. Örneğin, 1749-1789 yıllarında Fransız ithal mallarının yıllık olarak yaklaşık % 30'luk bir bölümü İzmir'den giriş yapmıştır. Bu eğilim yüzyıl biterken, 1776-1779 yıllarında, arttı ve ithalatta en büyük rakibi

---

[1] Archives de la Chambre du Commerce de Marseille, Marseille, I, 26, États des marchandisses venant du Levant et de Barbarie (1700-1747), 27 (1725-1759), 28 (1776-1779; 1786-1789). Bu arşiv bundan sonra ACCM olarak anılacaktır. Ayrıca bakınız, ANF, AE Biii 269 (1760, 1762), 272 (1763-1764), 273 (1766-1769), 274 (1770-1772).

[2] Ondokuzuncu yüzyılın başlarındaki ticaret rakamları için bakınız, J. G. Nanninga, *Bronnen tot de Geschiedenis van den Levantschen Handel, Vierde deel* ('S-Gravenhage, 1966), *passim*. Ayrıca bakınız, Archives du Ministère des Affaires Étrangères, Paris, CCC, vol. 35. Bu arşiv bundan sonra AMAE olarak anılacaktır.

İstanbul'un payı % 20'nin altındayken İzmir'in oranı % 34'e yükseldi.[1] İzmir'e gelen ithal mallarının değerinde Osmanlı iç pazarının büyümesini yansıtan mutlak bir artış vardı; bu, o dönemde yayılmacı döneminde olan dünya ekonomisinin bir parçası durumunda olan Osmanlı ekonomisinin genel büyümesinin ve artan ticarileşmesinin bir parçasıydı. Ondokuzuncu yüzyılın başlarında İzmir'in ithalatı o dönemin Osmanlı-Avrupa ticaretindeki dikkate değer büyümeye paralel olarak fazladan — bu kez dört kat — artış kaydetti.[2] Ancak, artık doğrudan ya da Malta üzerinden İzmir'in ticaretteki öncelikli partneri olan Fransa'nın yerini İngiltere almıştı.[3]

İzmir'in ekonomik büyümesindeki önemli bir faktör uluslararası ticaretin ihtiyaçlarını karşılayabilmesiydi. Batı Avrupa'da tekstil sektöründeki büyüme, kumaş üretiminde kullanmak üzere hammadeye ve bitmiş ürün için bir pazara ihtiyaç duyuyordu. İzmir ikisini de sağlayabilirdi. İmparatorluğun kıyı bölgelerini ve kara kütlesini kapsayan kısa ve uzun mesafe kara ve deniz yolu güzergahlarıyla İzmir, Avrupa kumaşlarını, çivit ve kırmız gibi boya maddelerini, Avrupa üzerinden gelen kahve ve şeker gibi sömürge mallarını ithal edip, büyük bir kitlesel tüketim potansiyelinin olduğu tüm Doğu Akdeniz'e Anadolu ve İran pazarlarının ücra köşelerine kadar dağıttığı gibi; pamuk, pamuk ipliği, ipek, tiftik ve yün toplayıp belli başlı Avrupa pazarlarına ihraç etti. Böylesi önemli bir dizi metanın ticareti, yerel olarak batı Anadolu'da ve Ege adalarında üretilip, genellikle nakit olan ödemelerinin malların Avrupa pazarlarına gönderdiği liman olan İzmir'de yapıldığı zeytinyağı ve buğday ihracatıyla destekledi.

Onsekizinci yüzyılın ikinci yarısında İzmir ekonomisindeki asıl sıçramayı yaratının büyük ölçüde, iyi kalite pamuk ve pamuk ipliğinin, genişleyen Avrupa, özellikle de Fransa tekstil sanayiine ithalatı olduğu söylenebilir. Örneğin, yüzyılın ilk yıllarında, 1700-1702'de İmparatorluğun Marsilya'ya toplam pamuk ihracatında İzmir'in payı yaklaşık %10'du; 1750-1754'te bu %44'e yükseldi ve 1785-1789'da, Osmanlı-Fransız ticaretinin zirve yıllarında, % 70'i geçti. Tahmin edileceği gibi, artan sadece İzmir'in pamuk ihracatındaki payı değil, aynı zamanda bizatihi pamuk ihracatının hacmi ve değerlydi: Endeksler 1700'deki 100'lük baz düzeyinden 1769'da yaklaşık

[1] ACCM, I, 19-20, *États des marchandises envoyées en Levant en Barbarie*, 1749-1789.
[2] AMAE, CCC, cild. 35 (1817-20).
[3] ANF, AE Biii 243, Konsolos Miège, Renseignements sur le commerce du Levant, Livorno, 13 Mayıs 1825.

1,040'a — her açıdan ticaretin zirve yılı olan — 1788'de 12,400'e ulaştı.[1] Pamuk ticaretindeki büyümenin pek çok nedeni vardı. Levant'ta ticaretin yürümesinde pamuk ve pamuk ipliği anahtar rolü gördü: Hem Osmanlı hem de Avrupa ekonomilerinde sınırlı sikke (yani nakit) vardı, takas yaygın bir değiş tokuş yöntemiydi. En karlı takas da, Avrupa kumaşı ile pamuk değiş tokuş edilmesiydi. Yakın çevresinde üretilen pamukta, Ankara menşeli tiftikte, limana Bursa'dan taşınan ya da İran'dan gönderilen ipekte genellikle yaşanan sorunlar yaşanmıyordu ve nakliye maliyetlerine tabi değildi. Sadece şehrin çevresinde üzun süreli bir silahlı çatışma, ki daha çok onsekizinci yüzyılın ilk yarısında yaşanmıştı; ya da daha çok yüzyılın ikinci yarısında görülen ciddi ve veba salgınları limandan pamuk ihracını ciddi biçimde kesintiye uğratabilirdi. Yerel ekonominin tepetaklak olmasına neden olan ve şehir piyasasının ve parasal alışkanlığın belirsizleşmesine katkıda bulunan bu olaylar yaşandı. Bu şansızlıklar aynı zamanda şehri demografik olarak da etkiledi. Ancak İzmir her zaman durumunu düzeltmeyi başarabildi. Nüfusunda artış olmadı bahsettiğimiz dönem boyunca yaklaşık 100,000 kişide sabit kaldı; ancak şehrin çevresinden sürekli insan çekebilmesi sayesinde nüfus azalması da olmadı, İzmir, geniş ardbölgesinden artan miktarlarda pamuk ve pamuk ipliği ihraç edebilme kabiliyetini de korudu.

Ancak, pamuk İzmir limanını üretmiştir demek, pamuğun yegane faktör olmayıp, çok önemli bir faktör olduğu, çok çehreli, daha karmaşık bir resmi aşırı basitleştirmek olacaktır. Aslında bir başka aslı faktör Avrupa-Osmanlı ticaretinin örgütlenmesi ve bunun İzmir'i etkileme tarzıydı. Belki de İzmir'in iş dünyasının en tanımlayıcı özelliği, rengini güçlü bir rekabetten alan ve her iki grubun — Osmanlı ve Avrupa tüccarlarının zaman zaman birbirleriyle rekabet edip, zaman zaman da işbirliğine girip zenginliklerini ve avantajlarını kattığı, iki temel ticaret grubunun arasında varolan ilişkilerin biçimiydi. Korumacı İngiliz ve Fransız ekonomileri Osmanlı tüccarlarının barış zamanında kendi kıyılarında yerleşmelerine ve kendi milliyetlerinden olanların ticari ağlarına katılmalarına izin vermediyse de, savaş zamanında istisnalar olabilirdi. İlaveten, ticaretin herkese açık olduğu Livorno limanından İzmir'e ticaret yapan Osmanlı tüccarlarıyla Fransız ve İngiliz tüccarları arasında, daha ziyade el altında yürütülen bir işbirliği de vardı. Bunların yanısıra, İngiliz ve Fransızlardan farklı olarak İtalyanlar ve Hollandalılar Osmanlı İmparatorluğu ile olan ticaretlerine Osmanlı tüccarlarının

[1]ANF, Marine B/7, 452, États des cotons en laines et filés du Levant à Marseille, 1782-1785; ayrıca bakınız, Elena Fangakis-Syrett, "The Trade of Cotton and Cloth in İzmir: From the Second Half of the Eighteenth Century to the Early Nineteenth Century" (der.) C. Keyder & F. Tabak *Landholding and Commercial Agriculture in the Middle East* (Albany, N.Y., 1991), s. 97-111, 209-214 içinde.

katılmalarına izin verdiler. Türk tüccarlar İzmir'i ardbölgelerine bağlayan iç ağlarda aktif olduklarından, Avrupa'nın liberal ticaret politikalarının avantajlarından yararlananlar çoğunlukla İzmir'le ticaretlerini Amsterdam, Roterdam, Ancona, Tryeste ya da Livorno'dan yürüten gayri-Müslimlerdi — Museviler, Ermeniler ve Rumlar —.

İngilizler ve Fransızlar yasal Kapitülasyonlar sistemiyle — yüzyılın büyük bölümünde — İzmir'in Batı ile olan ticari ağlarına hakimdiyseler, Osmanlı tüccarları da kendi hesaplarına hem iç hem dış ticarette limanın ardbölgesiyle olan ticari ağlarına hakimdiler. Ayrı fakat iç içe geçen ticari uzmanlık alanları olan, Avrupalı ve Osmanlı tüccarların günlük ticaret etkinlikleri birçok yönden karşılıkla ilişki içindeydi.[1] Avrupalılar esas olarak batıya giden gemilerle Osmanlı mallarını gönderip Avrupa'dan mal karşılamakla ilgileniyordu. Avrupalılar zaman zaman yerel tüccarlardan ve daha sık da şehrin çarşılarında ya da kervansaraylarında Osmanlı malları satanlardan mal alırken ve onlara kendi mallarını satarken bu işlemleri yürütecek simsarları olarak yerel tüccarları, istisnasız gayri-Müslim olanlarını, kullandılar.

Avrupalıların şehrin yakın ardbölgesi de dahil olmak üzere Batı Anadolu'nun içlerinde kendilerine ait, kalıcı bir ticari ağları ya da tesisleri yoktu.[2] Bu yüzden zaman zaman yapmış olabilecekleri gibi kendileri içerlere gittiklerinden bunu, bu durumlarda mihmandarları ve silahlı korumaları da olabilecek simsarlar ya da aracılar eşliğinde yaptılar. İçerlerdeki dil ve güvenlik sorunu — İzmir'in iç bölgeseleri kervanlar için güvenli olsa da, bireysel tüccarlar için her zaman güvenli değildi — onları bunu düzenli bir pratik haline getirmekten alıkoyan nedenlerden bazılarıydı. Avrupalıların şehir dışında daha fazla yerleşmelerinin önündeki daha önemli nedenler Anadolu'nun içlerindeki piyasalarla ilgili uzmanlık ve pazar bağlantılarının eksiklikleri ve yerel tüccar ağlarının güçlü rekabetiydi. Son olarak, finansla ilgili daha önemli başka bir neden vardı: Avrupa ekonomisinin onsekizinci yüzyıldaki sermaye birikim düzeyi veri alındığında, bu tüccarların Batıya ihraç edilecek malların alımı, toplanması ve limana ulaştırılması için etkin iletişim kanalları ve pazar bağlantıları tesis edecek sermaye kaynakları yoktu. Dahası, Avrupa

[1]Ondokuzuncu yüzyılda genç erkekler kendi hesaplarına, Avrupa'daki şirketlerinin temsilcisi olarak, İzmir'in de dahil olduğu Levant'a gidip, 8-10 yıl kalıyorlardı. Bunlar limandaki ünlü Frenk Mahallesinde yerleşmişlerdi. Genellikle atölye mekanın da kapsayan evleri rıhtımların yanında ve malları doğrudan yükleyip boşaltambilecek özel mülklerindeki iskelelere bitişikti. Evler aile için inşa edilmemişlerdi, bu ondokuzuncu yüzyılın başlarında başladı. Bundan sonra, Buca gibi şehrin civarındaki yerlerde sayfiye evleri inşa etmeye başlayacaklardı.

[2]Bazen komşu Ege adalarında ve daha çok da Midilli'de İzmir'den kontrol ettikleri acenteleri vardı. Örneğin, ACCM, S 72, N. Eydoux, Mytilene, 20 Kasım 1714.

pazarlarında Osmanlı mallarına artan talebe rağmen bu, batılıların içerlere yaptıkları seferleri sürekli olarak genişletmelerini garantileyecek ya da buna izin verecek ölçekte değildi. Pazar, hala belirsiz bir pazardı. Bazen, İzmir'deki Avrupalı ve yerel alıcılar arasındaki aşırı rekabet Osmanlı mallarının fiyatlarını Avrupa piyasalarında rekabet edemeyecekleri bir düzeye çıkarabiliyordu. Beklenen bir kervanın gelmemesi ticareti ciddi biçimde geriletecekken, birkaç Avrupa gemisinin beklenmedik gelişi pazarı canlandırabilir, ancak aynı zamanda onu batılı mallara ve sömürge ithal mallarına boğup, fiyatlarının satıcılar için karlı olmayan düzeylere kadar inmesine neden olabilirdi. İzmir'de ticaret yapmak, Levant'ın diğer bölümlerinde ya da aslında onsekizinci yüzyılda diğer Avrupa pazarlarında olduğu gibi, hala şans işi olabiliyordu. Kar, batılı da olsalar, Osmanlı da olsalar bütün tüccarların sürekli olarak gözden geçirdiği birçok faktörün tamamına bağlıydı.

İzmir'in süregelen önemine yol açan başka bir faktör de şuna dayanıyordu: Limanda bazıları Avrupalı tüccarların aracıları ve diğerleri ve simsarları haline gelen girişimci ve ekonomik olarak zengin, hareketli bir yerel tüccar topluluğu vardı. Böylece, yerel tüccarlar iç ekonomiyle bağlantı işlevi gördüler. Malları, ilişkileri, kredileri ve bilgileri kentin pazarlarındaki Avrupalılara taşıyıp, onların mallarını da daha içerlerde satılmak üzere diğer yerel tüccarlara sattılar. Aslında, neredeyse simsarlıkta bile uzmanlaşma vardı. Örneğin ithal malların satışı genellikle krediyle, ender olarak nakitle, müessese simsarınca; yani Avrupalı tüccarın simsarınca dışarıya ya da Osmanlı alıcının simsarına yapılıyordu.[1] Bu simsarlar münhasıran değilse de genellikle, gayri-Müslim Osmanlı tüccarlardı. Simsarları kullananlar sadece Avrupalılar değildi, onların uzmanlıklarından yerel tüccarlar da yararlanıyorlardı. Bu, süregelen ticari faaliyetlerin büyük bir bölümünde anahtar rolü oynayan bir meslekti. Dahası, simsarlar da sık sık kendi hesaplarına ticaret yapıyorlard.

Bütününde bu, o dönemde çok yaygın olan güven vermeyen alıcılara Avrupalıların krediyle mal satmamasın sağladığı gibi, yine Avrupalılara Osmanlı mallarını İzmir gibi rekabetçi bir pazardan en uygun koşullarla alma olanağı sağladığından karşılıklı olarak yararlıydı. Ek olarak, tüccar-simsar *ilişkisi*, Avrupalılara geri dönüş yolculuğunda gemilerinin tümüyle yüklenmiş olmasını garantiliyor, aynı zamanda Avrupa'dan getirecekler malları için pazarlar da sağlıyordu. Geri dönüş yolculuğunda geminin tümüyle

[1] *Parliamentary Papers, Tariffs*, vol. 2 (London, 1843), s. 98. Tanım onsekizinci yüzyıl için de tümüyle geçerlidir.

yüklenmesi garantisinin olması batılıları İzmir'e çeken önemli bir avantajdı. Daha sonrasında da bunlar yerel tüccarları limana çekti. Bu süreçte İzmir, Osmanlı içinde en iyi örgütlenmiş ve en yaygın tüccar ve mal ağının çekirdeği haline geldi.

Avrupalılar böylesi yerel ticaret ağlarını koparamazdı, koparmaları için neden de yoktu. Örneğin, Bursa ipeği ya da Ankara tiftiği Musevi, Ermeni ve Türk tüccarlarının tekelindeyken, İran ipeğinin ticaretini yapıp bunu taşıyanlar yalnızca Ermeni kervan tüccarlarıydı. Bu tüccarlar diğer yerel tüccarlaara satmak üzere İzmir'e mal getirdiler. Yerel tüccarlar muhtemelen başka aracılar ya da simsarlar kullanıp bunları Avrupalıların simsarlarrı üzerinden Avrupalı tüccarlara sattılar. Aslında Avrupalılar, kimi zaman Ege adalarından[1] zeytinyağı almak için yaptıkları gibi — Ege adalarında ardbölgenin ithalat pazarına yakınlığı Avrupalıların yerel üreticilere ulaşmadda gerekli bağlantıları kurmalarına olanak verdi —[2], bireysel olarak ya da İzmir'de konumlanmış batılı müesseselerin temsilcileri olarak doğrudan yerel üreticilere ulaştıklarında, yerel tüccar ağının sıkı rekabetiyle karşılaştılar. Türk ve Rum tüccarların Avrupalılarla zeytinyağı ihracatında rekabet ettikleri Girit örneği, Avrupalılarla yereller arasındaki ticari rekabet dinamiklerini göstermesi açısından iyi bir örnektir.[3] Bu durum ithalatta da aynıydı. Sakız örneğinin gösterdiği gibi, Avrupalıların İzmir'e getirdiği kumaşlar Ege adalarına onlar tarafından değil, çoğunlukla Rum olan yerel tüccar tarafından götürülürdü.[4]

Yerel tüccarların aracılar olarak konumunu güçlendiren bir başka neden daha vardı, bu neden Osmanlı ekonomisinin olduğu gibi onsekizinci yüzyıl Avrupa ekonomilerinin çoğunun da mali kaynaklarla ilgilenmesiydi. Bu gelişmenin önemli bir nedeni Avrupalı tüccarın Levant'la ticaretti kullanılabileceği sınırlı sermaye kaynaklarının olmasıydı. Bankacılığın o dönemdeki gelişme düzeyi göz önünde bulundurulduğunda, bu; Avrupa ekonomilerinin para arzında yaşadıkları periyodik daralmalara bağlıydı. Sonuç, Avrupalı; Hollandalı ve İngiliz tüccarlarından ziyade, özellikle Fransız tüccarların nakit ihtiyacı çekmeleriydi. Deniz taşımacılığının ya da uygun bir pazarın avantajlarından yararlanmak için Osmanlı mallarını satın almak isteyip de alacak nakdi ya da takas etmek için kumaşı olmayanlara istedikleri malları

---

[1] Patrick Boulanger, "L'île de Mytilène et le négoce français au XVIII siècle", (der.) D. Panzac, *Les Villes dans l'Empire ottoman: Activités et Sociétés* (Paris, 1991) cild. 1, s. 282-288 içinde.

[2] ANF, AE Biii 242, B. Jumelin, Commerce du Levant en général, 1812.

[3] Y. Triantafyllidou-Baladié, *Το εμπόριο και η οικονομία της Κρήτης, 1699-1795* (*The Commerce and Economy of Crete (1699-1795)* (Iraklion: Crete, 1988), s. 145-149.

[4] Elena Frangakis-Syrett, "The Economic Activities of the Ottoman and Western Communities in Eighteent-Century İzmir", *Oriente Moderno*, cild XVIII/1 (LXXIX), n.s. (1999), s. 11-26.

yerel tüccarlar sağladı. Bu bir çeşit krediydi, sadece yerel tüccarlar para sunmak yerine yaygın bağlantılarını kullanarak içerilerden krediyle aldıkları malları sunuyorlardı.[1] Avrupalı tüccar sadece takasla ya da nakitle mal almayıp, sık sık krediyle alım yaptığından, doğrudan Osmanlı alıcı ya da satıcılara gitmeyip her seferinde borç verebilen yerel tüccarla işleri sürdürmek daha anlamlı olabiliyordu. Bu biçimde, yerel tüccar İzmir'de ticaretin örgütlenmesinde kendine önemli bir yer edinip, mükemmel bir aracı haline geldi. Yerel tüccar, aynı zamanda kendi pazar bağlantılarını da sermaye olarak kullandı: İzmir piyasasının o dönemde bütün endüstri öncesi ekonomilerinde içkin olan sermaye kıtlığını süreç içinde aşmasını da sağladığı için böylesi bir durum herkes için faydalıydı.

Genelde, kredi, ciddi bir sikke kıtlığıyla karşılaştığında bile piyasanın işleyişinin sürmesine olanak vererek şehir limanında ticaretin örgütlenmesinde kilit bir rol oynadı; ek olarak, kredi karlı bir iş kaynağıydı. Çünkü o zamanlarda Osmanlı ekonomisi, kronik para sıkıntılarına Avrupa ekonomisinden daha fazla eğilimliydi. Bu, Avrupalıların da bir anlaşma bağlayabilmek için mallarının potansiyel Osmanlı alıcılarrına uzun vadeli krediler ya da takas ya da her ikisini birden önermelere gerektiği anlamına geliyordu. bu tip parasal koşullar ticaret pratiklerrini etkilemeleri bir yana, şehirde bir mali merkezin gelişmesine de katkıda bulundu. Bu İzmir'in Yakın Doğu'daki ekonomik konumunu daha da güçlendirdi.

Osmanlı ekonomisindeki para sıkıntısına bakıldığında bu sıkıntı, İmparatorluğun başka yerlerde olduğu gibi İzmir'in para piyasasında da Osmanlı parasıyla birlikte dolaşımda olan Batı paralarının ithaliyle kısmen aşılmıştır, bu paralar ticareti kolaşlaştırdığı gibi, ekonominin nakit ihtiyacı çeken diğer alanları da doldurmuştur. İzmir'in Batı pazarlarıyla ve İmparatorluk içindeki diğer iç pazarlarla yaygın bağlantıları onu İstanbul'u bile geride bırakarak İmparatorluğa sikke ithalinde mükemmel bir giriş limanı haline getirdi ve İzmir'e İmparatorluğun mali dünyasında özel bir yer sağladı. Bu ithalat özünde, o zamanlar meta ticaretinden bile daha önemli hale gelen, fark ödeyerek para takasıydı. Fransızlar bu ticaretteki en aktif katılımcılarken, Hollandalılar[2] ve İngilizler de para ticaretiyle ilgilendiler.[3] Levant Şirketi'nin bu gibi faaliyetlere ilişkin düzenlemeleri resmi olarak bunu yasakladığında bile, ki bu durum da para ticaretinin hangi ölçüde yaygın ve karlı olduğunu

[1]ANF, AE Bi 1052, Peysonnel, İzmir, 29 Ocak 1749 to Minister, Paris.
[2]ANF, F/12 549-550, Mémoire sur le commerce du Levant, 1777.
[3]Public Record Office, London, SP 105/337, Konsolos Anthony Hayes, Memorandum, İzmir, 15 Mayıs 1789. Bundan sonra bu arşiv PRO olarak anılacaktır.

gösteren bir kanıt niteliğindedir, İngilizler parayla ilgilenmeyi sürdürdüler.[1] İlaveten, bu hem Osmanlı hem de Avrupalı tüccarların yürüttüğü sikke ve değiş tokuş kağıtlarının arbitrajı ve diğer parasal spekülatif faaliyetler için bir cennet yarattı. O dönem Avrupa para piyasalarının hareketliliğiyle birlikte bu gibi pratikler onsekizinci yüzyılın sonunda ve ondukuzuncu yüzyılın başlarında daha yaygınlaştı. Bu, kısmen Fransız Devrimi (1792-1801) ve Napolyon Savaşları (1803-1814) yüzünden ve kısmen de Avrupa ekonomisinin genişlemesi yüzündendi. Bu gibi operasyonlar şehri zamanın belli başlı Avrupa mali piyasalarına bağlamaya ve İzmir'i İstanbul'dan sonra Levant'daki ikinci önemli mali piyasa haline getirmeye katkıda bulundu.

Eğer Osmanlı-Avrupa ticaretinin doğası ve örgütlenmesi Avrupalı ve Osmanlı tüccarları arasındaki ilişkinin dinamiklerini ve sonuçta şehir limanının ticari büyüme oranını büyük ölçüde etkileyen bir faktörse, savaşlar da İzmir'in ticaretini ve tüccarlarını etkileyen başka bir önemli faktördü. Deniz savaşları Ege Denizi'ndeki deniz taşımacılığı güzergahlarını, İmparatorluğun içinde yer aldığı savaşlar da İzmir'in geniş ardbölgesindeki kervan güzergahlarını kesintiye uğratabilirdi. Ancak, savaşlar ve özellikle de Avrupalılar arası deniz çatışmaları faydalı da olabiliyordu. Çünkü bunlar yerel tüccarlara büyük İngiltere ve Fransa ekonomilerinin korumacı sistemini altüst etmek ve uluslararası pazara tam olarak ve doğrudan ulaşmak için en uygun fırsatı sağladılar. Uygun bir örnek Yedi Yıl Savaşları'dır (1756-1763): İki Avrupalı gücün birbirlerine uyguladıkları hükümet destekli acımasız korsanlık ticari deniz güçlerini tahrip edip, de facto olarak onların mallarının diğer milletlerin gemileri tarafından taşınmasına yol açtı. Malları İngiliz ve Fransız gemileriyle taşımak yüksek sigorta bedelleri gerektiren tehlikeli ve belalı bir iş halince, tarafsız ve rekabetçi Hollandalı nakliyeciler boşluğu doldurmak için öne çıktılar. Ancak, İngiliz ve Fransızlardan farklı olarak Hollandılar Osmanlı tüccarların yanında ve Hollandalı nakliyecileri kullanarak İzmir'in Batı Avrupa ile ticaretine katılımlarının önünü büyük ölçüde açmasıydı.[2] Osmanlı müesseselerinin-Musevi, Rum ve Ermeni-Hollanda limanlarında yerleşik duruma gelmesi de bu dönemdeydi; süreç içinde Avrupa-Osmanlı ticaretinde bir dayanak noktası elde ettiler, barış yeniden tesis edildikten uzun zaman sonra da İzmir'le ticaret yapmayı sürdürdüler.[3]

---

[1]PRO, SP 105/118, Levant Company, London, 27 Nisan 1750 to Consul Crawley, İzmir.

[2]ARA, 2dd, De Scheepvaart en de Handel op Smirna, 1762 (der.) J.G. Nanninga, *Bronnen tot de Geschiedenis van den Levantschen Handel, Derde Deeel* ('S-Gravenhage, 1952), s. 761-763 içinde.

[3]ARA, 2dd, De Invoer en de Uitnoer met Nederlandschen Scheppen te Smirna, 1762, Nanninga, *Bronnen...*, (1952), s. 715-750 içinde. Ayrıca bakınız, ANF, F/12, 1850A, État général des maisons de commerce, İzmir, 1820.

İzmir'in yerel tüccar topluluklarının büyümesine katkıda bulunan bir başka faktör de, Yedi Yıl Savaşları boyunca, belgedeki İngiliz deniz operasyonlarının bir sonucu olarak ticaretin Marsilya'dan uzağa, porto franco olarak statüsü Osmanlı tüccarları da dahil bütün milletlerin ticaret faaliyetlerrine katılmasına izin veren, Livorno gibi İtalyan limanlarına yönlenmesiydi. Marsilya'nın, daha sonraları, Fransız Devrimi (1792-1801) ve Napolyon Savaşlarrında (1803-1814) İngilizlerce daha da sıkı ablukası, Marsilya ve İzmir arasındaki ticaretin tekrar, bir kez daha İtalyan limanlarına ve özellikle de Tryeste ve Ancona'ya yönlendirilmesine yol açtı. Ticarete ilişkin rakamlar gayet açıklayıcıdır. Amiens Barışı (1801-1803) sırasında Tryeste ve Ancona'nın, İzmir'in Avrupa'yla ticaretinin yaklaşık üçte ikisini karşlaması, Marsilya'nın savaşların ve Fransız Devrimi'nin siyasal çalkantılarının etkisinden kurtulamamasını yansıtmaktadır.[1]

Etkilenen sadece, tam anlamıyla Levant'a çıkış yolu olan Marsilya değildi. Amerikan Bağımsızlık Savaşı'nın son yılları olan 1781-1782'de limanları İngilizler tarafından abluka altına alınan Hollandalı tüccarlar İzmir'le ticaretlerinde kara güzergahına geri dönmeye zorlandılar. Bu güzergah onları Avrupa'dan Tryeste'ye ve oradan da deniz yoluyla İzmir'e getirip, süreç içinde Tryeste'yi de ticaretleri açısından önemli bir antrepo haline getirdi.[2] Livorno gibi, Tryeste ve Ancona de genellikle Musevi ya da Rum olan Osmanlı tüccarlarının ticaret müesseslerinin tesisine izin verdi. Bu tüccarlar üs olarak İtalyan limanlarının ticaret müesseslerinin tesisine izin verdi. Bu tüccarlar üs olarak İtalyan limanlarını kullanarak, daha önce Fransız ve Hollandalıların yürüttükleri İzmir'le ticaretin anlamlı bir bölümünü devraldılar.

Onsekizinci yüzyılın son döneminde ve ondukuzuncu yüzyılın başlarında İzmir'in yerel cemaatlerinin ekonomik büyümesine savaşların dolaylı yollardan yaptığı olumlu etkiler, Osmanlı İmparatorluğunu etkisi altına olan dünya ekonomisinin yayılmacı dönemiyle daha da güçlendi. Esasında bu, Osmanlı tüccarlarının büyüyen ticaretten giderek daha büyük bir payı devralmakta oldukları anlamına gelir. İzmir, süreç içinde Osmanlı iç ticaretinden olduğu gibi Osmanlı-Avrupa ticaretinden de giderek daha büyük bir pay alarak yerel toplulukla uyum içinde büyüdü.

*

---

[1] Frangakis-Syrett, *The Commerce of Smyrna...*, s. 274-276.
[2] ANF, Marine B/7, 446, Bertrand, 19 Ekim, 1782.

İzmir'in ondukuzuncu yüzyılın başlarında Doğu Akdeniz bölgesinde ve bütün olarak İmparatorlukta elde ettiği ekonomik zenginlik ve hakimiyet yirminci yüzyılın başlarına kadar devam etti. 1889'da İzmir'de yerleşen İngiliz Konsolosu şehrin süregelen ekonomik dinamizmi hakkında şu yorumlarda bulunmuştur:

> İzmir mıntıkası resmi olarak sadece Aydın vilayetini kapsıyorsa da, aslında ticari etkisi Türk Ege Denizi'nin tamamının yanısıra, Konya ve Antalya vilayetleri ile Ankara, Bursa ve Adana'nın bazı bölümleri de dahil olmak üzere Küçük Asya'nın en verimli bölümüne yayılmıştır. Bu ticari etki yıldan yıla artmaktadır....[1]

Bu, yüzyıl boyunca öyle ya da böyle anlatılan bir hikayeydi. İzmir imparatorluğun Batı[2] ile olan ticaretindeki en önemli liman olarak doğuşundan itibaren Osmanlı ticaretinde neredeyse tartışmasız bir yer tutmaya başladı. Ticari dinamizmi ve büyüklüğü sürekli arttı: Ondokuzuncu yüzyıl boyunca İzmir yalnızca Osmanlı İmparatorluğunun dış ticaret ağlarına hakim olmakla kalmadı, fakat aynı zamanda İmapartorluğun uçsuz bucaksız coğrafyasındaki iç ağların büyük bölümüne hakim olmaya da devam etti. 1840'larda İmparatorluğu Batıdan yapılan tüm ithalatın %24'ü ve tüm ihracatın %57'si İzmir limanından geçerken, 1900'de bu rakamlar sırasıyla %19 ve %55'ti.[3] İstanbul'un İmparatorluğun başkenti olarak çok işlevli olması, İstanbul'un rekabetine rağmen İzmir'in Osmanlı Türkiye'sinin en önemli ticaret limanı olarak kalmasına olanak tanıdı.[4] İzmir ticari bankacılık işlemleri açısından da

[1] *Parliamentary Papers, Accounts & Papers*, cild LXXVII (London, 1890), Annual Trade Report on İzmir for 1889, s. 2.

[2] ANF, AE Bi 1053, Peyssonnel, Mémoire, İzmir, 22 Kasım 1751; ayrıca bakınız, ANF, AE Biii 242, Fourcade, Mémoire, İzmir, c. 1812.

[3] Frangakis-Syrett, "The Port of Smyrna in the Nineteenth Century", s. 262.

[4] Ondukuzuncu yüzyılda yayınlanan literatüre bakıldığında İzmir'e ilişkin birçok çalışmaya rastlanır. D. Georglades, *Smyrne et l'Asie Mineure au point de vue économique et commercial* (Paris, 1885); C. Oikonomos, *Étude sur Smyrne*, çev. B. Slaars (Smyrna, 1868); F. Rougon, *Smyrne: situation commerciale et économique* (Paris, 1892); Ch. Scherzer, *La province de Smyrne* (Vienna, 1873).
İlk el kaynaklara referans veren literatür göz önüne alındgında, şu çalışmalar İzmir ekonomisinin ondukuzuncu ve yirmici yüzyıla ilişkin kısmının veçhelerini kapsar: Reşat Kasaba, *The Ottoman Empire and the World Economy: The Nineteenth Century* (Albany, NY, 1988) ve Orhan Kurmuş, "The Role of British Capital in the Economic Development of western Anatolia, 1850-1914" (Doktora tezi, London University, 1974); ayrıca bakınız, *idem, Emperyalizmin Türkiye'ye Girişi* (Istanbul, 1974) ve Elena Frangakis-Syrett, "Commerce in the Eastern Mediterranean from the Eighteenth to the Early Twentietth Centuries: The City-Port of İzmir and its Hinterland", *International Journal of Maritime History*, cild X/2 (1998) s. 125-154.

önemli bir merkez olmayı sürdürdü.[1] Ondukuzuncu yüzyılın son dönemlerinde ve yirminci yüzyılın başlarında imparatorlukta modern bir bankacılık sektörü gelişmeye başlıyorken, İstanbul'dan sonra en çok sayıda banka İzmir'de bulunuyordu.[2]

İzmir uluslararası piyasanın taleplerini her zaman esas olarak tarımsal ürünler ve hammadde ihracatçısı olarak karşılamıştı. Ondukuzuncu yüzyıldaki belli başlı ihracat mallarının zamanın ekonomik gereksinimleriyle birlikte değişmesi göz önünde bulundurulduğunda, İzmir'in temel ihracatı bu yeni ekonomik koşullara cevap verecek biçimde değişti. Avrupa dokuma sektörüne temel olarak pamuk, pamuk ipliği, yün ve diğer hammaddeleri ihraç etmekteyken, şehir limanı artık kuru üzüm, kuru meyve, incir, pamuk, kök boya, meşe palamudu ve afyon da ihraç etmekteydi; tahıl, sünger, zeytinyağı ve tütün de şehrin temel ihracatı arasındaydı. Pamuk hala önemli bir ihraç malı olarak görünse de, gıda maddeleri İzmir'in temel ihraç malları arasında en prestijli mevkideydiler. Şehir limanı, Amerika'nın güneyinden pamuk ihraç edilmesini engelleyen Amerikan İç Savaşı (1861-1865) sırasında artan miktarda pamuk ihraç edebilmesinin gösterdiği gibi, uluslararası piyasadaki geçici talep değişikliklerine bile her zaman cevap verebilecek durumdaydı. İzmir'in uluslararası pazarla ilişkileri ve entegrasyonu telekomünikasyon linkleri ve ulaşımdaki (hem demiryolundan hem de buharlı gemilerde) yeniliklerle ondukuzuncu yüzyıl boyunca güçlendirildi. Yirminci yüzyılın başlarında uluslararası piyasada pamuk fiyatındaki her değişiklik İzmir piyasasında da kaydediliyordu. Ancak İzmir ekonomisinin belirli karakteristikleri değişmedi. Onsekizinci yüzyılda İzmir'de ticareti karakterize eden, tüccarların tümü arasındaki keskin rekabet, ondukuzuncu yüzyılda ve yirminci yüzyılın başlarında da aynı derecede güçlüydü.[3] Bankacılık sektörünün ya da yirminci yüzyılın başlarında vadeli pamuk veya incir ticareti piyasasının rekabetçi özelliklerinin yansıttığı gibi, İzmir'in iş dünyası herkese açık kaldı.[4]

---

[1]ANF, AE Biii Felix de Beaujour, Inspection général du Levant, 1817; ayrıca bakınız, Henry Dearborn, *A Memoir on the Commerce and Navigation of the Black Sea and the Trade and Maritime Geography of Turkey and Egypt ...* (Boston, 1819), cild I, s. 110-111; Eugène Flandin, *L'Orient* (Paris, 1853-76), cild I, s. 45 ve Elena Frangakis-Syrett, "Banking in İzmir in the Early Twentieth Century", Business History Unit tarafından London School of Economics'de düzenlenen International Symposium in Honor of Alice Teichova'da sunulan bildiri, Londra, Eylül 2000.

[2]Frangakis-Syrett, "Banking in İzmir...".

[3]Elena Frangakis-Syrett, "Concurrence commerciale et financière entre les occidentaux à İzmir (XIXe-début XXe siècles)" (der.) J. Thobie, R. Pérez & S. Kancal, *Enjeux et Rapports de Force* (Istanbul, 1996), s. 117-127 içinde.

[4]AMAE, NS, cild 380, Annual Trade Reports in İzmir for the 1900s.

Ancak, ondukuzuncu yüzyılın ilk yarısında ticaretin İzmir'de ve Anadolu'daki iç bölgelerde örgütlenme biçiminin yanısıra Osmanlı-Avrupa tüccarları arasındaki ilişkilerde de önemli değişiklikler oldu. Bu gibi değişikler iç ticaret ağlarının ve vergi toplanmasının örgütlenme tarzında daha çok değişikliğe yol açtıysa da, İzmir'e ekonomik açıdan fayda sağlamaya, devamlı büyümesine katkıda bulunmaya devam ettiler. Hem batılılar hem de yerreller simsarları ticaret anlaşmalarında kullandıklarından simsarlık mesleği tümüyle ölmediyse de, bunlardan ilkinin Osmanlı'nın içlerinde çalışması için simsarlara ihtiyacı kalmamıştı, ikincisi de artık serbestçe ticaret yapabileceği uluslararası pazarla bağlantı olarak hizmet edecek batılı simsarlara ihtiyaç duymuyordu. Ondokuzuncu yüzyıln başlarında Endüstri Devrimi'nin yayılmasıyla, Avrupa'nın önde gelen ekonomileri daha önceki korumacı politikalarının yerine Serbest Ticaret politikaları uygulamaya başladılar. Sonuç olarak, İngiltere ve Fransa, İzmir'le Marsilya, Londra ve Liverpol gibi şehirlerdek yeni üslerinden ticaret yapan, çoğu gayri-Müslim Osmanlı ticaret müessesselerinin kendi kıyılarında yerleşmesine izin verdiler. Bu onlara İngiltere ve Fransa'nın büyüyen ulusal pazarlarrına olduğu gibi, uluslararası pazara da sınırsız giriş olanağı tanıdı. Bu, İzmir'le ticaret için diğer Avrupa limanlarında oluşturdukları acentelerde görünen ticari risklerrinin büyümesine de yol açtı.

Her ikisi de dünya ekonomisinin o dönemde yayılmasının sonuçları olan sermaye kaynaklarının gelişmesi ve ihraç pazarlarının büyümesi, İzmir'doki Avrupalı tüccarlarını ticaret faaliyetlerinin vizyon ve ölçek olarak büyümesine yolaçtı. İzmir'de üstlenmiş ve yerel tüccarları ajanları olarak kullanan batılılar — Avrupalılara daha sonra Amerikalılar eklendi —, şehri çevreleyen bölgeden Osmanlı mallarının toplanmasını örgütlemeye başladılar. Süreç içinde Osmanlı tüccarlarını by-pass edip, İzmir'de ve içerilerdeki pazarda dağıtmak üzere mal ithal etmeye de başladılar. Başlagıçta İzmir'in ardbölgesine yönelik böylesi girişimler deneme nitçliğindeydi, ancak yüzyıl ilerledikçe daha düzenli hale geldi ve batılı firmalarca ajanlar olarak kullanılan yerel tüccarlar sayıca arttı. Bu girişimleri güvenli yasal temellere oturtan şey Babıali'nin başlangıçta İngiltere ile, sonra da Fransa ve tüm diğer belli başlı Avrupa güçleriyle imzaladığı 1838 Ticaret Anlaşmasıydı.[1] Bu ticaret anlaşması ticareti herkese açtı ve Osmanlı tüccarlarının Avrupa üülkelerinin her yerinde ticaret yapmasına olanak verdi. Osmanlı içlerini de batılılara açtı.[2] Onsekizinci yüzyıldan farklı olarak, artık Avrupalıların sermayesi, yasal dayanakları ve

[1]Mübahat Kütüoğlu, *Osmanlı-İngiliz İktisadi Münasebetleri,* 2 cild (Istanbul, 1976), cild II, s. 7-38.

[2]*Parliamentary Papers, Tariffs* (London, 1840), cild II. Correspondence respecting ... the Commercial Treaty with Turkey, s. 39; ayrıca bakınız, *ibid* (London, 1843), cild II, Commercial Regulations, Treaties, s. 32-36.

kendi ülkelerinde sürekli büyüyen, çevreye yerleşip buralarda kalıcı yapılar kurmalarına olanak sağlayan pazarları vardı. 1838 Ticaret Anlaşması'nın yanısıra, 1830'larda Akdeniz'e buharlı gemilerin girmesi batılı tüccarların, bazı durumlarda de yerel tüccarların ticaretlerini içerilerde geliştirmelerine, hatta tesis edilmiş yerel ticaret ağlarının direncini kırmalarına yardımcı oldu.[1] Dahası, büyüyen pazarla birlikte, dışarıdaki tüketicilerle ve memleketlerindeki üreticilerle düzenli iletişim onsekizinci yüzyılda İzmir piyasasında varolan dalgalılığı ve belirsizliği gidermeye büyük ölçüde katkıda bulundu.

Ondukuzuncu yüzyılın ikinci yarısında Smyrna-Aydın ve Smyrna Kasaba Demiryolu Şirketleri'nin İzmir'in batı Anadolu Ardbölgesindeki ağları, ulaşılamayan alanları uluslararası pazara taşıyan batılı ya da Osmanlı bireysel girişimcilerin daha önceden başlamış olan ekonomik anlamda nüfuzlarını daha da güçlendirdi. Demiryollarının girmesiyle düzensiz ve tahmin edilemeyen kervan sistemiyle başa çıkmak için daha büyük bir stokla çalışmaya alışık olan içerlerdeki tüccarların böyle davranması için artık bir neden kalmamıştı. Bu yüzden pazara daha fazla mal getirebiliyorlardı. Demiryolları; malların taşınmasını düzenleyerek, maliyet-etkin ve daha az zaman gerektiren bir hale getirerek tarımsal ürünün daha fazla metalaşmasına katkıda bulundu. Bu, sonrasında, tarım sektörüne sıkıca bağlı olan İzmir ticaretini olumlu yönde etkiledi.[2] Demiryolları özellikle uluslararası pazardan üretim yerlerine değil, üretim yerlerinden uluslararası pazara mal akışında kullanıldı. Özellikle, yirminci yüzyılın başlarında bir sektör olarak büyüyen madencilik demiryolları tarafından desteklendi. Devam eden zinginleşmeyle birlikte demiryolları da şehrin yakın çevresindeki kentsel yerleşmelerin büyümesini destekledi.

Genel merkezi Söke'de olup, 1850'lerden itibaren ciddi büyüklükte meyan ihracatı yaptığı Batı Anadolu'nun içlerindeki birçok tesisi işletmekle olan İskoç firması MacAndrews Forbes & Co. ondukuzuncu yüzyılın ikinci yarısındaki batılı sermaye yatırımına ve etkinliğine iyi bir örnektir. Ancak, Mac-Andrews Forbes & Co. gibi geniş ölçekli bir ihracatçı bile küçük ölçekli yerel tüccarların rekabetinden etkilendi ve meyan kökü ticaretini hiçbir zaman tekelleştiremedi.[3] Benzer bir biçimde, denizcilik şirketleri, meşe palamudu ihracatı işletmeleri, halı imalatı işletmeleri, pamuk işleme ya da iplik boyama

---

[1]Elena Frangakis-Syrett, "The Implementation of the 1838 Anglo-Turkish Convention on İzmir's Trade: European and Minority Merchants", *New Perspectives on Turkey*, Nr. 7 (1992), s. 91-112.

[2]AMAE, CCC, cild 54, Consul Pelissier, İzmir, 28 Nisan 1882 to Hariciye Vekile A. de Freycinete Paris; ayrıca bakınız, Rougon, *Smyrne*..., s. 148-152.

[3]PRO; FO 195/1161, Consul Reade, İzmir, 11 Ekim 1878 to the Governor General, Vilayet of Aydın.

fabrikaları, krom ve zımpara taşı madenleriyle bütün batı Anadolu'ya yerleşen Charnaudlar, Whittallar, Patersonlar veya Reesler, sürekli yerel girişimcilerle rekabet halindeki batılı ekonomik faaliyetin örnekleriydi. Osmanlı döneminin sonlarında batılıların ekonomik etkinlikleri ve yatırımları içerilere yayılmıştı ve batılı kapatalistlerin varlığının hissedilmediği tarım hariç, muhtemelen ekonominin hemen hemen her alanına kadar uzanmıştı. Ancak, Müslim ve gayri-Müslim Osmanlı tüccarları şehrin ve hinterlandının bütün ekonomik sektörlerinde — hakim oldukları ithalattan etkin oldukları ihracata, madenciliğe, deniz taşımacılığına, halı imalatına, un değirmenlerine, gıda işlemeye, tabakçılığa ve hafif endüstri sektördeki bütün diğer ticari işlere kadar — aktif ve rekabetçi olmayı sürdürdüler. Batılıların hakim olmaya yatkın oldukları alan geniş sermaye kaynaklarına ve en gelişmiş teknolojiye ihtiyaç duyan altyapıydı.

İthalata bakıldığında, onsekizinci yüzyılın ortalarında İmparatorluğun temel ithalat limanı olarak ortaya çıkmasından bu yana İzmir, tekstil ürünleri başta olmak üzere, bir dizi batı mallarıyla, sömürge mallarını ithal etmekteydi. Bazı önemli değişiklikler olduysa da, bu durum geniş anlamda aynı kaldı. Ondokuzuncu yüzyılın sonlarına doğru, iç pazarındaki genişlemeyi ve şehir limanıyla ardbölgesinin öncesine göre ulaştığı ekonomik büyüme düzeyini yansıtan, gümüş işleri gibi, daha çeşitli bir dizi tüketim malı ithal ediliyordu.

Bu arada, şehrin ve bölgenin büyüyen hafif endüstri sektörünün ihtiyaçları için gerekli olan tarım makineleri ve petrol ürünleri gibi ithal ürünlerinde de bir artış vardı.[1] Ondokuzuncu yüzyılın sonunda ve yirminci yüzyılın başında, hiçbir zaman şehrin ticaret sektörüyle eşit düzeye ulaşmayan, batılı sermaye yatırım yaptıysa da, aslında geniş çapta Müslim ve gayri-Müslim yerel tüccarlarca finanse edilen ve daha çok küçük ölçekli işletmeleri içeren bir hafif sanayi sektörü doğdu. Halı imalatı sektörü, meyan kökü ve diğer hammaddeleri işleme fabrikaları doğrudan uluslararası pazara çalışıyorken, gıda işleme ve dokuma işletmeleri iç pazarı besledi. Yirminci yüzyılın başlarında İzmir ve çevresinde çok sayıda demir işliği, buz fabrikası, sigara, kiremit ve tuğla fabrikası olduğu gibi kuru meyve ihracatçılarının ihtiyacına yönelik paketleme yapacak işletmeler de vardı. Zeytinden ve susamdan yağ çıkaracak fabrikalar; sabun, makarna ve şekerleme üreten başka fabrikalar vardı. Dokuma fabrikaları ve boyama işliklerinin yanısıra baskı

[1]National Archives, Washington, DC, RG 84, cild 19, US Consul General G.B. Ravndal, Istanbul, 11 Mayıs 1912 to US Ambassador, W.W. Rockhill, Istanbul. Bundan sonra bu arşiv NA olarak anılacaktır.

presleri, çok sayıda tabakhane, tornahane vardı. İlk iki sektör, İzmir'in ve batı Anadolu'daki çevresinin uluslararası ticarette ünlü olduğu şehrin halı endüstrisinin bir parçası olduğu için gelişen alanlardı.[1] Un değirmenciliği, İzmir'i un ithal etmekten kendine yeterli ve artık ürününü Ege Adaları ve batı Anadolu kıyılarına gönderir hale getiren bir başka başarılı alandı.[2]

Ondokuzuncu yüzyılın ikinci yarısı ve yirminci yüzyılın başlarında şehir daha fazla gelişme ve modernleşmesinde katalizör işlevi gören ciddi düzeyde bir altyapıya kavuşurken, ticaret ve deniz taşımacılığı faaliyetlerinin düzeyi ve yaygınlığı, ki şehrin ekonomisinin daha sonraki farklılaşması ve büyümesinin bir parçasıdır, İzmir'in ekonomik önemindeki anahtar olmaya devam etti. Sektör büyük batılı sermaye tarafından başlatılan, gelişmiş ve kompleks teknoloji kullanan projelerden ibaretti. Ondukuzuncu yüzyılda ve yirminci yüzyılın başlarında Orduğu'nun en önemli şehirlerinden biri olarak İzmir'in altyapısı hem bu başarıya destek oldu, hem de kentin ekonomik başarısının sembolü haline geldi.

Ondokuzuncu yüzyılın ikinci yarısı gibi erken bir tarihte İmparatorluğun ilk demiryolu ağına sahip olan İzmir aynı zamanda ilk modern rıhtıma ve liman kompleksine de sahipti. Rıhtım ve liman kompleksi zamanında bir mühendislik harikası olarak görüldü. Bu, İzmir'i Akdeniz'in modern limanlarının ilk sırasına taşıdı. Daha çok özel mülk olan onsekizinci yüzyılın tahta dalgakıranları ve iskeleleri temizlenip limanın trafiği epeyce etkin hale getirildi. Mallar artık mavnalarla kıyıya taşınmadığından gemileri yükleyip başaltmanın aldığı zaman azalmıştı. İnşaat başladığında, 1868'de rıhtım projesini savunan bir Osmanlı memurunun raporu, liman bir kez yapıldığında gemiler için manevra zamanının (boşaltma ve yeniden yüklemenin) 20 günden 6 güne ineceğini ve gemilerin bundan ciddi biçimde tasarruf edeceğini doğru olarak saptamıştır. Rıhtım tamamladıktan sonra mallar daha az hamaliyeyle ve daha kısa sürede taşınacağı için, kayıp ve hırsızlık olasılığının azalmasından ve sigorta oranlarının düşmesinden de kazanç sağlanacaktı.[3] 1876'da proje tamamlandığında liman şehir planlaması açısından, deniz kıyısında biriken ve sağlık sorunu haline gelen durgun suların tahliyesine de olanak verdi. İskeleyi dolaşıp gümrük binasına giden bir

---

[1]PRO, FO 195/2134, Konsolos Cumberbatch, İzmir, 4 Aralık 1902 to British Ambassador Sir Gerard Lowther, Istanbul; ayrıca bakınız, Scherzer, *La province de Smyrne*... s. 170-172 ve Rougon, *Smyrne*..., s. 247-259.

[2]PRO, FO 195/910 Konsolos Cumberbatch, İzmir, 3 Feb. 1865 to W. Stuart, Istanbul; ayrıca bakınız, *Parliamentary Papers, Accounts & Papers*, cild CXVI (London, 1908), Annual Report for 1907, s. 9.

[3]PRO, FO 198/43, Report by Parnis Effendi on the Smyrna Quay Question, İzmir, 1 Temmuz 1880.

tramvayın çalışması şehir ulaşımı açısından bir avantaj olmasının yanında tüccarlar için de bir kazançtı. İlaveten, güzel konutların inşa edildiği ve piyasa yeri haline gelen rıhtım kenarındaki mülklerin fiyatları ciddi biçimde artarken, İzmir mordern bir iş merkezine kavuştu.[1]

Bütün avantajlarına rağmen rıhtımın birinci sınıf bir Fransız firması, Dussaud Kardeşler tarafından inşası şehirdeki İngilizlerin başını çektiği yerleşik çıkar çevrelerinin husumetini doğurdu. İngilizler o zamana kadar İzmir'deki altyapı projelerinin tekelini ellerinde tutuyordu: Hem demiryolu şirketleri hem de Gaz Şirketi İngiliz işletmeleriydi. Ancak başlangıcından itibaren rıhtımın inşasını savunan İzmir Belediyesi, Dussaudların yanında yer aldı ve projenin tamamlanmasını garanti altına almada aktif bir rol oynadı.[2] İzmir Belediyesi aynı zamanda İzmir limanının dolmasını engellemek amacıyla Gediz (Hermus) Nehri'nin 1885-1891'de kanala alınmasını gerçekleştirdi ve böyle liman ve rıhtım kompleksinin genel işleyişine yardımcı oldu.[3] Birinci Dünya Savaşı arefesinde İzmir ve batı Anadolu/Ege bölgesindeki daha küçük diğer kasabalar daha çok kamusal olanağa kavuşmuşlardı. Yerel buharlı gemi şirketleri Ege Deniz'ni doldurdu. İzmir tramvayla iki banliyösüne, Göztepe ve Karşıyaka'ya bağlanmış; hem Smyrna-Aydın hem de Smyrna-Kasaba Demiryolu Şirketleri yayılmış; İzmir ve ardbölgesindeki kasabalar telefon, ev ve işyeri kullanımı için gaz ya da elektrikle donanmıştı.[4]

Çevresiyle birlikte şehrın dünya ekonomisine entegrasyonunun ve ekonomik gelişmesinin bir kanıtı olan bir başka önemli gelişme de, yirminci yüzyılda oluşan sermaye yoğunlaşmasıdır. Bu süreç, İzmir'in en önemli ticaret alanında, yani ihracatta ve halı imalatında kartellerin ya da sendikaların kurulmasıyla sonuçlandı. Oriental Halı Dokumacıları Şirketi[5] ve Smyrna İncir Paketlemecileri Şirketi[6] 1900'lerde yaratılan ve bu sektörlerdeki hem Osmanlı hem de batılı şirketlerin çoğunu içine alan tröstlerin en büyük ikisiydi. Pek çoğu uzun süredir İzmir'de bulunan Osmanlı ve batılı girişimcilerce, İzmir

[1] İzmir rıhtımı ve limanı hakkında daha fazla ayrıntı için bakınız, Elena Frangakis-Syrett, "The Making of a Nineteenth Century Ottoman Port: The Quay of İzmir", *Journal of Transportation History*'de cild 22, sayı 1 (2001), s. 23-46.

[2] Örneğin, Baş Vezir Ali Paşa (1867-1871) başından itibaren altyapı projesinin kararlı bir destekleyicisiydi. Osmanlı İmparatorluğunun işin bütünündeki rolüyle ilgili olarak ayrıca bakınız, Mübahat Kütükoğlu, İzmir rıhtımı inşaatı ve işletme imtiyazı", *Tarih Dergisi*, cild 32 (1979), s. 495-558.

[3] Louis Godard, "L'irrigation en Turquie", *Le Génie Civil* (1909-1910), cild LVI, s. 283.

[4] *Parliamentary Papers, Accounts & Papers* (London, 1909) cild XCVIII, s. 10-11; *ibid.* (London, 1910), cild CIII, s. 19-20.

[5] PRO, FO 195/2360, Consul H.P: Barnham, İzmir, 7 Şubat ve 12 Nisan 1910 to Lowther, Istanbul.

[6] NA, RG 84, cild 19, Ravndal, Istanbul, 11 Mayıs 1912 to Rockhill, Istanbul; ayrıca bakınız ibid., cild 18, US Consul G. Horton, İzmir, 14 Feb. 1912 to Rockhill, Istanbul.

ekonomisinin belirli sektöründe kurulan sınırlı sorumlu şirketlerin bu dönemdeki hızlı artışı sermaye yoğunlaşmasına eşlik etmiştir.[1] Bu kurulan şirketlerin önemli bir kısmı ticaret sektörünü temsil ediyorsa da, diğer sektörlerde de, en belirgin olarak madencilik ve deniz taşımacılığında, şirketler kuruldu. Bu şirketlerde yerel girişimciler kurucu, yönetim kurulu üyesi ya da hisse sahibi olarak aktif olarak temsil ediliyorlardı. Sermaye kaynakları anlamında şirketler hem Osmanlı sermayesini hem de batılı sermayeyi temsil ediyordu. Daha fazla ekonomik büyümeyi teşvik etmeleri bir yana, bu şirketler — bazıları kısa ömürlü olsa da — sermaye birikim düzeyinin ve bölge ekonomisince ulaşılan modernleşme düzeyinin tezahürleriydi.

Kentin kesintisiz ticari büyümesi ve biriken karlar, toplumsal anlamda, tüketici olarak zevk düzeyi şehrin maddi yaşamını ve kültürel alanlarını büyük ölçüde etkileyen bir burjavazinin ortaya çıkmasıyla sonuçlandı. Bunlar emlaka, yeni şirketlere ve başka çeşit güvencelere yatıracak fazla sermayesi olan zengin ve sofistike bir iş ve profesyoneller eliti, potansiyel banka müşterileriydi. Dahası, kentin kültürel faaliyetlerine katılıp, zenginliğinden yararlananlar yalnızca Osmanlı girişinmciler değil, aynı zamanda yabancı girişimcilerdi. Çok-uluslu Avrupalı tüccarlar İzmir'de onyedinci yüzyıldan beri yer almışsa da, ondokuzuncu yüzyılda sayıları artıp, ticari dinamizmle birlikte şehre ününü kazandıran bir kozmopolit kültür ve kimlik verdi. Amerikalılar,[2] İngilizler,[3] Fransızlar,[4] Helenler,[5] Avusturyalılar, İtalyanlar, Hollandılar ve Almanlar İzmir'deki en önemli Avrupalı topluluklardan bazılarıydı. Mutlak sayılarla hiçbir zaman çok olmasalar da, sermaye, uzmanlık ve bağlantılar anlamında şehrin iş ortamının önemli bir parçasını oluşturdular. Bölge ekonomisinin dış ticaret, bankacılık, madencilik, deniz taşımacılığı, denizcilik sigortacılığı ve halı imalatı gibi sektörlerinde etkindiler.

---

[1] *Parliamentary Papers, Accounts & Papers* (London, 1912-13) cild C, s. 11.

[2] Elena Frangakis-Syrett, "American Trading Practices in İzmir in the Late Nineteenth and Early Twentieth Centuries", (der.) D. Panzac, *Histoire économique et sociale de l'Empire ottoman et de la Turquie (1326-1960)*, (Paris, 1995), s. 177-184 içinde.

[3] Elena Frangakis-Syrett, "British Economic Activities in İzmir in the Second Half of the Nineteenth Century and Early Twentieth Centuries", *New Perspectives on Turkey,* sayılar: 5-6 (Fall, 1991), s. 191-227.

[4] Serap Yılmaz, "XVII-XIX. Yüzyıllarda İzmir'de Fransızlar", *Çağdaş Türkiye Tarihi Araştırmalar Dergisi,* cild 1/3 (1993), s. 89-115; Marie-Carmen Smyrnelis, "Européens et Ottomans à Smyrne de la fin du XVIIIe à la fin du XIXe siècle" (der.) M. Anastassiadou & B. Heyberger, *Figures anonymes, figures d'élite* (Istanbul, 1999), s. 119-133 içinde.

[5] Hellenes terimi Osmanlı İmparatorluğundaki Sultanın tebaası olan Yunanlarda farklı olarak, bağımsız bir Yunan devletinin uyruğu olan Yunanlar anlamına gelir. İzmir'deki her iki Yunan grubunun ekonomik faaliyetleri hakkında bakınız, Elena Frangakis-Syrett, "The Greek Mercantile Community of İzmir in the First Half of the Nineteenth Century", (der.) D. Panzac *Les Villes dans l'Empire Ottoman: Activités et Sociétés* (Paris, 1991), cild I, s. 391-416 içinde ve *idem.,* "The Economic Activities of the Greek Community of İzmir in the Second Half of the Nineteenth Century and Early Twentieth Centuries", C. Issawi & D. Gondicas, *Ottoman Greeks in the Age of Nationalism* (Princeton, NJ, 1999), s. 17-44 içinde.

Birinci Dünya Savaşı arefesinde, İzmir ve ardbölgesinin ekonominin tüm sektörlerindeki büyümesi görünür nitelikteydi: Şehrin ekonomisine hakim olan ticaret sektöründeki büyüme ve artan modernleşmede; denizcilik ve sigortacılık gibi tamamlayıcı sektörlerin daha da büyümesinde; uluslararası pazarla olan telekomünikasyon linklerindeki hızın ve etkinliğin artışında; hafif sanayi sektöründeki büyümede; anonim şirketlerin patlamasında; şirketlerin birleşmesinde ve tröstlerin kurulmasında; kente hizmet veren demiryolu taşımacılığından kent içinde kitle taşımacılığına ve kamusal olanakların tesis edilmesine kadar uzanan, altyapının gelişmesi düzeyinde. Aslında, onsekizinci yüzyıldan farklı olarak, ondukuzuncu yüzyılda İzmir'in ekonomisi ve nüfusu ardbölgenin batı Anadolu'daki ve Ege Adaları'ndaki bölümlerini içine alıp, bir Büyük İzmir yaratacak ölçüde büyüdü. Böylesi bir ekonomik büyüme ve şehrin ve çevresinin yaşadığı nüfus büyümesiyle uyumluydu. Nüfus onsekizinci yüzyıldaki 100,000 kişiden, Birinci Dünya Savaşı arefesinde yarım milyona ulaştı.

Bu ekonomik verimliliğin yerel para piyasasına da faydalı sonuçları oldu. Önceki dönemlerin aksine yirminci yüzyılın başlarının İzmir'inde döviz kurlarında daha küçük dalgalanmalar olması ve daha düşük faiz oranları, o zaman için bile likit sermaye ve kredinin temin edilebilirliğinin kanıtı olarak değerlendirildi. Bu değişen piyasa koşulları büyük ölçüde, yatırımcılar ve tüketiciler arasında ekonominin uzun dönemdeki zenginliğine duyulan daha büyük bir güvenin eşlik ettiği, zinginleşen ve gitgide modernleşen bir ekonomiyle ulaşılan sermaye birikimindeki artışa bağlandı. Bu tip değişiklikler yüzyıl dönümünde İmparatorluğun belli başlı diğer kentlerinde olduğu gibi İzmir'de de gelişmiş olan, kurumsallaşmış modern bin bankacılık sektörünün büyümesine ve gelişmesine de bağlandı. Modern bir bankacılık sektörünün doğuşu, modernleşme sürecinin ve Akdeniz'in ve Yakın Doğu'nun en buyuk kentlerinden biri olan İzmir'in ulaştığı ekonomik büyüme düzeyinin nihai taç giyişi olarak görülebilir. Dahası bu, iki yüzyıl boyunca süren bir ekonomik büyümeydi.

APPENDIX A

Percentage Share of Exports of Ottoman Ports to Marseilles, 1745-1789 (in livres tournois)

and

Percentage Share of Imports of Ottoman Ports to Marseilles, 1749-1788 (in livres tournois)

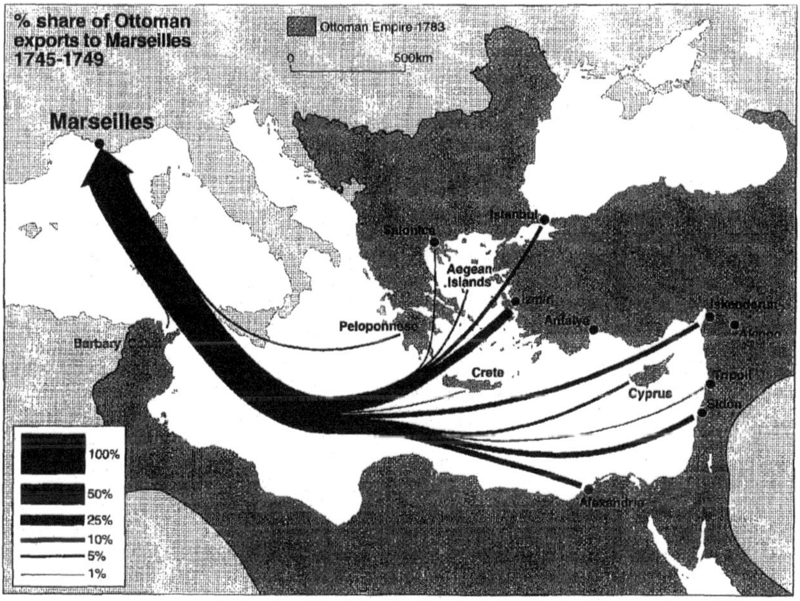

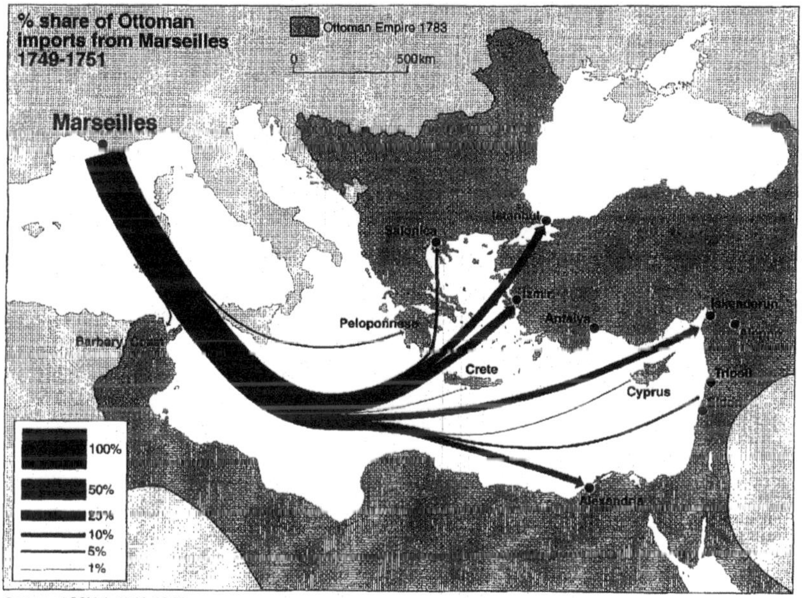

Sources : ACCM, I, 19-20, 26-28

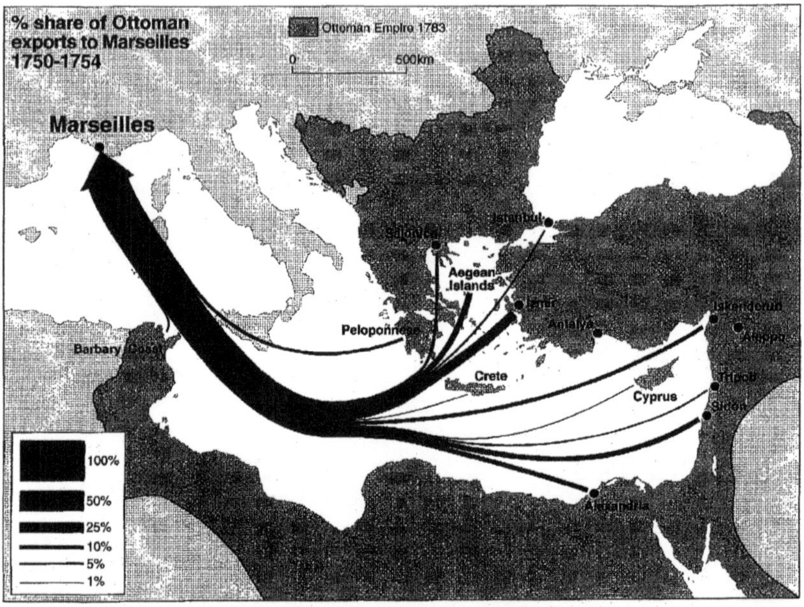

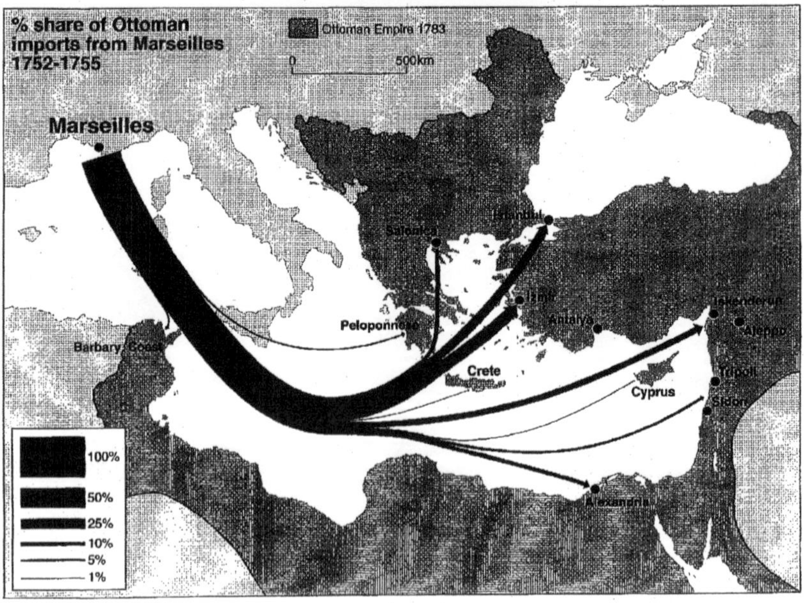

Sources : ACCM, I, 19-20, 26-28

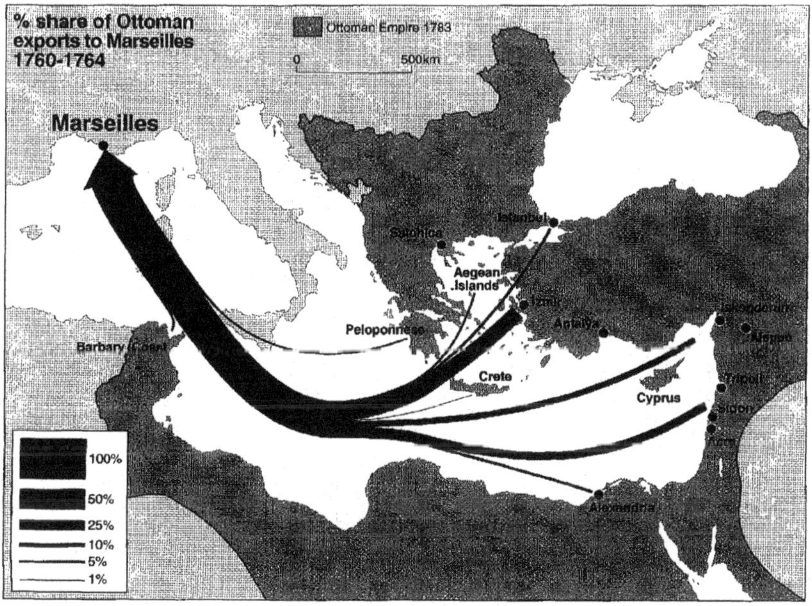

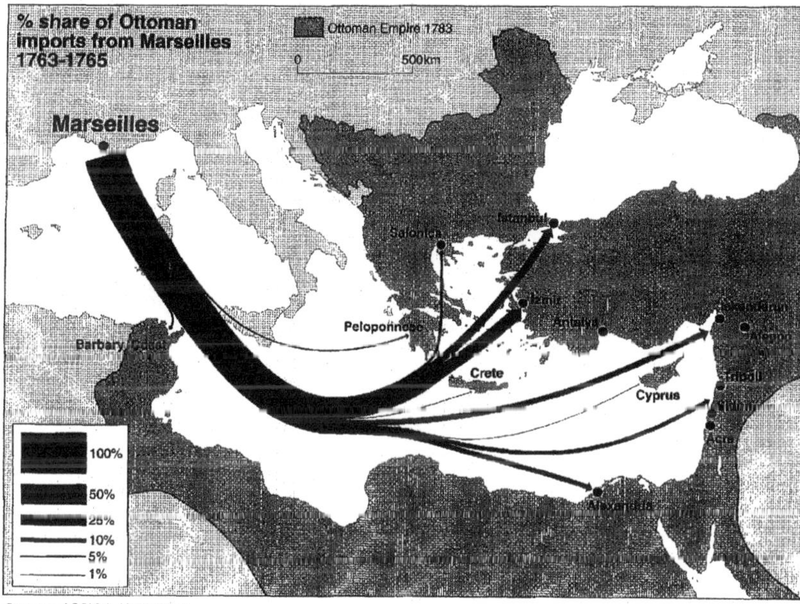

Sources : ACCM, I, 19-20, 26-28

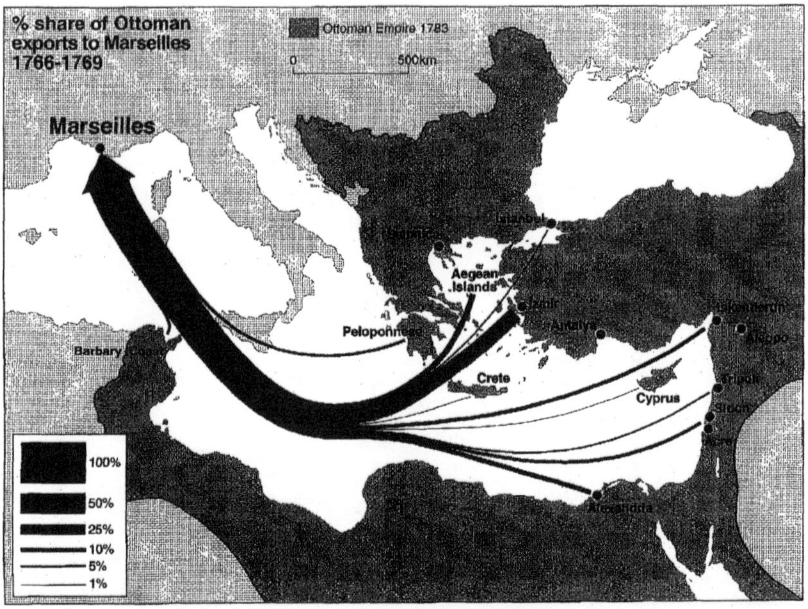

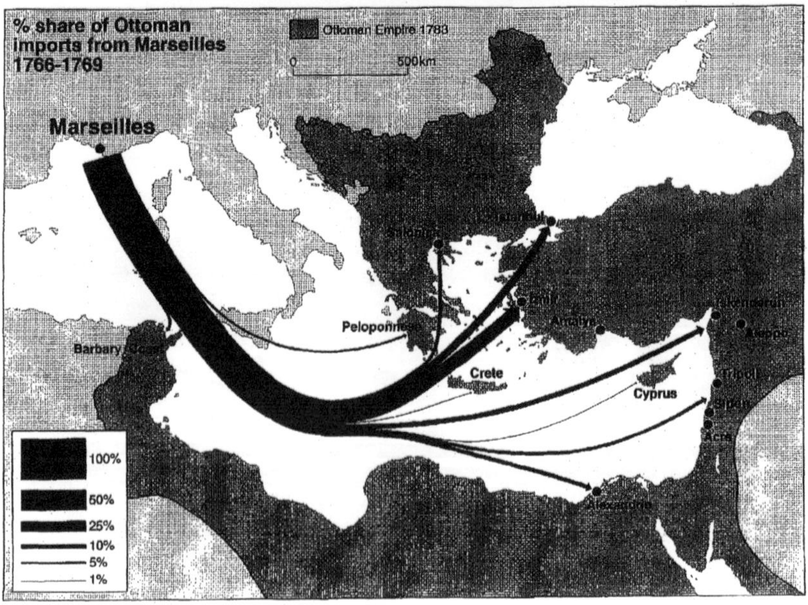

Sources : ACCM, I, 19-20, 26-28

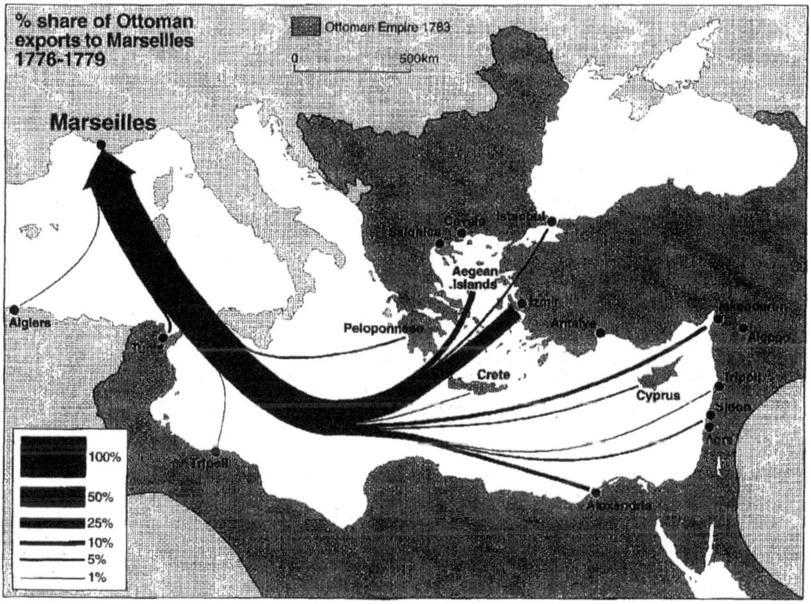

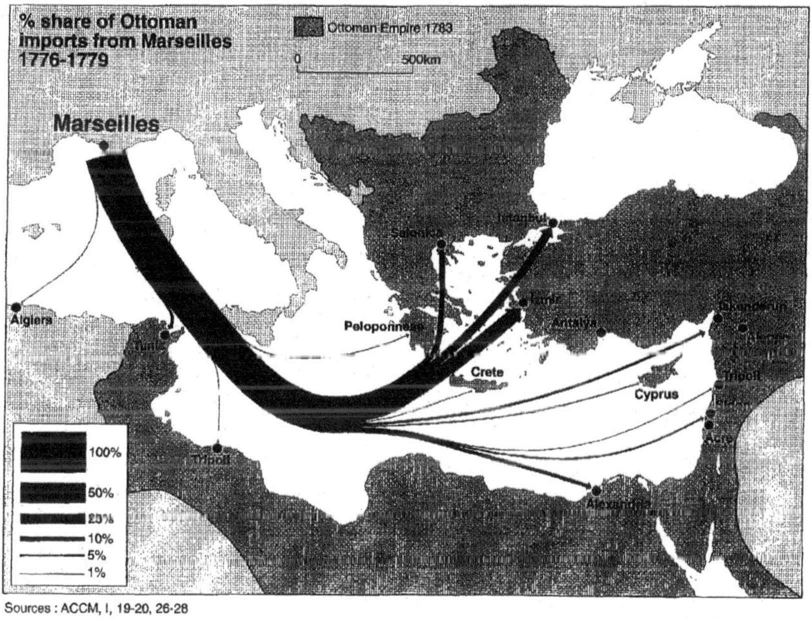

Sources : ACCM, I, 19-20, 26-28

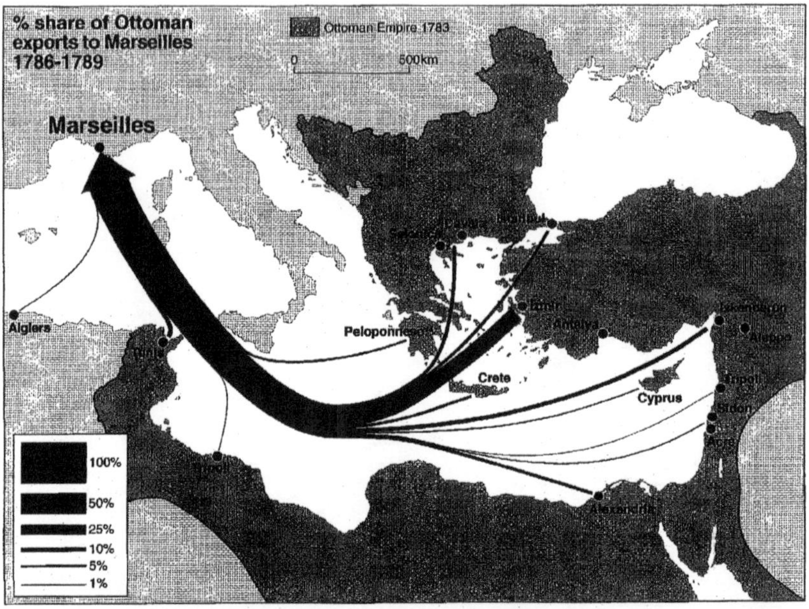

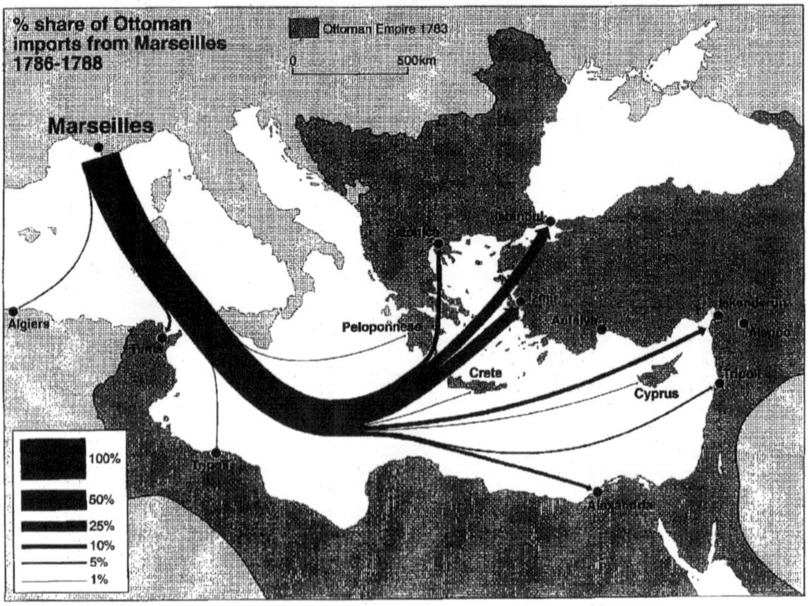

Sources : ACCM, I, 19-20, 26-28

APPENDIX B

Principal Annual Exports from İzmir to Marseilles as a Percentage of İzmir's Total Exports to Marseilles, 1721-1820

and

Principal Annual Imports to İzmir from Marseilles as a Percentage of İzmir's Total Imports from Marseilles, 1721-1820

Principal Annual Exports from İzmir to Marseilles as a percentage of Total Exports, 1721-1820

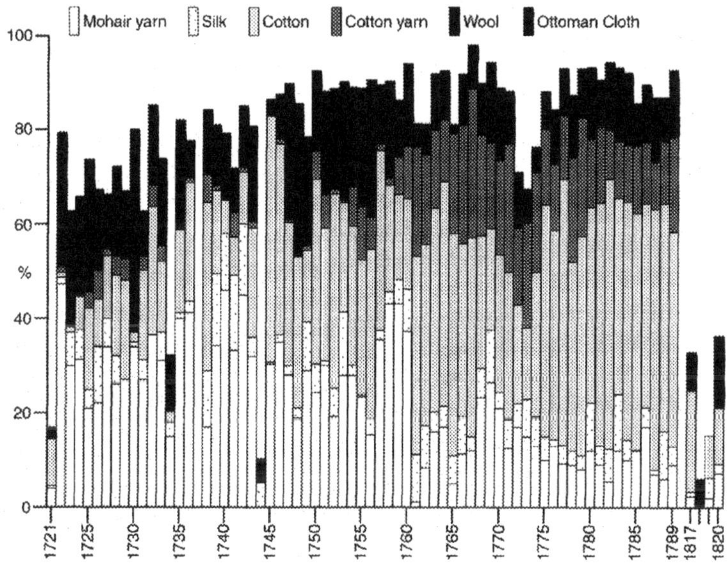

Sources : ACCM, I, 19-20, 26-28

Principal Annual Imports to İzmir from Marseilles as a percentage of Total Imports, 1721-1820

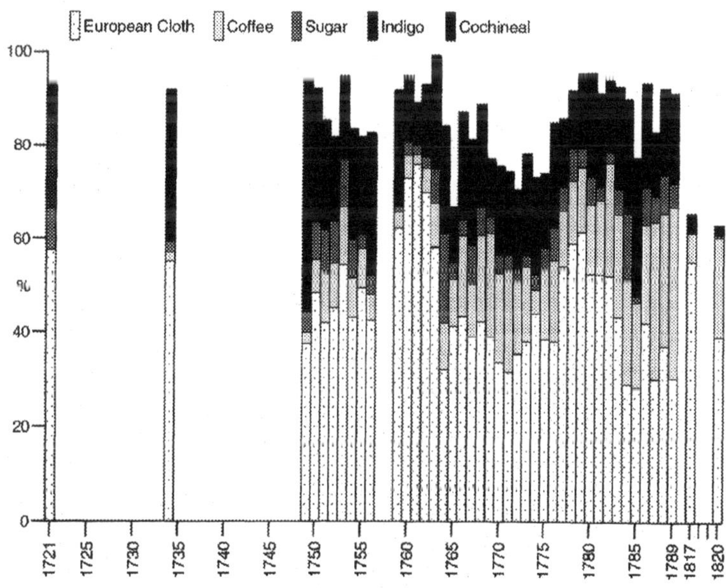

Sources : ACCM, I, 19-20, 26-28

APPENDIX C

Percentage Share of Total Annual Exports of İzmir to Western European Ports, 1775-1820 (in livres tournois)

and

Percentage Share of Total Annual Imports of İzmir from Western European Ports, 1775-1820 (in livres tournois)

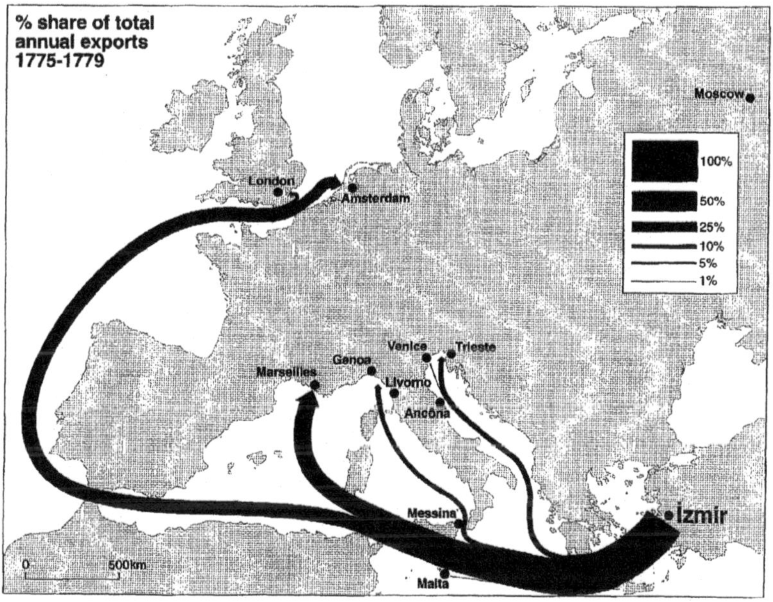

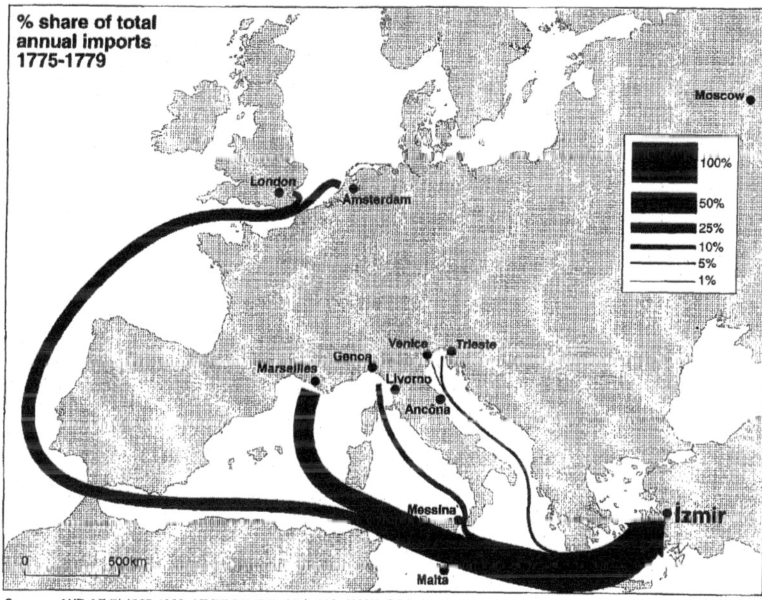

Sources : ANF, AE Bi 1065-1069; AE Biii 276-277; ARA, 168; AMAE, CCC, 35-36

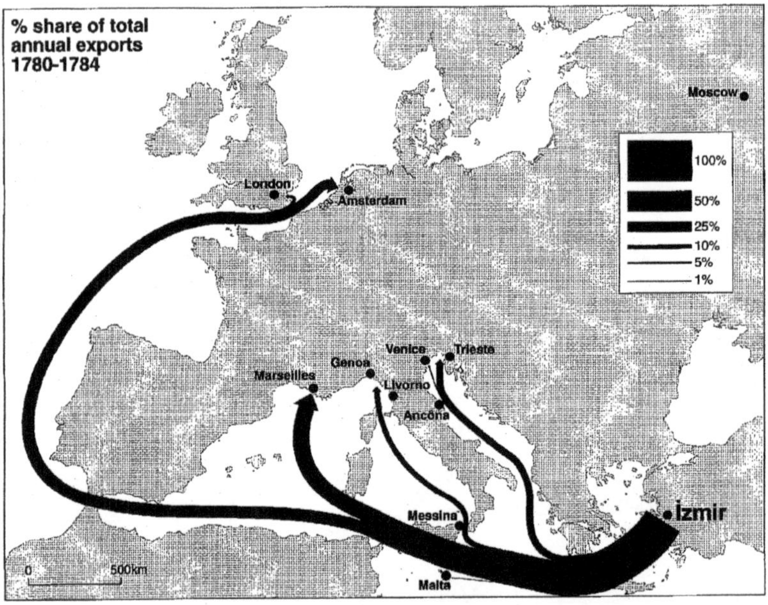

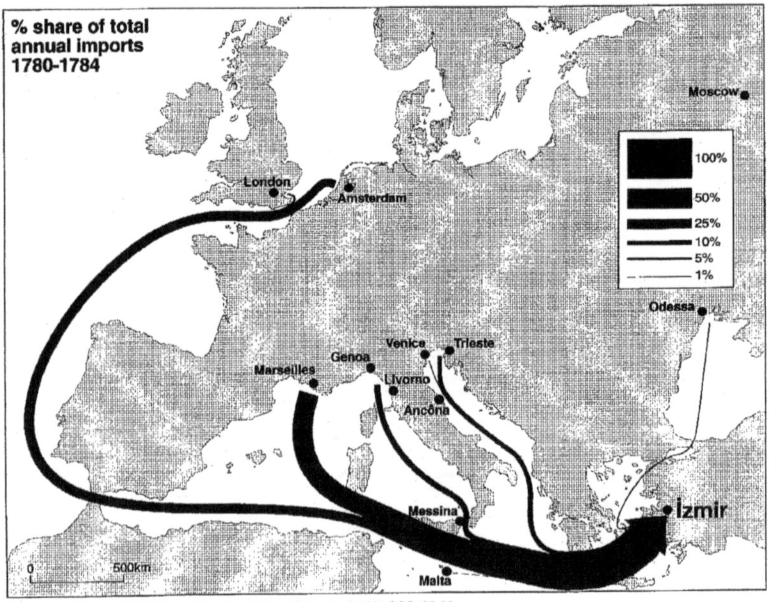

Sources : ANF, AE Bi 1065-1069; AE Biii 276-277; ARA, 168; AMAE, CCC, 35-36

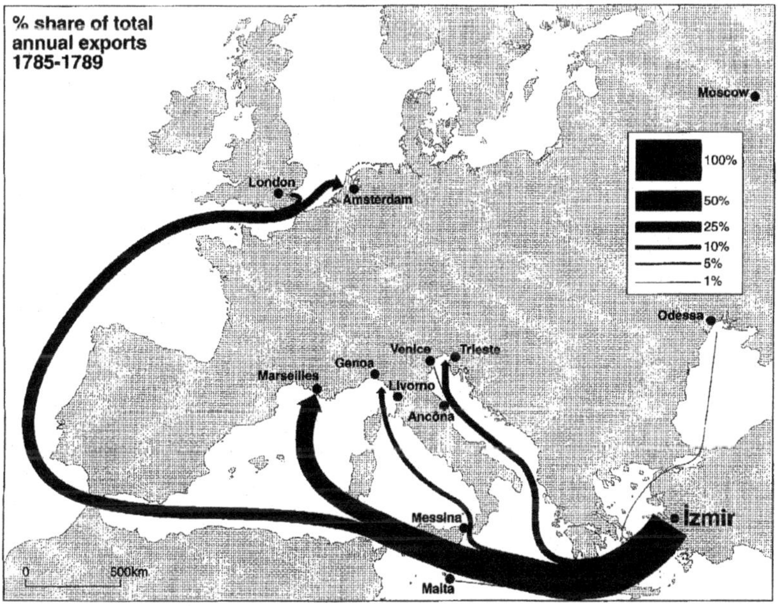

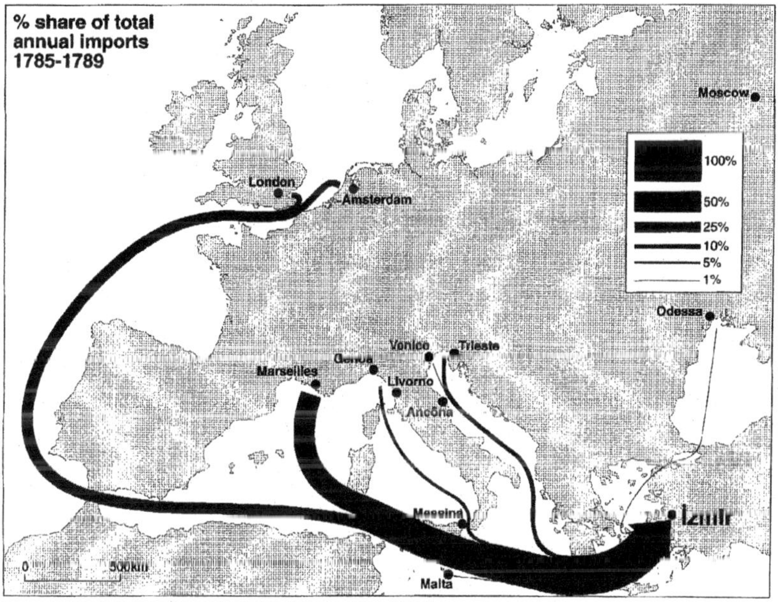

Sources : ANF, AE BI 1065-1069; AE Biii 276-277; ARA, 168; AMAE, CCC, 35-36

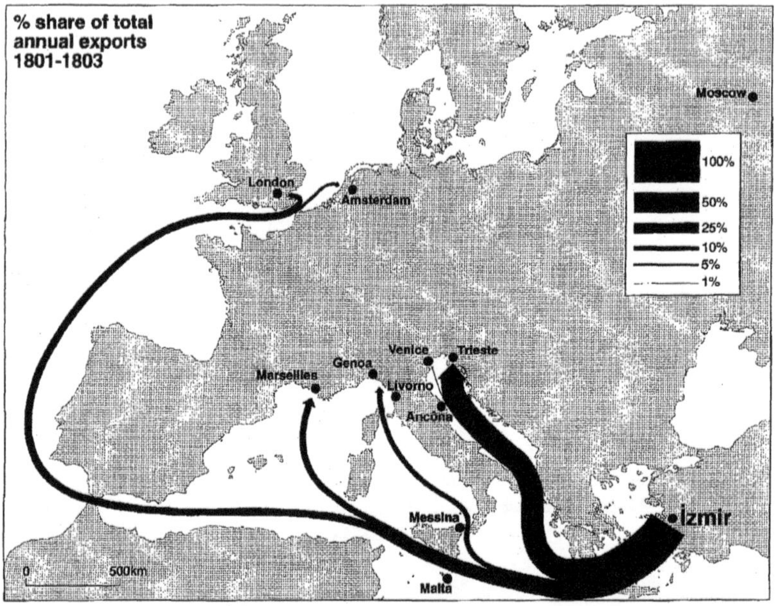

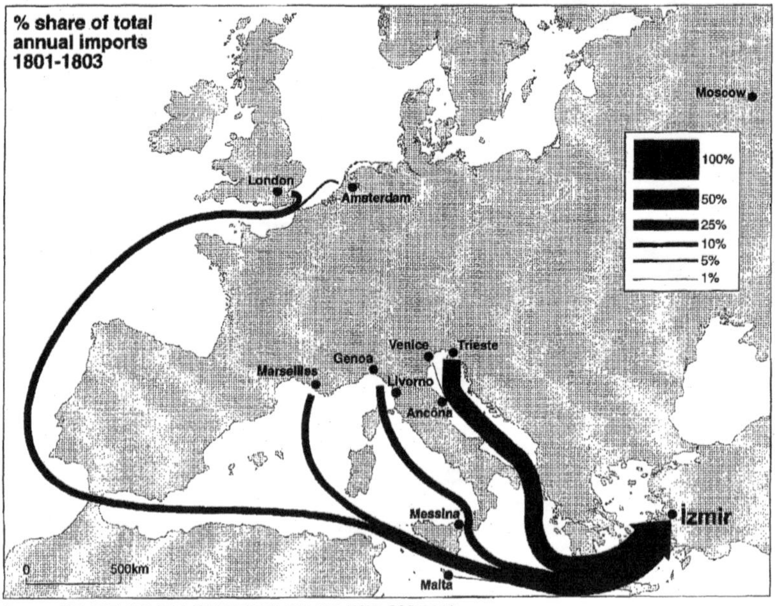

Sources : ANF, AE Bi 1065-1089; AE Biii 276-277; ARA, 168; AMAE, CCC, 35-36

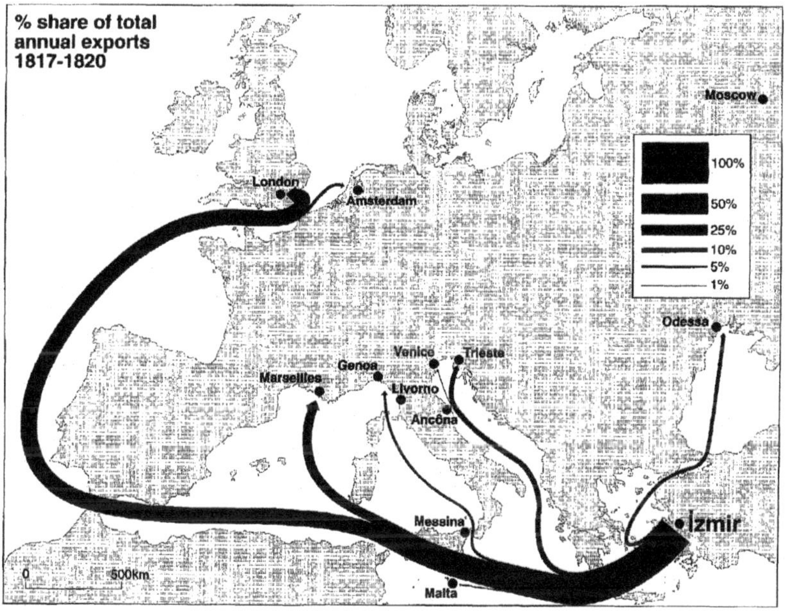

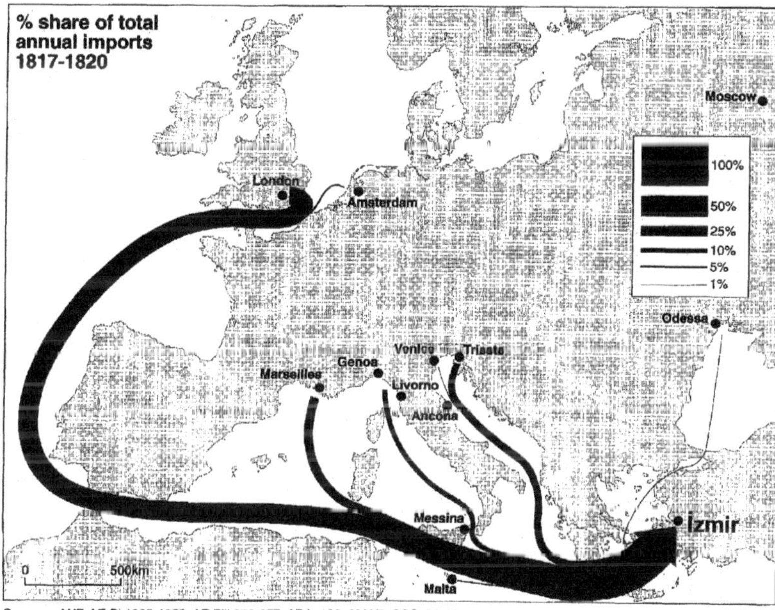

Sources : ANF, AE Bi 1065-1069; AE BIII 276-277; ARA, 168; AMAE, CCC, 35-36

www.ingramcontent.com/pod-product-compliance
Ingram Content Group UK Ltd.
Pitfield, Milton Keynes, MK11 3LW, UK
UKHW041131071026
15587UKWH00009B/424

9 781617 191022